An Ape's View of Human Evolution

Our closest living relatives are the chimpanzee and bonobo. We share many characteristics with them, but our lineages diverged millions of years ago. Who in fact was our last common ancestor?

Bringing together ecology, evolution, genetics, anatomy and geology, this book provides a new perspective on human evolution. What can fossil apes tell us about the origins of human evolution? Did the last common ancestor of apes and humans live in trees or on the ground? What did it eat, and how did it survive in a world full of large predators? Did it look anything like living apes or was it more like the fossil apes?

Andrews addresses these questions and more to reconstruct the common ancestor and its habitat. Synthesizing 35 years of work on both ancient environments and fossil and modern ape anatomy, this book provides unique new insights into the evolutionary processes that led to the origins of the human lineage.

Peter Andrews has always had a keen interest in fossils, and an encounter with Dr L.S.B. Leakey while working in the Kenya Forestry Department encouraged him to make the move to anthropology. He has spent much of his career at the Natural History Museum, London, where he was Head of Human Origins until his retirement in 2000. Since then he has been curator of Blandford Museum while retaining an Emeritus Research Associate position at the Natural History Museum, along with honorary professorships at University College London and the University of York. He has published ten books, two with Chris Stringer, and nearly 200 articles in the scientific and popular press.

An Ape's View of Human Evolution

PETER ANDREWS
The Natural History Museum, London

CAMBRIDGE
UNIVERSITY PRESS

CAMBRIDGE
UNIVERSITY PRESS

University Printing House, Cambridge CB2 8BS, United Kingdom

Cambridge University Press is part of the University of Cambridge.

It furthers the University's mission by disseminating knowledge in the pursuit of education, learning and research at the highest international levels of excellence.

www.cambridge.org
Information on this title: www.cambridge.org/9781107100671

First published 2015

Printed in the United Kingdom by TJ International Ltd. Padstow Cornwall

A catalogue record for this publication is available from the British Library

Library of Congress Cataloging-in-Publication Data
Andrews, Peter, 1940–
An ape's view of human evolution / Peter Andrews.
    pages cm
Summary: "Our closest living relatives are the chimpanzee and bonobo. We share many characteristics with them, but our lineages diverged millions of years ago. Who in fact was our last common ancestor? Bringing together ecology, evolution, genetics, anatomy and geology, this book provides a new perspective on human evolution. What can fossil apes tell us about the origins of human evolution? Did the last common ancestor of apes and humans live in trees or on the ground? What did it eat, and how did it survive in a world full of large predators? Did it look anything like living apes? Andrews addresses these questions and more to reconstruct the common ancestor and its habitat. Synthesizing 35 years of work on both ancient environments and fossil and modern ape anatomy, this book provides unique new insights into the evolutionary processes that led to the origins of the human lineage"– Provided by publisher.
ISBN 978-1-107-10067-1 (Hardback)
1. Human evolution. 2. Primates–Evolution. 3. Fossil hominids. 4. Paleontology–Miocene. 5. Physical anthropology. I. Title.
GN281.A54 2015
599.93′8–dc23 2015013762

ISBN 978-1-107-10067-1 Hardback

Contents

Contents

The colour plate section appears between pages 144 and 145.

Preface

It is common knowledge that our human ancestors descended from apes. It is also commonly thought that in the course of this transition, some ape men left the forests, in which their ancestors were living, and entered a life in the African savanna. In the course of this transition, so the story goes, our ancestors started walking upright on two legs, started making tools, and gradually became what we are today. I will be examining the evidence for these assertions, and in particular I will be looking at the evidence for what our ancestors were like and where we came from. In doing so I will try and dispel some of the confusion many people are in because of the long history and great variety of fossil apes, the group from which we arose. In particular, I will be looking at the evidence for our last common ancestor with the apes to try and discover when and where we came from. This will entail over 20 million years of human evolution dating back to the time when apes first appeared in the fossil record.

Many recent surveys of early human evolution take chimpanzees as a model for our ape ancestry. Living apes, and particularly chimpanzees, which are our closest living relatives, are one of the major sources of information about our last common ancestor, in particular identifying characters and behaviour shared in common, and these have been described in some detail in Chapters 2 and 16 based in part on work by Bill McGrew. It would be a mistake, however, to imagine that the last common ancestor looked anything like a chimpanzee, for it, like humans, has evolved from this ancestor by 'descent with modification' in the words of Charles Darwin. It was no surprise that when fossil remains of *Australopithecus anamensis* were found a few years ago, this 4 million-year-old human ancestor looked nothing like chimpanzees; however, it had similarities in its jaws and teeth to the Miocene apes that I was studying at the time. Since it also had human attributes such as adaptations for bipedalism, which is a uniquely human trait, it was completely different from the chimpanzee-like common ancestor that was (and still is for some people) the accepted interpretation of the human/ape common ancestor. I coined the phrase 'ecological apes' for such hominins (early human ancestors) to emphasize its ecological similarities with Miocene apes while recognizing at the same time its place in human ancestry.

Over and beyond such issues are questions about where our ancestors lived, what they ate and how they got their food. Were our remote ape-like ancestors living in trees or on the ground, and were they eating meat? Did they make or use tools, and if so what kind? How did they manage to survive in a world full of large predators? Most of this book will be about trying to answer these questions, but answering them is not always straightforward as the fossil record is notoriously patchy. We are unlikely to find the first organisms in a lineage, firstly because they would have been extremely rare, secondly because they may not look anything like what we predicted for them, and thirdly because they may be hard to distinguish from the organisms immediately preceding them: thus the earliest human ancestors would have been almost indistinguishable from the ancestral fossil apes.

A fourth human attribute, intelligence, is even harder to identify in fossils. There is a spectrum of intelligence from rudimentary life forms, such as reactions of unicellular animals to light or heat, to our conscious thought processes by which we anticipate problems and try to solve them. Even beyond that, we solve problems not by individual efforts but by working with other people: we may anticipate the need for communicating by telephone, but we have no idea, as individuals, how to make a telephone; what we anticipate is the process of going to the shops to buy a telephone that has been made by others. This issue will be taken up in Chapter 2.

Many of our questions about human evolution were formalized by two American anthropologists who between them changed the way we look at human evolution. In 1951, Sherwood Washburn proposed in his 'New physical anthropology' that the way to understand human origins required a multidisciplinary approach, with geneticists, anatomists, palaeontologists and social scientists all focusing on the question: where did we come from? This initiative was taken up by F. Clark Howell, who applied this multidisciplinary approach to field studies, emphasizing the need for understanding the context in which fossil humans were found, the nature of the geological deposits representing past environments and the need for good dating techniques. This book follows in their generalist tradition, relating the anatomy, behaviour and genetics of our human ancestors to the context in which they are found in the fossil record, and in particular relating these aspects to the environment in which our ancestors lived.

In these days of overspecialization, entire careers are built upon single fossil taxa, or even single parts of their skeletons, and it is easy to lose sight of the evolutionary picture in so doing. So much effort is placed on these narrow constraints that hypotheses can be built up without finding the need to go out into the field to identify background or underlying context. Many years ago, the Yale scientist Elwyn Simons commented on how few anthropologists visited his laboratory to work on his collection of fossil apes, and I can repeat his sad affirmation that in my 25 years curating the fossil ape collection at the Natural History Museum, with six type specimens, few visitors came to examine them even while writing articles about them. Even more is this true of anthropologists writing about ecological interpretations of fossil apes and hominins: few anthropologists have carried out ecological analyses of modern habitats before generating sweeping interpretations about past environments. The outcome has been many myths about the past, not least that of the origins of African grasslands and their significance in human evolution. I am no ecologist, but I have participated in ecological surveys ranging from forest (Kakamega) to grassland (Serengeti) and from river flood plains (Tana River) to disturbed habitats (Laetoli). All these, plus my forestry background, have provided insights into the extent we can and cannot delve into past environments.

Living species of ape, chimpanzees, gorillas, orang utans and gibbons are few in number, and there is only a single living human species. However, there is a great range of variation in fossil ape species, and indeed the time preceding the emergence of humans could be called 'the age of the apes', for they were the common primate species living in many places across Africa, Europe and Asia. A few years ago, Terry Harrison and I attempted to look at human ancestry from the bottom up, what we called the worm's eye view of human evolution. We approached human evolution from the point of view of the ape, looking not at the end products of human evolution, ourselves and our immediate ancestors, but at its beginnings from the fossil apes. This was the issue I raised when I coined the phrase 'ecological apes', for these ape-like early hominins should be compared ecologically with the Miocene apes rather than with later hominins. The problem with this is that there are many species of fossil apes extending back at least 20 million years, and the question then arises as to which ape.

Thirty-six species of Miocene apes are currently known, but this is only a fraction of the fossil apes that actually lived during this period. The number of Old World higher primates living today has been documented by Colin Groves as 141 species, and it is reasonable to suppose that in the past there may have been at least as many fossil species living at any one time. Multiply that number by 20 million years and it is a safe assumption that fossil ape diversity over the 15 million years preceding the split between humans and apes was many times greater than 36. It is unlikely, therefore, that the fossil apes known at present give a full picture of the morphological diversity present in the Miocene, but what I will be doing is to describe what we do know at present to illustrate the range of morphology from which both humans and chimpanzees were derived.

For those who are put off by the large numbers of fossil apes now in the literature, it may be a relief to know that I am not going to be looking at this 'multitude' in its entirety but shall concentrate on just three groups of fossil apes that seem to me to be particularly relevant to human evolution. I have selected those groups because I believe they can tell us about ape and human ancestry, and they come from sites ranging from the early Miocene to the Pliocene. In making these choices, I may cause offence to some scientists who feel that 'their' fossil ape has been neglected, but my choice has been dictated to a large extent by degrees of completeness of the fossil apes and by my first hand knowledge of the specimens. In cases where less well-represented fossil apes add information to the ape/human common ancestor they will be briefly mentioned. As far as possible, I will be avoiding taxonomic issues: two comprehensive books have been published recently with full descriptions of all presently known fossil apes and humans. These are *The Primate Fossil Record* edited by Walter Hartwig and *Cenozoic Mammals of Africa* edited by Lars Werdelin and Bill Sanders, and for the most part I have used the classifications currently in place in these two works. This has not always been easy, for names are changing all the time, particularly for the dryopithecines, but the names themselves are a peripheral issue in terms of the morphology and environment of the last common ancestor between apes and humans. Writing this book has given me a number of insights into the present state of fossil ape taxonomy, some of which may inadvertently emerge in discussion, but I have done my best to keep my opinions on ape taxonomy under wraps.

Chapter 1 of this book looks at the background to the study of common ancestry of apes and humans. The study of all forms of life rests ultimately on how we classify them, and this in turn rests on the assumption that life is structured. Although evolution has followed a random trajectory, the fact that life has evolved, one species giving rise to another, has led to the structure that we recognize when we classify birds as birds or fish as fish. If species had been created without this structure, each one would consist of a random set of characters: there might be cold-blooded birds, fish with legs, or for that matter fish and birds with shells. There would be no expectation of underlying shared structure, but biology has shown that all plants and animals have shared common ancestors with related species at some time in the past, and they have inherited characters from that ancestor, although we might not recognize them as belonging to that group. For example, all birds have feathers and wings, and an early bird fossil would be recognized as a bird if it had feathers and wings, but since these characters are exclusive to birds it cannot be the common ancestor that birds shared with dinosaurs since it is already a bird. This is the conundrum facing those who attempt to decipher evolutionary history. The common ancestor of apes and humans would be expected to share characters with both but not to have characters exclusive to one or the other or itself to be unique.

Part I provides the background to the study of apes, their anatomy and behaviour (Chapter 2), their genetics (Chapter 3), and a brief review of their taxonomy (Chapter 4). I will explain the taxonomic terminology used in this book in Chapter 3, but suffice it to say for now that I am using the term Hominidae, and its vernacular, hominid, as the family encompassing the great apes and humans. Together with the Hylobatidae (gibbons and siamangs) they are grouped in the superfamily Hominoidea. Some fossil hominids are recognized as apes, while those placed on the human lineage are designated hominins. Some late Miocene and Pliocene hominids are claimed to be human ancestors, but there is some doubt whether these fossil hominids precede the split between apes and humans or if they are early human ancestors. For the purposes of this inquiry, this is not an important distinction, for I will be looking at their morphology, not their taxonomic status. In another sense, however, knowing the time and place of the ape-human divergence can only be depicted by taxonomic decisions, however arbitrary.

Part II reviews the present and past environments of apes (Chapter 5). This both provides a classification of vegetation types and short introductions into the environments occupied by apes. Chapter 6 describes the methods by which the environments of living and fossil apes and humans are analysed and reconstructed. Throughout this book I will be emphasizing the environments to which fossil apes and humans were adapted, for only by this way can we build up a picture of what these fossil species looked like and how they behaved. I will therefore be relating the morphology of the fossil species to their associated environments in order to show how they inter-relate and how the changes giving rise to chimpanzees and humans are affected, or not, by changes in the environment. The numerous environmental indicators will be briefly described, with examples from the fossil record. They include: geological and isotope evidence; evidence from plants; environmental reconstruction from the functional anatomy of mammals (ecomorphology); and evidence from species richness, ecological diversity and community ecology.

Part III provides the detailed descriptions of the three groups of fossil ape. Chapters 7 to 15 give accounts of the fossil apes interspersed with chapters describing their environments. These chapters show where and when fossil apes were living, what they were eating and how they moved around on the ground and in the trees. In all these respects, the environments they were living in are critical to understanding their position in hominid evolution: I will show, for example, that the majority of known fossil apes were not forest dwellers but lived in woodland savanna of varying degrees of openness, and many of them were terrestrial as well as living in trees.

The distinction between woodland and forest in tropical environments should be explained, for it is an important one, and very few animal species are found today living in or adapted to both. (It is perhaps no coincidence that chimpanzees are one of the few mammal species able to exist in both forest and woodland savanna.) Tropical forest is generally multi-canopied, so that even quite large tree-living animals can follow aerial pathways through the different layers of the canopies, moving from one canopy level to another to pass from tree to tree. Tropical woodlands, however, have single tree canopies, and even when the crowns of the trees are in contact, the branches at the extremities of the canopies are too slender to support the weight of animals bigger than large squirrels (examples of woodland are illustrated in Chapter 2, Figure 2.3, and Chapter 5, Figure 5.3). Most fossil and living primates are too large to be fully arboreal in tropical and subtropical woodland habitats, and they must come to the ground when moving from tree to tree. This applies equally to subtropical and temperate forests, which in general have single canopies and structurally are more akin to tropical woodlands than to tropical forest. Getting back to fossil ape environments, as woodland dwellers there was no 'departure from forest to savanna', for the primary adaptation of most fossil apes was not to forest in the first place; there was no abrupt 'down from the trees' in the transition from ape to human, for as woodland dwellers the fossil apes living in the time preceding the transition must have had some degree of ground-living activity in their behaviour. The key human morphologies – upright bipedal locomotion, early increases in brain size and changes in the teeth – arose in woodland habitats with no major change of ecology, and they evolved from apes that were already partly dependent on moving about on the ground.

In Part IV, Chapters 16 and 17 provides an overview of the evidence for the acquisition of human characters and the environments in which this occurred. This is a personal inquiry bringing together the results of field and laboratory work that I have been involved in at many of the fossil localities mentioned here. I will therefore be citing my own work extensively in addition to that of many others throughout this book. I have been fortunate in being able to collaborate with many friends and colleagues in the course of my work, and my collaboration with Terry Harrison, for example, goes back more than 30 years, from the time when he was my first postgraduate student. I was very lucky in having three brilliant students during my early years at the Natural History Museum: Terry of course, Lawrence Martin and Stephen Dreyer, all of whom I co-supervised with Leslie Aiello (figure). Between them they have contributed much to my research, and if I have not always expressed my debt of gratitude to them, this is now an opportunity to do so.

I also benefited greatly, if indirectly, from my PhD supervisor, Dr L.S.B. Leakey, whose inspirational approach to research and life in general turned research into an adventure. I spent most of my time working on my docto-rate while I was living in Nairobi, and there I was also helped greatly by Alan Walker, who showed me the value (and hazards) of asking questions. The Van Couvering family enlivened my time at Cambridge, and Judy in particular (now Judith Harris) introduced me to taphonomy and good

The author with Leslie Aiello, Terry Harrison and Lawrence Martin at the conference Human and Primate Evolution in Context held in London on 21 September, 2009. Photo by Terri Harrison.

excavation processes, and I was also lucky enough to coincide with both David Pilbeam and Colin Groves during their short tenures in the Anthropology Department at Cambridge University. They were an inspiration that is still having its effects today. My time at the Natural History Museum brought me into contact with a variety of experiences, as anyone who has worked in such monolithic institutions will know all about, but my determined avoidance of the administration and office politics kept much at bay, while I was lucky enough to come in contact with some brilliant minds. Chris Stringer and I have worked in harmony for nearly 40 years and we have published several books together, to say nothing of the first publication of the fossil evidence for the 'Out of Africa' hypothesis that we published together in 1988. I am grateful to my many students, for some of whom I shared supervision duties with Leslie Aiello, and who have all contributed much to my research programme. I am also grateful to my many friends and collaborators, who each in their separate ways have also contributed much to my work: Jorge Agusti, Leslie Aiello, Rosa Maria Albert, Berna Alpagut, Songül Alpaslan, Libby Andrews, Miranda Armour-Chelu, Margaret Avery, Catherine Badgley, Marion Bamford, Peter Banham, Larry Barham, David Begun, Kay Behrensmeyer,

Lynne Bell, Ray Bernor, Alan Bilsborough, Bill Bishop, Rob Blumenschine, Louis de Bonis, Basak Boz, Douglas Brandon-Jones, Tim Bromage, David Cameron, Thure Cerling, David Chivers, Desmond Clark, Ron Clark, Juliet Clutton-Brock, Margaret Collinson, Sam Cobb, Jill Cook, Shirley Coryndon, Jack Cronin, John Damuth, Yannick Dauphin, Chris Dean, Eric Delson, Arzu Demeril, Christiane Denys, Peter Ditchfield, Patricio Dominguez-Alonso, Stephen Dreyer, Sarah Elton, Ayhan Ersoy, Yolanda Fernàndez-Jalvo, Mikael Fortelius, Eva-Maria Geigl, Insaf Gençtürk, Barbara Ghaleb, Phil Gingerich, Mireille Giovanola, Colin Groves, Judith Harris, Terry Harrison, Robin Harvey, Sylvia Hixson, Kathy Homewood, Jerry Hooker, Jenny Horne, Clark Howell, Louise Humphrey, Hugh Iltis, Emma Jenkins, Jay Kelley, Rick Johnson, Bill Kimbel, Tania King, Jonathan Kingdon, Richard Klein, Meike Köhler, George Koufos, Kristin Kovarovic, Robert Kruszynski, Michael Le Bas, Roger Lewin, Helen Liversidge, Jayne Lord, Orie Loucks, Josep Marmí, Henry McHenry, Bill McGrew, Lawrence Martin, Theya Molleson, Norah Moloney, Georgia Mortzou, Salvador Moyà-Solà, John Murray, Fred Njau, Kenneth Oakley, Eileen O'Brien, Paul O'Higgins, Colin Patterson, Charles Peters, Martin Pickford, David Pilbeam, Ana Pinto, Rosemary Powers, Jay Quade, Denne Reed, Lorenzo Rook, Antonio Rosas, Brian Rosen, Fred Rögl, Phil Rye, Bill Sanders, Freidemann Schrenk, Jeff Schwartz, Louis Scott, Elwyn Simons, Christophe Soligo, Ian Stannistreet, Chris Stringer, Anthony Sutcliffe, Mark Teaford, Ibrahim Tekkaya, Heinz Tobien, Alan Turner, Dick Vane-Wright, Suvi Viranta, Alan Walker, Lars Werdelin, Eleanor Weston, Tim White, Peter Whybrow, Jim Williams, Terry Williams, Bernard Wood and Levon Yepiskoposyan.

I wish to acknowledge the kindness of the following for allowing me to use illustrations from their work: Mikael Fortelius, Jay Kelley, Tania King, Salvador Moyà-Solà, Josep Marmí, Fred Rögl, Phil Rye, Gen Suwa and Tim White.

I would like to acknowledge the help of the following from Cambridge University Press: Megan Waddington, who helped steer me through the preparation of figures and text, Beata Mako, the production editor, and Penny Lyons who copy-edited the text. I am very grateful for all their help.

Finally, I wish to give special thanks to Terry Harrison, Sylvia Hixson and Kristin Kovarovic for reading drafts of this manuscript and providing many valuable comments and suggestions for its improvement.

Note added in proof

As this book was going to the printers, an article by McNulty et al. (*Journal of Human Evolution* 84, 42–61) attributed two species of *Proconsul* to a new genus: *Ekembo nyanzae* and *Ekembo heseloni*: see Chapter 7. This changes could not be made to the text.

Chapter 1
How can we recognize common ancestors?

There are many issues that challenge us today in our investigations of the natural world. One that has always fascinated me is the structure of the universe and our position in it; and in a way following on from this, we can ask what is the nature of life and in particular how did humans evolve. The first is the stuff of astronomy, and with advancing technology we see many things today that we could not even have begun to predict in the past. The second is driven by our fascination with the world around us and in particular with ourselves, our origins and our place in the world.

It used to be thought that all we need to know about our evolutionary history will be resolved by finding more and better fossils, in the same way as it used to be thought that to understand the universe all we need is bigger and better telescopes. For both lines of inquiry, however, it is increasingly being recognized that what we really need are new ways of looking at things, at stars and cosmic rays in the case of astronomy, and at our genetic history and fossil environments in the case of human evolution. It is not enough now to find earlier and better fossils of ancestral humans; we should rather be seeking to understand their place in the web of life and their interactions with the ecosystems in which they once lived. This can be followed through-out human evolution, but of particular importance is the time when the human lineage first appeared. Can we identify our common ancestor with our closest primate relatives, or as some put it, the missing link in human evolution?

There are in fact many 'missing links' in human evolution, and Charles Darwin devoted two chapters of his book *The Origin of Species* to the problems in identifying them. Missing links are transitional forms between species, and Darwin was concerned with their apparent absence, both in living species, which he discussed at length in Chapter VI, and between related fossil species, discussed in Chapter X. He did not consider either to be fatal to his theory of natural selection, for by their nature they would have been superseded and replaced by emerging species. He would have been gratified by the current fossil record of human evolution, which is replete with 'missing links'. Each one tells us something about how we evolved as a species, when transitions occurred, and where, but none of them tell us where we first came from.

Our closest living relative among the apes is currently recognized as the chimpanzee, and it is natural to look for intermediate forms between humans and chimpanzees, both in terms of shared morphology and behaviour, and in the fossil record. Darwin is very explicit on this: "I have found it difficult, when looking at any two species, to avoid picturing to myself forms directly intermediate between them. But this is a wholly false view; we should always look for forms intermediate between each species and a common but unknown progenitor; and the progenitor will generally have differed in some respects from all its modified descendants" (Chapter X, page 413, of the sixth edition of *The Origin of Species*). In other words it would be a mistake to consider that our common ancestor with chimpanzees looked anything like either ourselves or like chimpanzees, but it is reasonable to look to see how much we share with chimpanzees, both genetically and morphologically.

Another approach to studying human evolution takes as its starting point our knowledge of modern humans, our anatomy, behaviour and genetics, and works backwards in time to look for the 'missing links' in the human fossil record. It will be seen that the further back we go, the harder it becomes to distinguish apes from humans, and the time when the human lineage arose is still unknown. We do know, however, that our closest living relatives are the apes, and I believe we need to approach this issue by looking at human origins from new directions, both by looking from the ape's point of view and by applying the new methods and technologies that are increasingly becoming available. In this way, we can extract more and more information from the available evidence. I will be looking at living and fossil apes to find genetic and morphological patterns present in the past in relation to the origin of the human lineage, extracting the likely behaviour of these now-fossilized apes, and reconstructing their place in the ecosystems in which they lived. Key points in this regard are as follows:

- Throughout three quarters of their history, fossil apes differed greatly from living apes.
- The norm for apes as shown by the fossils spanning 15 million years of evolution was of quadrupedal monkey-like adaptations.
- Fossil apes were adapted both for life in trees and on the ground.
- They were adapted for a mainly fruit diet, but some had adaptations for leaves or harder food like nuts.
- The majority of known species did not live in tropical forest but in tropical to subtropical open canopy woodland.
- Sexual dimorphism was moderate to high in many fossil apes, indicating fluid social structures.

We can infer that the last common ancestor of apes and humans shared some of these characteristics, as did early human ancestors, and major differences first came about through the acquisition of adaptations for bipedal walking early in human ancestry.

History of investigations into human evolution

The question of human origins has intrigued people from before the time of Charles Darwin. Karl Linnaeus first formulated the question of man's origin when he assigned humans to the order Primates (then called Anthropomorpha) and described them just like any other plant or animal. This was not accepted by some early scientists, who placed humans in their own separate class, and even T.H. Huxley placed humans in their own group, the Anthropini, despite the fact that he recognized their similarities with the African apes. Charles Darwin in *The Descent of Man* took the view that "from a genealogical point of view it appears ... that man ought to form merely a family, or possibly even only a subfamily" in the order Primates. He says further that "If the anthropomorphous apes be admitted to form a natural sub-group, then as man agrees with them, not only in all those characters which he possesses in common ... but in other peculiar characters, such as the absence of a tail and of callosities and in general appearance, we may infer that some ancient member of the anthropomorphous sub-group gave birth to man." Darwin finally goes on to warn that we should not expect any ancestor that "was identical with, or closely resembled, any existing ape or monkey". It was generally recognized by these nineteenth century scientists, therefore, that humans are primates, are grouped with apes and their common ancestor resembled neither ape nor human.

With regard to *where* humans evolved, Darwin is more direct. "It is therefore probable that Africa was formerly inhabited by extinct apes closely allied to the gorilla and chimpanzees; and as these two species are now man's nearest allies, it is somewhat more probable that our early progenitors lived on the African continent than elsewhere." He further recognized that early humans were frugivorous (fruit-eating) and lived in a hot climate. T.H. Huxley agreed with Darwin's conclusions both with respect to Africa being the original home of mankind and to chimpanzees and gorillas being most closely related to humans (Figure 1.1). The German zoologist Ernst Haeckel, in his *History of Creation*, devised 22 stages in the evolution of life, and in the absence of fossil evidence, he placed apes in stage 20 and humans in stage 22. The acquisition of upright walking, the presence of a large brain and the power of speech marked their separation at stage 21. These early scientists were working with near absence of fossil evidence, but it was stemming from

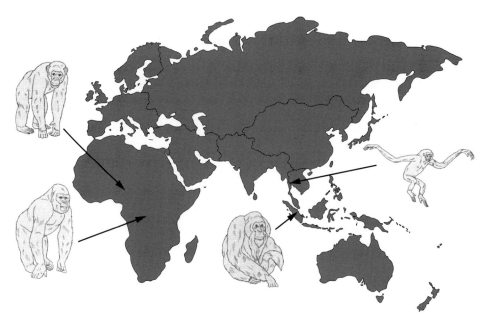

Figure 1.1 Distribution of the extant apes, chimpanzees and gorillas in Africa, and gibbons and orang utans in Southeast Asia.

their insights that early twentieth century scientists like Raymond Dart, Ralph von Koenigswald, Eugene Dubois and Louis Leakey devoted much time and expense looking for the 'missing link' or the common ancestor between humans and apes.

Eugene Dubois had been inspired by Haeckel's work, which provided him with what we would call today a 'search image'. Neanderthals did not qualify for his search image, as he thought that they were only a low sort of human, a primitive race. For Dubois, "Only the fossil remains of the transitional form between ape and man could prove evolution irrefutably. There could be no denying evolution, with such a fossil in hand. To find the right fossil, the one with anatomy that was half-man, half-ape … what a grand thing it would be, to be the man who found the missing link!"

In 1887, Eugene Dubois set out to Indonesia (at the time the Dutch East Indies) with the express purpose of finding the missing link between humans and apes, and against all the odds he was successful. First he found a molar tooth which he thought looked like a chimpanzee tooth. Soon after he found a skull cap which must have housed a brain very much larger than that of any living ape, and a leg bone which indicated that his fossil had been an upright two-legged walker. These are two elements of Haeckel's stages, and Dubois could hardly be blamed for not finding the third, as evidence of speech does not fossilize, at least not at this early stage. After some juggling with names, Dubois eventually named his fossil *Pithecanthropus erectus*, which translates as erect ape man. He claimed it was neither ape nor human but was the transitional form that must have existed between man and the anthropoids.[1] Despite its large brain, nearly twice the size of even the largest gorilla, he never accepted it as a human ancestor, although most others did so over time.

The earliest fossil human found was not in fact greeted with acclaim but was largely ignored. This was the Neandertal skull found in 1848 in Gibraltar. Many claims were made for it, but when it was first found it was not even identified as a human ancestor. It was thought by many to be a pathological modern human, with its great brow ridges and robust skull, and in fact there was little interest in it. A few years later, a similar skull was found in the Neander valley in Germany (Neander Tal). It was named by Professor William King as *Homo neanderthalensis* at the 33rd meeting of the British Association for the Advancement of Science in 1863. King described the fossil in more detail the following year, and T.H. Huxley provided an account of the Neandertal skull in *Man's Place in Nature*. He identified some of its characters as ape-like, although he recognized its human qualities: "In no sense can the Neanderthal bones be regarded as the remains of a human being intermediate between men and apes."

At the same time as these early Neandertal fossils were being found, the first fossil apes came to light from much older Miocene deposits in Europe (Figure 1.2). Some of these have been claimed to be ancestral to living apes and even humans, but all too often the search for the chimpanzee–human common ancestor has been sidelined by using the chimpanzee as a model. Such a procedure was in fact first suggested by Huxley, but using one of the descendant species like this as a model for the common ancestor would be putting the cart before the horse, for it not only does not answer the question of what the common ancestor was like, but it also actually prevents us from even asking the question. In fact, few mammalian lineages have remained unchanged since the time of the late Miocene, and it is simplistic to assume that the hominin lineage has undergone significant evolutionary change since the common ancestor but the chimpanzee lineage has not. Robert Broom was equivocal on this matter: "there is much difference of opinion as to whether the ancestor was a higher anthropoid such as the gorilla or chimpanzee, (or) an earlier anthropoid like the fossil Miocene ape *Dryopithecus*", although he had previously rejected all dryopithecines as possible ancestors on the grounds that they had

---

[1] Anthropids are the Old World monkeys and apes, the superfamilies Cercopithecoidea and Hominoidea.

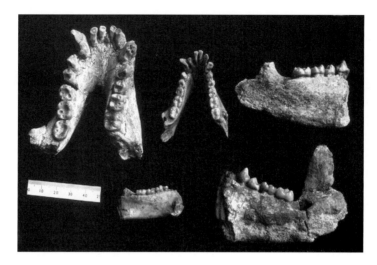

Figure 1.2 The first fossil apes of *Dryopithecus* and *Pliopithecus* found in southern France during the nineteenth century, consisting only of jaws and teeth. These fossils were known to Darwin and Huxley, but they did not comment on them.

large canines and shearing third premolars, and he considered this condition could not be reversed to arrive at the australopithecine and human condition.

Other workers took a more balanced view of human origins. W.K. Gregory observed that: "Many anthropologists have specialized almost exclusively in their own field and have not acquired a practical knowledge of the evolution of the mammals, so far as it is known in many orders and families of mammals throughout the Tertiary and Quaternary Periods. Such specialists are impressed by the great and obvious differences between mankind and the existing anthropoids. They often magnify the phylogenetic importance of these differences, sometimes to the extent of supposing that the derivation of man is still veiled in complete mystery, ... (and that) chimpanzee and gorilla have retained, with only minor changes, the ancestral habitus in brain, dentition, skull and limbs, while the forerunners of the Hominidae, through a profound change in function, lost the primitive anthropoid habitus, gave up arboreal frugivorous adaptations and early became terrestrial, bipedal and predatory, using crude flints to cut up and smash the varied food." I believe that it is a deeply buried assumption in the views of many scientists that humans are indeed 'different' from the rest of the animal kingdom, and this is in fact a throwback to nineteenth century thinking, which classified humans in their own family.

Björn Kurten, a remarkably perceptive biologist, proposed in his book that "Man did not descend from the apes. It would be more correct to say that apes and monkeys descended from early ancestors of man. The distinction is real: in the traits under consideration, man is primitive, apes and monkeys are specialized." Louis Leakey was another perceptive biologist, and he brings out two issues that give many people cause for concern when regarding our relationship with the apes when he said:

> People will stand in front of a chimpanzee in a zoo, or a stuffed gorilla in a museum, and say: 'I just could not believe that I am descended from that!' Scientists do not believe it either, nor do they ask anyone else to believe it; but they do claim that the great apes and man had a common ancestor long ago. But man on the one hand and apes on the other represent different branches and different specializations that have arisen from that common stock . . . . It has been all too common to write or speak of the great apes as PRIMITIVE members of the ape-human stock, and from this to argue that physical characters that occur in the apes are also PRIMITIVE characters, and as such, characters which one might expect to find in pre-human fossils that were in the direct line leading to man himself.

Mike Rose made a particularly telling point when he said: "When I look at the postcranial bones from the Miocene apes, I get a fairly consistent pattern from many species, but it is nothing like what we see in modern apes. Maybe we should consider the ones that survived as the bizarre ones." I believe we should indeed take the Miocene apes as 'normal' and their present survivors as highly derived, which means most emphatically that we should not use any of the living apes as a model for the ancestral pattern for humans.

Fossil apes and human evolution

Now we should consider how much fossil apes can tell us about human evolution and what kind of information we can expect to get from a study of fossil apes. For a start they provide an approximate age *when* a particular lineage arose, including the human lineage; they also tell us *where* it existed in the past; and therefore they tell us where and when the ancestors for two lineages may have lived, and in particular where and when the last common ancestor of apes and humans lived. In addition, they tell us *which adaptations* were present in different lineages of fossil ape, which can then be compared with the adaptations seen in early humans, the order in which adaptations appeared and which were important to the life of the animals. This is important in itself, but if the adaptations are related to the *environment* with which they were associated, they should allow us to interpret the place fossil apes and humans occupied in that environment. These issues are based on the assumption that morphological adaptations relate to habitat and can be interpreted for fossil apes by comparison with living primates.

In contrast to all these things that the study of fossil apes tells us about ape and human evolution, it needs to be stated that most species of fossil ape tell us little about the evolutionary relationships of living taxa. The evidence for this comes from genetics and morphology of living species; although I will provide some background on this, the main part of this book is about the fossils, and therefore the main emphasis of this book will not be on evolutionary relationships but on the adaptations and the environment of the ape ancestors of humans. This is based on my belief that any realistic assessment of the last common ancestor of apes and humans must be interpreted in terms of where, when and how it lived, and this means its location and environment. I will be describing the ranges of adaptations present in fossil apes in relation to their environment, and in interpreting the types of habitat occupied by the Miocene apes I will be drawing upon my years of work in Kenyan forestry. I should explain a little about my work in Kenya as a background to the ecological interpretations I will present later in this book.

My first job in Africa was in the Kenyan Department of Forestry, at a remote forest station high up on the slopes of the Aberdare Mountains: Kiandangoro Forest Station is set in the midst of montane forest at an altitude of 2400 metres. There are dense bamboo thickets through which elephants had carved pathways, and following these paths was virtually the only way of penetrating them; by contrast the montane forest was easier to get through except that it seemed to be mostly growing on near vertical slopes. I had many close encounters with the local wildlife, including a close inspection from a leopard one night while asleep in a rather flimsy tent. I also had the good fortune to walk through a large herd of buffalo in dense vegetation without seeing a single one. The forest guards who had gone on ahead and who were safely perched up in trees could see the whole event unfolding, which they told me about in graphic detail afterwards.

My next posting in Kenya was to assist with the running of the Nyeri Division, which controlled the montane forests of Mount Kenya and the Aberdares. Although collectively described as forest, in fact the vegetation ranged from magnificent camphor forests on the southeast mountain slopes, where the moisture-laden winds blowing in from the sea dumped most of their water load, to the dry cedar forests of the northwest, the winds having deposited most of their moisture content before reaching there. On the northern slopes there are no trees at all, the dry forest having been replaced by ericaceous vegetation. Above the upper limits of the tree line, at about 3000 m, was a wonderful landscape of heathers, giant groundsel and *Senecio*.

My third posting was to western Kenya, both to seek out new areas to set aside for planting new forests around the shores of Lake Victoria and to manage Kakamega Forest. Kakamega Forest is an 'island forest', the furthest eastern outlier of the Central African and Ugandan lowland forests (technically part of the Guinea-Congolian lowland rainforest). It officially extends over 240 km^2 and has a great variety of habitats: species-rich areas in broad river valleys (Yala River), intermediate semi-deciduous forest with less complex canopy structure covering much of the area away from the valleys and more open areas of bushland on rocky outcrops. Local farmers have excised much of the land, both officially and unofficially, for settlement, so that well under half of this area is now under forest. The mammal fauna has been well documented by Jonathan Kingdon in his magnificent series on East African Mammals, and the monkeys have been extensively studied, including the formation of mixed-species groups of monkeys. What is particularly interesting about this region is that the forest vegetation is interrupted by grass glades, areas with stable borders of *Acacia* and tall herbaceous vegetation. These may have been the result of clearing of the forest, although where the forest is being cleared at present for agriculture, the trees grow back if given the chance. The surrounding forest has many pioneer tree species that rush to fill any clearing, for example *Maesopsis eminii*, which is a common species at Kakamega, and which is known to readily expand into surrounding grasslands. The glades have shallow dry soils, unlike the grass dambos of the Central African forests, which are part swamp. Since rainfall over the Kakamega Basin is in excess of 2000 mm, spread evenly throughout the year, with even the driest month receiving about 100 millimetres, it is evident that the grass glades are not climatically controlled but are present as a result of some other factors. As far as I know, this has not yet been studied, but other possible solutions are that there is a hard pan close to the surface of the soil, which impedes drainage of the soil and prevents the growth of deep-rooting trees, or there may be chemical contaminants in the soil preventing growth of trees (Figure 1.3).

Kakamega Forest is in the north of Nyanza Province, and in the south there were almost no forest areas receiving any protection. My job was to locate suitable areas and to persuade the local population of the benefits of building up forests. This was not an easy task, and while a measure of agreement was reached for several areas, in the long term the needs of the local people for land to grow crops on has prevailed. In the course of my work in the region I met many interesting people, and one of the lessons I learned was the tragedy of living with contradictions. Subsistence farming was the norm in that part of Kenya, and the farmers were able to feed their families by expanding into the woodlands surrounding their farms. They did this by cutting down the trees, and they could tell me of several instances where the clearing had destroyed their water supplies. They were well aware of cause and effect, the existence of

Figure 1.3 Kakamega Forest, Kenya. (a) The interior of the semi-evergreen forest, which is classified as intermediate tropical forest, i.e. intermediate between lowland and montane forest. (b) The forest edge, with rainforest stepping down to a line of Acacias and down again to a line of high herbaceous (*Acanthus*) vegetation, and finally down to grassland. (c) The transitional border is more or less permanent, and fires started in the grassland do not penetrate into the forest. Grass glades are very extensive within the forest boundaries, and they appear to be edaphic in origin rather than climatic, but the nature of the soil factors is not known at present. A black and white version of this figure will appear in some formats. See plate section for colour version.

perennial streams being dependent on tree cover on the hills and watersheds, and they had observed for themselves how the streams dried up when the trees were cut down, but the farmers were forced to expand into the woodlands to provide for their sons and daughters. In theory they welcomed my proposals to set aside areas for forestry, but in practice they needed the land for growing food.

While working for the forestry department, I encountered extensive areas of sediment with fossils exposed due to erosion (helped by removal of the trees), in areas like Songhor, Rusinga Island and Maboko Island. Because I also had an interest in fossils, I collected some of those that I had found and showed them to Dr L.S.B. Leakey in Nairobi. Louis was always interested and supportive of the ignorant amateur, so when in 1967 my position with the forestry department was 'africanized', that is, the replacement of expatriates by qualified Kenyans, Louis encouraged me to switch from forestry to anthropology. He helped me get a place in his old college at Cambridge, St John's College, and promised me a job describing the big collection of Miocene fossil apes when I returned to Kenya. This all duly came to pass and led to my PhD dissertation, which he supervised in his own inimitable way: my 'supervisions' involved waiting outside his office and then trotting after him as he walked to his next appointment along the outside corridors of the old Centre for Prehistory and Palaeontology. To my great regret, Louis died the year before I completed my dissertation and long before I was ready to publish my results.

I wrote my dissertation on fossil apes from western Kenya, describing new species and revising others. At the same time, I analysed the environments in which the fossil apes lived, thus combining anthropology with my forestry background. This was useful also when I described the modern flora of Rusinga Island, one of the principal fossil ape sites, and when I joined Colin Groves and Jenny Horne on an expedition to the lower Tana River in Kenya to work on the plant and animal ecology. The Tana River forests have a disjunct distribution, being similar to those of Central Africa several thousand kilometres away, and the species of colobus monkey and mangabey living there have a similar disjunct distribution. The small mammal fauna living in the forests was also remarkable in that the dominant species of rodent was the spiny mouse (*Acomys*), which is normally found in arid and semi-desert conditions, which was an early lesson in the adaptability of mammals to environments far outside their 'normal' ones.

My background in both forestry and anthropology has coloured my perspective on the last common ancestor of apes and humans, viewing it not as an abstract entity that was in some way intermediate between, and ancestral to, apes and humans, but as a fossil species that was living and adapted to a particular environment. For example, human beings are now completely terrestrial, but did we develop this bipedal walking because we were already terrestrial, or did we become terrestrial because we were becoming bipedal? Interpreting the environment in which the ancestral apes lived is key to understanding this conundrum and what it means to human origins (see Chapter 5).

Jonathan Kingdon makes the point that:

> The habitats of today's species may differ in many important ways from those of ancestral species, but the fact that modern chimpanzees are forest-dwelling fruit-eaters while omnivorous humans live in more open habitats has led to a widespread assumption about the course of human evolution. The favourite image is of forests drying out and the four-legged, forest-living ancestors of humans adapting to more open conditions by becoming erect. This in my view must be wrong; chimpanzee ancestors were not always tied to the rain forest, and human ancestors could not have moved out into open environments until they were already bipedal.

There is now increasing evidence (as far as it is known at present) that Miocene apes did not for the most part live in tropical forests but are mostly associated with woodland habitats; and the types of woodland they occupied were similar to those occupied by the earliest hominins. In other words, there was no great environmental change in the transition from late Miocene ape to late Miocene hominin. This will be one of the main themes of this book.

Common ancestors

Chimpanzees are generally accepted as being our nearest living relatives, and when comparisons are made with human evolution, the implicit assumption is sometimes made that chimpanzees have not changed greatly from the common ancestor shared with humans and that there has been great change within the human lineage. We know the latter to be true, for there is now an extensive fossil record of human fossils, but we know next to nothing about the chimpanzee lineage, which may have passed through comparable degrees of change. Present-day genetic variation in chimpanzees, for instance, is greater than that present in humans, despite the fact that the distribution of chimpanzees today (and probably in the past) is limited to a narrow band of equatorial Africa, whereas humans and human ancestors have long had a continental or global distribution. We do not know how the genetic changes manifest themselves in chimpanzee anatomy. In the absence of fossil evidence, we have to work out which of the two descendant species, humans or chimpanzees, retains more ancestral characters than the other, and we must be cautious before jumping to conclusions on this subject, both in terms of morphology and genetics.

The common ancestor of chimpanzees and humans undoubtedly shared characters with both but was also different from both. We can identify some characters of our common ancestor with chimpanzees by comparing them to humans to see what they have in common and how they are different (see Chapter 2). This comparison can be extended back to the relative next in line, gorillas, by outgroup comparison. From a theoretical perspective, however, it may be argued that any common ancestor is essentially unknowable, because the characters by which it may be linked with its descendant species are not yet present. Closely related species are certain to share many characters as well as having developed different characters after their separation, but by the time that any one of these characters are present in a putative ancestor, it is no longer the common ancestor but belongs to one or other of the descendant lineages. For example, one of the most visible morphologies distinguishing living apes from all other primates is the loss of the tail, and any fossil primate lacking a tail cannot be the common ancestor between monkeys and apes but must already be considered an ape. However, the common ancestor could have had a tail without being placed on the line leading to monkeys, for all other primates have tails, and this is the ancestral condition for all primates primitively retained by monkeys. It is likely, therefore, that the common ancestor of apes and monkeys had a tail, but this does not help to identify it, just as lack of tail would disqualify it as the common ancestor. It is interesting that tails in primates come in all shapes and sizes, but once lost, as in apes, it seems that it is lost forever. The characters present in a common ancestor, therefore, can only be identified if they are either ancestral retentions from an earlier common ancestor (such as a tail) or if they are characters shared uniquely by the two descendant species. An example of the latter in the hominoid clade is the presence of a vermiform appendix, which is a character shared by all apes and humans but absent in other primates.

In the past 50 years, many hominin fossils have been identified as human ancestors, but there is still little agreement as to their relationships with each other and with modern humans. I use the term hominins for humans and their immediate ancestors, that is, all fossils that are more closely related to modern humans than they are to anything else. Fossil hominins may be links on the chain leading to modern humans, or they may be side branches off the main line leading only to extinction, but if they are more closely related to humans than they are to apes, they cannot be the common ancestor of apes and humans. It is in the clade encompassing apes and humans that we must look for their common ancestor, and we need to consider the evidence for which ape. Towards the end of the twentieth century, there was debate about whether it was the African apes that were most closely related to humans, as first suggested by Darwin and Huxley, or whether it was the orang utan. The matter appears to have been resolved with the advent of DNA studies, which demonstrate that chimpanzees have the greatest genetic affinity with humans, but there remains a body of morphological evidence, and some genetic, that suggests a closer relationship between orang utans and humans, so some doubt remains about this conclusion. What is clear is that many characters appear in parallel in the living apes, and this makes it difficult to decipher the exact path of ape and human evolution. This is expressed as the presence of high degrees of homoplasy in hominoid evolution, that is, the independent evolution of character states through evolutionary convergence.

There is less doubt about the timing and location of the common ancestor of the African apes and humans. It has been widely assumed from the time of Darwin and Huxley that the location was somewhere in Africa: the early fossil record for humans from 5 to 2 million years ago is exclusively African, but the fossil record of the African apes during the same period is almost non-existent. During the previous period, 12 to 8 million years ago, few fossil apes are known from Africa whereas at the same time there is an abundance of fossil apes in Europe and Asia. This has led some anthropologists to suggest that the common ancestor of the African apes and humans was derived from European fossil apes such as *Dryopithecus*, which re-entered Africa in the late Miocene. Recently, however, several fossil finds have been made in Africa that begin to bridge the gap, and these will be briefly reviewed in Chapter 15 along with several other hominid species that are currently identified as hominins, that is, direct human ancestors. Now, however, we must return to the central question of this book, how can we identify the last common ancestor of apes and humans?

Firstly, we have to set up a working phylogeny of the extant taxa based on their similarities derived from common ancestry. These are characters present through common descent, so that they can be deemed to be genetically and biologically the same (homologous characters). Not all shared similarities are homologous, however, for some may have arisen independently like the wings of birds and bats, and viewing similarities without an understanding of how they arose can produce misleading results. This is the difference between phylogenetic and phenetic similarity, clade versus grade. The subject of Palaeoanthropology has suffered considerably from the confusion over this dichotomy, as some scientists continue to support the grade concept through their insistence on maintaining the separation of the great apes in Pongidae and humans in Hominidae. This was partly due to Gregory's influence and partly because of their perception of the radically different adaptive and behaviour zones occupied by humans and chimpanzees. The two family names are still used by some to this day, but an increasing number of researchers have proposed alternative taxonomies that are consistent with currently recognized relationships among the extant hominoids.[2] To truly reflect evolutionary history these phylogenies must be based on homologous characters inherited from recent ancestors and convergent, or non-homologous, homoplasies must be discarded. Further to this, the characters shared between two species are only significant in evolutionary terms if they were uniquely shared with their common ancestor, so that they are both homologous and derived (synapomorphies) relative to other species. Homology can sometimes be clearly evident, as for instance in the loss of the tail in all apes, but examples will be given below of cases where the evidence is ambiguous, as in the case of the facial similarities between the fossil ape *Sivapithecus* and the orang utan. These two apes share many characters of the face that are often assumed to be homologous, derived characters shared uniquely by them, but the postcrania in the fossil ape are nothing like that present in the orang utan, which shares many characters related to its orthograde (upright) posture with chimpanzees and gorillas. If *Sivapithecus* is indeed on the orang utan lineage, these postcranial characters must have evolved in the orang utan independently of the other great apes and humans. This is quite possible if, for instance, the great ape and human common ancestor lacked orthograde specializations. Molecular evidence is not immune from this problem of homoplasy, as will be discussed in the next chapter.

This illustrates some of the difficulties in identifying common ancestors. It can be seen that the degree of proximity of an extinct taxon to the last common ancestor of chimpanzees and humans is inversely related to the number of phylogenetically informative characters that either link them or are unique to either, and so it is to be expected that earlier stem hominins (that is, those at the base of the hominin lineage) become increasingly more difficult to recognize in the fossil record based on such characteristics. It means that we are faced with the regrettable situation that the earlier the hominin, the more complete will have to be the fossil material in order to identify possible hominin characters.

Taking as an example the split between monkeys and apes for which we have more evidence, we can potentially provide better evidence on their

---

[2] References are given in my publication with Terry Harrison, from which parts of this section are derived.

ancestral morphotypes. Based on extant anthropoids, the group that includes both monkeys and apes, it is equally possible to reconstruct individual characters of the ancestral hominoid morphotypes as being more like Old World monkeys, more like hominoids, intermediate, or uniquely different from the extant forms or their nearest outgroup. For example, the ancestral anthropoid condition may have had lower molars with a tiny hypoconulid (fifth cusp), which was subsequently enlarged in hominoids and lost in cercopithecids. This inferred intermediate ancestral state is a perfectly reasonable supposition given that this is the condition in other primate outgroups, that is, species that diverged at earlier evolutionary stages. However, the occurrence of large hypoconulids in stem anthropoids, that is, fossil species that are clearly anthropoid but neither ape nor monkey, and the evidence from the earliest fossil monkeys demonstrate that a large hypoconulid on M_1 and M_2 was the primitive condition for the last common ancestor of extant catarrhines, just as in fossil and modern hominoids. Similarly, Old World monkeys are distinctive among modern anthropoids in having specializations of the foot, which are functionally associated with increasing the stability during extreme bending of the foot. These features are lacking or poorly expressed in all other extant primates, and based on this it would be reasonable to conclude that these are unique characters present only in the monkey lineage and absent in apes. However, these characters are also typically found in fossil ankle bones from the early Miocene of East Africa belonging to stem hominoids, so that when fossils are introduced into the analysis these characters of the foot seem likely to have been present in the common ancestor of monkeys and apes (unless we accept the improbable scenario that early Miocene fossil apes, including *Proconsul*, are more closely related to monkeys).

What these examples demonstrate is just how labile the list of individual traits is that make up the ancestral morphotypes, especially as new data are introduced into the analysis. The potential for error is compounded once the individual traits are combined into an ancestral morphotype. With this in mind, it is important to view ancestral morphotypes as approximations with relatively low resolution, rather than precise and accurate formulations of the ancestral condition. This is particularly important in stem forms where the proportion of potentially phylogenetically meaningful characters is small in relation to the number of primitive features, and the level of resolution may, therefore, exceed the capability to confidently differentiate their preserved anatomy from the ancestral morphotypes. If this is the case, there is a serious danger that the outcome of phylogenetic analyses might be influenced or skewed by the introduction of a few characters of uncertain or dubious utility.

Summary

- The last common ancestor of apes and humans was that species of fossil hominid that was ancestral to humans and our closest living ape, the chimpanzees.
- Based on their shared geographical location, it is inferred that the last common ancestor lived in Africa, and it combined primitive characters present in apes generally; characters present in the great ape and human clade (e.g. loss of tail, increasingly upright posture); and characters shared uniquely by humans and chimpanzees.
- Only the last of the three sets of characters are diagnostic of the last common ancestor of apes and humans, as the others are retained from earlier ancestors.
- All these characters need to be interpreted in terms of their functional relationship with the environment occupied by the fossil hominids in order to understand their place in the environment.
- Throughout the evolution of the apes, their preferred habitat was woodland rather than forest; and most species were partly terrestrial. The last common ancestor of chimpanzees and the earliest fossil hominins were also partly terrestrial woodland dwellers.

Part I
Apes: their morphology and behaviour

Chapter 2
Morphology and behaviour of living apes

We have seen in the previous chapter that in order to reconstruct the relationships of living apes and humans, it is necessary to look both to the living species and to fossil apes. The next two chapters are entirely concerned with the morphology, behaviour and genetics of living apes, gibbons, orang utans, chimpanzees and gorillas, with some notes on humans (upright bipedal apes) as well. This will lead to their formal classification, which also includes some of the fossil apes that are discussed in Chapter 4.

Extant apes

Living species of apes have an exclusively tropical distribution and are divided between the Asian apes, living in tropical forest environments in Southeast Asia, and African apes, living in varied wooded habitats across Central and West Africa and extending into the western borders of East Africa. Living apes and humans are distinguished from other primates through morphological features such as the absence of a tail and presence of an appendix. They share a number of specializations of the skeleton, which are useful as diagnostic characters because bones and teeth are the most readily preserved parts in the fossil record. Orthograde (upright) body posture, broad chests, mobile shoulder regions and short, stiff lower backs are present in all living apes and distinguish them from monkeys. The clavicle (collar bone) is long, the shoulder bone is situated on the back rather than the sides of the chest and the wrist is modified for mobility of the joint. The lumbar vertebrae have robust pedicles, caudally inclined spinous processes and dorsally oriented transverse processes arising from the pedicle. Synapomorphies of the skull include the deep arched palate and relatively small incisive foramina. The teeth are generally primitive, except in the broad incisors and enlarged molars. Recently, it has been demonstrated that soft-tissue anatomy also distinguishes within and between apes and humans, but unfortunately soft tissues do not generally fossilize.

Asian apes include the gibbons and orang utans. They retain many primitive ape characteristics and have also developed a number of unique characters that are different from any other ape, in particular those related with brachiation in the gibbons. There are thirteen species of gibbon (*Hylobates*) divided into four subgenera or genera (*Hylobates Nomascus, Hoolock, Symphalangus*) occupying most parts of Southeast Asia where primary forest still remains. They are strictly arboreal, and they move about in the trees suspended by their greatly elongated arms in a type of locomotion called brachiation. They have many adaptations to brachiation, for example, the automatic hook formed by their hands when they extend their arms – they literally cannot extend their fingers when their arms are extended, an excellent device for hanging securely on to branches. Their arms are relatively long compared with the size of their bodies. They also appear to have long legs as well and they often move bipedally on larger branches of trees. Geometric morphometric measurements of the skull show that when size is removed, gibbons are similar to gorillas, probably the ancestral condition for apes. Humans and orangutans differ most greatly from this.

The combination of characters present in all gibbons indicates that they all share a single common ancestor, but little is known of the gibbon fossil record. They are distinctive in sharing large-scale chromosomal rearrangements, and speciation models based on this indicate a divergence date of 5 million years ago. The minimum age for the gibbon radiation is also indicated by a shared genetic mutation of the uricase gene, which occurred in the middle to late Miocene, between 10 and 5 million years ago. This led to increases in serum uric acid, which enhanced the ability to convert fruit sugars to fat stores, and it would have provided selective advantage for fruit-eating animals living in seasonal environments since it improved their ability to survive periods of food shortage by building up fat reserves during times of plenty (see Chapter 4).

Two species of orang utan are known from the tropical rainforests of Borneo (*Pongo pygmaeus*) and Sumatra (*Pongo abelii*), but fossil orang utans are also known from mainland Asia. Both species are largely arboreal despite their great size, which ranges in body weight from 88 to 308 lb (40 to 140 kg), and they are therefore restricted to multi-canopy rainforest.

The orang utan is strictly arboreal, and although it has slightly elongated arms relative to its body weight, it lacks the brachiating adaptations of gibbons. Also unlike the gibbons, the orang utan's legs are short relative to body size, so that its arms appear disproportionately long. They have a suite of characters enabling them to move in trees by hanging on with all four hands and feet, as the foot is strongly grasping and functions in part like a hand. Other characters are a stiff lower back, a broad chest, rib cage broad and flattened from front to back and into which the spine is embedded, scapula on the back rather than the sides of the chest and elongated clavicle. These characters are present also in African great apes and humans, and they are often claimed as evidence that all great apes and humans passed through a suspensory phase of evolution, but recent fossil evidence suggests that these

should be viewed as pre-adaptations for suspension and that suspensory locomotion has been acquired independently by several hominoid lineages. It is
upright (orthograde) posture that is the common inheritance of the great apes
and humans. These similarities with the African great apes have led in the past
to them being grouped in the same family, the Pongidae, and the whole group
classed as brachiators like the gibbons; however, it is likely that the suspensory
characters in the orang utan lineage were acquired independently of other
apes and the characters present in the African apes and humans have nothing
to do with suspensory activity.

The differences separating the orang utans from other apes are in part
genetic (for example, some aspects of their DNA) and in part morphological.
Soft-tissue morphology, for example, conclusively supports the molecular
evidence in distinguishing the orang utan from the African apes, but it
has also been shown to share many characters with humans, more for
instance than are shared between chimpanzees and humans. However, the
deep face, enlarged premaxilla, narrow distance between the eyes, massive
zygomatic bones, smooth floor of nose and enlarged central incisors are
characters unique to the orang utan, and in all of these traits the African apes
and humans retain what is interpreted to be the primitive ape condition.
Orang utans also differ from humans and other apes in the angle the face
makes with the base of the skull. The highest degree of bending is present in
humans (the condition known as klinorhynchy) and least degree in orang
utans (airorhynchy). In this respect the African apes are more similar to
humans than to the orang utan, although there is considerable variation,
related in part to the degree of prognathism, that is, the extent to which the
lower face projects beyond the front of the cranium. We do not know what
the primitive condition was for Hominoidea, and evidence from fossil apes is
ambiguous (see Chapters 12 and 16).

There are two (or probably three) species of chimpanzee (Figure 2.1).
Bonobos (*Pan paniscus*) are confined to the southern loop of the Congo River,
living in impoverished forest that is growing on Kalahari sands, indicating that
the area was very different in the past. The common chimpanzee (*Pan troglodytes*) has the widest distribution in East and Central Africa, and now the
western chimpanzee populations are named as a separate species, *Pan verus*.
Habitats range from lowland evergreen forest (Equatorial Guinea, the Tai
Forest), intermediate evergreen forest (Budongo, Kibale), dry forest (Mahale),
mixed forest and woodland (Gombe), riverine forest in arid savanna (Senegal)
and Miombo woodland (Ugalla). The last named site is sometimes referred to
as 'savanna' and so we get 'savanna chimpanzees', but in fact the vegetation at
Ugalla is Miombo woodland, which is described by Frank White as transitional
woodland 10 to 20 metres in height. In all habitats, chimpanzee diet remains

Figure 2.1 Chimpanzee eating figs in the Budongo Forest, Uganda. Most living and fossil apes were fruit-eaters, and figs are an essential element of their diet. Figs are common in forest and in savanna woodlands, where they may grow to great size along water courses. Their unique form of fertilization (by species of fig wasp exclusive to the species of fig) and the fact that individual fig trees produce fruit asynchronously with other fig trees means that figs are available at most times of the year.

remarkably consistent with some regional differences: the chimpanzees of the Tai Forest, for example, do not appear to hunt duiker even though they are hunted in other areas; and the scavenging of already dead animals and digging for underground storage items may be slightly greater in more arid habitats, although rare in general.

African apes are distinguished from orang utans by specializations of the wrist, elbow, hand and frontal sinus and the development of thick brow ridges. They have a series of unique modifications of the elbow, wrist and hand that are related to knuckle-walking. Their legs are reduced in length (relative to body weight) so that their arms appear long in proportion to the rest of their body, although in fact their arms are no longer relative to body weight than in other higher primates. The effects of the apparent arm length are further increased both by elongation of the fingers of the hand and by the fact that when they walk quadrupedally on the ground they support their weight on the middle phalanges of the hand. This raises the body to a semi-upright position even when the animals are walking on all fours, and this trend to upright posture may be a precursor to the fully upright posture in humans. The orang utan, which parallels the leg reduction in African apes, has proportionally longer arms relative to body weight; while Tom Rein has shown that relative to gibbons and the spider monkey (*Ateles*), which are the two primates which have the greatest degree of suspensory behaviour, the forearms of orang utans are not as long as indicated by their behaviour.

Chimpanzees and gorillas combine upright posture with possible adaptations for suspensory locomotion in their elongated hands, adaptations of the elbow and shoulder joints and the circular cross-section of the humerus shafts. Similar adaptations are present in the orang utan (but not in humans). Outgroup comparison, first comparing humans with chimpanzees, then both with gorillas, and then all three with orang utans, parsimoniously shows that whereas the ancestor of the great ape and human clade had orthograde adaptations, it is less clear if it had suspensory adaptations. Well-developed suspensory adaptations are present in several lineages of fossil apes, in all cases associated with upright posture, but not all of them could be ancestral to the living great apes and humans. If so, it it is likely that their suspensory characters were either primitively retained in the great apes and in humans or that they were convergent. If they were not ancestral to later hominids, or if the hominid common ancestor lacked suspensory characters, it suggests that suspension was not a significant characteristic of human and great ape ancestry.

The second scenario of common ancestry of apes and humans is through adaptations to knuckle-walking. This is a unique form of locomotion by which chimpanzees and gorillas support themselves on the dorsal surfaces of the middle phalanges of the hand (not actually their knuckles as the name suggests). William Gregory described this peculiar form of locomotion in 1916 as a prelude to bipedalism in humans, and since that time it has received much support as a characteristic of the ape/human common ancestor. The adaptations present in chimpanzees and gorillas for this form of locomotion are similar in both, and this similarity has been put forward as evidence both of their sister-group relationship, based on the assumption that the shared characters are homologous. If this is the case, both the common ancestor of the African apes and humans, and the last common ancestor of chimpanzees and humans, were probably knuckle-walkers, on the basis of this being the most parsimonious evolutionary change.

Several authors have challenged this view and suggested that the knuckle-walking characters in chimpanzees and gorillas were acquired independently, and this has been tested by Scott Williams based on the morphologies of the hand and wrist. He showed not only that many of the supposed 'knuckle-walking characters' are present in many other primates associated with other forms of locomotion, but also that they are variably developed in chimpanzees and gorillas and do not always occur together in a strongly correlated way. It is likely, therefore, that they developed independently in chimpanzees and gorillas, that is, they are not homologous; furthermore, they do not provide evidence of sister-group relationship between them, contrary to early thinking on this subject.

Knuckle-walking characters present in chimpanzees and gorillas include wrist adaptations such as fusion of the os centrale with the scaphoid and dorsal extension of the articular surface of the capitulum, and the development of dorsal ridges on the metacarpals of the hand to limit dorsiflexion. There are, however, a number of differences in the wrist anatomy that cannot be put down to differences in behaviour. Two of the wrist bones in gorillas are relatively shorter throughout growth (ontogeny), and there are differences in the sizes of articular facets. These differences in body weight transference during knuckle-walking and the fact that they arise during growth indicate that knuckle-walking evolved in parallel in chimpanzees and gorillas. In addition, some of the supposed knuckle-walking characters may have been adaptations for climbing large vertical supports.

The great range of diets in chimpanzee populations has been demonstrated through the analysis of carbon isotopes in chimpanzees living in the Kibale Forest, Uganda. The isotope values differ from both those of leaf-eating and fruit-eating monkeys, and they are apparently influenced by a great variety of features in the habitat. In contrast to this, the oxygen isotope values show chimpanzees as canopy feeders and distinct from terrestrial feeders such as warthogs, baboons and duikers. These results will be seen in Part IV to be relevant to the interpretation of fossil ape diets.

The great habitat range of chimpanzees is unusual, for few mammals are known that can live in both forest and non-forest habitats. Very large mammals like the African elephant and the black rhinoceros live in both, as well as some carnivore species such as leopards, the ultimate all-rounder, but no African primates live in both apart from chimpanzees. This begs the question as to the environment of origin for chimpanzees: was it forest, as many researchers suppose, with chimpanzees hanging on in supposed marginal woodland habitats? Or were they originally woodland-adapted species, managing to survive in forest during the last few thousand years as the African woodlands have been gradually decimated by human populations? Jonathan Kingdon has suggested their existence in forests may be analogous to that of the Okapi, a clearly non-forest-adapted relative of giraffes marooned in tropical forest as rainfall increased and the Central African forests expanded after the last major dry period in Africa.

The vegetation and climate of Mt Assirik in Senegal is described as mixed gallery forest, deciduous woodland, bamboo, grassland and bushland plateau, with woodland and grassland making up over 90% of the habitat (Figure 2.2). This compares for example with the environment at Gombe, which is a

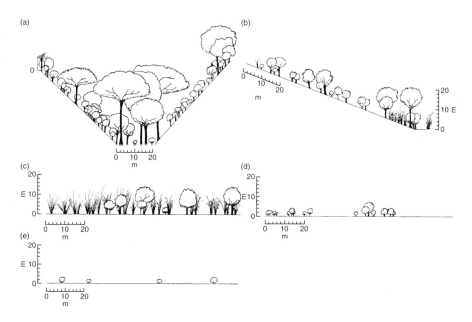

Figure 2.2 Vegetation profiles at Mt Assirik, Senegal showing the five principal vegetation types occupied by chimpanzees: (a) gallery forest with woodland on upper slopes; (b) woodland; (c) bamboo mixed woodland; (d) grassland; and (e) plateau grassland. Reproduced with permission from McGrew et al. 1981.

mixture of evergreen forest, semi-deciduous forest, Miombo woodland and grassland with scattered trees, with the latter making up 39% of the habitat. Several other chimpanzee habitats have been analysed in the same way, such as those at Ugalla, Kasakati and Mahali, which are also predominantly woodland and grassland (85 to 90%).

Tropical woodlands vary greatly in structure and species composition, but from a chimpanzee's point of view, perhaps the most important thing they have in common is that they have abundant and varied ground vegetation (Figure 2.3). This contrasts with the frequently sparse ground cover in tropical forests. It is unfortunate that little is known about the past range of chimpanzees, but they have been recorded in middle Pleistocene deposits in Kenya, 600 km to the east of their present range and associated with open woodland to arid environments. There is a very real possibility that chimpanzees have long been adapted to a wide variety of habitats, only one element of which is tropical evergreen forest, and this has been true throughout their evolutionary history. They have catholic diets, and in an analysis of the diet of Liberian chimpanzees it has been shown that the isotopic signal was surprisingly homogeneous, with little differences between young and old, or between males that consume most meat and females that consume less, or between

Figure 2.3 Tropical deciduous woodland dominated by small-leaved *Acacia* species. The tree canopy is 60 to 80% closed. The crowns of some trees are in contact, gaps between trees are small, and even where canopies interconnect, the branches are too small to support the weight of any of the known fossil apes. There is a partly evergreen bush community and ground vegetation is mainly grass and herbs.

groups inhabiting rainforest and those in woodland habitats. In other words, they appear to be happy eating almost anything.

One common element to most habitats occupied by chimpanzees is the presence of fig trees (see Figure 2.1). Fig trees have a symbiotic relationship with fig wasps, each species of fig having their own unique species of wasp that both pollinates the fig flowers and eats their fruits. The wasps benefit through gaining a safe refuge inside developing figs, and the trees benefit by having guaranteed pollination. The life cycle of fig wasp species in tropical environments is to a large extent independent both of life cycles of other fig wasps and of variations in climatic seasons, so that production of fruit by African figs can occur at any time of the year, independently of time of fruiting of other fig trees. Therefore, in a large enough expanse of woodland or forest with a sufficient number of fig trees, there are always some fruiting figs throughout the year, and it is this more than anything that allows fruit-eating animals such as chimpanzees to survive even in apparently hostile environments.

Gorilla species are also confined to tropical Africa, and the genus is divided into the eastern gorilla (*Gorilla beringei*) and the western lowland gorilla (*Gorilla*

gorilla). Some scientists distinguish these species at the subspecies level, but the current trend is to see them as distinct species. The gorillas are the largest of the primates, with body weights ranging from 165 to 396 lb (75 to 180 kg), whereas chimpanzees at 88 to 110 lb (40 to 50 kg) are much smaller. The differences in size between males and females, termed sexual dimorphism, are related to aspects of behaviour in the apes, and to some degree they may also form the basis for identifying behaviour in fossil apes (Figure 2.4).

Body mass dimorphism varies in all primate species, and males are generally larger than females. Human males are on average 15 per cent larger than females, but in gorillas and orang utans this increases to 50 per cent, making them highly sexually dimorphic. Gorilla social groups are dominated by single large males called silver-backs because their backs are covered by white hair, which control and defend a group of females and their offspring for exclusive mating rights. The silver-backs are distinguished not only by their larger size and distinctive hair colour, but also by their larger canine teeth, which are used in displays against other males. Chimpanzees have lower levels of sexual dimorphism; although males may act aggressively towards other males, they tolerate each other for the most part and live in multi-male groups. Gibbons are the least dimorphic of the apes, and like humans they have monogamous life styles. This minimizes rivalry between males and hence the need for males to become large and aggressive. There is thus a degree of association between sexual dimorphism and behaviour in living primates relating to some aspects of territoriality, competition and dominance behaviour. Sexual dimorphism may be expressed in certain aspects of the teeth and limb bones, and where these body parts are available for fossil apes and humans, estimates of dimorphism can be made, particularly from measurements of the canine and femur. This issue will be discussed for some of the fossil apes where samples are big enough to estimate dimorphism, and its consequences will be disussed further in Chapter 16.

It has been mentioned above that evidence from hard tissues such as bones and teeth seem to support a relationship between gorillas and chimpanzees, whereas soft-tissue anatomy and DNA support a relationship between chimpanzees and humans. It has also been shown by John Grehan and Jeffrey Schwartz that the orang utan shares more non-DNA characters with humans than do chimpanzees. These differences in the interpretation of evidence from morphology and DNA make it problematic when interpreting fossil evidence, which is almost entirely based on bones and teeth. For example, if there are few shared derived characters from the hard tissues linking humans and chimpanzees, that is, characters shared only by them and with no other primate, how can it be possible to identify fossils belonging to the same clade? Soft tissues and DNA do not usually fossilize from these early time periods and

(a)

(b)

Figure 2.4 (a) Tropical forest showing multiple tree canopy structure and ground cover within the forest; (b) ground water forest in Tanzania. The forest is situated in an arid zone and the forest is supported by water flowing off the adjacent rift valley highlands. Species zonation is evident with larger evergreen trees along river courses leading down to the lake in the background.

so are not available for analysis. This is a critical issue when considering fossils, for it is often assumed that chimpanzees have changed less from their last common ancestor with humans, and humans have changed more, so that the last common ancestor would have looked more like a chimpanzee. This will be discussed further in Chapter 16, but it can be noted here that chimpanzees are highly derived in a number of characters, for example in their lower vertebral column, their hand proportions and their teeth.

Multivariate analysis of 171 morphological characters support human–chimpanzee relationship. It has also been considered in the past that chimpanzees and gorillas formed a sister group, based on their shared presence of knuckle-walking adaptations. However, some of the modifications of the wrist appear to be different in the two African apes, and the analyses of soft-tissue anatomy that indicated closer relationship between chimpanzees and gorillas are not supported by statistical analysis. Another soft-tissue analysis of the muscles of the head and neck and upper limbs also did not support a chimpanzee–gorilla clade, but it failed to identify any characters shared by chimpanzees and humans. What it does support is the African ape and human clade, and it further identifies six characters unique to humans compared with three unique to chimpanzees, which is presented as evidence that humans have changed more than chimpanzees since their divergence.

Many of the adaptations for upright posture have been attributed to suspensory or knuckle-walking locomotion. For example, Susan Larson has listed 34 characters said to be associated with suspensory locomotion and/or upright posture, including broad chests, shoulder bone situated on the back, stiff lower back elongated clavicle, broad sternum, wide glenoid fossa, large, round humeral head, strong medial and lateral ridges on the distal humerus, deep olecranon fossa, short olecranon process of the ulna, projecting coronoid process, round radial head, great range of movement at the elbow joint, elongated hands and reduced styloid process. Only seven of these characters are unique to living apes, however, while another eleven are present also in spider monkeys, a suspensory New World monkey. The remaining characters are shared with other, non-suspensory primates, and while they enable suspension, they are not diagnostic of the behaviour.

Mention must also be made of the possible significance of below-branch suspension in ape and human evolution. This is sometimes known as brachiation, but this is a description both of a form of behaviour, that of swinging below branches of trees, and of an anatomical functional complex, specifically that of gibbons. When first used by W.E. Owen he intended the behavioural aspect to refer only to gibbons, but at the turn of the century Sir Arthur Keith classed orang utans as brachiators and chimpanzees as having the pattern of brachiators, although excluding them as actual brachiators; later still the American anthropologist William Gregory classed both chimpanzees and gorillas as brachiators. It was not until the mid-twentieth century, when John Napier finally defined brachiation, that all apes were classed as brachiators, together with some monkeys such as spider monkeys. He later modified this by distinguishing 'true' brachiators such as the gibbons from 'modified' brachiators such as the great apes, with semi-brachiation being applied to monkeys such as the spider monkey. This was an arrangement based either on anatomy or on behaviour, sometimes both, and sometimes with a taxonomic element such as when monkey behaviour is distinguished from that of apes. The distinguishing characters, however, both in behaviour and anatomy, relate to suspension by the arms in trees (behaviour) and the adaptations that make it possible. However, some of these supposed brachiating characters, such as the short, stiff lower back, are absent in gibbons, the most suspensory of the apes. These adaptations of the trunk are in fact related to upright posture and not necessarily to suspensory activity in trees, although it may be a pre-adaptation to vertical climbing in all the living apes.

Chimpanzees in fact pass through a series of locomotor types as they mature into adults. They habitually use suspensory locomotion as juveniles, with orthograde posture and use of the arms for suspension. As they mature, however, they change to quadrupedal locomotion, the main change taking place at adolescence, and by age 12 or 13 they are fully quadrupedal. They are almost unique in this degree of change during development; gorillas show limited change during development, and by age two they are fully quadrupedal, while orang utans show no change at all in locomotor behaviour. The adaptations that are related to suspension may therefore be a relic of past evolutionary history and not related to what chimpanzees actually do in their locomotor behaviour. This does not clarify the issue of which came first, orthogrady, which enables suspensory locomotion, or suspensory activity, which required the development of orthogrady for greater efficiency.

The fourth hominid to be considered is *Homo sapiens*, the human species. Humans are found throughout the world at the present time, but fossil evidence shows that until about 70 000 years ago they were restricted to Africa. Other species of the genus *Homo* had been present in Europe and Asia in earlier times, and Neandertals were living in Europe when modern humans arrived, but only our own species survived to the present day. All, however, shared similarities in their bipedal locomotion (walking upright on two legs) and increasing brain size. The environments associated with fossil hominins will be reviewed in Chapter 15.

Bernard Wood and Terry Harrison list the characters by which fossil members of the human lineage might be recognized as follows: shortening of the face, forward position of the zygomatic process (cheek region), enlarged brain, forward position of the foramen magnum (where the spinal column connects with the brain), vertically implanted incisors, reduced canines, loss of premolar shearing function with the upper canine, enlarged molars and bipedal specializations of the hip, legs and feet. This is an impressive list, but as Wood and Harrison point out, every one of these characters, except brain enlargement, is present on one or other fossil ape or other primate. This highlights the subject of homoplasy again and the importance of determining whether characters are the result of common ancestry or convergence.

Tool making, meat-eating and cannibalism

It used to be thought that humans were the only primates that used or made tools: hence Kenneth Oakley's classic article 'Tools makyth man'. What Oakley had in mind in his *Antiquity* article was of course stone tools, not bits of twig. This all changed, starting with Jane Goodall's observation of the use of sticks by the Gombe chimpanzees when fishing for termites. It was one of Louis Leakey's far-sighted convictions that in order to gain some knowledge of the behaviour of the last common ancestor between apes and humans, one had to look to ape behaviour in comparison with our own. In this conviction he was following sound phylogenetic principles, more usually applied to morphology but equally applicable to behaviour. It was for this reason that he initiated a series of field studies on living apes, starting with Jane Goodall's work on chimpanzees at the Gombe reserve in Tanzania. He was also following the ideas of Sherwood Washburn's 'new anthropology'. Although Washburn was more interested in monkey behaviour than that of apes, Leakey always had the evolution of humans in mind, and he therefore focused on the primates closest to humans, the apes. Behaviour in terms of food intake and locomotion will be discussed later, but first I will mention two aspects of chimpanzee behaviour which do not fossilize but which may cast light on the last common ancestor with humans; first is their liking for meat, for which they may scavenge or engage in organized hunts; and second is their tool using and tool making abilities.

In fact, the killing and eating of vertebrate prey ranks low in chimpanzee carnivory, and insect prey makes up a far larger proportion of their diet. There is also little evidence for scavenging animal carcasses. Observations of chimpanzees over an 11-year period at Kibale National Park showed scavenging on only four occasions, even though they had the opportunity to scavenge approximately 40 times during this period. Similar results have been found at other locations occupied by chimpanzees, and it is not clear why they ignore animal carcasses that might offer potential food. This behaviour is quite different from human hunter-gatherer groups, and it may be that the chimpanzees simply do not recognize certain dead animals as potential food. The four carcasses consumed by chimpanzees at Kibale were two duikers and two red colobus monkeys, both animals they may prey upon. In other places, such as Gombe and Mahale, larger animals like bushbuck have been seen to be scavenged.

Jane Goodall observed the first chimpanzee hunt at Gombe when from a distance she saw a big male chimpanzee in a tree eating a baby pig. The adult bush pigs were voicing their displeasure at the base of the tree, suggesting that the chimpanzee had just stolen one of their infants, and suggesting further that the adult pigs themselves had no fear of chimpanzees, which were limited to preying on infants. Subsequent studies showed that chimpanzees engage in cooperative hunts, for example of colobus monkeys, during which individual chimpanzees take on different roles to distract or head off the monkeys while other individuals chase and catch the chosen individual. Their success rate with a large group of hunters is nearly 100 per cent, whereas hunting success by a single chimpanzee is only one third that. They eat the whole animal, including gnawing on bones. Several studies have shown that the tooth marks left on the bones after chimpanzee feeding are very similar to the marks left after human chewing. For example, marks characteristic of human chewing include puncture marks, both single and multiple, bent ends, peeling, superficial linear marks and chewed ends. Many of these modifications may be caused by other agents when found on their own, but in a study that I carried out with Yolanda Fernández-Jalvo from the Museo Nacional de Ciencias Naturales, we showed that it is the combination of these marks that is important. Found together, they are characteristic not only of human chewing but also of that by chimpanzees.

So far there has been no evidence that gorillas and orang utans either hunt or eat meat, and although there are well-documented occurrences of both in other primates, for example baboons and capuchin monkeys, neither seems to be widespread in primates. Two things single out hunting by chimpanzees; one is that hunts are cooperative and seemingly organized events; and the other is that the food may be shared with non-participating individuals. Both aspects are common to human hunting, and it may be inferred, therefore, that this is shared derived behaviour in humans and chimpanzees and that it would have been present in their last common ancestor.

Many primates are vegetarian, but it is likely that most also eat animal food in the form of insects, at least to some degree. Animal protein has high nutritional value, and it has been observed that chimpanzees eat meat more frequently during the dry season when their staple diet of fruit is most difficult to come by. In other words, meat, particularly in the form of insects, may be a fall-back food that is taken when preferred food is not available. The same is true incidentally of human hunter-gatherer societies, where there is greater reliance on the products of hunting during seasonal shortage of other foods, and where division of labour between males and females is well established. It is interesting in this connection that male chimpanzees may get preferential access to females if they share some of the meat with them after making a kill, and this is likely to have been a strong incentive for sharing as well as the potential beginnings of sexual division of labour.

A recent study has shown that eating meat has consequences for age of weaning in mammal species. Carnivores have an earlier age of weaning than herbivores, and humans fit the carnivore pattern, with weaning at about 2.5 years. Weaning in the living great apes occurs at more than twice this period and fits the herbivore pattern. Reducing the time to weaning shortens the period between births, and this can result in more rapid reproduction, which in turn affects population dynamics. It is particularly interesting in this study that no difference was found between herbivores and omnivores, which eat up to 10% meat, and this implies that eating a small amount of meat makes no difference to age of weaning; the change occurs when there is a significant increase from 10 to 20% meat, which is the proportion that defines significant carnivory. The percentage of meat in chimpanzee diets is not clear: in one study, 3% of the time chimpanzees spend eating they are eating meat, but given the high nutritional value of meat, its contribution to chimpanzee diet must be higher than that. Presumably it is less than 10%, so that meat would have no effect on age of weaning in chimpanzees, but at some stage in the human lineage there would have been a marked increase in the amount of meat eaten that took humans into the carnivory bracket. This may have occurred at around 2.5 to 3 million years ago, when stone tool technology is first recognized in the fossil record, and this is the time when meat consumption by hominins is actually recognizable by cut marks left on bones after butchery. We would fail to recognize hominin access to meat earlier than this, when hominins and apes were using unrecognizable or perishable implements such as unmodified stones and pieces of wood.

The eating of meat also has consequences for brain size (Figure 2.5). Primates in general have relatively larger brains than other animals, and this trend is continued in the apes. Both may be connected with the consumption of animal protein. Similarly, the increase in brain size in later stages of human evolution has been linked with increased meat in their diets by Leslie Aiello and Peter Wheeler. Their expensive tissue hypothesis suggests that enlarging the brain, which is a tissue requiring large amounts of energy, could only have come about at the expense of other tissues, particularly the gut, which is another expensive tissue. Meat is a highly nutritious food, requiring smaller and shorter guts to digest it, so that increase in meat in the diet led to

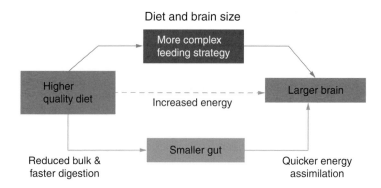

Figure 2.5 The relationship between brain size and diet. The brain is an expensive tissue in terms of the energy needed for its functioning, and the larger the brain, the greater must be the energy supply (fuel) to drive it. In humans this has been achieved by reduction in the gut (another expensive tissue) and increase in quality of diet through change to eating more meat. Redrawn from Aiello & Wheeler 1995.

reduction in the gut which in turn allowed (although it should be emphasized did not necessarily promote) increase in brain size. The exchange took place in human evolution about 2 million years ago, for it is at this time that we see the first expansion of brain size. Before that time, fossil hominins had brain sizes similar to that of apes, and this would have been a feature of the last common ancestor of apes and humans.

There is some evidence of cannibalism in chimpanzees, first shown by Jane Goodall in 1977 at Gombe. This has been followed up by further observations on chimpanzees in the Mahale Mountains, Kibale National Park and Budongo Forest. These show hostile encounters occurring between males along territory boundaries, with groups of males specifically targeting infants, often letting the infants' mothers escape. No clear explanation exists for the subsequent cannibalism, but the simplest explanation is nutritional, for the manner of killing and eating the infant chimpanzees is exactly the same as when other animals are the prey. This is the logic by which nutritional cannibalism has been identified in prehistoric human populations at Fontrégoua in France and at Gough's Cave in southern England, and while other motivations might play a part in chimpanzee behaviour, there is no strong indication as to what these might be.

Meat-eating by itself does not necessarily imply hunting behaviour, for early hominins may have been scavenging during the Pliocene period, long before they were making stone tools. By this means, they would have had secondary access to carcasses if they were able to compete with other scavengers such as hyaenas. It is also possible that carcasses were more plentiful at that time, for there were specialized hypercarnivores such as sabre-tooth cats that would have left plenty of meat on abandoned carcasses. It is possible, but not verifiable, that the last common ancestor of humans and chimpanzees was close to the threshold of greater carnivory; although chimpanzees remained below the threshold, early hominins soon passed above it, providing the selective advantage of more rapid reproduction rates and improved nutrition. Whether this is the case or not, it is almost certain that the last common ancestor had developed tools to hunt with, as both humans and chimpanzees do today.

Tool use is known for a great variety of animal species, but the manufacture of tools for specific purposes is not. A quick summary of tool types used by the chimpanzee populations in Gombe, Mahale, Tai, Bossou and Goualougo includes between fifteen and twenty-five different types of tools, leading to a number of propositions encompassing tool use by chimpanzees:

- apes as well as humans are dependent on tools for their survival during some periods of the year;
- apes as well as humans fashion tools following arbitrary cultural rules rather than in a purely adaptive way;
- population differences in tool use, such as for ant dipping, are cultural rather than adaptive;
- chimpanzees as well as humans use tools to access underground storage organs, which may indicate higher cognitive abilities; it is most frequent in more arid habitats, and while it also occurs in forest habitats, the chimpanzees do not appear to use tools to dig up the food;
- chimpanzees habitually sit upright to crack open nuts, using one hand to hold the hammer stone and the other to control the target area; the freeing of the hands by this method may have been pre-adaptive to stone knapping;
- chimpanzees as well as humans use tools to hunt, for example at Fongoli, Gombe and Tai; and
- chimpanzees as well as humans may combine more than one tool to attain a single goal, or conversely they may use one tool for more than one purpose.

It may be that the difference between chimpanzee and human use of tools is not so much qualitative as quantitative, and the transition from ape to human was a shift in emphasis rather than something completely new. For example, it has recently been shown in a study that the ability to learn from others of the same species, and to make technological improvements, is partly dependent on group size. Large social networks allow humans to learn from others to a degree far greater than is possible with small groups, and it may be that chimpanzee social groups have never been big enough, or cohesive enough, to achieve this ability to learn and improve by imitation of other group members. It would certainly be the case that the last common ancestor of humans and chimpanzees used and made tools at least to the extent of chimpanzees.

Recent work has shown that gorillas and orang utans also use tools, but to a more limited extent than chimpanzees. Gorillas have been seen to test water depth using a stick, and orang utans may use pointed sticks to prise open fruits with protective hairs or spines, but so far no evidence has been presented showing the manufacture of tools by these great apes. There is a major conceptual difference between tool use and tool making, where the tool has to be visualized in the unmodified stick or stone and then fashioned to fulfil the desired purpose. It may be concluded that tool use is a great ape character, rudimentary in the case of gorillas and orang utans and more advanced in chimpanzees, which have also developed cultural differences in the making of tools. It is likely, therefore, that the ancestors of the great ape and human clade were also tool users, and it is interesting to speculate how far back in time this went. In other words, were any of the Miocene apes described here tool users? This question will be taken up in Chapter 16 after I have reviewed what we know about the fossil apes.

Three other aspects of chimpanzee behaviour are shared with humans, although whether they could be counted as shared derived characters is uncertain. The first of these, described by Jane Goodall, is their inter-group rivalries that can lead to extreme violence. In the 1960s, there began a process by which a group of male chimpanzees tended to spend much of their time in the northern part of the Gombe Reserve, while others remained in the southern part. Over time, the two groups became separated effectively into two territories and there was little interaction between them, but then hostilities began along the borders between the two groups. This amounted to little more than noisy demonstrations when the groups were the same size, but when there was a numerical superiority on one side or the other, the weaker group would be attacked. On occasions, roving bands of chimpanzees were observed from one group entering the territory of the other group, searching for and attacking lone individuals if they could find them. Territorial conflicts are common in many animal species, but they do not usually result in the targeted death of individuals or in the complete annihilation of one group by the other. However, this is precisely what happened in this case. This is a very human attribute, and it also puts in mind the birth cohort of *Kenyapithecus kizili*, which is described in Chapter 11. This intrusive group of nine fossil apes was preserved in the same deposits as a much larger group of unrelated fossil apes. Nine individuals were at the same developmental age (young adults) and had identical double hypoplasias on their incisor teeth, formed during the same stages of their development; these differed from the hypoplasias observed in the common species, indicating exposure to differing environmental conditions. The question can be asked if this was a marauding group of apes that came to an abrupt end far away from their home.

A second behavioural observation on chimpanzees is based on nest distributions in woodland habitats. Certain areas of the woodlands were repeatedly used for nest building, with 90% of nest sites being used again and again, whereas other areas of woodland were not used at all. What is interesting about this is that the spatial distribution and concentration of nests is similar to archaeological distributions at fossil hominin sites and might well represent hominin choices of living areas. Concentrations of archaeological materials are often interpreted as home-base areas or butchery areas, but on this analysis, the former is more likely.

Finally, it has been shown above that sexual dimorphism may provide indications of the social structure of living apes. Gibbons and humans, for example, live in monogamous family groups and have low levels of dimorphism in both body size and canine lengths. Gorillas and orang utans by contrast have polygynous social structures and high levels of dimorphism. Chimpanzees have multi-male groups based on temporary alliances, and their social structure is fluid. This is termed fission–fusion social groups where temporary sub-groups are set up for many different purposes. They have lower levels of sexual dimorphism, for although males may act aggressively towards other males, they tolerate each other for the most part.

Summary

- Living apes have tropical distributions in Africa and Asia.
- Gibbons are strictly arboreal, live in evergreen rainforest in Asia, eat fruit and have monogamous social groups; low sexual dimorphism.
- Orang utans are strictly arboreal, live in evergreen rainforest in Asia, eat fruit and have polygynous social groups; high sexual dimorphism.
- Gorillas inhabit forested areas of Africa, with some populations/species terrestrial, others partly arboreal and partly terrestrial, and have polygynous social groups; there is some evidence for tool use; high sexual dimorphism.
- Chimpanzees are partly arboreal and partly terrestrial, live in African forest and non-forest woodland environments and have multi-male fission–fusion social groups; they use and make tools, hunt and eat animal prey, may engage in cannibalism and practice a form of warfare; spatial distribution of nests suggests occupation of core areas; intermediate sexual dimorphism.
- Humans are strictly terrestrial, but retain some capacity for climbing trees, live in a wide variety of habitats and commonly have monogamous social groups and low sexual dimorphism.

Chapter 3
Human and ape phylogenies

We have seen that the living apes share many characters with humans, and since the time of Darwin it has been generally recognized that they are our closest living relatives. Their morphology, however, does not demonstrate clearly which of the apes is our closest relative, and while the shared behaviours of chimpanzees and humans are suggestive, it is not conclusive proof of relationship. It has also been mentioned above that there is no known fossil ape that can unreservedly be shown to be ancestral of any living species of ape or human, as the evidence available from the known fossils is ambiguous, although it must be stressed that they provide much essential information on other aspects of ape evolution. The evidence for relationships comes from comparisons of living apes and humans with each other based on their morphology, behaviour and genes. It is this last line of evidence, the molecular biology of apes and humans, that will be covered in this chapter.

Morris Goodman set the application of genetic markers for human evolution on its way in the 1960s, and his book *Molecular Anthropology* was a landmark in primate phylogenetic studies. Goodman was very clear that humans were most closely related to African apes, but early methods lacked sufficient detail to differentiate between chimpanzees or gorillas as man's closest relative. Later work on immunological responses came to the same conclusion, but interestingly the level of responses of human with gorilla genetic markers was less than that with chimpanzee (1.09 for gorilla:human compared with 1.14 for chimpanzee:human, taking human:human as 1). For the first time, however, an attempt to put a date to the human/ape divergence was made, and assuming that immunological divergence increases at a constant rate, a date of 5 million years ago for the split was indicated. In the nearly 50 years since this figure was published, it has remained close to the centre of a range of values proposed by numerous studies, some older and some younger.

It was first proposed that chimpanzees and humans share almost 99% of their genome based on a measure of genetic distance. Almost more important than this conclusion was the observation that genetic distance did not coincide with observable morphological differences, and it was concluded from this that mutations alter the level of gene expression by modifying regulatory genes rather than changes in base pair substitutions. This is still the accepted interpretation of the DNA evidence, which has recently been greatly augmented by the DNA sequencing of the chimpanzee genome by The Chimpanzee Sequencing and Analysis Consortium 2005. This has now been able to document many different levels of DNA change, from single-base substitutions to segmental duplications. Estimates of genetic divergence between chimpanzees and humans vary, and as Steve Jones shows in his book on Charles Darwin, "such figures underrate the real divergence of the two species. Changes in the number and position of inserted, repeated or deleted segments mark both lines. There are three times as many alterations of this kind as of single-base changes, which puts the overall difference between men and chimps at around 4 per cent." Humans have gained many hundreds of gene copies since the split with chimpanzees.

Molecules versus morphology

Before going any further with this line of evidence, the difference between molecular and morphological evidence should be mentioned. The shared presence of discrete morphological characters as evidence for phylogenetic relationship is based on homology, that is, characters inherited from a common ancestor. The presence of five fingers and toes is a character shared by most mammals; it was evidently present in the common ancestor to all mammals and it is a discrete character. It contrasts with analogous characters, such as the wings of birds and bats, both because the bones forming the wings are different in the two groups and because they did not share a common ancestor. Some molecular characters are like this, for example chromosome number, which is different in humans and chimpanzees, but distance measures quantify DNA similarity based on probabilistic models and not on discrete characters that can distinguish between homology and analogy.

Colin Patterson was one of the earliest to face up to contrasts between morphology and molecules in reconstructing phylogeny. He recognized that homology between molecular sequences is not based on discrete characters but is quantifiable, and reconstructing phylogeny entails "reconstructing ancestral sequences which will produce the descendant sequences with the *minimum* of evolutionary change". This is the principle of parsimony, which is a principle of reasoning rather than an inference about nature, and it only became possible as a practical method of phylogenetic reconstruction with the development of computers. In my contribution to Colin's book in 1987, I compared distance measures unfavourably with observations on morphological characters, and even though there is a wealth of DNA sequencing data available now, I still continue to question the ways in which it is sometimes analysed. It is not the principle of parsimony that I question so much as the assumptions of homology that ensue from quantifying ancestral sequences. In a tree based on parsimony, the genetic characters shared by sister species (as defined on the tree) are assumed to be homologous, and they may be uniquely shared (from their common ancestor) or they may be retentions from an earlier ancestor. There is no way of distinguishing them. Characters shared by one of the pair with a third species are assumed not to be homologous and not evidence of relationship with this species. In other words, this definition of homology is arbitrary and based on numbers, as Colin pointed out above, and it has no reality in biology. Homology can only be identified after the most parsimonious tree is built, and a different tree would result in different sets of homologous characters. As a biologist, I find this an unsatisfactory solution to what is admittedly an intractable problem.

DNA analyses

Returning now to the main subject of this chapter, inferring phylogeny from DNA (deoxyribonucleic acid), we recognize that there are three kinds of DNA that can be studied. The first type is the DNA in the nucleus of our body cells, called nuclear DNA. This DNA contains the blueprints for most of our body structure, and we inherit a combination of it from both of our parents. As nuclear DNA is copied during cell division, copying mistakes are made, and if the changes are not lethal, these mutations are then also copied on. They thus accumulate through time and their number used to estimate the time involved in their accumulation. The second type is Y-chromosome DNA, which lies on the chromosome that determines the male sex in humans. The DNA on this chromosome can be used to study evolutionary lines in males only, without the complication of inheritance from two parents. Recent research suggests that variation in Y-chromosome DNA is relatively low. The third type is mitochondrial DNA (mtDNA), which is present in the mitochondria outside the nucleus of cells and which is inherited through females only. The mito-chondria are the manufacturing centres of the cell, which provide the energy for each cell. Their DNA is passed on in the egg of the mother when it becomes the first cell of her child; no mtDNA is present from the father's sperm, so that mtDNA essentially tracks evolution through females only.

In recent years, DNA sequences have been analysed in many different labora-tories. One of the early types of DNA analysis, DNA–DNA hybridization, provided phenetic evidence for DNA divergence. Phenetics identifies relation-ship based on greatest overall similarity, as against phylogenetics which attempts to identify relationship based on common ancestry. These phenetic analyses are based on the *implicit assumption* that the similarities are phylogen-etically meaningful, but more recent discoveries of changes in gene regulation, rather than modifications of the genes themselves, are more soundly based. For example, regulatory genes have been shown to have undergone strong positive selection along the human lineage, especially those involved in speech, brain development and skull musculature.

An analysis of nuclear DNA used 22 DNA sequences from humans and African apes and showed that humans are most closely related to chimpanzees, with an estimated divergence date of just less than 5 million years ago. This similarity is not quite as simple as first supposed, for it has recently been shown that both bonobos and the common chimpanzee separately share 3% of their genomes with humans that are not shared with each other. In other words, there was some interbreeding between the earliest human ancestors with ancestors of both bonobos and chimpanzees, although today the two apes have completely separate ranges of distribution. The earlier divergence of gorillas was estimated at just over 7 million years ago, but both these dates depend on correct calibration of the 'molecular clock' (see below).

The sequencing of the male-specific region of the chimpanzee Y-chromosome has shown that it differs greatly in humans and chimpanzees; for example, the chimpanzee Y-chromosome contains only two thirds as many genes or gene families as the human Y-chromosome, and only half as many protein coding transcription units. This seems to be due both to gene acquisition in the human lineage and gene loss in the chimpanzee lineage. This level of difference is huge, and in other species such a difference implies divergence times of hundreds of millions of years. This is clearly not the case with the human/chimpanzee split, and it was not predicted and cannot account for the rapid divergence of chimpanzee and human lineages. Their divergence can be related to several factors: multiplied by sperm competition in chimpanzees, in turn related to chimpanzee societies where several males mate with females in oestrus, and the implications here are that the common ancestor of chimpanzees and humans lacked this high evolutionary turnover of the Y-chromosome and that both are highly derived relative to their common ancestor.

Apart from the anomalous results from the Y-chromosome, most molecular data support divergence of humans and chimpanzees between 4 to 6 million years ago (Figure 3.1). These estimates have been calibrated by some 'known' point in time taken from the fossil record, and the ones usually chosen are the split between monkeys and apes, 30 to 25 million years ago, and the orang utan split from the African apes and humans, at 15 to 12 million years ago. If these dates were to be changed, the dates from the molecular clock would need to be changed also. However, much of the fossil evidence is still disputed, and there are no Miocene apes known at present that can unequivocally be placed on any of the extant ape lineages. Even the separation of apes and monkeys is open to doubt; fossil primates preceding separation tell us nothing about the

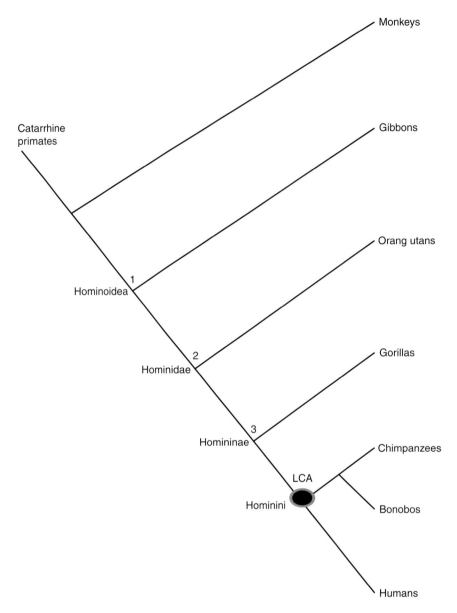

Figure 3.1 Phylogeny of the apes. Apes and monkeys are classified together as catarrhine primates, and the date of the split between monkeys and apes is best provided by the earliest fossils of either group (1). New evidence suggests this may be 25 Ma, but the evidence is stronger for a date of close to 20 Ma. Similarly, the likely divergence date for the orang utan (2) is 12 Ma or earlier, and calibrating the divergence date of apes and humans (LCA, last common ancestor) based on these two calibration points gives a date for the earliest hominin (human ancestor) between 4 and 5 Ma. There are no fossil chimpanzees or gorillas that provide evidence of dating for their lineages.

timing of the split, and the presence of the earliest known fossil for any lineage only gives the latest age for the origin of the group, never the earliest, for there may be earlier fossil apes yet undiscovered.

Until recently, the earliest known fossil monkey was from deposits between 19 and 20 million years old from Napak, Uganda. Recently, however, a monkey-like tooth has been described from the Rukwa Rift in southern Tanzania dated to 25 million years ago, and from the same site at Rukwa is a fossil tooth row of an anthropoid similar to the Miocene proconsulids. If these identifications are verified, it would indicate a divergence date of apes and monkeys about this time or earlier, but no comparisons have been made with the older monkey-like teeth of *Parapithecus grangeri*, to which the Rukwa specimen appears very similar, and I have my doubts about the hominoid status of *Rangwapithecus* (see Chapter 7). There is nothing to verify the hominoid status of the latter other than a superficial similarity with proconsulids, and some aspects of its teeth distinguish it from other hominoids. Statistical models have predicted the amount of time by which an actual divergence date may have pre-dated the earliest known fossil evidence based on the diversity patterns of the fossil species, but the low (known) diversity of both early hominins and early apes makes it problematic applying these models to these two branching points.

Similarly, the divergence of the orang utan is dated from the appearance in the fossil record of *Sivapithecus*, which has orang utan-like features of the skull. The earliest record of this genus and other fossil apes with orang utan-like skulls is about 12 million years ago, but the postcranial skeletons of these apes have none of the great ape characters generally considered to have been present in great ape ancestry. If *Sivapithecus* really is on the orang utan lineage, the postcranial features the orang utan shares with the African apes (which were the basis for their original grouping in Pongidae) must be convergent. However, another group of fossil apes combines orang utan-like postcranial skeletons with relatively primitive skulls. This is the Dryopithecinae, and there are two divergent views on how to interpret this: one group in Spain links the dryopithecines with the orang utan, and another group in Canada links them with the African apes (see Chapter 12). The earliest record of dryopithecine fossils is about 12 million years ago, and applying the statistical models to the diversity pattern of 12 million-year-old dryopithecines (N = 3) and sivapithecines (N = 2) gives estimates of possible orang utan divergence of 14.4 million years for the former split, and 13.2 million years for the latter.

These two calibration points from the fossil record may therefore be more recent than currently thought, and when used to calibrate the molecular clock, subsequent divergence dates, as between chimpanzees and humans, would have to be reduced to closer to 4 million years. The splitting of humans and chimpanzees has even been proposed to be as recent as 3 million years ago by one molecular study. This has obvious implications for the identification of some proposed early hominin ancestors older than 6 million years, such as *Orrorin tugenensis* and *Sahelanthropus tchadensis*.

What is really needed here is some other method of finding divergence times, and two have recently been proposed. One is based on generation times in African apes and humans, using the known parentage information from chimpanzees and gorillas that have had long-term studies in the wild to infer their generation times and to calculate mutation rate per generation. Generation time is the average time between two consecutive generations in a population. It can be represented by the average age of parenthood, by the difference in age between parents and offspring in successive generations, or by the average age at which population members reproduce (the mean age between onset of puberty and female menopause). In human populations, the generation time typically ranges up to 30 years, and for the apes it has been calculated as averaging 24 years for chimpanzees and 19 years for gorillas and gibbons. Mutation rates per generation is either calculated based on numbers of mutations in two lineages since they shared a common ancestor, or by direct observation of mutations in present-day individuals. For humans these two rates differ substantially, with the present-day mutation rate lower than the figures suggested by their evolutionary history: for example, humans have accumulated 30 per cent fewer mutations than baboons since the time of their common ancestor. This may be linked to the different generation times in baboons and humans, being 10 to 12 years in the baboons and 28 to 30 years in humans. The intrinsic mutation rate is not known at present for the living apes, but with shorter generation it may be expected to differ from that of humans.

There is no way at present of calculating mutation rates in fossil apes, but based on mutation rates observed in human generations, and assuming also that these same rates pertain to fossil apes and humans, the separation of chimpanzees and humans is calculated to have taken place 7 to 8 million years ago. We do not know, however, what the generation time was for fossil apes, and still less do we know the mutation rate during ape evolution, and both factors would have affected the divergence times of the living apes.

Partly in consequence of the longer generation time in humans, it has been shown that genetic variability is less in human populations, with their global distribution, than it is in chimpanzees, despite their limited geographical distribution. Genetic variation on the X-chromosome, as measured by the number of differences between any two individuals, is 3.7 in the global human population as opposed to 13.4 for chimpanzees distributed across equatorial Africa. In other words, any two chimpanzees have nearly four times as many differences from each other as do any two humans. These differences are in the non-coding region of the chromosome, however, and so they do not necessarily translate into morphological differences, but clearly something very different was occurring between humans and chimpanzees after splitting from their common ancestor. It may be that the chimpanzee level of difference was already present in the common ancestor, and primitively retained in living chimpanzees, but through genetic drift or a bottleneck in human evolution much of this variation was lost.

Further complications arise from the possibilities of hybridization following the speciation of humans and chimpanzees from their common ancestor, but so far there is no evidence supporting this and the idea has been criticized by some molecular biologists. The genome studies also show that for some genes, humans are more closely related to either bonobos on the one hand or to chimpanzees on the other, but the usual conclusion is that the two ape species are more closely related to each other than either are to humans. The bonobo–chimpanzee split is estimated at between 1 and 2 million years ago, at about the time of the formation of the Congo River which today separates the two species.

A second method of calibration is based on substitution rates in mitochondrial DNA within a lineage. This depends on quantifying rates of change in relation to well-dated events within the lineage and building a statistical model taking account of the heterogeneity within the lineage. It also requires of course the extension of the method to nuclear DNA, and this will come in the future.

A speculation

Chimpanzees have greater genetic diversity than humans, with three distinct races or species. It may be, of course, that 50 000 years ago humans had comparable diversity with the three species coexisting: *Homo sapiens*, *Homo neanderthalensis* and *Homo floresiensis*, but now only we remain. An interesting scenario, and a good plot for a book, is to think what might have happened in the absence of humans if one of the chimpanzee species had started to expand its range in the same way as humans. Jennifer Caswell and others have shown that Central African chimpanzees have expanded their range since they split off from the chimpanzees of West Africa about half a million years ago; the latter population has been declining since then while that of Central Africa has expanded by a factor of four during the same time. It is probably no coincidence that genetic variation in the Central African chimpanzee species is more than twice that of the western species and is also greater than that present in humans today, although its morphological variation is less. It is interesting to speculate what might have happened if the small populations of early hominins died out through some catastrophe, leaving the field clear for chimpanzees.

Classification of the apes and humans

The taxonomy followed here is based on two splendid taxonomic compilations including fossil apes, one on African mammals edited by Lars Werdelin and Bill Sanders, and the other on all fossil primates, edited by Walter Hartwig. It also is taken in part from my recent publication with Terry Harrison, and it reflects my current view of hominoid taxonomy. Some of the fossil families are undoubtedly paraphyletic, that is, the species included in them probably did not come from a single common ancestor; for example Afropithecinae is taken here to include a number of middle Miocene species that were advanced with respect to early Miocene apes but lacked the specializations of contemporary and later fossil apes. It is likely that the subfamily Dryopithecinae as depicted here is also paraphyletic. Terry Harrison groups afropithecines with proconsulids, both groups preceding the divergence of gibbons and the great apes and humans, and there is a lot to be said for this, but I would like to stress again that this book is not concerned with ape taxonomy but rather it aims to set out the ranges of morphological variation present during the Miocene as the stage from which the common ancestor of apes and human emerged. The alternative scheme, which I prefer here, is to classify proconsulids as stem hominoids and afropithecines as hominids, together with kenyapithecines, dryopithecines, and the extant great apes and humans, and so I have shown them here. *Rangwapithecus* is grouped with proconsulids, although I believe there is some doubt about that, and *Oreopithecus* is grouped with the dryopithecines.

It is a relatively simple matter to draw up an extensive list of morphological traits that distinguish modern humans from their extant sister taxon, the chimpanzee. They can be found listed by Aiello and Dean in their text *An Introduction to Human Evolutionary Anatomy*; many are autapomorphies or uniquely derived features that distinguish humans from all other hominoids. However, it is important to note that chimpanzees are also derived relative to the last common ancestor, whereas in some respects humans retain the inferred primitive hominoid condition. To take two examples, the human hand retains the primitive proportions of the fingers of the hand, particularly the relatively long thumb, all of which are present in fossil apes from the early Miocene onwards, while chimpanzees have greatly lengthened hands but reduced thumbs; and in the back bone, humans have five lumbar vertebrae on average, which is probably the primitive number of five or six present in gibbons and some fossil apes but that has been reduced to four in chimpanzees. Among the human specializations, the most prominent, at least in terms of skeletal anatomy, are the changes in the hip, knee and foot related to development of upright posture and obligate bipedalism, the greatly enlarged relative brain size, the reduction in the size of the canines and the loss of canine/premolar sectorial function (along with a corresponding modification in the form of the canines and anterior premolars). Among chimpanzee specializations, the most prominent are the enlarged incisor teeth, the vertebrae as mentioned above and the specializations of the elbow, wrist and hand associated with knuckle-walking.

Superfamily Hominoidea		
Family Proconsulidae		
	Proconsul, Rangwapithecus	
Family Hylobatidae		
	Hylobates	**Gibbons**
Family Hominidae		
Subfamily Ponginae		
	Pongo	**Orang utan**
	Lufengpithecus, Sivapithecus	
	Khoratpithecus	
Subfamily Kenyapithecinae		
	Kenyapithecus	
Subfamily Afropithecinae		
	Afropithecus, Morotopithecus	
	Equatorius, Griphopithecus	
Subfamily Dryopithecinae		
	Dryopithecus, Pierolapithecus	
	Anoiapithecus, Rudapithecus	
	Oreopithecus	
Subfamily Homininae		
Tribe Gorillini		
	Gorilla	**Gorilla**
Tribe Hominini		
Subtribe Panina		
	Pan	**Chimpanzee**
Subtribe Hominina		
	Homo	**Humans**

Chapter 4
Review of fossil apes

Fossil apes are known from over 20 million years ago up to very recently. The discovery of the first fossil ape, *Dryopithecus fontani* found in France in 1854, predated Darwin's *The Origin of Species* by 5 years. During the second half of the nineteenth century and the first half of the twentieth century, many more fossil apes were found and described, leading to a proliferation of names. No evolutionary scheme gained general acceptance during this time, leading to confusion about the significance of fossil apes generally. Stemming from this period of name proliferation, the impression arose that fossil apes have little to offer to the understanding of human origins.

Two classic papers brought order to the classification of fossil apes. In 1954, the great Swiss palaeontologist Johannes Hürzeler published his synthesis of the Pliopithecidae, a group of ape-like anthropoids that may have been close to the anthropoid ancestors that gave rise to monkeys and apes. Hürzeler's synthesis of pliopithecid taxonomy illuminated their evolutionary significance. I was lucky enough to meet and work with Hürzeler while I was studying at Cambridge, and his systematic approach to ape taxonomy greatly influenced me. At that time he was also working on a revision of the dryopithecines, but he never completed the work, and in the 1960s Elwyn Simons and David Pilbeam produced their revision of the dryopithecines, which brought order into the chaos of names, where males and females of the same fossil ape were sometimes placed in different species (or even genera). Both studies eliminated many redundant names that had been erected by enthusiastic scientists over the previous 100 years, established a new framework for the study of fossil apes and formed the foundation on which subsequent research has been based.

Fossil ape taxonomy has changed out of all recognition since the papers by Hürzeler and Simons and Pilbeam, and there are now more names in the literature than there were before their pioneering work. Many of the newly named species are undoubtedly valid, but some are less so. I do not intend to review the current taxonomic status of all these fossil apes, however, as Lars Werdelin and Bill Sanders have done this for Africa and Walter Hartwig has reviewed all fossil primates in two recent edited volumes. Instead, I am going to briefly outline three major groups of fossil ape, without going into detail about their names and relationships. Part III of this book will describe in some depth the morphology and ecology of these three groups of fossil ape, both to provide some insight into the nature of the animals belonging to the groups, and to show how they provide the necessary morphological background to understanding from whence came the common ancestor to apes and humans.

Before doing this, brief mention should be made of the sparse fossil evidence for the great apes. A small number of fragmentary fossils are all that we have of fossil chimpanzees and orang utans, with nothing at all for gorillas. This is the biggest barrier to furthering our understanding of ape and human evolution, for if we had a fossil record for chimpanzees comparable to that for humans, many questions we still have for the latter would be answered (although an equal number or more new questions would doubtless be raised). The single fossil chimpanzee known so far is a case in point, for it was found in middle Pleistocene deposits about half a million years old in Kapthurin, Kenya. There are only three isolated teeth, which do not tell us much about the anatomy of the fossil ape, but its location many hundreds of kilometres from the present range of chimpanzees requires explanation, as does its presence in a relatively open woodland environment. Kapthurin is a site in the eastern rift valley, well beyond the present range of chimpanzees, and environmental indicators are of an arid climate and woodland vegetation. In the same stratigraphic horizon of the Kapthurin Formation are human fossils, suggesting that chimpanzees were coexisting with humans at this time and place. The human fossil record from this period and earlier is replete with fossils, and later species were clearly at home in the fragmented rift environments, but the fossil record of the Central and West African forest environments is still unknown, both for chimpanzees and humans. Either or both may have been present in these western forests, and it is premature to place their environmental dichotomy in time or space in the absence of evidence from these other parts of Africa.

There is also a single femur of unknown context from the Kikorongo Crater in western Uganda, which may represent a late Pleistocene chimpanzee ancestor. A fragment of hominoid mandible from Niger in West Africa, which comes from an unknown site and is broadly late Miocene in age, may be another chimpanzee ancestor. Radiographs of the latter specimen suggest that it is indeed a hominoid primate, but there are too many uncertainties around its discovery to be able to come to any conclusions about its significance. There is just a hint here, however, that chimpanzees were formerly more widespread in tropical Africa and that they may have had a broader range of habitats.

There are also Pleistocene fossils of the orang utan, showing that it too had a wider distribution than it does today. As well as Borneo and Sumatra, where they occur today, orang utan fossils have been recovered from many sites in China, Vietnam, Laos, Cambodia, Thailand and Java, mostly from middle to late Pleistocene sites. Most recently they have also been found in cave sites in the Malay Peninsula, which further extends their former range. This extensive distribution across Southeast Asia could also suggest that orang utans had a broader habitat tolerance than the equatorial forest to which they are presently restricted. The fossil orang utans are essentially modern in appearance and tell us nothing about the origin of their lineage. To understand something of ape origins as well as human origins, it is necessary therefore to look to the fossil apes from the Miocene and Pliocene, spanning the period 20 to 5 million years ago.

The three groups of fossil ape that will be considered here are the proconsulids from the early Miocene of East Africa; the kenyapithecines and afropithecines from the early middle Miocene of Africa and Europe; and the dryopithecines from the late middle Miocene of Europe. These three groups span about 12 million years, and although a few Miocene apes are known subsequent to this period, they provide little insight into the origin of the extant apes.

Proconsulids

The earliest known fossil apes come from the early Miocene of East Africa, and they are generally considered to be stem hominoids, that is, apes that preceded any of the splits between living species. For this reason they are accorded a family name of their own: Proconsulidae, in parallel with the two families of living apes: Hylobatidae (gibbons or lesser apes) and Hominidae (great apes and humans). *Proconsul* is the best known of these primates, and the sites from which it comes are located in the area where I worked for the Kenya Forestry Department. The genus *Proconsul* has been divided into two genera as this book was going to press, with a new genus *Ekembo* named for the two best-known species, *Ekembo nyanzae* and *Ekembo heseloni*, both from Rusinga Island (Figure 4.1). This reflects modifications of their teeth which indicate an evolutionary advance over earlier species of *Proconsul*.

The recent description of *Proconsul meswae* from more than 20 million-year-old deposits in Kenya provides the earliest record of this group (excluding for the moment the proposed hominoid from Tanzania: see Chapter 3). This species differs from other species of *Proconsul* by its low crowned incisors, broad molars and premolars, with a more pronounced degree of buccolingual flare, and relatively deep mandibular body. Six to eight species of *Proconsul* are known (Table 4.1), and they share many primitive characters with living apes. Possible shared derived characters with apes are in the bones of the shoulder, elbow and foot, which have been demonstrated for at least two of the species of *Proconsul*, and the loss of the tail, which has been demonstrated for *Proconsul heseloni*. This means that two things can be said about ape evolution: firstly, the

Figure 4.1 Judy Van Couvering (now Judith Harris) pointing out fossils in the Kulu Formation on Rusinga Island.

apes had already differentiated from the other primates by the time *Proconsul* lived 20 million years ago, or sometime earlier; and secondly, the initial modifications that characterized them as apes were postcranial. This is interesting, because it is in their postcranial anatomy that living apes show their greatest specializations, both as a group and as individuals.

Kenyapithecines and afropithecines

These two middle Miocene subfamilies are grouped here because they combine derived characters (with respect to proconsulids) such as robust jaws and enlarged molars and premolars with thickened enamel. They share these characters with early hominins, although their significance is uncertain. In addition, the two *Kenyapithecus* species share another suite of characters that are derived with respect to both afropithecines and proconsulids: *Kenyapithecus wickeri* from Fort Ternan in Kenya (Figure 4.2) and an early non-African fossil ape, *Kenyapithecus kizili* from Paşalar in Turkey. I excavated at both of these sites, the former with Alan Walker and Judy Van Couvering, and the latter with Berna Alpagut and Lawrence Martin. *Kenyapithecus* is rare at both sites, but a

Table 4.1 The species of *Proconsul* and related forms from the early Miocene

Locality	Age (millions of years)	Fossil ape species	Other species
Kipsaraman	14.5	*P. gitongai*	
Maboko, Fort Ternan	15–14	*Proconsul* sp.	
Moroto	18–17		*Afropithecus turkanensis*
Rusinga Island	18.5–17	*P. heseloni, P. nyanzae*	*Nyanzapithecus vancouveringorum, Dendropithecus macinnesi*
Mfwangano Island	18.5–17	*P. heseloni, P. nyanzae*	*Dendropithecus macinnesi*
Songhor	20–19	*P. africanus, P. major*	*Dendropithecus macinnesi, Limnopithecus evansi* *Rangwapithecus gordoni* *Kalepithecus songhorensis*
Koru	20–19	*P. africanus, P. major*	*Micropithecus clarki, Limnopithecus legetet, Kalepithecus songhorensis*
Napak	19.9–19.7	*P. major*	*Micropithecus clarki*
Meswa Bridge	22–20	*P. meswae*	

Werdelin, L. & Sanders, W.J. 2010. See text for replacement of *Ekembo* for some species of *Proconsul*.

second fossil ape species present at Paşalar and at Çandir, also in Turkey, was extremely abundant, and it shares many ancestral characters with middle Miocene afropithecines such as *Equatorius africanus* and *Nacholapithecus kerioi* (Table 4.2). The Paşalar deposits consisted of rapid flood accumulations of locally derived material followed by the formation of palaeosols, which indicate tropical to subtropical conditions during the Miocene with a strongly seasonal (wet–dry) climate (see Figure 4.2).

Dryopithecines

The dryopithecines are the third group of middle and late Miocene fossil apes that will be considered here. This includes the genus *Dryopithecus*, and a

(a)

(b)

Figure 4.2 (a) Louis Leakey (standing) at Fort Ternan showing the site to Dick Hay who is examining one of the fossiliferous palaeosols, which is located at the level of his head. Photograph courtesy of Anthea Gentry. (b) The excavation at Paşalar. The students are excavating the fossiliferous sands, which can also be seen in vertical section behind their heads.

number of similar taxa that have been distinguished from it: *Hispanopithecus, Pierolapithecus, Anoiapithecus* and *Rudapithecus* (Table 4.3). The teeth of some of these taxa have similarities with *Proconsul* teeth, but the skull and postcrania are different and in some cases share characters with the living great apes. Although first described from St Gaudens, France, dryopithecines are now best known from sites in Hungary and Spain. I excavated at the Hungarian site, Rudabánya (Figure 4.3), with Ray Bernor and David Cameron and did a detailed taphonomic and palaeoecological analysis of the site and its fauna.

Table 4.2 Middle Miocene fossil apes from Africa (top five rows) and Europe (bottom three rows)

Locality	Age (millions of years)	Fossil ape species	Other species
Fort Ternan	14	*Kenyapithecus wickeri*	
Kipsaraman	14.5	*Equatorius africanus, Proconsul gitongai*	*Nyanzapithecus pickfordi*
Maboko Island	15	*Equatorius africanus*	*Nyanzapithecus vancouveringorum*
Nachola	16–15	*Nacholapithecus kerioi*	*Nyanzapithecus vancouveringorum*
Ad Dabtiyah	16–15	*Heliopithecus leakeyi*	
Paşalar	16.5–16	*Griphopithecus alpani, Kenyapithecus kizili*	
Çandir	16.5–16	*Griphopithecus alpani*	
Engelswies	17–16	*Griphopthecus* sp.	

Werdelin, L. & Sanders, W.J. 2010.

It is dated to between 9 and 10 million years, and the sedimentary environment indicates woodland swamp vegetation. Two of the Spanish sites, Can Llobateres and Can Ponsic, are the same age as Rudabánya, between 9 and 10 million years old. The fossils preserved at both sites are fragmentary and crushed, but the presence of ribs and vertebrae together with skulls and mandibles suggests absence of transport in the accumulation of the fossils.

There is some difference of opinion on the relationships of the dryopithecines with living great apes. Traditionally they have been viewed as primitive apes, but two claims for relationship are now in place. David Begun considers that the skull has similarities with the African great apes, and he has proposed that the African apes originated in Europe from some part of the dryopithecine lineage and migrated back to Africa to give rise to the African great apes and humans. Salvador Moyà Solà however considers that some of the Spanish dryopithecines share characters of the postcranial bones that are most similar to that of the orang utan. A third view is that they are stem hominids, fossil apes preceding the split between orang utans, the African apes and humans.

Table 4.3 Middle to late Miocene species of *Dryopithecus* and related forms from Europe

Locality	Age (millions of years)	Fossil ape species	Other species
Çorakyerler	8.8–7.3	*Ouranopithecus turkae*	
Baccinello	8.3–7.5	*Oreopithecus bambolii*	
Udabno	9.1–8.7	*Udabnopithecus garedziensis*	
Pyrgos	9.4–9.3	*Graecopithecus freybergi*	
Ravin de la Pluie	9.4–9.3	*Ouranopithecus macedoniensis*	
Can Llobateres	9.8–9.4	*Hispanopithecus laietanus*	
Nikiti	9.7–8.7	*Ouranopithecus macedoniensis*	
Sinap	9.9–9.7	*Ankarapithecus meteai*	
Can Ponsic	10.4–9.8	*Hispanopithecus crusafonti*	
Rudabánya	11.5–9.7	*Rudapithecus hungaricus*	*Anapithecus hernyaki*
Polinyà	11.6–11.1	*Hispanopithecus laietanus*	
Castell de Barberà	11.8–11.1	*Dryopithecus fontani*	
Hostalets de Pierola	11.9–11.8	*Pierolapithecus catalaunicus* *Dryopithecus fontani* *Anoiapithecus brevirostris*	
La Grive Saint-Alban	13.0–11.1	*Dryopithecus fontani*	
Saint Gaudens	13.0–11.1	*Dryopithecus fontani*	

Werdelin, L. & Sanders, W.J. 2010.

Late Miocene apes

Late Miocene fossil apes are poorly known, and in Africa and Europe they disappeared from the fossil record about 8 million years ago. Three taxa that have been identified as apes are present in Africa during the period 9 to 10 million years ago, but there is little evidence from their morphology to indicate their relationship with living and fossil apes, and there is even less information about their environment (Table 4.4). There are also several hominid species from the late Miocene of Africa, which have been described as hominin ancestors, but which are hard to

Table 4.4 Late Miocene fossil hominids from Africa

Locality	Age (millions of years)	Fossil ape species
Beticha, Ethiopia	10.5–10	*Chororapithecus abbyssinicus*
Samburu Hills, Kenya	10–9.5	*Samburupithecus kiptalami*
Nakali, Kenya	9.8–9.6	*Nakalipithecus nakayamai*
Toros-Menalla, Chad	7.2–6.8	*Sahelanthropus tchadensis*
Tugen Hills, Kenya	6.2–5.6	*Orrorin tugenensis*
Awash, Gona, Ethiopia	5.8–5.2	*Ardipithecus kadabba*

Werdelin, L. & Sanders, W.J. 2010.

Figure 4.3 Miklos Kretzoi and Hernyak, the discoverers and first excavators at Rudabánya, Hungary.

differentiate from apes, for example *Ororrin tugenensis* from northern Kenya, *Sahelanthropus tchadensis* from Chad and *Ardipithecus kadabba* from Ethiopia. They share many primitive characters with Miocene fossil apes that are associated with arboreal life, but from their location and age it is possible that they are close to the common ancestor of African apes and humans.

Ape dispersals

There is every reason to believe that apes originated in Africa, as all of the earliest fossil apes known at present come from Africa and were restricted to this continent for the first 6 or 7 million years of ape history. The earliest dispersal of fossil apes was in the middle Miocene, about 16 million years ago, seen with the appearance of *Kenyapithecus kizili* and *Griphopithecus alpani* in Turkey. This was followed by an apparently independent dispersal out of Africa at the end of the middle Miocene with the first appearance of the dryopithecines in Spain and southern France. It is likely that the orang utans and gibbons arose out of one of these dispersals, but the evidence is ambiguous (for the orang utan) or absent (for gibbons). What is particularly interesting about these early dispersals is why and how did the fossil apes move out of tropical Africa? What was their environment like, and what were the motivating forces that led to their intercontinental dispersal? I will try to answer these questions by first looking at the environments of fossil apes to see if there is any evidence for environmental forcing, and then considering a genetic mutation that affected all hominids in the middle Miocene.

Ape environments

What will become clear from later chapters is that most of the fossil apes known at present from Africa, including the most common species, are associated in the fossil record with woodland habitats, not forest. For example, many of the early Miocene fossil apes have been recovered from sites where the environmental interpretations point to deciduous woodland habitats and there are only a few sites where forest is indicated; even here the evidence suggests that the forests were local rather than regional, either montane forests on high ground or high water-table (edaphic) forests. This points to a factor in palaeoecological studies that is sometimes ignored, habitat heterogeneity. Where a mosaic of habitats is present within the movement ranges of fossil species, a greater number of species may be present. In Africa and North America, where species richness patterns have been studied, the species richness of mammals, birds and other vertebrates is consistently found to be greatest in areas of topographic relief, where changes in altitude bring about changes in habitat over relatively short distances. It will be seen in Chapter 6 that in Africa, in particular, species richness of mammals is greater in the varied topography of the rift valleys than in tropical rainforest.

Primate species richness is today greatest in lowland tropical forest, and I should introduce a word of caution at this point that it may be that in sampling the fossil record we have mainly found non-forest sites and faunas. Few Miocene sites are known in Central and West Africa, and it may be that if and when they are found and excavated, the environmental history of fossil apes will change. However, Judy Van Couvering and I demonstrated in 1975 that the early Miocene sites of East Africa were situated within the tropical forest zone extending eastwards from Central Africa. Based on evidence available at present, therefore, it appears that most fossil apes were living in woodland and forest/woodland mosaic habitats.

During the middle Miocene, some species of fossil ape emigrated to Europe and Asia, and there too they are associated with vegetation types that are structurally analogous to tropical woodlands. The evergreen subtropical forests of southern Europe, for example, included many deciduous species (the swamp cypress is a deciduous conifer) and were highly seasonal. They had simple tree canopy structures analogous to those of tropical woodland, while other species in Asia were living in summer rainfall monsoon forests, which are highly seasonal. In both cases, it is likely that the forests had local distributions, again indicating high levels of habitat heterogeneity. This feature will be discussed in more detail in Chapters 6 and 16.

APES VERSUS MONKEYS

It may be seen from Tables 4.1 to 4.4 that there is a significant reduction in numbers of fossil ape species present in Africa during the Miocene. There were from nine to ten species in the early and early middle Miocene of Africa, the number falling to four in the later middle Miocene and three in the late Miocene. This trend was reversed in the middle and late Miocene in Europe and Asia. In 1981 when many of these fossil apes had not yet been found, I plotted the regression of species numbers against time for African apes, which showed that ape diversity was declining throughout the Miocene, so that they were well on the way to extinction by the Pleistocene (Figure 4.4). At the same time as the decline in fossil apes in Africa, there was an increase in numbers of species of fossil monkeys, from two in the early Miocene to nine or ten in the late Miocene, about 30 in the Pliocene and over 60 today. The regression lines in Figure 4.4 are taken from my 1981 paper, based on numbers of fossil and recent apes known at that time, and for comparison I have put in the comparable proportions for apes and monkeys based on the numbers recognized today. There is little difference between the two sets of figures, and it remains true that in Africa apes flourished in the early Miocene to a greater extent than any time since.

A particularly significant factor concealed in these numbers of fossil apes is that at some early Miocene sites, there are four or even five species of fossil ape apparently coexisting with smaller primate species. After the early Miocene, the most species from any one site is two. Monkeys were rare throughout the Miocene but have now taken over most of the areas once occupied by apes, and today only two ape species coexist in the tropical forests of Africa and Asia.

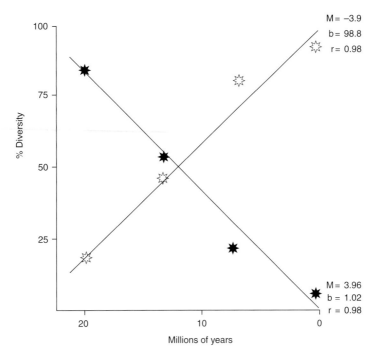

Figure 4.4 Comparison of the relative proportions of apes and monkeys throughout the Miocene. The vertical scale gives the percentage numbers of species of fossil apes and fossil monkeys plotted against time as first published in Andrews (1981), and the relationship between them is shown by the regression line. The original numbers of living species were based on Napier and Napier's (1967) assessments, and the numbers of fossil species were based on the fossils available in 1981. Many more fossil ape and monkey species have been discovered since this diagram was first produced, as listed in Tables 4.1 to 4.4, and the proportions of ape to monkey based on these newly discovered fossil species are shown as black stars for fossil and living apes and open stars for fossil and living monkeys. There is little change from the regression line based on my 1981 publication.

Numbers of middle Miocene ape species are gradually increasing as additional sites are excavated, but each site has only a single ape species. This suggests that the environments occupied could only support single ape species, and conversely, where there were more than two, a richer environment is indicated – either tropical forest, which today supports twelve to fifteen primate species, or heterogeneous habitats, which provide a varied environment allowing species with different habitats to coexist.

There are one or two exceptions to these singleton sites, for example the middle Miocene site at Paşalar in Turkey and a late Miocene site in Hungary. I will show in Chapter 11 that two ape species were present at Paşalar, one extremely abundant and a second rare species, but there is evidence that the two apes were living in separate places and not coexisting (see Chapters 3 and 11 where this issue is described in some detail). The two ape species present at

Rudabánya provide a different case. They had similar diets, locomotor and positional behaviour, and they overlapped in size. There is some indication that they differed in fall-back foods, with one species increasing leaf consumption during lean periods, and the other less palatable fruits, but it also appears that they were only partly sympatric. Although they occur together in two levels at Rudabánya, they are present in different frequencies, each being common at one level and rare in the other. This could be a function of habitat heterogeneity or, since different time periods are represented at the two levels, displacement of one by the other.

The significance of habitat heterogeneity is important in another respect, that of possible effects of rates of dispersal. It has been proposed that there is a relationship between habitat heterogeneity, level of foresight and likelihood of dispersal in fossil hominins, and it is likely that the same would apply to hominid apes and the common ancestor with humans. High habitat heterogeneity was shown to select for increased foresight (for example in locating where and when different food items would be available) and this in turn would tend to reduce the likelihood of dispersal (why go away when the present habitat offers abundant resources). Dispersals of apes out of Africa during the middle Miocene may have been prompted by reduction in habitat heterogeneity (perhaps due to global cooling) and dispersal away from more homogeneous environments.

Extending their ranges into the higher latitudes of Europe and Asia is just as significant a feature of ape evolution. Well away from the tropics, there would have been much greater seasonality, both in terms of temperature (periods of cold during winters) and rainfall (summer rainfall regimes resulted in long dry periods during the winter). Clearly the dispersing species of fossil ape had to adapt to survive, let alone thrive, in such seasonal habitats, and they managed it in part by changing their diets to food items that were harder and tougher to eat, recognized today by changes in their jaws and teeth, and perhaps aided by a mutation affecting their capacity to convert sugars in their diet to fat and promote storage of food.

A middle Miocene mutation

In the middle Miocene, a genetic mutation occurred in the lineage leading to the great apes and humans. This was a mutation of the gene that controls the production of the enzyme uricase. Uricase (urate oxidase) metabolizes uric acid, which is a purine metabolic product that is generated during the degradation of DNA. In most mammalian species, uric acid is metabolized by the enzyme to generate allantoin. However, there is evidence that there was a progressive reduction in uricase activity due to mutations in the promoter region during

A speculation

From the middle Miocene onwards, we have seen that the common pattern for fossil apes was one species per fossil site. We have also seen that the number of known fossil apes undoubtedly under-represents the actual number of species at any one time, but for most of the fossil ape sites we can be confident that the species represented was probably the only fossil ape present at those sites. In other words, there were no unknown species hiding in the wings. Furthermore, the distribution pattern of living apes is also one of single species per site: the only apparent exception to this is the sympatry of chimpanzees and gorillas, but observations in the wild show that where they are present together in one region, they tend to occupy different parts of the environment and rarely meet up with each other.

We will see in later chapters that the earliest hominins were ecologically still ape-like, and they also appear in the fossil record as one species per site. We may ask the question, therefore, as to whether our earliest ancestors existed as a single lineage or whether there were multiple lineages, as found at later stages of human evolution. The answer according to present evidence is that there was only a single lineage evolving from the common ancestor with chimpanzees, but it seems likely that within a million years this had diverged into two or more lineages evolving in different parts of Africa. For example, hominins in southern and eastern Africa appear to be distinct lineages; and hominins such as *Australopithecus afarensis* living in woodland environments may have occupied different environments from *A. anamensis* and could have coexisted in the same general region (see Chapter 15). The question then becomes which lineage gave rise to later hominins and eventually to us, but that question is beyond the scope of this book.

hominoid evolution, and this was followed by complete silencing of the gene from mutations in the coding region. In the great ape and human clade, the silencing mutation occurred in codon 33 of exon 2 approximately 15 million years ago, whereas the mutation in the hylobatids occurred in codon 18 of exon 2 approximately 9 million years ago. The consequence of loss of uricase is the accumulation of the purine waste product, uric acid, during metabolism. The loss of uricase both results in a higher baseline level of uric acid in the blood and less ability to maintain uric acid within set levels. The presence of high levels of uric acid has particular consequences when fructose is an important element in the diet. Since fruits were a major staple in the diet of fossil apes, Rick Johnson and I decided to investigate the implication of their interaction with uric acid for fossil apes during human evolution.

Fructose is the primary sugar present in fruit, and when it is eaten it is converted to glucose and stored in the blood. Excess glucose is stored in the liver as glycogen and released back into the blood as the levels of stored glucose diminish. In the presence of uric acid, much of the fructose entering the body is not broken down into glucose, because the production of ATP by the mitochondria in the cells (this is the process by which the glucose is exchanged into energy) is interrupted by uric acid. Instead of producing energy by the release of glucose, much of the fructose that is eaten is converted and stored as fat. This was obviously beneficial to animals living in seasonal habitats, increasing their ability to put on weight in times of plenty to see them through lean times, and so the increased levels of uric acid in fruit-eating hominoids would have had survival value, especially as they moved into more seasonal habitats. In modern humans, who eat too much sugar, it is now of great concern, and it is one of the contributing causes of the obesity epidemic sweeping through modern human populations.

There is a twist to this tale, however, and this is the interaction of fructose with ascorbate (vitamin C). One of the actions of vitamin C is to block the metabolic interaction between uric acid and fructose to increase fat stores, reducing the effects of high uric acid levels in the blood. However, the ability to synthesize vitamin C was lost in all higher primates some time back in the late Eocene, which was another period of pronounced global cooling, and as with the later uricase mutation, the loss of vitamin C synthesis may have provided survival advantage to animals needing to rapidly increase fat stores. Vitamin C is present in fruit, but its concentration decreases as fruit ripens, which is also when amounts of fructose increase; hence, to get maximum advantage from fruit, animals lacking uricase should wait for the fruit to ripen or even to become over-ripe. This is the feeding strategy of living apes, and it may well have been adopted in the middle Miocene soon after the uricase mutation occurred. This coincided both with the onset of global cooling in the middle Miocene and the time when fossil ape species flourished in Europe and Asia, where seasonal temperature fluctuations were far greater than occur today in tropical Africa.

Returning now to the changing fortunes of apes and monkeys during the Miocene, it is possible that the uricase mutation provided sufficient selective advantage for the apes to allow them to survive changing environmental and climatic conditions. It has also been suggested that the apes increased in body size as competition with monkeys increased, but it will be shown in later chapters that even in the early Miocene, fossil apes almost matched living apes in body size and were only exceeded post-Miocene by male gorillas and orang utans. I am proposing that the Miocene apes selected ripe fruit, with its higher fructose content and lower vitamin C content, and with the high levels of serum uric acid resulting from the uricase mutation, they were able to store fat more readily and adapt to the increasingly seasonal environmental conditions.

Summary

- The early history of descriptions of fossil apes is briefly outlined, followed by an account of the sparse evidence of fossil chimpanzees and orang utans.
- Three groups of fossil apes are briefly described, proconsulids, afropithecines and kenyapithecines, and dryopithecines.
- Most of the fossil apes are associated with woodland habitats, or woodland/rainforest mosaic habitats.
- Future sampling in West or Central Africa may provide evidence of forest-adapted fossil apes, but there is some reason to doubt this.
- It is suggested that it was their ability to survive in tropical woodland habitats, with high seasonality, that enabled fossil apes to spread outside tropical Africa and into Europe and Asia.
- Late Miocene hominids are briefly mentioned.
- The trends in ape diversity in Africa show the decline in numbers of species through the Miocene, and a possible survival mechanism is proposed through the uricase mutation. This occurred about 15 million years ago and increased the ability of the fossil apes to survive in highly seasonal habitats.

Part II
Environments and palaeoenvironments

Chapter 5
Structure and composition of ape environments

The species of living ape described in Chapters 2 and 3 have been well studied, both their behaviour and their ecology. Their inter-relationship with their environment is key to understanding how they function, and in this chapter I am going to set out a simple classification of present-day environments in relation to the living apes, and this will then form the basis for interpreting past environments of fossil apes. It is my strongly held belief that our inter-pretations of the past can only be based upon what we can see around us today. This is not to say that environments in the past were identical to present-day environments, for many are demonstrably different, but they differ in ways that can be interpreted by our knowledge of present ecologies. Records of fossil plants, for example, show us when particular species of plants first appeared, and whether they were related to present-day forest or wood-land species, but they do not tell us about the structure, the ecophysiology, of the environment. For this we need evidence from other sources that will be described in the next chapter.

Modern environments

In order to relate fossil and recent apes to their environment, it is necessary to provide a brief classification of the terms used here. There are numerous classifications of vegetation structure as applied to ape and human environ-ments, and it seems that every work on palaeoecology adopts one or other of them, never the same. The one that Judy Van Couvering and I used in 1975 was modified from Peter Greenways's 1943 vegetation classification of East African vegetation, and it is the one I have used ever since. Thure Cerling has recently proposed one that combines his carbon isotope ($\delta^{13}C$) work with the classification by Frank White of African vegetation for the UNESCO vege-tation map of Africa. This is the seminal work on African vegetation, and I have combined it with my earlier scheme to produce the following classifica-tion. It will be restricted to just four biomes (major regional ecological com-munities of plants and animals), which have similar types of vegetation as a result of similar climate regimes. This is often as far as palaeoecological inter-pretation can go, but where evidence is good it may be possible to recognize different types of plant formation within these biomes. Sometimes there is botanical evidence (pollen, leaves, seeds) and this may provide details of plant associations.

Forest biome

The forest biome is characterized by a continuous stand of trees (trees have single stems as distinct from shrubs with multiple stems). Aspects of physiognomy include evergreen or deciduous, degree of crowns intermingling (density), canopy complexity and canopy height. The main canopy is at least 10 m tall; in some formations a higher emergent canopy up to 50 m may be present, and more commonly there is a lower tree canopy and a shrub layer; ground vegetation is sparse, consisting of herbs; and grasses are rare and are usually C_3 species (see Chapter 6). Forests grow in areas of high precipitation with a relatively short dry season; in subtropical to tropical climatic regimes, frost-free; in the subtropics with summer monsoon rainfall; in the tropics with one or two periods of rainfall following the movement of the sun, or more specifically of the intertropical convergence zone (ITCZ); and they are usually found on well-drained soils.

TYPES OF FOREST
- Lowland evergreen forest grows below about 1500 m in the tropics but is restricted to near sea level in subtropical climatic regimes; different tree associations make up the three tree canopies, the tallest of which is up to 50 m.
- Semi-deciduous intermediate forest grows at 1500 to 2000 m in the tropics (see Chapter 1, Figure 1.3).
- Edaphic forest with low species diversity grows on sandy soils or in areas subject to flooding, while evergreen swamp forest (and riparian forest) is similar in physiognomy to tropical evergreen forest, up to 45 m tall but with discontinuous canopy structure.
- Montane forest is evergreen, growing above 2000 m in the tropics, with precipitation ranging from 800 mm to >2500 mm. Two broad types include dry montane forest with conifers and broad-leaved forest similar structurally to temperate dry forest growing at sea level in South Africa.
- Dry evergreen forest grows in areas of marginal rainfall at 600 to 900 mm, and it often has low diversity tree associations including species with adaptations to withstand longer dry seasons; up to 15–25 m in height.
- Deciduous forest grows in areas with rainfall 600–900 mm; tree canopy up to 20 m, discontinuous but with a dense lower canopy.
- Evergreen coniferous forest may be associated with swamp conditions in subtropical regions.

- Ground water forest is usually composed of broad-leaved trees, is evergreen and similar to lowland or intermediate forest, but grows in arid regions and is dependent on ground water.

Savanna biome

The savanna biome vegetation has variable amounts of grasses and woody plants. Both woody and grass elements are always present, but the greater the wooded element the fewer grasses in the ground vegetation and the more herbs. Woodland elements may be trees (with single trunk) or shrubs (with multiple stems). Woodland is included here in the savanna biome although many authors treat it as distinct. Formerly widespread in Africa, much of the woodland has been destroyed to make way for agriculture. Tree–grass mixtures are regarded as fundamentally unstable, and the relative contributions of wood and grass are in a state of flux with many factors pushing in different directions, sometimes towards greater tree cover, and sometimes towards more open grassy conditions. The contribution of woody species may be measured by percentage canopy cover or by a leaf area index.

African savanna generally occurs where rainfall is highly seasonal, with a distinct dry season: summer rainfall (monsoon) in subtropical regions, winter rainfall in the far north and south of the continent; within the tropics there may be two rainy seasons, but the dry season is always long. It occurs within subtropical to tropical temperature regimes with a low incidence of frost. Note that alpine meadows with frost-controlled grasslands are not part of the savanna biome and neither are dambo grasslands where periodically high water-tables produce flooded grasslands. Shallow soils support savanna in areas of high precipitation, and deeper soils are needed to support savanna in dry areas. The root systems of trees vary with soil type, but may extend as much as ten times beyond the canopy diameters. Freely drained soils support the richest and tallest woodland savanna formations; impeded drainage areas have low diversity woodland contributions with low canopy structure.

Types of savanna are as follows:

- Deciduous woodland has closed canopies or at least 40% canopy cover and a minor shrub understorey and herbaceous ground vegetation with grasses reduced in extent and diversity; tree canopy 10–20 m, rarely up to 30 m.
- Sclerophyllous woodland is closed canopy evergreen woodland or shrubland growing in highly seasonal winter rainfall areas.
- Tree or woodland savanna has open tree canopies, few shrubs and diverse and extensive grass ground flora.

- Bushland has a thick cover of shrubs with at least 40% cover, generally deciduous, and occasional trees 3 to 8 m tall; grasses and herbs constitute the dominant ground cover.
- Shrub savanna has open to closed shrub canopies and extensive grass ground flora.
- Savanna grassland has scattered trees and extensive grass ground flora.

Two major processes influence the development of savanna – fire and animal predation. Fire has been an important factor in savanna development since the time of the spread of grasses. In areas of high rainfall, fire has the effect of reducing tree cover because the abundant ground vegetation produces hot burns. In more arid areas, fire may encourage the spread of woody vegetation, although if fires are infrequent, the resulting hot burns my cause widespread death of trees. Total exclusion of fire generally allows the spread of trees.

Two very different sized animals dominate animal predation on plants in savanna habitats: termites are the major herbivores, as are grasshoppers in some years, followed in Africa by browsing and grazing mammals. Mammals may range from selective feeders, for example small-sized browsers with narrow pointed faces, to large-sized bulk feeders such as horses, some bovids, rhinos and elephants. About half of African bovids are intermediate feeders to some degree. Elephants may destroy trees by tearing off branches or uprooting them in their quest for food, and where high concentrations of elephants occur tree cover may be totally destroyed. This has happened in recent times in Tsavo National Park, where dense woodland cover, which was present in the 1960s when I worked there, was replaced by open grassland by the end of the century.

Grassland biome

The grassland biome is defined here as an open sward of grasses and other perennials, lacking shrubs or trees over most of the area. As a result of the absence of woody vegetation, open grassland is exposed to high solar radiation, with C_4 grasses and perennials tolerant of exposure to light. This applies both to perennial grasses and to annuals. The grassland biome has a restricted distribution in Africa, and where it occurs it is usually the result of biological or animal (including human) activity, fire or soil/water factors (edaphic). Fire-induced grasslands often form on deep soils high in nutrients, so that the grass sward is dense and high, resulting in hot burns that kill any trees and shrubs; large areas of the Guinea-Congolian forest have been destroyed and replaced by grassland, and when patches of forest remain, the combination of forest and grassland may be designated forest–savanna mosaic. Human-induced grasslands occur where woody vegetation has been cleared for agriculture, including use of fire, for example the Athi Plain in Kenya. Animal-induced grassland is produced by a combination of large mammals such as elephants and intensive termite activity. The extent of grassland may be local, for example concentrations of animals around water holes may leave open areas even in forest environments, or it may be widespread, as in the case of the Tsavo and Mara grasslands. The open grasslands of the Mara region north of Serengeti reverted to woodland and thicket in the early twentieth century as a result of the devastation of wild and domestic mammal herds by Rinderpest. In 1963 the disease disappeared from the region, and with the reintroduction of elephants soon after, the open grassland returned. Edaphic grasslands occur as a result of flooding, where water levels are periodically high for long enough to kill the roots of trees; dambos along river valleys and flood plains are two examples of this. Grasslands may also occur naturally in tropical Africa on soils with strongly impeded drainage; for example, where drainage is blocked by hard-pan development, such as calcretes, trees cannot survive and open grasslands result, as in the short grass plains of Serengeti. Finally, alpine grasslands or high latitude grasslands occur where frost damage kills trees.

Desert biome

The desert biome has sparse ground cover on a rocky or sandy substrate; trees and bushes are absent except where edaphic conditions allow. Semi-desert has low branching shrubs and trees up to 3 to 4m and ephemeral cover of succulents and annual herbs and grasses. This biome is not likely to have figured largely in ape or human evolution.

Habitat heterogeneity

In two scientific papers I wrote with the late Bonnie O'Brien, we investigated the possible connections between numbers of mammal species present in Africa (species richness) and the environment in which they lived. We counted species numbers per unit area, each unit being $25\,000\,km^2$, and there were as few as 6 to nearly 200 mammal species for each of the 1079 equal area units. The numbers of species, however, did not correlate closely with the vegetation; numbers were high for the units sampling tropical rainforest, but they were even higher for the units that included within their borders areas of high topographic relief, and the greatest of these were along the rift valleys running north to south through eastern Africa (Figure 5.1). There is little forest in the rift valleys, but there is great variety of vegetation types because in the tropics vegetation changes quickly with changes in altitude. At each level, slightly

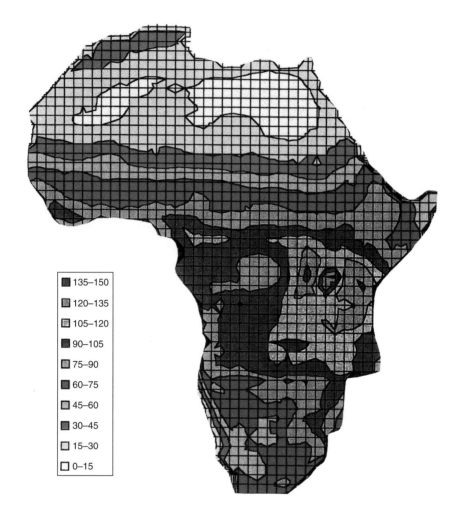

135–150
120–135
105–120
90–105
75–90
60–75
45–60
30–45
15–30
0–15

Figure 5.1 Numbers of mammal species per unit area for Africa. Numbers were calculated from range maps superimposed on an equal area grid of 1079 grid cells (excluding those with overlap over lakes or the sea). Highest species richness is shown by the browns and greens running north-south along eastern Africa. North of the equator there is a clear latitudinal gradient of diminishing species richness, but in southern Africa this gradient is affected both by the eastern highlands and the western desertification. A black and white version of this figure will appear in some formats. See plate section for colour version.

different associations of mammals occur, so that where altitude change is of the order of hundreds or thousands of metres, the plant and animal associations show many changes over limited horizontal distances. It is this variety that gives rise to high habitat heterogeneity and is the driving force behind the high numbers of mammal species and genera along the rift valleys shown in Figure 5.1. We shall see in Chapter 16 just how important it is.

A special case of habitat heterogeneity is that of dispersal of fig trees in tropical Africa. Figs can occur in almost any environment provided sufficient water is available. It was pointed out in Chapter 2 that fig trees have symbiotic relationships with fig wasps, each species of fig having their own unique species of wasp. Since the life cycles of fig wasps in tropical environments differ from those of other wasps, fruiting by African figs can occur at any time of the year, independently of time of fruiting of other fig trees. As a result, in any environment where fig trees are present fruit is available throughout the year.

The Miocene environment

Evidence of the vegetation present during the first part of the Miocene is limited. At the beginning of the Miocene, Africa was still an island continent separated from Europe and Asia by a wide stretch of sea, the Tethys Sea. The opening and closing of land bridges connecting Africa to continental Eurasia allowed faunal migrations between the continents, and it also had a major impact on ocean currents and consequently on climate change in the region. Palaeogeographic reconstructions of the circum-Mediterranean area show how tectonic movements have altered the area of the Tethys/Mediterranean (Figure 5.2). In the late Eocene, the Tethys Sea was a wide expanse of ocean, with Africa and India far to the south and southern Europe a series of more or less small islands to the north. In the early Miocene, at a time when fossil ape species were flourishing in East Africa, the first land bridge formed, and faunal interchange took place, with gomphotheres, deinotheres and primates (but not hominoids) moving into Eurasia and rhinos entering Africa. The *Gomphotherium* land bridge, as it is called, closed again as sea levels rose about 16 million years ago, the so-called Langhian transgression, and Africa was cut off, but just before the transgression, hominid primates migrated out of Africa and into Central Europe and western Asia. It will be appreciated that a land bridge connecting Africa to Europe acted as a barrier to foram dispersal while enabling land animal dispersal. A permanent land bridge was established across the Arabian Peninsula in the middle Miocene, about 15 million years ago.

Fossil plants from East Africa show the presence of both forest and deciduous woodland in the early Miocene (Figure 5.3). There are indicators of tropical forest associated with the fossil ape *Proconsul*, although the geological evidence suggests it was growing locally as gallery or ground water forest. In the middle to late Miocene, 12 to 6 million years ago, the Ngorora flora is interpreted as forest, based on an assemblage of 58 leaf morphotypes as well as twigs and fruits, but most environmental evidence indicates widespread woodlands associated with fossil apes. Other sites later in time show

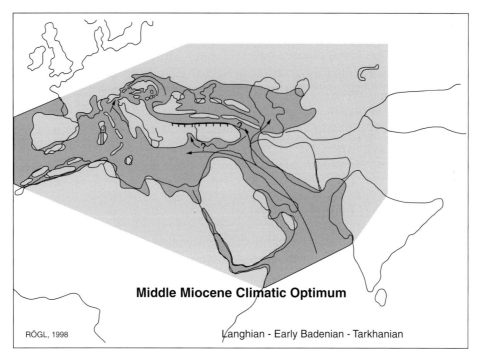

Figure 5.2 Palaeogeographic reconstruction of the Mediterranean (Tethys) sea way at the time of the sea level rise known as the Langhian transgression about 16 million years ago. The connection between the Atlantic and the Indian Ocean is demonstrated by many shared species of foraminifera (shown by the arrows). Africa was cut off from Europe and Asia and migration between the continents ceased. Reproduced with permission from Fred Rögl 1999.

(a)   (b)

Figure 5.3 (a) The late Bill Bishop at the Ngorora Formation, Kenya. He was a hugely influential figure in the description and understanding of Miocene deposits in East Africa, having first worked in Uganda and latterly in Kenya, leading the Bedford College geological surveys along the Baringo rift valley. (b) The Kerio Valley Acacia woodlands, part of the Baringo rift valley system.

the presence of woodland rather than forest, with only a few sites indicating the presence of forest.

In the Middle Awash region, between 6 and 5 million years ago, carbon isotope values indicate the presence of woodland associated with a proposed early hominin ancestor, *Ardipithecus kadabba*. In sediments of the Omo-Turkana Basin, analysis of isotopes showed that some open habitats in a generally woodland setting existed for long periods, spanning the period of divergence of apes and humans and part of the early hominin fossil record. The spread of C_4 grasses (see Chapter 6), however, and evidence of open grassland did not occur until well into the Pleistocene, after the emergence of *Homo* and long after the split between apes and humans. The woodland habitats during the late Miocene and Pliocene appear little different from those of the middle and late Miocene apes, and there is no evidence, for example, during the time of transition from ape to hominin that the environments associated with them changed to any great extent. This is consistent with the low degree of climate change during the same period, and it suggests both that the common ancestor to apes and humans was living in this kind of woodland habitat, and that the evolutionary pressures leading to the divergence of the hominins was not the result of climate forcing.

In contrast to the situation in tropical Africa, more severe and more strongly seasonal changes occurred in Europe. During the early Miocene and the beginning of the middle Miocene, southern Europe had a subtropical climate, and subtropical coniferous forests covered the eastern Mediterranean region, with *Sequoia* species growing along the shoreline, much as it does today in northern California. Further to the west there was warm humid deciduous forest with elms and *Zelkova* the dominant species. The climate was strongly seasonal, with pronounced wet and dry periods based on evidence from Paşalar in Turkey (Figure 5.4), and towards the end of the Miocene, cooler and more temperature-seasonal conditions were occurring in Eurasia. In Central Europe the mean annual temperature fell 7°C to a mean of 15°C. Conditions worsened in Europe during the mid-Vallesian crisis during which up to 30% of mammalian genera became extinct, so that mammalian faunas after about 11 million years changed dramatically. Subtropical forest changed to deciduous woodland as temperature and rainfall decreased. There were also more open environments locally in Spain and southern Europe, but in the Vallès Penedès region of northeastern Spain subtropical summer rainfall forests persisted to the end of the Vallesian, with warm temperate forests to the north; fossil apes persisted for some time in these relic areas. The *Sequoia* forests were gradually replaced by more temperate species, so that by the time of the Pliocene the vegetation pattern across Europe was much as it is today, with forest cover to the north of the Mediterranean and open environments to the south. *Taxodium* forests

Figure 5.4 The site at Paşalar after 5 years' excavations. The main fossiliferous unit is the white sand, which is exposed in mid-section, with an upper calcareous silt above the top step of the excavations and a lower calcareous silt forming the floor of the excavation at the level of the road in the foreground. The calcareous silts are gleyed (pale colour due to anaerobic conditions resulting from waterlogged deposits), but they also contain many calcareous nodules that formed from calcium deposition when the sediments were dry. These two deposits therefore indicate that both waterlogging and seasonal drying occurred at these levels, which points to a highly seasonal monsoon climate. The legs belong to Erick Bestland.

(swamp cypress) were common at low altitude/latitude, deciduous forest at mid-altitude/latitude and ericaceous moors at high altitude.

These changes in the region of the Tethys Sea, brought about in part by the interruption of oceanic currents between the Atlantic and Indian Oceans, were associated with widespread cooling and build-up of the East Antarctic ice sheet. Africa during the early Miocene was warmer and wetter than it is at present. The rise in diversity of Miocene faunas has been shown for the North American faunas to have started in the late Oligocene, with the temperature peaking at 17 to 15 million years ago, and this was followed by long-term cooling, leading to decline in mammal diversity. The decline is most marked during the Eocene followed by a stable period during the Oligocene and into the first part of the middle Miocene, and then another rapid decline at the end of the Miocene (Figure 5.5). Global cooling was occurring worldwide, including expansion of the Antarctic polar ice cap and the formation of deserts in North Africa, but the Miocene temperature decline is attributed to changes in ocean currents rather than expansion of the ice sheet. Consequences for terrestrial ecosystems are not completely straightforward, for it must be assumed that ocean–atmosphere

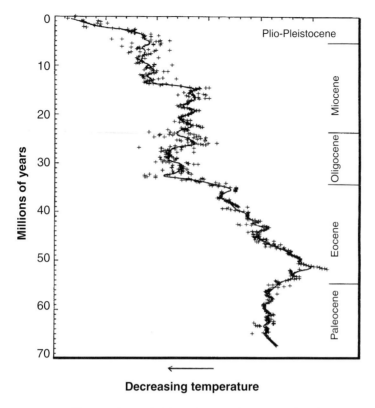

Decreasing temperature

Figure 5.5 The benthic $\delta^{18}O$ record compiled from deep sea drilling records in the Atlantic Ocean. The records show a temperature peak in the early Eocene and several cooling stages interspersed with periods of stasis. At the time of emergence of the apes in the Oligocene to early Miocene there was little temperature change, but there were sharp falls during the middle Miocene after 15 Ma, when apes first left Africa, and in the late Miocene to Pliocene after 5–4 Ma, when apes and humans diverged. The cooling is attributed to expansion of the ice sheets and changes in ocean currents. Redrawn from Denton 1999.

reorganizations co-occur with, or even cause, simultaneous changes in the greenhouse gases of the atmosphere.

As a result of declining temperatures, African tropical forests, which once covered much of the equatorial region, became greatly reduced in extent, although there were areas of relic tropical rainforests remaining in tropical Africa which did not disappear and which would not have driven any new adaptations for forest-living primates. Conversely, the African woodlands spread at the expense of forest, providing more opportunities for woodland-adapted primates. The rate of change in African vegetation would have increased greatly with the last temperature decline towards the end of the Pliocene about 2 million years ago. In Europe, the late Miocene temperature decline manifested itself in the transition from subtropical evergreen forests in the middle Miocene to the deciduous broad-leaved woodlands we see today, and this was accompanied by the large-scale turnover in the mammalian fauna designated the mid-Vallesian crisis. This included the extinction of fossil ape species throughout Europe and Asia with one or two exceptions, which managed to hang on for a time in refuge areas.

At issue here, and this forms one of the main themes of this book, is whether Miocene apes were a forest-adapted group struggling to survive in a changing world, or whether they were a woodland-adapted group taking advantage of global cooling and expansion in Africa of tropical woodlands. Contrary to much work linking early fossil apes to forest environments, mine as well as others, many of the Miocene apes may have radiated in the early Miocene as woodland-adapted species. It will be seen in later chapters that they and later fossil apes are largely associated with non-forest environments, interpreted in the literature as various forms of woodland, ranging from open to closed, and deciduous to evergreen. They would then have been well positioned to take advantage of the cooling trend during the Miocene and to extend their range both in the expanding African woodlands and into subtropical to warm temperate climates. However, this runs counter to the evidence presented in Chapter 4 for long-term decline in ape species richness in Africa, and so the situation was evidently more complicated than this.

It will be seen in Part III that many fossil apes occurred as single species in their respective faunas. The exception to this is in the early Miocene of East Africa, where up to five fossil apes may be found in some localities (see Chapter 8). By analogy with living primates, this number of species (or greater) is only found in forest environments, and the evidence is strong that at this stage tropical forest environments were a significant habitat for early Miocene apes. For much of the later history of fossil apes, however, no more than one species has been found at most sites, and in the two cases where two have been found, there is good evidence that they were derived from different environments (see Chapters 10 and 13). Living apes also tend to live as single species; for example it has been observed that where chimpanzees and gorillas occupy the same region, they tend to keep to different parts of the environment. This appears to be the case for early hominin species as well, although it is evident that two or more species were able to coexist for large periods of time during human evolution. This restriction in the number of species of fossil ape and hominin is consistent with their presence in woodland environments as opposed to forest.

But if fossil apes were living in relatively open woodland environments, what was the driving force that led to their emigrations out of Africa and into Europe and Asia? Woodland environments are structurally more homogeneous than tropical forests, as well as being more widespread, and although the woodlands of southern Europe would have been structurally similar to those from tropical Africa, the degree of seasonality would have been greater, in particular the food shortages during the northern cooling. It has long been known that animals feeding on highly dispersed food items, for example fruit or insects, have relatively larger brains and apparently greater intelligence and/ or memory to be able to find their food compared with animals that eat a widely available food type such as leaves. This in turn may lead to higher levels of foresight in such populations, and it would appear that high levels of habitat heterogeneity, where food items are more widely dispersed, also leads to a higher level of foresight for exactly the same reason. A link has now been proposed in human populations that high habitat heterogeneity and foresight leads to reduced dispersability, whereas by contrast, homogeneous environments may increase the likelihood of populations dispersing. When applied to ape and hominid populations, the prediction is that dispersal out of Africa may have been driven in part by high degrees of homogeneity of the environment. This issue will be brought up again in Chapter 16.

Summary

- This book is as much about the environments lived in by apes and early humans as it is about their evolution. This is because I believe that only by seeing them in the environments to which they are adapted can we understand how and why they evolved.
- Arising from this, modern environments have been described in some detail, particularly the forest and savanna biomes in which all apes live today and which almost all fossil apes occupied in the past.
- Habitat heterogeneity is recognized as a factor at least as important as identifying vegetation types.
- There is some evidence that chimpanzees may have been as much adapted to life in savanna woodlands as to the tropical forests where they are most abundant today.
- The evidence for Miocene and Pliocene environments is briefly described, showing the possibility that Miocene apes were adapted for tropical woodland habitats, and that the common ancestor to apes and humans also occupied the same kind of habitat.
- The divergence of hominins from the common ancestor also occurred in a tropical woodland habitat. The low degree of climate change during this period in the Pliocene supports the idea that there was little habitat change at this time.
- Relatively homogeneous woodland habitats and diets of widely dispersed fruits may have led to increases in brain size in early fossil apes and prompted the dispersals of apes out of Africa.

Chapter 6
Environmental indicators

When we discover a new fossil hominid, we want to know more than just what it is called. We want to know what it did, how it lived, what it ate and what kind of environment it lived in. All these are the subject of palaeoecology, the study of the inferred interactions between past organisms and their environments. These interactions provide evidence on the relationship between palaeoenvironments and fossil apes and fossil humans, and they are essential to the understanding of how evolution operates. In other words, it is not enough simply to know that a particular fossil existed at a time and place and that it might be ancestral to later forms, for this tells us little about how it lived and how it functioned in its environment. For this we need to attempt to reconstruct the environment with which it was associated and its place in the ecosystem. For human evolution in particular, we would like to know whether we are descended from forest apes or woodland savanna apes, whether we became bipedal in wooded environments or in open savanna, whether we learned our social behaviour in trees or on the ground, whether we have vegetarian ancestry or were meat-eaters, and many other questions that can only be anwered if we know what kind of environment we evolved in.

There are several lines of inquiry providing evidence on past environments and those that are most useful in interpreting fossil ape and human environments are briefly reviewed here. Some like sediment or faunal analyses may be directly linked with hominid remains, but others are only rarely found associated with hominid fossils. Some lines of inquiry have limitations that have to be considered, for example community analysis of point versus regional assemblages, fossilized ecosystems and accounting for bias in fossil faunas. It is generally recognized that mammals may not be the best source of evidence on hominid palaeoecology, but at least they are consistently there, and it is for this reason that so much work has gone into devising new ways of extracting ecological information from mammalian faunas.

Sediments and soils

The nature and structure of sediments are a primary source of information about past environments. Sedimentary structures can be observed at first hand today, and we still follow the principles first expressed by James Hutton that "the past history of our globe must be explained by what can be seen to be happening now". Charles Lyell formulated this as the principle of uniformitarianism, and we use this principle to interpret past events by observing the processes operating today.

Structures in the immediate vicinity of fossil sites provide evidence on the local environment. For example, evidence of rivers or channels may be present, or there may be drainage features in the sediments, outflow or spring deposits (Figure 6.1). Soils may be formed in the past and preserved as palaeosols, and these may be regarded as trace fossils representing past ecosystems. Lignites and black clays may form in waterlogged soils, and calcareous horizons or nodules in the soil profiles may form under conditions of seasonal drying of the soil. Calcretes or hard pans may form in the soil, sometimes so thick that they impede further drainage of water through them, resulting in local flooding.

Figure 6.1 Spring deposit through the Paşalar deposits formed as an inverted cone. Vertical stratification is present in the spring deposits with secondary calcareous deposition forming horizontal bands. The bottom of the cone is resting on the Mesozoic marbles that form the basement rock at the site, and the spring penetrated through the lower calcareous silt and the fossiliferous sands. The deposits within the spring are similar to those of the fossiliferous sands, and excavation of the upper levels of the sands failed to distinguish them. Another spring deposit from the same site was seen to continue through the upper layers, so that they are composed of a mixture of the fossiliferous sands and the upper calcareous silt. No fossils were found in the spring deposits. Andrews & Alpagut 1990.

One example that brings together these features is well illustrated in the work of Rob Blumenschine and Ian Stannistreet and the Olduvai Landscape Paleoanthropology Project (OLAPP) team at Olduvai Gorge. This showed that the sediments at FLK 22 accumulated on a peninsula between a river and a freshwater marsh. Good drainage on the peninsula permitted the establishment of woody vegetation including trees, while mixed sedge/grassland occurred in the open lower-lying channel. This variation in habitat provided opportunities for the diverse plant and animal assemblages in the region and this study shows just how valuable the landscape approach is and how much it adds to interpretations based on single sites (Figure 6.2).

In another example, Dick Hay investigated the geomorphology of the Laetoli area in northern Tanzania, and he showed that the Pliocene sediments at Laetoli were deposited on an uneven surface with low relief, dissected by shallow valleys, with a broad shallow valley running from east to west and a 250 m valley to the south cut into basement rock. The development of palaeosols and the presence of fossilized termite nests show that the land surfaces were stable with good drainage, enabling the development of vegetation for periods of several thousands of years.

Marion Bamford and I investigated the modern vegetation in the Laetoli region in relation to the existing topography for comparison with the geomorphological structures described by Hay (Figure 6.3). The modern vegetation has great variability of woodland types, all existing under one climatic regime: riverine woodlands and gallery forest; broad-leaved deciduous woodlands on

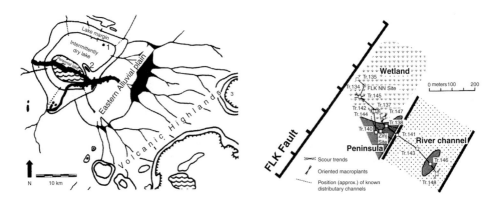

Figure 6.2 Reconstruction of the *Zinjanthropus* level below tuff 3 at Olduvai Gorge. The geological features mapped at the landscape level indicate an alluvial plain between the volcanic highlands to the east and an intermittent lake to the west. Hatched lines show the present position of Olduvai Gorge. A narrow peninsula intruded into the Olduvai lake and wetland, with a river channel behind. The fossil hominin (*Zinjanthropus boisei*) was recovered from the peninsula area, where the plants and mammals indicate the presence of dense canopy woodland. This is a high-precision association of a fossil hominin with local and regional environments. Reproduced with permission from Blumenschine et al. 2012.

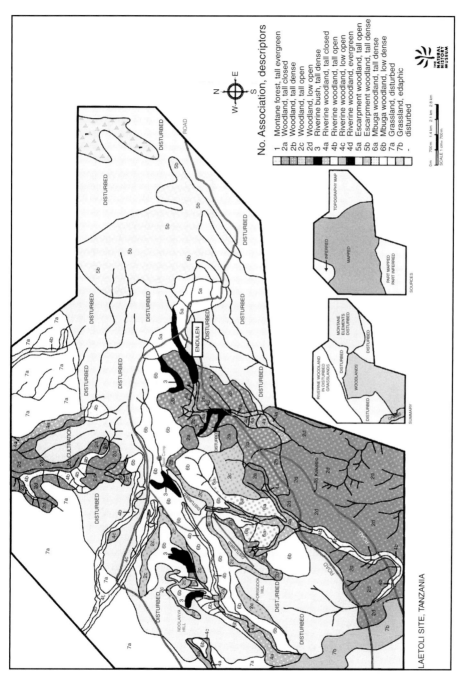

LAETOLI SITE, TANZANIA

No. Association, descriptors

1   Montane forest, tall evergreen
2a Woodland, tall closed
2b Woodland, tall dense
2c Woodland, tall open
2d Woodland, low open
3   Riverine bush, tall dense
4a Riverine woodland, tall closed
4b Riverine woodland, tall open
4c Riverine woodland, low open
4d Riverine woodland, evergreen
5a Escarpment woodland, tall open
5b Escarpment woodland, tall dense
6a Mbuga woodland, tall dense
6b Mbuga woodland, low dense
7a Grassland, disturbed
7b Grassland, edaphic
-   disturbed

Figure 6.3 Distribution of Laetoli vegetation at the present time. The distribution of vegetation in relation to the topography of the area can be used as a guide to past vegetation when combined with past topographical features. The area today has broad-leaved woodland (Combretaceae) as the predominant vegetation type on freely drained slopes, *Acacia* woodland widespread on valley flats with impeded drainage and along seasonal river channels, and high gallery forest where permanent springs come to the surface. Extensive sections of all vegetation types have been replaced by invasive weed herbs as a result of human clearing. Andrews & Bamford 2007. A black and white version of this figure will appear in some formats. See plate section for colour version.

85

thin well-drained soils; *Acacia* woodlands on valley bottoms with impeded drainage; limited areas of grassland on soils with well-developed calcretes (Figure 6.4); and increasing forest elements in the flora to the east with increasing altitude (and rainfall). We then could compare the existing vegetation/geomorphology relationships with the Pliocene geomorphology reconstructed by Hay, and by making predictions on the climate we were able to reconstruct the mixed woodlands present at Laetoli in the past. For some levels it was possible to check our predictions against fossil plant remains, for example fossil wood, grass and sedges, and pollen.

Miocene deposits in the Siwalik Hills were investigated to see how environmental and/or climatic events shape species and ecosystems over millions of years. It showed that the Siwalik sediments and fossils were deposited in a large river system comparable in size to the modern Indus River. Multiple river channels and smaller braided rivers drained the hills that were being uplifted by the contact between the Indian subcontinent and mainland Asia, with widely varying rates of water flow and depositional conditions. Alluvial fans and flood plains with low local relief formed along the lower reaches of the rivers, and where conditions allowed, soils formed on the flood plains. The sediments indicate increasing seasonality through time during the period 10 to 5 million years ago, with wooded habitats, seasonally wet habitats and closed woodlands in drier areas. These environments were occupied by fossil apes (see Chapter 14), which had to be adaptable to cope with an ever-changing environment.

Isotopes

The analysis of stable isotopes in soil carbonates and organic matter measures proportions of C_3 to C_4 plants present. In tropical environments, C_3 plants include nearly all trees, shrubs and herbs, together with grasses where there is a cool growing season, while C_4 grasses grow in open, unshaded places. Present environments globally have a significant proportion of C_4 vegetation in tropical savannas, temperate grasslands and semi-desert scrublands. The carbon isotope composition of carbonates in fossil soils shows that C_4 vegetation was present in Africa by about 9 million years ago, but it began to expand only after about 7 million years ago. Expansion to levels seen today took place after 1.7 million years. In other words, vegetation was mainly trees and shrubs during the Miocene, and there was no evidence of extensive grassland until well into the Pleistocene, after the emergence of *Homo* and long after the split between apes and humans. It is now even possible to quantify the relative proportions of trees and grasses in past environments by relating the present-day

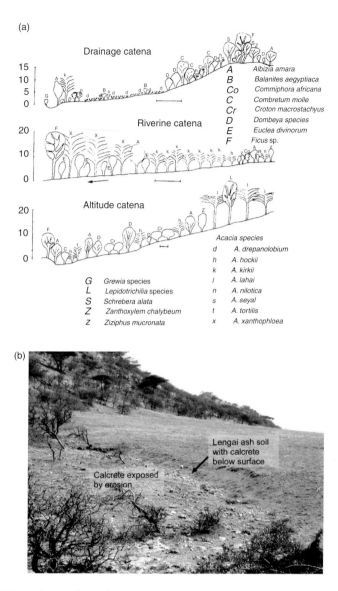

(a)

Drainage catena

A	Albizia amara
B	Balanites aegyptiaca
Co	Commiphora africana
C	Combretum molle
Cr	Croton macrostachyus
D	Dombeya species
E	Euclea divinorum
F	Ficus sp.

Riverine catena

Altitude catena

Acacia species

d	A. drepanolobium
h	A. hockii
k	A. kirkii
l	A. lahai
n	A. nilotica
s	A. seyal
t	A. tortilis
x	A. xanthophloea

G	Grewia species
L	Lepidotrichilia species
S	Schrebera alata
Z	Zanthoxylem chalybeum
z	Ziziphus mucronata

(b)

Lengai ash soil with calcrete below surface

Calcrete exposed by erosion

Figure 6.4 (a) Vegetation profiles at the present time at Laetoli. We identified three vegetation catenas based on variations in topography. The drainage catena ranged from dense broad-leaved *Combretum* woodland on shallow soils on hill slopes to low *Acacia drepanolobium* woodland (1 to 5 m) on the valley flats below and tall *Acacia* woodland (10 to 15 m) in the (dry) river channels. The riverine catena varied from low mixed bushland at the headwaters of the channels to tall *Acacia xanthophloea* woodland on the lower reaches of the channels, and where there was perennial water, broad-leaved gallery forest. The altitude catena varied from *Acacia* or *Combretum* woodland at low altitude, to broad-leaved woodland on intermediate slopes, *Acacia lahai* woodland on the lower slopes of the eastern mountains and montane forest on the mountains: Andrews & Bamford 2007. (b) An example of the dramatic effects of drainage can be seen on the lower slopes of a low hill in the Serengeti ecosystem, with trees on the well-drained slopes of the hill with little or no soil, and short grass plains on the deep volcanic ash soils lapping up against the hill.

$^{13}C/^{12}C$ (δC) values to actual vegetation on a broad spectrum of recent tropical soils, showing the degree of shift from closed tree cover to open grassland. When past environments are placed within the $\delta^{13}C$ spectrum the amounts of tree cover can be estimated (although it should be noted that the spectra differ between soil organic matter from decaying plant material and soil carbonates from the mineral composition of the soil).

Carbon isotope proportions can also be investigated in the enamel of herbivorous mammals, which provides an indication of the vegetation the animals were eating at the time when their tooth enamel was forming. An animal eating mainly grass has C_4 enamel, and an animal eating mainly leaves from trees and bushes has C_3 enamel, and this applies in the same fashion to all mammals, regardless of their taxonomic position. For example, investigating the teeth of ten mammal species from member 1 at Swartkrans showed that 44 individuals had C_3 diets in member 1 and 15 with C_4, giving an indication of the greater availability of C_3 versus C_4 plants in the vicinity of the site. Similarly, 500 specimens from Pliocene deposits at Laetoli had a mix of C_3 and C_4 signals on the teeth from 23 large mammal species: suids had mixed and C_4 diets; giraffes had only C_3 diets; equids had mainly C_4 diets; different bovid tribes ranged from C_3 to C_4; and monkeys, proboscideans and rhinos had mixed diets. Ostrich egg shells had an exclusively C_3 signal. In other words, there was a mixture of grasses and trees at Laetoli, and together with other evidence shows that the environment at this early hominin site (see Chapter 15) comprised woodland with some open areas.

A large number of herbivore teeth were also analysed isotopically from Pliocene deposits at Dikika in Ethiopia, from which is known the same hominin species as at Laetoli. These sites span several hundred thousand years, and the carbon isotope results show that a range of wooded savanna habitats was present at the site, but there was no indication of forest or closed canopy woodland and C_4 grasses made up nearly three quarters of the animals' diets. The relative proportions of wooded versus grassed habitats changed through time, and the oxygen isotope (see below) values suggest that the climate was wetter than earlier in the Pliocene and wetter also than at present. Clearly, the hominins associated with these faunas, both at Dikika and Laetoli, were adapted to a wide range of savanna habitats.

A final example from the Miocene is from the carbon isotopes of sixteen species of herbivore, frugivore and carnivore from a sample of teeth from Miocene deposits at Paşalar, Turkey. They showed a range from strongly C_3 to intermediate with C_4, indicating that the area was well wooded. C_4 grasses, however, were not abundant until 7 to 6 million years ago, and so these values at Paşalar may rather be due to water stress (see Chapter 11).

The oxygen isotopes in the tooth enamel of fossil mammals from Paşalar showed that some species were feeding in the open, including giraffes feeding on the tops of the trees which were exposed to sunlight, and a species of bovid was grazing in open grassland. The oxygen isotope composition of bone is largely determined by the $\delta^{18}O$ value of environmental water, although it is also affected to a limited extent by the metabolic processes in different species. Plant foliage can be enriched in ^{18}O by evaporation from the leaves, so that an animal feeding on leaves exposed to the sun has enriched $\delta^{18}O$ values. This is the case, for example, with giraffes, which feed high up on the tree canopies, and the fossil giraffe from Paşalar showed the highest $\delta^{18}O$ values. This effect has also been shown for tree-living monkeys living in closed canopy forest environments in the Tai Forest. Differences in $\delta^{18}O$ values between species correlated with the different canopy levels occupied by those species, which demonstrates that it might be possible in future studies to identify the canopy levels occupied by fossil species.

Nitrogen isotopes are also analysed to investigate the presence of meat and/ or marine foods in diets of fossil animals. This has been useful in determining variations in diets of omnivorous species such as bears, and it might have been expected that this would also be a useful tool to establish the degree of meat-eating in chimpanzees, but in an analysis of isotopes in chimpanzee populations, no difference in isotope values has been found between male and female chimpanzees despite the fact that the males have been observed to eat six or seven times more meat than females. The explanation for this might be that tooth enamel, which is the tissue that is isotopically analysed, is formed during infancy, and infants and juveniles are not usually allowed to share meat. It has also been found that elevated $\delta^{15}N$ values may be mimicked by pathological states affecting the nitrogen balance, as well as fasting or breast-feeding.

Trace fossils and taphonomy

Trace fossils are the imprints left by living organisms in sediment where the organisms themselves have disappeared. The most commonly found trace fossils are animal burrows in the sediment that have later been infilled by different sediment, so that they stand out with different colour or texture. Just occasionally, the actual burrowers are found buried in their burrows. Similar to this are the impressions made by plant roots, which form both in the sediment and on the surfaces of bones preserved in the sediment. The marks left by roots are visible as branching grooves with rounded profiles on the surfaces of the bones (Figure 6.5a). Sometimes whole trees are preserved, not as fossil wood

(a)

(b)

(c)

buzzard

(d)

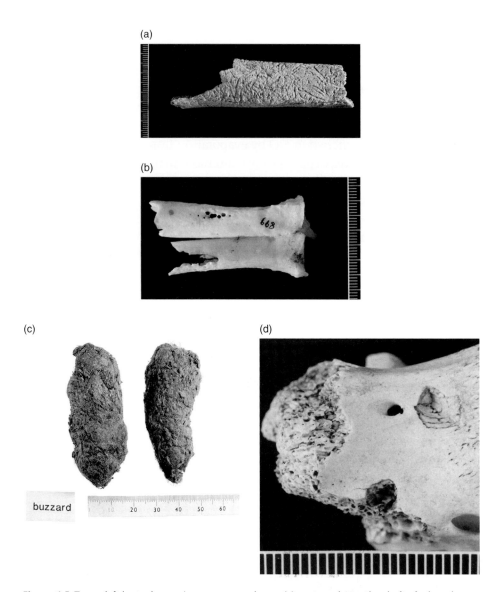

Figure 6.5 Traces left by taphonomic processes on bone: (a) root marks on the shaft of a long bone; (b) effects of acid corrosion on a bone in wet heathland; (c) predator pellets; (d) tooth marks puncturing the end of a bone. In most of these cases, the agent producing the modification was not present, but its presence could be inferred from the nature of the modification.

but as infilled cavities left after the decay of the wood. There is an example of this described by Alan Walker at the fossil ape site Rusinga Island in Kenya, and this will be described in Chapter 8.

The classic example of trace fossils in human evolutionary studies is the presence of footprints preserved in the footprint tuff at Laetoli. Mary Leakey showed that the footprints were made by an upright hominin that walked on two legs. This is the earliest unequivocal evidence for bipedalism nearly 4 million years ago at Laetoli in northern Tanzania. Tracks, trails and footprints of many species of mammals and birds are also preserved at Laetoli, and these were shown to men from a local community still engaged in hunting-gathering life style. They were able to identify the tracks and build up a picture of the movements of animals across the Pliocene land surface.

Traces of carnivore activity may be present on fossil bones with chewing marks (Figure 6.5d), and these may provide an indication of predator species present at the site. Digestion of teeth and bones of prey animals may show the presence of a predator species even in the absence of that predator in the fossil record. The pellets and scats left by birds and mammals (Figure 6.5c) are called coprolites, and Terry Harrison has shown that many of the coprolites preserved at Laetoli retain enough of their original shape for them to be identified at least to family. For example, he has shown the presence of coprolites of felids, canids and hyaenids at the site, and many of these include partly digested bones of a small antelope and a hare, which are the two most abundant animals at Laetoli. Figure 6.6 shows a coprolite with an exposed bone in a hyaena scat (Figure 6.6a), and a scatter of fossil bones from the break-up of a carnivore coprolite (Figure 6.6b). I have made a particular study of pellets and scats from birds and mammals, and in some cases it is possible to infer the presence of a particular type of predator in a fossil assemblage even though no fossils of that predator are preserved. Non-carnivore chewing of bone is seen when herbivores chew the ends of bones or rodents gnaw on bones.

Taxonomic evidence

Reconstructions of palaeoenvironments based on the perceived ecologies of selected animal species (so-called indicator species) have been commonly made in the past. They vary from being based on a few 'significant' species or may be applied to larger sections of the total assemblage. Reconstruction of palaeoenvironments through analysis of species lists assumes ecological equivalence between fossil organisms and their living relatives, and the same representation of habitats between past and present. This may be justified for plants or for recent fossil faunas, since the species may still be alive today, in which case there is direct evidence as to their ecological attributes. For example, Marion Bamford documented an area of grassland at Olduvai dated to 1.8 million years ago, with plant remains of sedges, grasses and woody

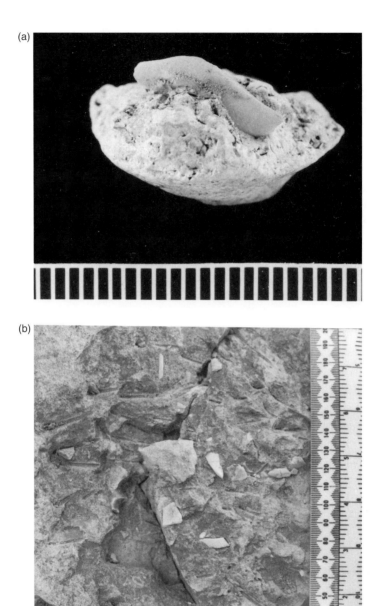

Figure 6.6 (a) Coprolite from Pleistocene deposits of the Lower Hyaena Stratum, Tornewton Cave, Devon, with digested fossil bone exposed in the coprolite. (b) Scatter of digested fossil bones from the break-up of a middle Miocene coprolite, Yeni Eskihisar, Turkey.

plants and palm phytoliths, and this flora is very similar to ones existing today. Mammals are more problematic, and although ecological assessments are based on intuitive knowledge of the ecological adaptation of the animals concerned, the method is unsystematic and cannot be reproduced by other scientists, for each will have their own intuitions.

Pollen is widely used for habitat reconstruction, but it is rarely preserved at the same levels as mammals. It is often the case that even though the species composition of floras may be well documented by pollen analysis, the structure of the vegetation may still be ambiguous, especially if there is some indication that the pollen comes from many different locations and habitats and is spread over a long period of time. Pollen is transported by the wind, sometimes for considerable distances, and since some pollen types are lighter than others, some may be blown in from different environments.

Shapes and sizes of fossilized leaves may provide a more direct insight into rainfall, as in tropical Africa the physiognomy of leaves is related linearly to moisture variables, providing evidence both of seasonality and total rainfall. Regression models of the relationship between leaf area and annual precipitation calculated for living floras have been applied to fossil sites in the Tugen Hills, Kenya, generating rainfall predictions for comparison with independent identifications of fossil vegetation. Similarly, the presence of teeth along leaf margins is related to annual temperature, with untoothed leaves being more common with increased temperature. Analysis of leaf type from the Miocene of Rusinga Island, following Raunkiaer's classification, shows that all the leaves recorded so far are untoothed. These methods are independent of plant identification and are equivalent to the ecomorphology of animals that will be considered below.

Invertebrates and lower vertebrates may provide a valuable source of taxonomic evidence on past environments. Land gastropods are ecologically conservative and many have highly specific habitat requirements, although because they are small and not very mobile they can be found in microenvironments controlled more by edaphic or topographic features than by climate. Bernard Verdcourt has analysed East African gastropods in some detail, and he has shown that some groups, for example, streptaxid carnivorous snails, have high levels of diversity only in faunas restricted to forest environments. Identifying the taxonomic composition of entire communities of snails provides good insights into the environments in which they lived.

Taxonomic analysis is still generally used for small mammal Pleistocene faunas. Changes in taxonomic composition of successive faunas in a sedimentary sequence may be due to differences in vegetation and hence to differences in climate, but since small mammal assemblages are commonly accumulated as the prey of predators, and different predators may have varying prey choice or hunting areas, the observed differences in faunal composition may be due to change in predator, not change in environment. Multivariate methods have been applied to the taxonomic composition of large rodent assemblages from the early to middle Miocene of Spain; by extrapolating from predominant adaptive strategies of related taxa, inferences were drawn about climatic change during this period. This study assumed, however, that the means of accumulation of the rodent assemblages was the same at all levels, an unlikely eventuality over such a long time, and some of the changes observed may have been the result of different predators targeting different species of rodent.

A similar approach has been used for the large mammals in the long Omo sequence spanning the end of the Pliocene and into the early Pleistocene (from 4 to 2 million years ago). This study was based on species abundances as well as species numbers, and it assumed that the taphonomic biases obviously present in the fossil faunas were similar throughout the sequence. These workers from the Smithsonian Institute in Washington showed that changes in the abundances in pigs, monkeys and bovids showed vegetation changes from more forested environments to more open woodland environments. They attributed these changes to climate change and related the pattern of change to evidence from the marine record of isotopes. The periods of high species richness also have high abundances of many species, while periods of lower species richness have only one or two very abundant species. These two aspects of diversity, species richness and species equability, often go together, but they can be measured by separate diversity indices, and both are dependent on sample size. There is also potential for confusion if body size is not taken into account.

Another taxonomic index is based on the proportions of bovid tribes in fossil faunas: alcelaphines and antelopines (such as wildebeest and gazelles) compared with tragelaphines and reduncines (such as bushbuck and waterbuck). The first two tribes contain almost entirely grazing species whereas the second two contain mainly browsing species, making this a quasi-ecomorphological approach. The index of one to the other shows the relative proportions of grazers to browsers and hence the relative proportions of grass and wooded vegetation, leading to climatic inferences as well. The link with vegetation and climate is tenuous at best, however, since grass is the dominant ground vegetation in all phases of savanna, and in fact closed woodland and open grassland can exist side by side within the same climatic regime based on differences in soil, topography and altitude. It is also supposed by some workers that alcelaphines are indicators of open grassland, as in the open plains of Serengeti, but over most of their range alcelaphines live in wooded or bushed environments, eating the grasses forming the major ground cover.

Lars Werdelin has recently given a fascinating account of changes in carnivore diversity in Africa. He showed that the carnivore fauna in the Miocene was very different from what it is now: between 7 and 8 million years ago, there were sabre-toothed cats, long-limbed hyaenas, giant bear dogs and a leopard-sized member of the badger family, with many smaller carnivores as well. Three million years later there were members of the cat family like modern lions and leopards in addition to sabre-toothed cats, modern-looking hyaenas, several dog species and a giant civet. Carnivore diversity peaked at between 3 and 4 million years ago, but after 2 million years numbers of species declined steeply, with the loss of the sabre-tooths and other giant forms and the modern carnivore faunas emerged. By analysing the functional adaptations of the carnivores at these different stages, it could be seen that the hypercarnivores were in drastic decline, with modern carnivore faunas filling far fewer ecological niches than their Miocene counterparts. One of the reasons for this decline could be climate change, since the climate cooled during this period; however, I have shown in work I did with Bonnie O'Brien that carnivore species richness in Africa today is not correlated with climatic factors. We looked at species richness patterns of all mammals in Africa and related them to seventeen climate and geographical variables, and whereas some groups of mammal had distributions highly correlated with such variables as seasonal temperature, annual rainfall or seasonal energy budget, the carnivores showed no change in relation to any of these variables. It is interesting, however, that the period of greatest decline in the carnivore faunas occurred at the time of emergence of the genus *Homo*, with evidence of more sophisticated tools, increased meat-eating and probably greater reliance on hunting. Was *Homo* then the new hypercarnivore, replacing the Pliocene fauna?

Numbers of species per unit area (Figure 6.7) may provide climatic or habitat information, but there are many confounding issues to contend with. The correlation of species numbers with climate has been seen in Chapter 5 to be influenced by mountainous areas or even areas with modest topographic relief (Figure 5.1). In addition, different types of mammal have different relationships with climate and habitat, so that, for instance, arboreal frugivore species richness is most highly correlated with presence of forests whereas terrestrial herbivores are more highly correlated with habitat heterogeneity; similarly, small mammal species richness is correlated most highly with precipitation, whereas large mammals are correlated with minimum monthly temperature. Another issue is that the greatest species richness in Africa is found where topographic relief is greatest in contrast to plant species richness, which is highest in high temperature/rainfall conditions, that is, in tropical forests. Without first knowing some of this background information, the interpretation of palaeoecology from species richness is highly problematic.

Two attempts to reconstruct past communities through analysis of species lists were habitat spectra and the taxonomic habitat index. Both weight fossil

(a)

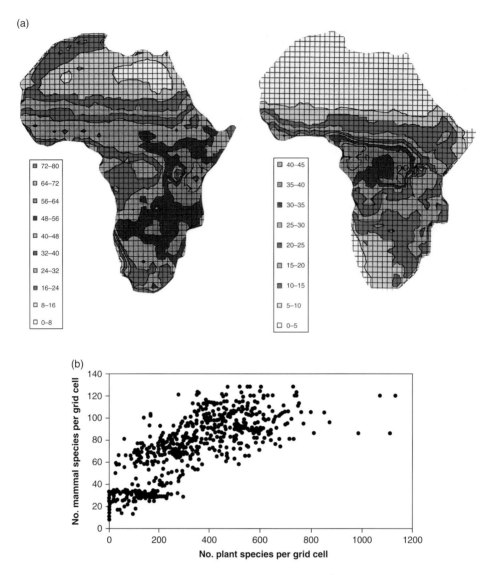

(b)

Figure 6.7 (a) Numbers of mammal species per unit area (25 000 km² grid cells) in Africa. On the right are numbers of arboreal and scansorial (both tree-living) mammal species; and on the left are numbers of terrestrial species. The isoclines depict numbers of species per unit area as indicated on the scales to the left of each map. The highest species richness of tree-living species is in the forests of west Central Africa and the western edge of the western rift valley; and the highest species richness of ground-living species is in heterogeneous habitats of East Africa and along the eastern rift valley. The difference between the two distributions is highly significant (p = 0.0001). A black and white version of this figure will appear in some formats. See plate section for colour version. (b) Numbers of mammal species for all of Africa compared with numbers of woody plants, both per unit area (r = 0.79, p > 0.0001). Andrews & O'Brien 2000, 2010.

species according to their degree of relationship to living species. For habitat spectra, living species were given a weight of 6, and their habitat preferences were weighted by this amount. Extinct species were given weights of 5 if their genus was still extant and four if it was not, and decreasing still further to subfamily and family relationships. Habitat preferences modified by this weighting were calculated for all species in a fossil assemblage and a spectrum constructed for the sum of the habitat weightings. The taxonomic habitat index (THI) is derived from the habitat weightings for all living species in Africa, and the weighted averages for all species in a series of recent faunal assemblages are added together and divided by the number of species in each fauna to give average ordination scores for the faunas. For fossil faunas, the THI is based on degrees of relationship of the fossil species with living taxa of known habitat: extant species in the fossil fauna keep their habitat ranges unchanged, but extinct species are given scores averaged for all species in the genus; extinct genera have scores averaged for all species and genera in a subfamily, and so on. For example, an extant monkey species such as the red tailed monkey (*Cercopithecus ascanius*) is scored 1 for forest habitats; an extinct species of *Cercopithecus* is weighted for the genus, which averages 0.9 for forest and 0.1 for woodland; and an extinct cercopithecine genus has a score based on all genera in the subfamily (Figure 6.8).

Ecomorphology

Ecomorphology of mammals examines the functional morphology of species in relation to the environment without reference to their taxonomic identity. By comparing the pattern of morphologies obtained for fossil species with the patterns in recent species of known habitats, inferences are drawn about the range of probable adaptations present in the fossils. The relationship between function and morphology is not straightforward, however, as different taxonomic groups achieve the same behaviour with different adaptations. For example, adaptations of the femur for running in carnivores are not the same as the adaptations for the same behaviour in equids, and they are different again in bovids. In other words there is limited phylogenetic equivalence between taxa, for even if their function is similar, they may adapt to it in different ways. As a result, the selected skeletal elements to be analysed must first be assigned to a taxonomic group, for example bovids or suids, and fossil bone comparisons can only be made within the same group.

Tom Rein has examined the limiting factor of phylogenetic equivalence in detail. He investigated the functional correspondence between forelimb morphology and different forms of locomotion and then estimated the

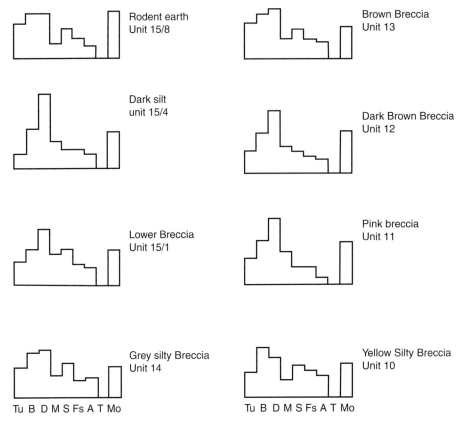

Figure 6.8 Taxonomic diversity indices for eight mammal faunas from eight time-successive stratigraphic levels of early middle Pleistocene deposits at Westbury-sub-Mendip Cave, Somerset. The Unit 10 fauna near the bottom of the sequence is most heavily weighted towards cool boreal forest and steppe habitats, but Units 11 and 12 immediately above have faunas that are weighted towards deciduous forest and appear to represent warmer conditions. The two following units, 13 and 14, have cool to cold values, and they are followed by two faunas in the bottom of Unit 15 that indicate even warmer conditions than in Unit 11. The uppermost unit, 15/8, has a fauna with high tundra and boreal forest weighting. The variations in taxonomic habitat index represent cyclical change in climate up through the cave sequence of cool-warm-cool/cold-very warm-cold. The range of habitats is displayed at the bottom of the diagram, as follows: Tu, tundra; B, boreal forest; D, broad-leaved deciduous woodland; M, Mediterranean evergreen woodland/bush; S, steppe; Fs, forest and steppe; A, arid environments; T, tropical; Mo, montane environments. Andrews 1990.

degree of phylogenetic signal present in each trait-behaviour in regression models. These models were then applied to fossil apes and monkeys to estimate their behaviour. He found, for example, that suspension by the arms in apes like gibbons is important in shaping forelimb morphology because of the tensile strain being placed on the limbs, and lengths of long bones (but not humerus length) and proximal phalanges increased with increased suspension. These characters are to a large extent independent of phylogeny, although he noted that the arm length of the orang utan is not as great as might be expected in relation to its behaviour. For other types of behaviour, he found that the height of the glenoid fossa is linked with leaping behaviour, and characters of the elbow (length of the olecranon process) and shoulder (humeral torsion) are linked with terrestrial locomotion. Curvature of the phalanges is associated with arboreal behaviour, but there is a strong phylogenetic signal in this character, which makes it difficult to generalize across different species.

Paul Harvey and Mark Pagel provide an example of the kind of pitfall encountered when taxonomic differences are not taken into account. Hawks, shrikes and Australian shrike tits have similar hooked beaks, which might be taken to indicate similar diets in all three; however, whereas the first two feed on small mammals, using their hooked beaks to tear open their prey, the shrike tits feed on tiny insects which they eat whole. Shrike tits use their beaks to rip bark off trees to get at the insects rather than on their prey, so although the function of the beak is the same, to tear and rend, its application is different. This example could be extended to other species with hooked beaks, such as owls, that swallow prey whole, or to parrots and lovebirds, which use their beaks to open up fruit.

The strength of ecomorphology as a method of palaeoenvironmental reconstruction is that it is quantifiable. Measurements can be taken on different parts of animal skeletons or teeth that can be functionally related to the activities of different groups of animal, both their forms of locomotion and their diet. An example of the first is John Kappelman's work on the bovid femur: the barrel-shaped femoral head on the hind limb of bovids that live in open habitats is an adaptation for fast running, for it restricts movement of their legs to backwards and forwards. Forest or closed cover bovids, however, are able to twist and leap through thick vegetation, and they have a more spherical head giving greater ranges of movement at the hip joint. A quite different suite of characters has been used to distinguish between adaptations in climbing, digging and running in carnivores: arboreal carnivores have strongly curved claws, shorter metatarsals and longer proximal phalanges, while terrestrial species have short claws, longer metatarsals and short phalanges (Figure 6.9). These shape differences can easily be measured and quantified, and the measurements related to these different functions (Figure 6.9). The relationship of these functional morphologies with the environment can be applied to fossil bones, and without even knowing the species of bovid or carnivore, predictions can be made as to how they moved and in what kind of environment.

Ideally, combinations of analyses of different taxonomic groups are used to indicate palaeoenvironments. For example, several recent studies have been

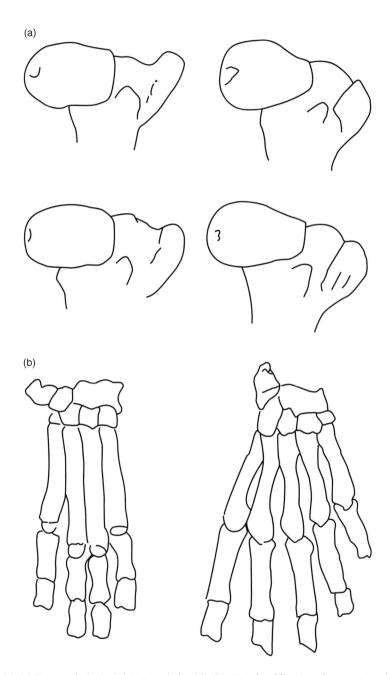

Figure 6.9 (a) Ecomorphological characters in bovids showing the differences between running and leaping adaptations in the head of the femur in bovids: left, cylindrical femur heads, which restrict movement at the hip joint to forwards and backwards, is adaptive for species that run fast over open ground; right, rounded femur heads, which allow movement sideways as well as forwards and backwards, are better adapted for leaping and dodging in closed cover habitats but are inefficient for running fast. (b) Ecomorphological characters of carnivore foot bones: left, long metapodials and short phalanges and the bones all parallel are adaptive for movement in one plane, as in running in open habitats; right, arboreal species with the bones more spread out and the phalanges longer for gripping branches. Adapted from Kappelman 1988 and Van Valkenburgh 1987.

done on the ecomorphology of mammal faunas from Laetoli: the ecomorphology of the phalanges, astragalus and radius of bovids indicate that these animals were adapted for living in continuous regional woodland cover at Laetoli, with a decrease in cover in the upper deposits, although the area was still wooded; another analysis of the ecomorphology of nine bovid skeletal elements gives a similar result, showing these animals to be adapted for heavy cover woodland-bushland. Once again, these closed environments were present during deposition of the lower Laetolil Beds, giving way to light woodland-bushland at the time of the Ndolanya Beds.

Most work on ecomorphology targets specific body parts, but in a major study of ruminant functional morphology, Meike Köhler has analysed the ecomorphology of many body parts for large samples of recent and fossil ruminant species. She has defined three morphological types based on analyses of body profile, horn types, upper and lower jaws, morphology of the limb extremities, and proportions of the limb bones, and these three types are related to a finely graduated habitat change from closed to open habitats. Fossil ruminants can then be analysed in the same way, with the same division into habitat types, and when the distribution of these types is combined for a single fossil locality a spectrum of probable habitats is built up.

In another study, sabre-tooth cats were compared with modern felids showing that their incisor and carnassial morphology indicate extreme flesh specialization but lack of bone crushing ability, while their postcranial adaptations indicate non-cursorial leaping modifications. This is taken to imply a distinct carnivore community in the past that was dominated by sabre-tooth cats in closed habitats, as shown above.

Functionally effective teeth are essential for survival in mammals, and destruction of tooth enamel leads to the eventual loss of teeth. The inability to process food in the mouth can be a major cause of death in old individuals, perhaps not starvation itself but weight loss, malnutrition and greater susceptibility to disease, and it is thought that thickened enamel and heightened tooth crowns (hypsodonty) prolongs the life of teeth. Degree of hypsodonty of the molars is strongly related to habitat in many groups of mammals. Hypsodonty is a measure of how high the crowns are on mammal teeth, and generally speaking, the higher the crown the longer the effective life of the tooth for animals feeding on abrasive material. Hypsodonty is also linked with the amount of soil ingested during feeding, which may be greater for animals feeding in open habitats where their food source is close to the ground, but this does not necessarily imply grass; for example, the pronghorn antelope (*Antilocapra americana*) has highly hypsodont teeth but it eats little grass, and the hypsodont teeth present in this antelope are more probably due to the soil

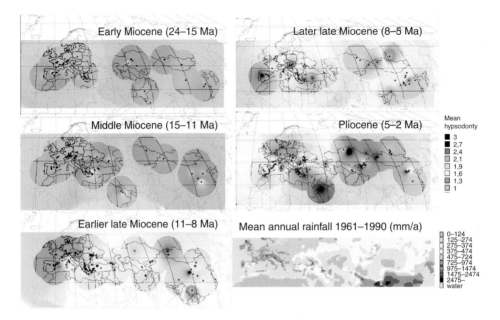

Figure 6.10 Hypsodonty maps showing change over time from the early Miocene to late Pliocene. The colours show the degrees of hypsodonty, with blues and greens indicating low hypsodonty (low crowned teeth) and yellows and reds indicating high hypsodonty (high crowned teeth). Distributions for five time periods, from early Miocene to Pliocene, are shown compared with a map of mean annual rainfall at the present time (bottom right), with blues and greens indicating high rainfall and yellow and red indicating low rainfall. The colours are not intended to be equivalent to hypsodonty levels of the mammals, but there is a parallel change which suggests that hypsodonty increased in the past as rainfall diminished. Reproduced with permission from Fortelius et al. 2002. A black and white version of this figure will appear in some formats. See plate section for colour version.

grit in its food. Browsing herbivores, by contrast, feed on leaves of trees or bushes well above ground level.

Mikael Fortelius and colleagues make use of degrees of hypsodonty as a proxy for degrees of aridity in European and Asian faunas (Figure 6.10). They show that there is a relationship between hypsodonty and rainfall at the present time, that predicted rainfall based on hypsodonty is concordant with other climatic evidence and that changes in climate, for example between the north and south sides of the Tibetan plateau, are reflected in changes in hypsodonty in herbivorous mammals. In another ground-breaking study, measures of hypsodonty have been combined with evidence from stable isotopes from the teeth of fossil mammals at an early Pleistocene site at Venta Micena in Spain. The hypsodonty index indicated that seven herbivores had grazing adaptations, two were mixed feeders and two were browsers; however, when the carbon isotopes present in their teeth were analysed, it was found that all eleven species consumed exclusively C_3 vegetation. Differences in their oxygen and nitrogen isotopes revealed further differences in uptake of water or

Figure 6.11 Scanning electron microscope photo of the enamel surface on a molar tooth of a fossil ape from Paşalar showing pits and striations of microwear. The large size of the pits and their high proportions relative to striations provide an indication that the diet of this fossil ape consisted of hard objects in need of crushing (e.g. hard fruits). Reproduced with permission from Tania King.

consumption of aquatic plants, showing that it is possible to reconstruct some elements of past behaviour and trophic patterns.

The relationship between enamel thickness and diet is not straightforward, however, for extensive research has failed to find a direct link between them or between enamel thickness and the environment occupied. It is generally considered that abrasive or hard object diets in fossil apes are associated with thicker enamel to withstand the destructive effects of their food (Figure 6.11). Thin enamel, however, may be associated with increased degrees of shearing or blade-like morphology of teeth, and this may be related to type of food being eaten; for example, teeth with sharp blades producing a high degree of shear are adapted to tear open tough food like grass. A shearing quotient distinguishes primates that eat leaves from those that eat fruit (an example is shown in Figure 7.10), and this is based on the degree of blade development on the teeth. For example, primates that eat leaves (folivores) either have high pointed cusps, as in apes, or high ridges, as in Old World monkeys, and enlarged crushing basins between the cusps or ridges. These adaptations provide a shearing mechanism by which tough food objects such as leaves can be sliced up and crushed during chewing. Frugivores, however, have lower cusps with more flattened crowns by which softer food can be broken up. Food that is abrasive but brittle rather than tough is associated with more flattened crowns, so that blades are not needed for its breakdown.

Percy Butler developed the link between microwear and diet in 1952. Since then, numerous studies have established it as a means of identifying diet, and the use of scanning electron microscopy has been crucial to the development of the method. The relationship between microwear and food is based on the jaw mechanics and the angle of the upper and lower teeth (Figure 6.11), although microwear patterns for primates with a known diet of large hard objects are not diagnostic. Recent developments in the analysis of mesowear and microwear measure the heights and shapes of cusps and the sizes and depths of microscopic scratches and pits on the surfaces of the teeth (Figure 6.11). Microwear provides dietary information shortly before the death of the individual, since microwear traces are quickly obliterated by subsequent meals. Mesowear, however, provides dietary signals throughout the life of the individuals and distinguishes between the teeth of browsers (low rounded cusps) and grazers (high pointed cusps), with intermediate categories as well; it has been applied to bovids and cervids, later on to horses and primates, particularly the differences between cercopithecine and colobine monkeys.

Dietary signals from microwear may also be affected by the ingestion of grit with the food, similar to the hypsodonty patterns mentioned earlier. The presence of grit in the food of grazing mammals is easily explained because their food is at ground level, and when they pull up a clump of grass they would be likely to pull up some earth with it; however, fruits and seeds are not usually that close to the ground and would be unlikely to be contaminated with grit. In addition, many claims have been made that the heavy wear, thick enamel and abundance of pits on the teeth of some Miocene apes are due to their feeding on hard objects, but this may not be the case. A recent study by Peter Lucas and colleagues has shown that most plant remains have little impact on the formation of microwear features. Even hard shells and seeds have only about one tenth the hardness of enamel, and they are therefore not hard enough to scratch surface enamel. It is probably tiny particles of dust ingested with food that is likely to be the cause of many microwear features, and over time they may even obliterate deeper scratches and gouges formed when the soil grid is ingested with underground or close-to-the-ground food items.

Incisor morphology in primates is also related to diet, and it has long been known that frugivorous species have relatively larger incisors than leaf-eating species, particularly marked when colobine monkeys are compared with cercopithecines. The same difference is seen when gorillas are compared with chimpanzees and orang utans. Frugivores and hard object fruit-eaters also have more strongly curved incisors, both side to side and from top to bottom, while soft-object fruit-eaters have less curved incisors. Leaf-eating primates have the flattest incisors, and the spectrum of differences in living primates is similar to that seen in Miocene apes.

Species richness

Species richness is a measure of the numbers of species in ecosystems. There are several aspects to this, however, and applying measures of species richness to fossil faunas depends on the ecological strategies of different parts of the fauna, turnover of species across space and time, the size of the area sampled and equability of the faunas.

The first aspect of species richness is the measure of alpha diversity, the number of species in an assemblage for a given time and place. Most animal and plant taxa show diversity gradients, and these have been interpreted in terms either of physico-chemical factors, such as latitude or climate, or as a result of biological interactions such as competition or predation. An early analysis of richness gradients for mammals was made by G.G. Simpson for North American mammalian faunas, and he found a mixture of latitudinal and longitudinal gradients, the former based most probably on temperature change and the latter based on topography, i.e. the presence of north–south running mountain ranges. Diversity gradients of woody plants in Africa in relation to climate have been studied by Bonnie O'Brien, who showed that water-energy dynamics account for a large proportion of woody plant species. Woody plant species richness increases per unit area as energy from the sun increases up to the limit of water availability. This pattern may be interrupted by variations in topographic relief, where habitat heterogeneity allows greater variety of plant species into geographical areas. Species richness of mammals does not exactly follow the same trajectory as plants, as they are secondary consumers of energy, dependent ultimately on plants for their food. In the work I did with O'Brien, we found that maximum species richness of mammals is based partly on amount and seasonality of rainfall but partly also on woody plant species richness, for which climatic factors form only a partial contributing factor. In addition, different types of mammals relate differently to plant richness and climate. For example, arboreal species are more frequent, and form a greater proportion of mammal faunas in forest environments, whereas terrestrial species are more frequent in woodland and savanna (Figure 6.12); and similarly, browsing herbivores and frugivores also dominate

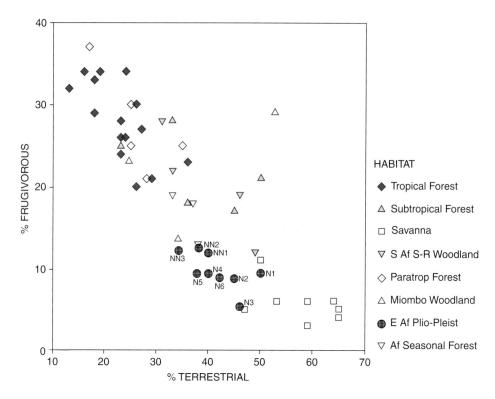

Figure 6.13 Ecological diversity plot of proportions of frugivores plotted against proportions of terrestrial mammals in eight modern environments. These are compared with nine fossil faunas from middle and upper Bed I at Olduvai Gorge. The modern faunas form three main groups, evergreen tropical and paratropical forest, subtropical deciduous seasonal forest and tropical woodland, and savanna habitats. The Olduvai faunas form two clusters, with middle Bed I faunas (labelled NN1 – 3) on the edges of the subtropical forest cluster and the upper Bed I faunas (labelled N1 – N6) on the edges of the savanna cluster.

which have many mammal species all more or less abundant (more equable), and open grassland faunas, which are dominated by few species. The present-day mass herds of reindeer in the arctic tundra, bison in the American prairies and wildebeest in the Serengeti plains are cases in point.

Finally, estimates of species richness are also affected by sampling problems. In an ideal world, the representation of animals or plants at a site is best shown both by the species present and by their abundances. Many habitats are dominated by relatively few species, and it is these that are most representative of that habitat, while uncommon species may be there by chance or be occupying marginal niches. The best information from plants and animals therefore comes from the ones that are most abundant, but there are major problems with abundance data; even making observations or collections today with living faunas, what you see one year may not be the same as is present the following year, because populations rise and fall due to complexities in the local ecology. In the fossil record, the problem is even worse, for there is no guarantee that the plants and animals present at a fossil site were actually living at that place. For example, they may have been transported to the site by water or by a predator: in the first case, their presence may be dictated by the ease of transport of their remains after death; and in the second case, their presence is controlled by the predator's hunting preferences.

There may also be selective destruction of certain sizes of bones from dead animals, both before and after fossilization. For example, at Laetoli, the rarity of hominin fossil remains has been attributed in part to their taphonomic destruction by scavengers and in part to the slow rate of accumulation of sediments, so that bones were exposed on the ground surface for many years and were destroyed by weathering. The large bones from bigger mammals were exposed on the surface for longer and are relatively rare, while smaller mammal bones that were buried more quickly are relatively more abundant. This may of course not be the whole picture at Laetoli, for the site is unusual in the absence of nearby lakes or rivers, so that there would have been no permanent source of water in the vicinity of the site.

Sample size is also critical when assessing animal abundances, for in general, the larger the sample the higher will be the number of species present. This is particularly important in fossil assemblages where sample size is often limiting. For example, the sample of mammals from the Miocene deposits at Paşalar, Turkey, has 52 species and these were represented by around 500 individuals in the collections made between 1983 and 1989, so that the diversity index of the fauna is 0.1. Two further species have been added in later excavations while the number of specimens has almost doubled, so that the diversity index is now 0.06. For these reasons, both taphonomic and sampling size, the use of abundance data in the fossil record is of limited use.

Community ecology

One of the earliest taxon-free methods to be used in palaeoecological reconstruction was my work on ecological diversity published in 1979. The development of this method came about as a result of friendly rivalry with Judy Van Couvering (now Harris), for we were both convinced that we had to find a better way of reconstructing past environment than the crude methods then available. We had used such methods to describe the environment of Rusinga Island following our excavations there in 1971, but it was evident to both of us that we needed a more rigorous method to provide a realistic picture of the environment. We both devised taxon-based methods, Habitat Spectra in Judy's case, and taxonomic habitat index which I developed with Libby Evans (both have been described above: Figure 6.8). In addition, I hit upon the concept of ecological diversity when going through the ecological literature and finding two publications describing mammal faunas in a way that I thought could be applied to fossil faunas. One of these was a publication by J.L. Harrison which demonstrated how mammals on different continents shared similar ecological niches and as a result shared convergent morpho-logical adaptations even though they were unrelated; for example, in lowland tropical forests in Asia, America and Africa, there are rodents with gliding (flying) adaptations belonging to different families, the Anomaluridae and Sciuridae; the sloth-like arboreal species such as the Bradypodidae in South America and the Manidae in Africa and Asia have similar habits and diets and similar adaptations; and the anteaters such as the Myrmecophagidae in South America and the Tubulidentates in Africa show remarkable morphological similarities in the way they feed. In all these cases, similar adaptations arose independently in unrelated groups of animals in response to similar environ-ments. This degree of convergence allows habitats to be compared or recog-nized based on the functional adaptations of constituent faunas even where the faunas are made of unrelated species. The second publication was a paper by Fleming that used this principle to develop habitat-specific patterns of mammals across the world, showing how these patterns were similar for similar habitats.

Charles Darwin in his *The Origin of Species* recognized the principle of convergence long ago, and it was commented on at length by Richard Dawkins in *The Blind Watchmaker*. Convergent evolution results in the pro-duction of similar adaptations in phylogenetically unrelated organisms sub-ject to similar agents of natural selection. The degree of convergence is constrained by the availability of genetic variability in the converging lin-eages and sufficient time for it to act. Extending this to whole communities, mammalian communities in similar habitats tend to show similar sets of adaptations even where no species are held in common between them. For example, degrees of frugivory or terrestriality (Figure 6.12) and other ecological adaptations could be analysed at the community level, and the proportions of the different adaptations within communities then indicate the range of ecological niches occupied by that community. Since many of these adaptations can be distinguished in fossil mammals, particularly their body size and ranges of adaptation, these form the basis for interpreting the community structure of the fossil faunas (Figure 6.13).

These are qualitative assessments, comparing morphologies of fossils with a range of morphologies in living mammals, and ecomorphology, described in the previous section, arose out of this approach by seeking to quantify these comparisons. Ecological diversity has been applied to a series of fossil faunas from the Eocene and Miocene to the Pleistocene, and has provided a more rigorous and semi-quantitative analysis of these faunas. For example, the ecological diversity of nine faunas from Olduvai Bed I spanning approximately 60 000 years has been analysed, and this showed that the proportions of frugivores, browsing herbivores and arboreal mammals distinguishes between the dense woodland of middle Bed I and the open savanna of upper Bed I. The former is associated with *Zinjanthropus boisei* and the latter with the first appearance of *Homo habilis* (Figure 6.13).

In an ideal world, ecological diversity would be based on the ecological adaptations demonstrated by ecomorphology and analysed at the community level. For this to happen, however, it is only possible to use those characters that are comparable between taxonomic groups, and the phylogenetic constraints mentioned earlier have to be taken into account. In an analysis with Sylvia Hixson, she took the same sets of measurements for 92 mammal species in six taxonomic groups (carnivores, bovids, suids, horses, rhinos and primates) with the aim of testing whether a set of 27 measurements, which were known to be significant adaptive characters in at least one of the taxonomic groups, could be applied across some or all family groups. She also tested the ecomorphological data for entire faunas to see if they produced patterns that distinguish, for example, a woodland fauna from a forest fauna. This is a broad-brush approach that limits the number of niche-related variables to those that are consistent with the morphologies of all the species being used in the analysis. Multivariate analyses (PCA) of the complete set of mammal species showed that the discrimination was much reduced when all taxa were considered simultaneously and morphological space was similar for every habitat type. When each taxonomic group was looked at separately, there was a good separation between open and closed habitats and this suggests that phylogeny was influencing the results. The information from the separate taxonomic analyses can be combined additively, which visually describes the space-use distribution of the 92 species, but in doing so the relationship between the ecological variables and the individual distributions is lost, although it was evident that the different taxonomic groups produced parallel patterns of habitat distributions.

The importance of sample size has been mentioned already, but sample composition is also important, and allowances can be made for perceived imbalances. Mammal communities have limited metabolic constraints such that they have size and energetic limits, and these limits were established for a large series of mammal communities by John Damuth. Fossil mammal communities can then be compared with them to see if they fall within the same limits. For example, Christophe Soligo has demonstrated that many Pliocene and Pleistocene mammal faunas fall outside these limits, showing that they are biased in some way, and only some of the Olduvai faunas fall within the limits. Allowance can be made for these biases, once they are determined, for example by comparing size distributions, randomizing the faunas so that they have similar size profiles and resampling them. When this was done for Olduvai Bed II, for example, the differences perceived initially in the faunas above and below the unconformity in this bed disappeared, and their palaeoecological reconstruction of dry woodland appeared the same at both levels.

Community analysis of point faunal assemblages

Fossil assemblages can generally be considered to be point accumulations, that is, the animals or plants making up the assemblages are collected from one place. They may not have all lived in one place, for many assemblages can be shown to have originated from two or more different localities, and it is the job of taphonomy to distinguish their sources. Despite this potential bias, John Damuth has shown that, in general, fossil faunas preserve community structure to a surprising degree. The question is how far fossil assemblages can be compared with modern ones and what kind of modern assemblage should be used. It is often the case that modern 'communities' are compiled from regional lists of animals and plants, for example lists of species from National Parks, or lists of species from arbitrary grid cells, and it is questionable if they form valid comparisons with fossil point assemblages. One way of dealing with this problem is not to use regional data at all but to use point collections from the present time. This was the option I chose in my initial work on ecological diversity, but many studies have used regional assemblages because there have been so few comprehensive collections where both large and small mammals have been collected from single locations, and the question needs to be asked how well do these regional assemblages reflect community structure. Juka Saarinen has addressed this problem in part by comparing regional fossil mammal faunas in 50×50 km grid cells with single fossil faunas present in the grid cells. The purpose was to discover how representative the point assemblages are. It was found that the single fossil sites contained about 60% of the fossil species in the grid cells, and that community structure could be estimated accurately from this. In other words, the regional fauna provides a good approximation of the community structure of the mammal fauna. This analysis compared fossil faunas with other fossil faunas, where the nature of the communities was unknown, but I have compared recent point assemblages with regional collections to see which is better.

The point assemblages that I used varied from single time/place collections, such as the one I made with Colin Groves at the Tana River flood plain, to single collections from National Parks. The regional collections are based on species present in equal area grid cells within which the point localities are situated. Figure 6.14 shows that the point localities contain between 29 and 70% of the mammal species present in the corresponding grid cells, and since the habitat reconstructed by ecological diversity can be compared directly with the known habitat, it is possible to say with confidence that even the most poorly represented point assemblage is still large enough to provide a good estimate of the community structure of the fauna. The opposite is not necessarily true, however, for the locality with the lowest number of species compared with the regional fauna, the Serengeti short grass plains, differs from the regional fauna because it is a local fauna (on a regional scale) that is atypical of

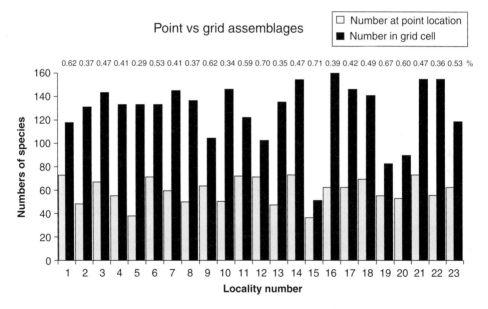

Figure 6.14 Comparison of numbers of mammal species in 25 000 km² grid cells compared with 23 point collecting localities. The 23 point assemblages are located in each of the grid cells, one within each. In all cases, the grid cell assemblages are larger than the point assemblage within the grid cell, and the proportions of one to the other are shown above each set of data: the point assemblages make up between 29 and 71% of the fauna recorded from the grid cells in which they are situated. The lowest proportions are where the point locality assemblage comes from an environment that is atypical of the grid cell fauna, e.g. the Serengeti short grass plains faunal assemblage, which is situated within a regional environment dominated by woodland (number 5). The 23 localities are listed in Andrews et al. 1979, table 2, and the grid cell data are from Andrews & O'Brien 2010.

the region as a whole. The same would be true of any point assemblage that is sampling a local habitat differing from the regional ecology.

Fossilized ecosystems and accounting for bias in mammal faunas

The assumption is made with all these methods of palaeoecological recon-struction that the present is a guide to the past. This is in fact all that we have to go on, for there is no actual way of viewing past environments directly, but it is an assumption that must be made with caution. There have certainly been many types of environment, ecosystem or habitat in the past that have no modern counterparts, and none of the methods outlined here can reconstruct exactly what they would have been like. Even from the Pleistocene we have found evidence for types of environment different from any existing today, such as the earlier example of the Olduvai woodland in middle Bed I. The structure of the woodland faunal community has no match in any of the modern woodland communities compared with it, and it seems to be inter-mediate between deciduous woodland and semi-deciduous forest. In cases like this, it may be possible to interpolate evidence within and between modern habitats to try and reconstruct what the nature of these unknown habitats was like.

A way of taking account of ecosystem differences, as well as accounting for possible biases in fossil assemblages, is to artificially reconstruct faunal assem-blages from different modern habitats by reducing the size of the faunas or by mixing species from different habitats. I ran a series of simulations based on work with Stephen Dreyer, which showed the extent to which habitat signals varied as a result of faunal impoverishment (Figure 6.15). A range of modern faunas had size biases introduced into them by systematically removing large or small species, and these biased faunas can then be used for comparison with fossil faunas to see if they match more closely than unbiased assemblages. I removed species from 23 recent faunas representing five habitat types, for example, by removing small species progressively, starting from the smallest, until well over half of the species had been removed in each case (Figure 6.15). Tropical forest faunas retained their forest signal with over half their species removed but had lost part of the signal with only one quarter of their species remaining. Removing large mammals progressively, starting from the largest, produced even less of a change in the habitat signal, for the remaining small mammals were sufficiently diagnostic ecologically to indicate the presence of forest. There was less change in woodland and bushland faunas, and greater ambiguity, for it is difficult distinguishing them even with intact faunas; however, at the other end of the ecological spectrum, the habitat signal for

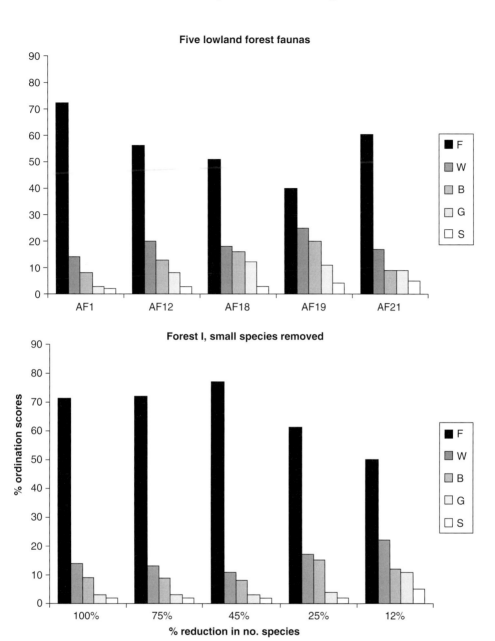

Figure 6.15 Top, taxonomic ordination scores for five tropical lowland forest faunas from Africa and Asia showing the variation in taxonomic scoring. Ordination scores are combined for five tropical habitat types, as follows: F tropical evergreen forest; W, tropical deciduous woodland; B, deciduous bushland; G, grassland; S, semi-desert. Tropical wet evergreen forests score highest for the forest signal, e.g. AF1, while intermediate semi-deciduous forests (e.g. AF19) have the lowest forest scores. Bottom, the complete fauna AF1 is shown on the left, and the four figures to the right have had small mammal species removed progressively by 25%, 55%, 75% and 88%. Even for the most strongly reduced fauna from AF1, the far right figure where the number of species has been reduced to 12% of the complete fauna, the distribution of habitat types is still within the limits of the five modern forest faunas and would have been recognizable as representing a forest fauna. Andrews 2006.

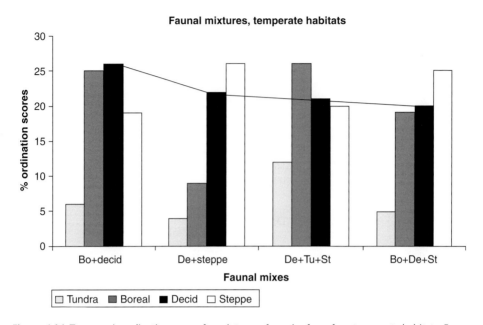

Figure 6.16 Taxonomic ordination scores for mixtures of species from four temperate habitats. From left to right, the figures show equal numbers of species from boreal and deciduous forest faunas; equal numbers of species from deciduous forest and steppe faunas; equal numbers from each of deciduous forest, tundra and steppe faunas, one third from each; and equal numbers of species from boreal forest, deciduous forest and steppe faunas, one third from each. In each case species were scored for just four habitat types, shown in the legend, and in all cases species were chosen at random from respective faunas to construct the mixed assemblages. Andrews 2006.

grassland faunas actually became clearer after removal of species, particularly when large species were removed.

The deliberate mixing of faunas from different habitat types also produced interesting results. In all cases the resulting mixtures produced greater variability in habitat representation, and this is shown here for a series of temperate faunas from Europe (Figure 6.16). Mixtures of boreal coniferous and temperate deciduous woodland with tundra and steppe faunas shows how the ecological signal varies with assemblage composition. This greatly extends the range of modern habitat representations, and based on similar faunal mixing of tropical faunas, I was able to demonstrate that the fauna from the Laetoli Beds (Pliocene deposits at Laetoli, Tanzania) was closer to the equal mixture of semi-deciduous forest and woodland faunas than to the fauna from any single modern habitat. The Ndolanya fauna from the same site, by contrast, was most similar to the mixture of two thirds bushland and one third grassland faunas. There are several ways of interpreting these results, but it suggests dense woodland with patches of forest for the Laetolil Beds and bushland with patches of grassland for the Ndolanya Beds.

Summary

The following sources for the reconstruction of palaeoecology have been reviewed:

- Sediments and soils
- Isotopes
- Trace fossils and taphonomy, foot prints, coprolites
- Taxonomic evidence of palaeoecology – evidence from plants, pollen, phytoliths, wood, seeds and fruit, leaves, gastropods, lower vertebrates, mammals, birds
- Ecomorphology of mammals – postcrania, hypsodonty, macrowear, microwear
- Species richness, alpha and beta diversity, relationship with climate, vegetation and habitat heterogeneity
- Ecological diversity of mammals
- Community analysis of point faunal assemblages
- Fossilized ecosystems and accounting for bias in mammal faunas

Part III
Review of fossil apes

Chapter 7
The view from the early Miocene

The genus *Proconsul* was first named by Arthur Tindell Hopwood from the British Museum (Natural History), now the Natural History Museum, in London. He was sent a small collection of fossils by E.J. Wayland that had been collected in western Kenya by a local doctor, H.L. Gordon. Hopwood recognized one of the fossils as the upper jaw of an anthropoid ape derived from Lower Miocene sediments, and the potential of the site became immediately obvious. Hopwood subsequently visited the site, Koru in western Kenya, and collected more fossils. He named the original ape upper jaw as *Proconsul africanus* and named two other taxa as well.

Wayland had visited Rusinga Island, Lake Victoria, in 1927, and he informed Louis Leakey about the fossil deposits he found there. Leakey at that time was based in Cambridge and was conducting a series of archaeological expeditions to Kenya. In 1931/32, on his third archaeological expedition, Leakey visited Rusinga Island with his assistant Donald MacInnes, and they immediately started finding fossil apes. Some of these finds were described by MacInnes in 1943, and in 1947 Leakey set up the Kenya Miocene expeditions in collaboration with Wilfred Le Gros Clark. These expeditions ran for 5 years, and they were continued off and on by Leakey for a further 15 years. Louis had supported my studies at Cambridge, and in 1969, after I completed my anthropology degree, he employed me as his research assistant to describe the Kenya Miocene fossil apes which had accumulated over the 20 years of collecting. I published my work in 1978 after I had moved to the Natural History Museum in London, and at that stage I recognized ten species of fossil ape and ape-like creatures, although this number has now more than doubled as a result of subsequent discoveries. Aided by my forestry background in Kenya, much of my work on fossil apes was combined with investigations into the environment inhabited by the apes, and when this is linked with the morphologies of the different ape species it gives us a good idea of how they lived.

The best-known fossil ape from Rusinga Island is *Proconsul heseloni*, named after Louis Leakey's field assistant Heselon Mukiri who excavated many of the fossil apes, including the skull shown in Figure 7.1. It was originally attributed to *P. africanus* described by Hopwood from the earlier site at Koru, but it lacks the specialized canine/premolar morphological complex seen in this species.

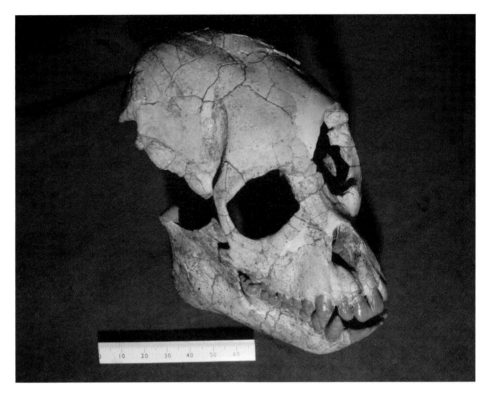

Figure 7.1 The skull of *Proconsul heseloni* from Rusinga Island, Kenya. It was crushed during preservation in the sediments.

This skull, and an associated partial skull and skeleton found in another part of the island in 1948, were the two best fossil ape specimens known at that time, but there are many additional specimens now that fill in many of the missing parts from the skeleton. The following descriptions of the morphology of *Proconsul* are based mainly on *P. heseloni*, and where other species are referred to they will be identified in the text. This is in part justified by the observation by Alan Walker in his descriptions of new material in 1983 that, for known parts, *P. nyanzae* is a scaled up version of *P. heseloni* with no major shape or proportional difference. Other fossil apes are listed in Table 4.1 and are mentioned where appropriate, but I should just repeat that I am not attempting to provide a full account of all fossil apes that have ever been found, but simply to describe the salient points of their morphology.

The skull and teeth of early Miocene apes

The partial skulls of *Proconsul heseloni* have a moderate degree of mid-facial prognathism (this is the degree to which the face projects forward below the eyes) and a low degree of alveolar prognathism (the degree to which the lower face projects below the nose). The size of the brain is $167 \, \text{cm}^3$, much smaller absolutely than any of the great apes, but this does not tell us much unless we relate brain size to body size, what is called the encephalization quotient or EQ. *Proconsul heseloni* was smaller than most living apes, with an estimated body weight of about 10 kg, and it has an EQ that overlaps the upper ranges of monkeys and the lower ranges of apes living today. Old World monkeys and apes have larger brains than other primates, and also primates have larger brains (relative to body size) than other mammals, so that the relatively large brain in *Proconsul heseloni* shows that increase in brain size occurred early in the lineage leading to living apes.

In other respects, the *Proconsul* skull has little to distinguish it as either monkey or ape. It is lightly built, lacks brow ridges and ridges or thickening of bone for the attachment of the jaw muscles. There is a broad incisive canal, which connects the nasal passage with the mouth, and this is the primitive condition for apes. The incisors are relatively large, broad and spatulate compared with monkeys, and the canines are high crowned and projecting beyond the level of the tooth rows. The lower third premolar is single cusped and occludes against the back of the upper canine, although this so-called premolar honing is less strongly developed than in *Proconsul africanus*. Canine/premolar honing primitively had a slicing action when the blade-like upper canine rubbed against an elongated lower premolar, and this is seen in many living monkey species and in *Dendropithecus macinnesi*, an ape-like species which coexisted with *Proconsul* species on Rusinga Island. This function has been reduced in most fossil apes except for *P. africanus*. The Rusinga Island proconsulids have been assigned to a new genus, *Ekembo*, as this book went to press. It demarcates the evolutionary transition in the canine/premolar honing function. Stem catarrhines and some monkeys have a specialized honing function which is retained in *Proconsul africanus* but strongly reduced in *Ekembo heseloni* and even more strongly reduced in later apes.

The molars have the typical ape-like pattern of four cusps on the upper molars and five on the lowers, and it was largely on this basis that *Proconsul* was first recognized as an ape, but it is now realized that this pattern predates the earliest *Proconsul* by at least 10 million years and it is probably a retained ancestral character in the apes. Prominent upper molar lingual cingula and lower molar buccal cingula are well developed on all species, the molar cusps are distinct and often angular and enamel thickness varies from thin to moderately thick. There is in fact little to identify any of the *Proconsul* species as apes based on skull and dentition alone.

Summary of the skull and teeth

- The *Proconsul* skull is gracile, with no brow ridges and only moderately prognathic (projecting) upper face

- Alveolar prognathism very low
- Brain size is relatively larger than in monkeys
- Incisors relatively large and adaptive for fruit-eating
- Canine/premolar honing is greatest in *P. africanus*, reduced in *Ekembo heseloni*
- Molars have well-developed cingula and differ little from prehominoid catarrhine ancestors

Postcranial skeleton of early Miocene apes

The forelimb of *Proconsul* indicates that this fossil ape was adapted to life in trees. Among its many arboreal adaptations in the upper arm are the torsion of the head of the humerus, lack of curvature of the shaft and the morphology of the distal end. The latter in particular shows strong similarities to living apes, with the strongly rounded capitulum and expanded trochlea, and this contrasts with the degree of torsion at the proximal end of the humerus, which links it with monkeys rather than apes. However, an isolated head of a humerus from Rusinga Island indicates that it came from a mobile shoulder, with less medial torsion than was inferred for the broken bone in the *P. heseloni* skeleton which suggests that it should not be attributed to this species. In the forearm, the neck of the radius is somewhat elongated, the styloid process of the ulna is elongated and the length of the radius compared with the humerus (brachial index) is lower than is found in most living anthropoids. Several patellas are known for both *P. heseloni* and *P. nyanzae*. They are broad and flat and also rather thin, similar to chimpanzee patellas and different from the thicker bones present in monkeys. This adaptation in monkeys is linked with powerful extension at the knee joint such as happens during running or leaping. The condition in *Proconsul* indicates its poor ability to leap or run, and it is seen also in other fossil apes for which the patella is known, and it seems to be a general ape condition.

A partial skeleton of *Proconsul nyanzae* shows that this species had at least six lumbar vertebrae as in monkeys, unlike living great apes, which have four, and humans and gibbons (and early hominins), which have five. Also differing from living apes is the position of the transverse processes on the lumbar vertebrae; they originate from the dorsal edge of the vertebral bodies, and the vertebral bodies are wedge-shaped, the ventral side of the bodies being shorter than the dorsal side. Both these conditions are shared with monkeys, and the wedging results in the back being curved, which is a monkey-like feature present in *P. heseloni* (Figure 7.2). The scapulae (shoulder bones) are placed on the sides of the narrow chests of monkeys. The narrow pelvis in *P. nyanzae* is monkey-like, indicating that this fossil ape also had narrow bodies (from side to side) and that they were quadrupedal and largely arboreal.

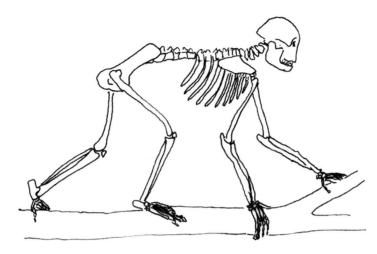

Figure 7.2 Reconstruction of the skeleton of *Proconsul heseloni*, now *Ekembo heseloni* (see text), showing its long curved back and narrow chest region.

The head of the femur is angled upwards (at 138°), more steeply than in monkeys, and this allows greater mobility at the hip joint, an adaptation for vertical climbing in trees. The articular surface of the femur head in *P. nyanzae* differs from the condition in both monkeys and apes. This suggests that the way these fossil apes moved was not exactly the same as in monkeys and also that *Proconsul* was not a strong leaper. What can be concluded on the basis of present knowledge is that *Proconsul* was adapted for habitual, careful movement through the trees but with extensive limb movements, using all four legs, and moving in quadrupedal fashion.

It has been mentioned earlier that lack of a tail is one of the most obvious features distinguishing apes from monkeys, and it has been confirmed that *Proconsul heseloni* did not have a tail. This is shown by the narrowing of the sacrum at the end of the spine, for species with tails have larger sacral canals for the passage of nerves and blood supply to the tail. There are few other characters that link any of the *Proconsul* species with the apes, and some anthropologists doubt the hominoid status of these species. Be that as it may, this mix of characters shows that *Proconsul* was neither fully ape-like nor fully monkey-like, but it does show that in terms of its way of life, it was adapted to life in trees. Its limb bones, however, are relatively robust for so small a primate, and in combination with its mobile joints, allowing extensive movement at the shoulder and hips, it supports the conclusion that *Proconsul* was a powerful but relatively slow climber.

The hand from the *Proconsul* skeleton has eighteen bones preserved, enough to provide a good reconstruction of the hand (Figure 7.3). This is important, for as we shall see later, the hand is of particular significance in hominin

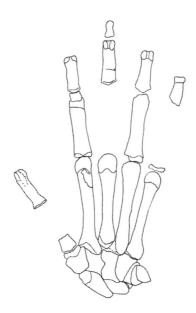

Figure 7.3 The *Proconsul* hand as reconstructed by Napier and Davis (1959). Additions recovered from the same individual by Alan Walker (2005) include the first metacarpal which confirms Napier's interpretation that the thumb in *Proconsul heseloni* was long and strongly built and unlike the great ape thumb.

evolution. The hand in *Proconsul* is relatively shorter than in chimpanzees except for the thumb, which is not reduced in length. As John Napier observed, the hand shows neither the long metacarpals and short phalanges as in baboons, nor the short metacarpals and long phalanges in New World monkeys (and in dryopithecines as will be shown later). However, the *Proconsul* hand is short relative to the forearm, and in this feature it differs from other anthropoid primates, both monkeys and apes. The morphology of the trapezium and its degree of medial rotation in the wrist indicates that the thumb was strongly opposable, and given its greater length relatively speaking compared with the chimpanzee thumb, it suggests that *Proconsul* had a strong grip. However, the articular surface is almost cylindrical in shape, limiting movement and restricting the rotatory movement of the thumb seen in the human hand, so that it would appear that the movement of the thumb in opposition to the other fingers would have been limited to abduction and adduction, that is, towards and away from the rest of the hand. The other wrist bones are in general monkey-like, with the scaphoid separate from the os centrale and the pisiform elongated and stout and articulating with the ulnar styloid. These are all interpreted as retained ancestral characters.

The distal ends of the metacarpals are smooth and rounded, as in chimpanzees, but they are pinched dorsally and not broad as in chimpanzees. This restricts their articular contacts with the phalanges when the fingers are

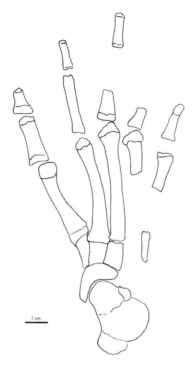

1 cm

Figure 7.4 The bones of the foot from the same individual as the hand shown in Figure 7.3. Redrawn from Walker & Shipman 2005.

extended and, therefore, their capacity for weight bearing. The broad articulations in chimpanzee metacarpals are probably related to their terrestrial knuckle-walking, during which the hands and arms have to carry the weight of the animals. The morphology in *Proconsul* is more similar to that of monkeys, both terrestrial and arboreal, and it is probably a retained ancestral character.

The phalanges cannot easily be distinguished from those of monkeys. The proximal phalanx of the thumb is long and cylindrical, and the head is narrower than the neck. This is an unusual combination of characters, but as mentioned above it shows that the thumb was long and not reduced in length as in chimpanzees. The proximal and middle phalanges of the fingers are slender and oval shaped, lack flexor ridges ventrally and have narrow distal ends. All this is in marked contrast to the condition in chimpanzees and is similar to arboreal monkeys, showing that *Proconsul* was primarily an above-branch quadruped, that is, it moved about in trees on the tops of branches rather than hanging below them as do brachiating apes.

The foot of *Proconsul* (Figure 7.4) has long slender metatarsals and phalanges with a strongly grasping and long big toe. The big toe is widely divergent, indicating a strongly gripping foot, and the metatarsals and tarsals are laterally compressed, indicating a narrow foot. The flattened proximal end of the first phalanx restricted side-to-side movement of the toes, so that movement was mainly in the dorso-plantar direction (that is, up and down) and used for gripping branches. The powerful flexor muscles on the hands and feet, as well as the robust intermediate phalanges and relatively broad terminal phalanx of the big toe, all indicate slow powerful movement in trees.

Summary of the postcrania

The morphology of *Proconsul* indicates that it lived in trees, moving on the tops of branches, and was not an habitual leaper but moved slowly and powerfully in the trees. The following are key points:

- Medial torsion of the humeral head
- Mobile shoulder joint
- Mobile elbow joint
- Narrow chest
- Long curved back
- Relatively long thumb
- Opposable thumb, non-rotatory
- Non-weight-bearing wrist and hand
- Relatively short hand
- Narrow gripping foot
- Powerful flexor muscles for gripping branches

Body size and sexual dimorphism of early Miocene apes

The body size of *Proconsul heseloni* is estimated at about 8 to 14 kg, comparable in size to siamangs, some of the larger Asian colobine and macaque monkeys, and baboons. Siamangs, like their cousins the gibbons, are uniquely adapted for life in trees by their extreme adaptations for brachiation, hanging by their arms below branches, but unlike gibbons, their greater body weight restricts their movement to larger branches in trees; smaller branches might break under their weight. Baboons are primarily ground living, but they are adept in moving about in trees. I once spent a few days watching a baboon that was separated from its group and had adopted a group of red tail monkeys (*Cercopithecus ascanius*) as its social group. It was quite sad to see the extreme efforts made by the baboon to keep up with the much more agile monkeys as they moved through the trees. Baboons lack some of the finer adaptations to life in trees, and they are simply too heavy to be able to use trees as locomotor pathways, although they are perfectly adept at climbing trees to feed. *Proconsul heseloni* had many adaptations to life in trees, but its body weight must have been a limitation. It had no adaptations for brachiation, as in siamangs, and it lacked a prehensile tail that enables New World monkeys of comparable size to move comfortably through trees, and it would appear from its limb morphology that it was restricted to slow climbing in trees. It is likely that it went frequently to the ground, like some arboreal monkeys do today, in order to move from one tree to another (see Chapter 8, Figure 8.3).

The issue of size becomes more marked when larger species of *Proconsul* are considered. The body weight of *P. nyanzae* is estimated at 28 to 46 kg, which is up to the size of chimpanzees, and *P. major* was even bigger, up to 80 kg, which is larger than chimpanzees (Figure 7.5). Chimpanzees and gorillas may feed in trees, but they spend much of their time on the ground, and their principal means of locomotion from one feeding tree to another is on the ground. This is undoubtedly because of their large size. However, the foot of the largest of the *Proconsul* species, *P. major*, has striking adaptations (deep calcaeo-cuboid pivot, plantar flexed talar head and medially angled talar head) similar to orang utan feet. These adaptations in the orang utan enables them to use their feet like another set of hands as they move slowly and carefully through trees. Orang utans are also restricted to dense tropical rainforest, where tree canopies are closely connected enough that they are able to move from tree to tree, and it will be shown below that the environments from which *P. major* are known are the only ones in the early Miocene to provide evidence of widespread forest habitats. Many of the environments associated with the other species of *Proconsul* are non-forest types of woodland, and because they were bigger than most monkeys living today, their body size would have limited their capacity for movement in trees. This leads to the conclusion that these species of *Proconsul* may have been partly terrestrial, with the larger species even more so.

So far I have described *Proconsul heseloni* in some detail and mentioned three other species, *P. africanus, P. nyanzae* and *P. major* (Figure 7.5). The size variation within each of these species is high, although probably not as high as in some later, middle and late Miocene apes, but it is similar to levels seen in the living great apes (the size differences between males and females gives a measure for sexual dimorphism). The size range of the most sexually dimorphic tooth, the lower canine, is shown in Figure 7.6, and shows the extent of size dimorphism of *Proconsul nyanzae;* this may provide some understanding of the kinds of social groups present in these fossil apes, for the degree of canine dimorphism is related to competition between males for access to females. Where there is strong competition, as in gorillas and baboons, males tend to have larger canines compared to females, sometimes with no overlap in size, and this in turn is related to body size dimorphism.

(a)

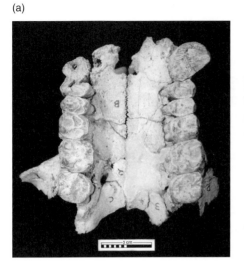

(b)

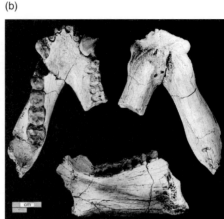

Figure 7.5 The two larger species of *Proconsul, P. nyanzae and P. major.* (a) The brilliantly reconstructed palate of *Proconsul nyanzae* by Peter Whybrow. He dismantled the bones of the palate, having first numbered each of the broken and distorted fragments prior to taking the palate apart. He then restored the fragments in their correct anatomical alignment. (b) Three views of the lower jaw of *Proconsul major.* Some authors suggest this species is sufficiently different from other species of *Proconsul* to merit placement in a separate genus. Whybrow & Andrews 1978.

In groups where a single male controls many females, competition is high as males have to fight to keep control; in these cases, males may be as much as twice the weight of females. Monogamous species like gibbons, where groups comprise single males and females, have low levels of body size difference and low canine dimorphism. The canine dimorphism in proconsulids is comparable to that of gorillas and orang utans, where one male may mate with many females, and it is likely that they had male-dominant societies as in these great apes.

Mention can be made of *Rangwapithecus gordoni* (Figure 7.7), which appears very distinct from *Proconsul* species. The biggest mistake I have made in the course of my work on fossil apes was in the description of a lower jaw that I found in 1972 at Songhor. I was in the process of describing the new species *Rangwapithecus gordoni* from Songhor, which had a very good upper jaw but only fragments of lower jaw, and I badly wanted my new specimen to belong to this new species, but in so doing I ignored obvious indications that it had greater similarities to *Proconsul africanus*. This was corrected in a paper I wrote with Alan Walker in 1993, and recently a fine lower jaw has been recovered which shows just how different this species really is. I wonder now if we are not making an even bigger mistake at present in identifying *Rangwapithecus* as a proconsulid, for there

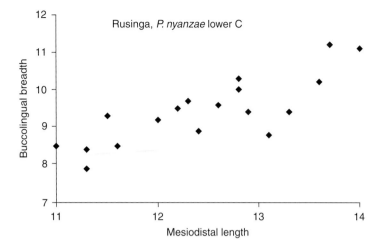

Figure 7.6 Length by breadth dimensions of the lower canine of *Proconsul nyanzae*. This is the most dimorphic tooth in the tooth row, that is, the tooth that is most likely to show the size difference between males and females. In this fossil ape, the largest canines are probably from male individuals and the smallest from females, but the size distribution is continuous, with no gap separating males from females, so that the intermediate individuals cannot be sexed. The measurements are in millimetres.

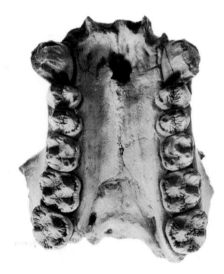

Figure 7.7 The palate of *Rangwapithecus gordoni*. This fossil ape comes from the same site as *Proconsul africanus*, and it is about the same size, but note the massive blade-like canine and the elongated premolars and molars with high cusps and strongly developed ridges, which are shearing adaptations for cutting through tough objects.

is no evidence in favour, other than superficial similarity, and some evidence from its teeth against. It may prove to belong to a group of catarrhine primates distinct from both monkeys and apes.

131

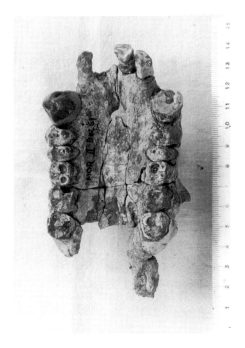

Figure 7.8 Palate and upper jaw of *Morotopithecus bishopi* from Moroto, Uganda.

There is a fifth species of *Proconsul*, *P. meswae*, that Terry Harrison and I described a few years ago. This comes from deposits older than 20 million years based on faunal evidence and is the earliest representative of the genus. It is assigned to *Proconsul* based mainly on shared primitive characters so that it forms the primitive sister taxon to all other species of the genus. I have described the circumstances of the discovery of this fossil elsewhere, but suffice it to say here that having been shown the site in 1978, and arrangements made and a grant obtained to return the following year to excavate it, we were somewhat dismayed when we arrived to find an empty hole in the ground where the site had once been. The bulk of the deposits at Meswa Bridge had been removed in our absence by our colleague, and our excavation that year was restricted to the edge of the channel in which the fossils were located. This is the only site where this ape has been found, and who knows how much was lost in the process.

All of the fossil apes described so far are known only from Kenya, but a form very similar to *Proconsul major* is also known from Napak in Uganda. There appears to be little difference between them and the specimens from Kenya. There is another fossil ape from Uganda, however, which is quite different, and this is *Morotopithecus bishopi* known only from Moroto. The teeth and palate (Figure 7.8) differ little from large species of *Proconsul*, and on this basis it was

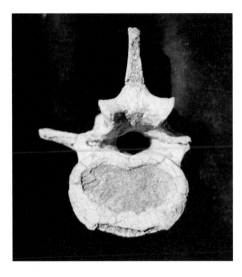

Figure 7.9 The most complete lumbar vertebrae from Moroto, Uganda. Note the robust vertebral body and the origin of the transverse processes above the level of the body, although not as high as in apes.

initially assigned to *Proconsul major*. One of the lumbar vertebrae from Moroto (Figure 7.9) has a great ape-like vertebral body (i.e. not wedge-shaped) and transverse processes arising from the junction of the pedicle and the vertebral body. This indicates a straighter, more robust lower back, as in living great apes, and an adaptation to more upright (orthograde) posture. The position of the transverse processes has some similarities with the larger New World monkeys, where the pedicle originates from the junction of body and pedicle, and these species are also more upright; however, it is not exactly the same as in the great apes, where the transverse processes originate more dorsally on the pedicle. The most conservative interpretation is that this morphology parallels that of the living great apes, and that upright posture is an independent acquisition in this Miocene ape (that is, it is not a derived character shared with living apes and humans).

Diet and behaviour of early Miocene apes

Several sources of evidence as described in Chapter 6 are available to reconstruct aspects of the behaviour of proconsulids in the early Miocene of East Africa. Their teeth are not adapted for shearing through tough food objects such as leaves (with one exception) but have lower cusps with more flattened crowns by which softer food such as fruits can be broken up. Looking at the whole spectrum of shearing adaptations of Old World higher primates, leaf-eating colobine monkeys from Africa and Asia are at one end of the spectrum, while frugivorous

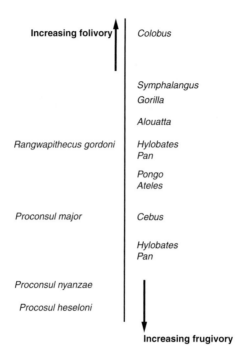

Figure 7.10 The shearing quotient measures the degree of shear, or cutting edge, on teeth, and the higher the quotient the greater the degree of shear. This is shown here on an ordinal scale, with greatest shear, signifying greatest amount of leaf-eating, at the top of the scale, and least shear, and greater fruit-eating, at the bottom. Living ape and monkey species are positioned to the right of the line, indicating their degree of shear, while fossil apes are shown on the left. Adapted from Kay 1977.

apes and monkeys are at the other end of the dietary spectrum; gorillas and siamangs are the most folivorous of the living apes, but they lack the extreme modifications of leaf-eating monkeys. Most of the species of *Proconsul* group with the frugivores, and in fact they appear even more extremely frugivorous than most of the living primates. This is shown here in Figure 7.10 on an ordinal gradient showing extreme folivory at the top of the gradient, and frugivores at the bottom. The living species are shown on the right of Figure 7.10 and fossil species on the left. The three *Proconsul* species all overlap and extend beyond the most frugivorous of the living primates, but the scale of adaptations in the Miocene might not correspond exactly with that of living primates, for it is unlikely that the proconsulids were any more frugivorous than living apes. What can be seen, however, is that *Rangwapithecus gordoni*, whose teeth have more pointed cusps and greater shear potential, falls towards the folivorous end of the spectrum for early Miocene apes. Since it in turn appears less folivorous than living species, it would appear that the scale for fossil apes is shifted up towards frugivory. *Rangwapithecus* is not known from Rusinga Island, but the closely related species *Nyanzapithecus* (formerly *Rangwapithecus*) *vancouveringorum* is present. Its high pointed cusps and greater shearing crests are similar to those of *R. gordoni* and this suggests that it too was partly a leaf-eater.

Rangwapithecus gordoni also has differences in its incisors, which indicate that it had a more folivorous diet compared with *Proconsul*. Incisor shape and curvature is related to dietary proportions of food eaten, and although *R. gordoni* has narrower incisors than other proconsulids, their overall shape indicates that it also was in part a fruit-eater. This is not a surprising result, for many dedicated folivores also eat fruit when it is available, and the pattern in this fossil ape is most similar to that seen in lowland gorillas. The other *Proconsul* species and *Morotopithecus bishopi*, the large ape from Moroto, all appear to be frugivores by these criteria.

Many features of microwear distinguish between fruit and leaf diets, and *Proconsul* species have molars with high frequencies of pits, indicating frugivorous diets. *Proconsul nyanzae* molars have higher pit frequencies than those of *P. heseloni*, suggesting that its diet contained more hard fruits. There is a trend of increasing proportions and sizes of pits as diets pass from soft fruit to hard fruit. At the macro level, this is consistent with wear patterns, since *P. nyanzae* has a greater wear gradient (i.e. the molars wear more rapidly so that the first molar is already quite worn by the time the third molar erupts) than the other species. In contrast to this, folivores have the highest proportions of striations on their molar teeth, which is the condition on *Rangwapithecus* teeth. *Rangwapithecus gordoni* is also different in having relatively thinner enamel than *Proconsul*, which is consistent with its more folivorous diet. It has been suggested in the past that all *Proconsul* species had thin enamel, but in a landmark study in 1998, David Beynon showed that proconsulid enamel is slightly thicker than the 'average', neither as thick as in some fossil hominin species nor as thin as in gorillas, but similar to *Sivapithecus* and human teeth. He also showed that root formation in the third molar of *P. heseloni*, the last of the permanent teeth to erupt, was complete between 6 and 7 years, so that their early life history was much shorter than in living apes.

An interesting speculation about the diet of *Proconsul* is that it almost certainly still retained a functional uricase gene. The mutation leading to the final deactivation of the uricase gene in the great apes was probably about 15 million years ago, several million years after the time of *Proconsul*. The significance of this has been described in Chapter 4, where it was shown that the loss of the uricase gene led to build-up of uric acid in the body, which in turn promoted the storage of fat from fructose, an evolutionary advantage in fruit-eating primates living in seasonal habitats where it is necessary to build up fat stores in times of plenty in order to survive the lean periods. This might not matter for primates living in tropical forest with low seasonality, but the loss of uricase would benefit fruit-eating animals in seasonal habitats. It will be shown below that this is the kind of environment that *Proconsul* and other early Miocene apes were associated with, seasonal woodlands and forest.

Summary

- The proconsulids were fossil apes that were monkey-like in their post-cranial morphology.
- Skull and teeth differ little from ancestral catarrhine condition.
- Brain size is relatively larger.
- Canine/premolar honing reduced in some species but not in *Rangwapithecus gordoni* or *Proconsul afrianus*.
- Quadrupedal slow climbers living in trees and ranging in size from the size of gibbons to larger than chimpanzees on the tops of branches.
- Body sizes from 8–14 kg to 63–83 kg, equivalent to siamang size to larger than chimpanzees, moderate to high sexual dimorphism.
- Some degree of terrestrial activity is indicated, particularly the larger species which were as big as chimpanzees or even bigger.
- The hand had similar proportions to the human hand, including long and probably powerful thumbs, but the thumb was non-rotatory.
- The hand had the manipulative capacity to use tools, which as has been suggested in Chapter 2 was a characteristic of the great ape and human clade, but there is no evidence that they did so.
- Most species were soft fruit frugivores, teeth had low degrees of shearing and microwear shows that they primarily ate soft fruit.
- There is some indication that *P. nyanzae* had a slightly harder fruit diet than *P. heseloni*, and good evidence that *Rangwapithecus gordoni* (and possibly *Nyanzapithecus vancouveringorum*) was a partial folivore, both from the higher degree of dental shearing and from its microwear.
- Dental development in proconsulids was complete by the age of seven.

Chapter 8
The environment in the early Miocene

The environments associated with early Miocene fossil apes are described here following the methods outlined in Chapter 6. It is important to remember that the operative word here is 'associated', for while the geology, plants and animals may all indicate specific habitats, it can not be known for certain that the fossil apes associated with the specific environmental evidence were actually living in these habitats. In some cases there is direct association between fossil ape and environmental evidence, for example when specimens of fossil ape are found together with plant remains, but in many cases they are found at different levels or different parts of the site, and association is inferred. However, if the fossil apes can be shown to be associated, time after time, with a particular habitat, there may be a strong presumption that they did indeed occupy that habitat.

Geological evidence

Geological evidence on the environment present at Rusinga Island has been provided by Michael Le Bas and by McCall, who described the formation of the large carbonatite volcano that was the source of the sediments on Rusinga Island (Figure 8.1): "Before the onset of Tertiary volcanism, the area has been subjected to peneplanation since the Mesozoic . . . there is no evidence of any derived sediments. At that time drainage was to the west and Lake Victoria did not exist." The sediments making up the Miocene deposits on Rusinga Island consist of volcanic sandy strata, on some of which fossil soils developed. The volcano is estimated to have been a large, low relief dome up to 20 km in diameter, and the sediments on which the fossil soils formed have been dated to about 18 million years and are listed as follows, from top to bottom:

Kiangata Agglomerate: thick deposits of agglomerate and ash flow (no fossils);
Kulu Formation: finely layered lake deposits with abundant fish but few terrestrial animals;
Hiwegi Formation: tuffaceous deposits in a riparian setting with abundant fossils of plants and animals in fossil soils; flood plain deposits and debris flows;

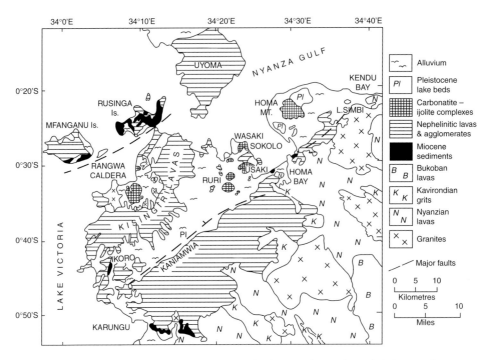

Figure 8.1 Major structural features of the Rusinga Island region during the early Miocene. The centre of volcanism was at the Rangwa dome with the Kisingiri lavas spreading out in all directions, including Rusinga and Mfwangano Island. Lake Victoria was not present, and drainage was to the west into a large shallow basin. It is likely that this basin drained westwards until cut off by the rise of the western rift valley highlands. Reproduced with permission from Le Bas 1977.

Rusinga Agglomerate: massive deposits but no fossils;

Kiahera Formation: tuffaceous deposits with few fossils on Rusinga Island, more abundant and more fossiliferous on Mfwangano Island;

Basal fluvial gravels and overbank clayey deposits (no fossils).

The great majority of fossil apes from Rusinga Island come from the Hiwegi Formation – flood plain deposits for the most part with fossil soils developed on them. The sediments have abundant fossils, so that as one walks over the outcrops they seem to occur everywhere. This is not what one sees today while walking over apparently equivalent flood plain areas, and in 1972 I teamed up with Colin Groves and Jenny Horne to investigate a modern flood plain to better understand the ecology of the Rusinga deposits. We spent 3 months on the Tana River expedition investigating the flood plain and observing and trapping the mammal and bird fauna, digging soil pits and measuring topographic profiles over the surface of the flood plain. Periodic flooding limits tree growth to areas raised above the level of the flood plain and the predominant vegetation over most of the flood plain is grass, but on areas elevated by no more than a couple of metres trees can survive the flooding. The raised areas are on sandy levees formed along the banks of past river channels and ox-bow lakes, and rich associations of forest and woodland develop on them. Both the tree species and parts of the mammal fauna have affinities with the Central African forests, including species of red colobus monkey and mangabey, and this disjunct distribution probably arose many thousands of years ago when climates were wetter and there was some degree of ecological continuity with Central Africa. Our 1972 expedition provided a fascinating insight into flood plain ecology, but one of my central concerns, finding and mapping bone distributions on the flood plain, was a non-starter, for despite intensive searching we found no bones at all. The reason for this disappointment, predictable enough with hindsight, is that the annual flooding of the river (not quite annual, for some years the river does not flood) very quickly buried any bones lying on the surface. However, this does not answer the question as to how such high concentrations of animal bones came to accumulate in the Rusinga deposits. The answer is probably that they were not linked with the river system and its periodic floods, but with the subsequent soil and vegetation development on the flood plain.

The fossil soils or palaeosols that formed on the Rusinga sediments during periods of volcanic quiescence or freedom from flooding may have taken hundreds of years, sometimes thousands of years, to develop. The longer the periods without volcanic activity, the deeper the soils and the less disturbed. There are many calcareous horizons in the soil profiles, which form under conditions of seasonal drying of the soil. The highly calcareous deposits were rich in sodium and calcium carbonates, which formed the raw material for the calcretes observed today in the sediments. Measuring the depths of these horizons provides an indication of the rainfall existing at that time, and it is estimated to have been at least 600 to 700 mm per year, although the physiognomy of fossil leaves from the Hiwegi Formation indicate rather higher rainfall. Recent work by Kieran McNulty's group on collections of fossil leaves has predicted much higher rainfall during this time, but the geological evidence shows that the area of sediment accumulation had a high water-table, not unexpected in flood plain conditions. In other words, the forest that is shown to have been present by the remains of tree trunks and leaves was a ground water forest existing under local, edaphic conditions, and so its presence does not indicate high rainfall.

Carbon isotope analyses of the sediments derived from organic matter in the fossil soils show them to be at the limit of the C_3 photosynthetic pathway, close to the values seen in mixed C_3/C_4 soils. The values of $\delta^{13}C$ are usually highly variable where such mixtures occur today, but in the case of the Rusinga palaeosols there is little variability. In addition, at this time in tropical Africa, there is no evidence that the C_4 pathway had emerged. It would appear, therefore, that the plants growing on the soils and contributing to the organic matter in the soils were C_3 plants, that is, bushes and trees for the most part, but the isotope values at the top of the range for C_3 plants show that the vegetation was growing under environmentally stressed conditions, such as water stress and high seasonality.

The sediments present on Mfwangano Island are essentially the same as those on Rusinga Island, being part of the same volcanic system. The other groups of sites from which species of *Proconsul* are known are the Songhor-Koru deposits, which were formed around the Tinderet volcano, a nephelinite volcano very different from Kisingiri, although the volcanic airfall ashes that make up large parts of the Songhor-Koru deposits were again highly calcareous. Little sedimentological work has been done on these deposits, but it is clear that soils were formed to considerable depths and the soils were red rather than the grey of the Rusinga sediments, indicating well-aerated sediments. At least nine different levels are present in the Songhor sediments, all superficially alike and hard to correlate because of numerous small faults, and I spent an arduous but pleasant season tracing the units on the ground. I mapped them with Martin Pickford, based on the regional geology map produced earlier by the late Bill Bishop; working with these two outstanding field geologists was a wonderful experience. Although the Songhor palaeosols also had prominent calcretes, it is not known how much of this was a function of climate and how much due to the abundance of calcium carbonate. Rainfall was probably considerably higher than at Rusinga Island.

Summary of geological evidence

- The Rusinga Island sediments accumulated on the flanks of a volcano 18 million years ago.
- Fossil soils were developed on the sediments and indicate moderate rainfall, at least 600 ml, with a seasonal climate.
- The water-table was high, consistent with edaphically wet conditions.
- Analysis of carbon isotopes indicates that the vegetation consisted of trees and shrubs probably growing under conditions of water stress.
- There is some evidence for the presence of forest, particularly from Mfwangano Island and the Songhor and Koru sediments on the flanks of Tinderet volcano, which were laid down 19.6 million years ago and had well-aerated soils developed on them and higher rainfall.

Flora and fauna

The Rusinga Island Miocene deposits have a rich fauna and flora that have been extensively studied to reconstruct the environment. Kathleen Chesters worked on the early collections of plant fossils recovered from many of the sites on Rusinga Island. She described the flora as uniform across the island but with differences on Mfwangano Island, and this is the only site differentiation that she records. Chesters first pointed out the abundance of climbing plants, and because climbers are not particularly abundant in primary rainforest she suggested that they could indicate that the local flora represented either forest margin habitats or gallery forest along a river. She also noted the great abundance of species of the Apocynaceae, the seeds of which are adapted for water dispersal, and she states further that "Almost without exception the trees are mentioned (by Richards) as growing in, or on, the edge of forests." Some of the trees might be found in forest habitats, but for the most part they represent environments beyond the forest limits and are part of the widespread woodland communities that used to be common in tropical Africa. Some tropical rainforest was undoubtedly present at this time, as indicated by the presence of large forest trees in the Mfwangano Island flora (e.g. species of *Entandophragma* and *Sterculia*) and the presence of forest-adapted mammals in a few Rusinga Island faunas (see next section), but overall the plant species Chesters records are more consistent with woodland vegetation rather than forest.

This was put to the test when Libby Evans and I excavated the fruit and nut bed in 1981. Martin Pickford and the palaeobotanist Margaret Collinson joined us in the field, and we made an extensive collection of fossil plants from five levels in the fruit and nut bed, but it was not until 20 years later, when Marion Bamford joined us, that we finally got around to publishing our results. The site is in the Hiwegi Formation, terrestrial sediments with immature soils developed, and in this respect they are similar to the Okoko palaeosols described by Erick Bestland and Greg Retallack, which these authors interpreted as stream-side soils developed under deciduous broad-leaved woodland (Sudano-Zambezian woodland to give it its technical name) with a relatively dry climate (Figure 8.2a).

Our excavation in the major plant-bearing horizon (Figure 8.2b) yielded abundant small twigs, and cracks in the twigs showed that they were broken in places. They were associated with nearly 200 fruits and seeds. Distribution plans of the twigs show a scatter of remains at all levels, with no order or direction, and they were lying almost flat or with no more than a 10 degree slope (Figure 8.2c). We took this to indicate that the flora was preserved as an undisturbed surface litter accumulation of "fruits and seeds, mixed with twigs of various sizes with random orientations and very low depositional dips, wood and bark fragments and decomposed leaves. There has been minimal transport and the flora evidently accumulated as litter beneath vegetation (and) therefore represents the local vegetation." There is little sign of water action, either in the sediments or in the distribution of the plant remains, and neither is there any indication of mixed sources from the list of plant taxa.

(a)　　　　　　　　　　　　　　　　　　(b)

(c)

Figure 8.2 The fruit and nut bed on Rusinga Island. (a) The sediments are poorly exposed, and we made a surface collection with reference to a single datum line. Lake Victoria can be seen in the distance in the first picture. (b) The excavation of the fruit and nut bed on Rusinga Island. (c) Surface collecting: the scatter of white objects consists of fragments of wood.

Retallack estimates that the duration of soil development was about 100 years, but there is no indication from the plant species that the vegetation was early in the ecological succession as Retallack suggests.

The nearest living relatives (NLR) of the fruits and seeds indicate closed woodland vegetation with trees, shrubs, lianas and climbers. Climbers are represented by twining stem fragments as well as by a wide variety of distinctive fruits and seeds. There were very few thorny twigs (only 3% of the twig collections), and no *Acacia* species or forest tree species. Deciduous broadleaved woodland with continuous canopy is strongly indicated for this flora, which is contemporaneous with and in close proximity to the sites from where the fossil apes were recovered.

More recently, excavations on Rusinga Island have resumed under the direction of Kieran McNulty. Analyses of fossil leaves from the Hiwegi Formation on Rusinga Island have identified sixteen morphotypes of leaves. These include forms similar to *Phragmites* and *Typha*, wetland reeds and bulrushes requiring permanent water to grow, and trees with untoothed leaves. The proportion of trees with untoothed leaves is high compared with toothed (serrated edges of the leaves), which indicates high annual temperature. Similarly, the relatively large leaf size, which includes moderately large and small leaves but only two morphotypes with large leaves, indicates broad-leaved trees (as opposed to trees with small leaves such as Acacias) such as are present in forest or woodland. At one site on Rusinga Island (R3) the dense remains of tree stumps and roots in a brown soil indicate the presence of forest with closed canopy on a stable land surface. There is leaf litter that does not seem to have been transported, leaf mass per area that suggests the trees were evergreen and leaf types that have been identified to at least 29 morphotypes. This could indicate extensive areas of forest during the early Miocene, but as seen above, the sedimentary structure shows the deposits were accumulated with a high water-table, which could indicate localized ground water forest or, by analogy with the Tana River forests, it could indicate island forests of limited extent growing on a seasonally wet flood plain in a highly seasonal and relatively dry climate. Most significantly from the point of view of fossil apes is the direct association of several specimens of *Proconsul heseloni* with the forest environment indicated by the plant remains, and the earlier finds of *Dendropithecus macinnesi* from a nearby site can also be correlated with the same forest environment.

Closed canopy woodlands were once common in East Africa, but many of them have long been cleared for agriculture. Woodlands differ from forest in having a single tree canopy and sometimes with extensive grass ground vegetation, although no evidence of grass was present in the Rusinga flora. The restriction to a single canopy is an important difference for tree-living animals, which have complex pathways through the multiple canopies present in tropical forest. Single tree canopies, even in closed woodland, do not offer the same opportunities for arboreal pathways, except to small animals such as squirrels, as the interconnecting branches in the single tree canopy are too thin to support the weight of larger animals. Apes the size of *Proconsul*, even the smallest species, would have been unable to move any distance through the tree canopy in this kind of environment without coming to the ground (Figure 8.3).

Land gastropods are common in most Rusinga deposits and were studied by Bernard Verdcourt, but he sampled the gastropod faunas by locality and provided no record of stratigraphic variations. In general, the Hiwegi

Figure 8.3 View upwards into a woodland canopy. This woodland has about 90% canopy cover, greater than the minimum definition of at least 40% cover, but even so it can be seen that the interconnecting branches between adjacent trees are thin and incapable of supporting the weight of any animal greater than one or two kilograms. Since the smallest fossil apes known from the Miocene and later are at least 10 kilos, it is apparent that to move from one tree to the next would have required descent to the ground. Any ape inhabiting woodland habitats, therefore, must to some extent have been adapted for ground living.

Formation has at least two types of gastropod assemblage preserved in different levels: one dominated by achatinids, indicating a range of savanna environments, and the other by streptaxids, a family of carnivorous gastropods, for which high species richness indicates forest environments. They indicate a varied environment of open country and forest, including some areas of wet evergreen forest. The lack of stratigraphic control means that the distribution of these vegetation types is not known, and it is also not known which of them may have been associated with the fossil apes. The significance of this will be seen when the mammals are described.

Collections of fossil mammals have been made on Rusinga Island since the 1930s, and a large number of collecting localities have been identified. Most are in the Hiwegi Formation but some are in the underlying and slightly older Kiahera Formation, which is better represented on Mfwangano Island. Louis Leakey undertook a number of excavations on both islands, but the main collections resulted from surface collecting where the locality was recorded but nothing else.

(a)

(b)

(c)

Figure 1.3 Kakamega Forest, Kenya. (a) The interior of the semi-evergreen forest, which is classified as intermediate tropical forest, i.e. intermediate between lowland and montane forest. (b) The forest edge, with rainforest stepping down to a line of Acacias and down again to a line of high herbaceous (*Acanthus*) vegetation, and finally down to grassland. (c) The transitional border is more or less permanent, and fires started in the grassland do not penetrate into the forest. Grass glades are very extensive within the forest boundaries, and they appear to be edaphic in origin rather than climatic, but the nature of the soil factors is not known at present.

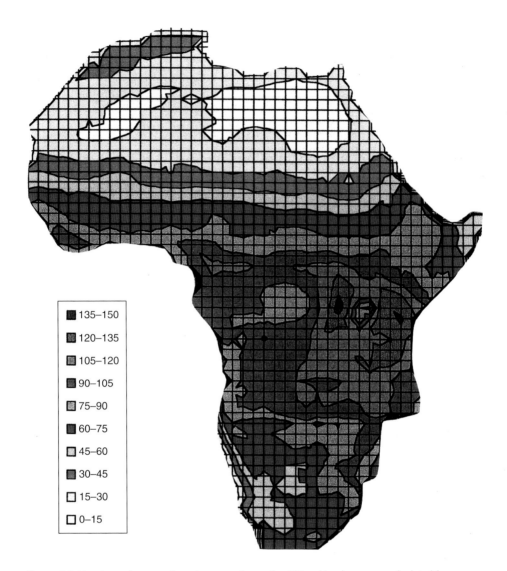

Figure 5.1 Numbers of mammal species per unit area for Africa. Numbers were calculated from range maps superimposed on an equal area grid of 1079 grid cells (excluding those with overlap over lakes or the sea). Highest species richness is shown by the browns and greens running north-south along eastern Africa. North of the equator there is a clear latitudinal gradient of diminishing species richness, but in southern Africa this gradient is affected both by the eastern highlands and the western desertification.

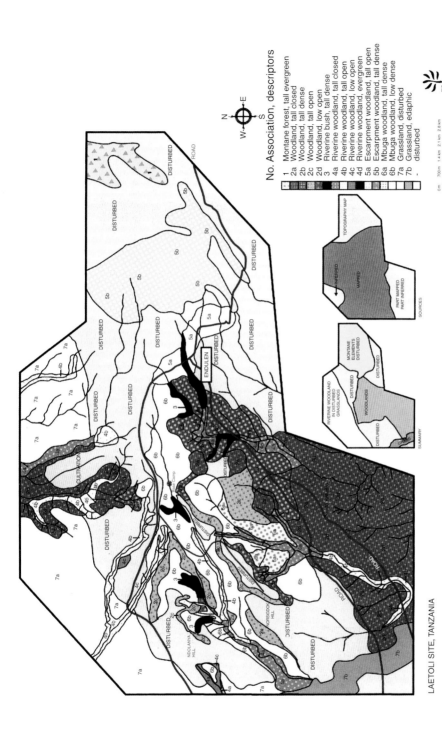

LAETOLI SITE, TANZANIA

No. Association, descriptors

1   Montane forest, tall evergreen
2a   Woodland, tall closed
2b   Woodland, tall dense
2c   Woodland, tall open
2d   Woodland, low open
3   Riverine bush, tall dense
4a   Riverine woodland, tall closed
4b   Riverine woodland, tall open
4c   Riverine woodland, low open
4d   Riverine woodland, evergreen
5a   Escarpment woodland, tall open
5b   Escarpment woodland, tall dense
6a   Mbuga woodland, tall dense
6b   Mbuga woodland, low dense
7a   Grassland, disturbed
7b   Grassland, edaphic
-    disturbed

0m   700m   1.4 km   2.1 km   2.8 km
SCALE 1 cm= 700 m

Figure 6.3 Distribution of Laetoli vegetation at the present time. The distribution of vegetation in relation to the topography of the area can be used as a guide to past vegetation when combined with past topographical features. The area today has broad-leaved woodland (Combretaceae) as the predominant vegetation type on freely drained slopes, *Acacia* woodland widespread on valley flats with impeded drainage and along seasonal river channels, and high gallery forest where permanent springs come to the surface. Extensive sections of all vegetation types have been replaced by invasive weed herbs as a result of human clearing. Andrews & Bamford 2007.

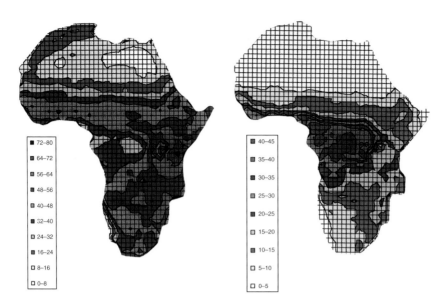

Figure 6.7 Numbers of mammal species per unit area (25{ts}000 km² grid cells) in Africa. On the right are numbers of arboreal and scansorial (both tree-living) mammal species; and on the left are numbers of terrestrial species. The isoclines depict numbers of species per unit area as indicated on the scales to the left of each map. The highest species richness of tree-living species is in the forests of west Central Africa and the western edge of the western rift valley; and the highest species richness of ground-living species is in heterogeneous habitats of East Africa and along the eastern rift valley. The difference between the two distributions is highly significant (p = 0.0001).

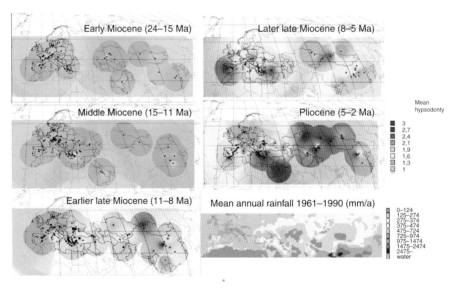

Figure 6.10 Hypsodonty maps showing change over time from the early Miocene to late Pliocene. The colours show the degrees of hypsodonty, with blues and greens indicating low hypsodonty (low crowned teeth) and yellows and reds indicating high hypsodonty (high crowned teeth). Distributions for five time periods, from early Miocene to Pliocene, are shown compared with a map of mean annual rainfall at the present time (bottom right), with blues and greens indicating high rainfall and yellow and red indicating low rainfall. The colours are not intended to be equivalent to hypsodonty levels of the mammals, but there is a parallel change which suggests that hypsodonty increased in the past as rainfall diminished. Reproduced with permission from Fortelius et al. 2002.

This collecting method produced large collections but little stratigraphic or contextual information, and in 1971 Judy Van Couvering (now Judith Harris) and I carried out several fine scale excavations in the fossil soils from single stratigraphic horizons within the Kaswanga sequence to try and obtain good associations between the fossil animals that we discovered. We recovered three distinct faunal assemblages from four excavations: the first was a waterside assemblage, with crocodiles and pleurodire turtles; the second contained many fossil taxa with arboreal and frugivorous adaptations, related to forest-living species today, such as galagine bush babies, rhynchocyonine elephant shrews, tragulids, anomalurid flying squirrels and a high diversity of rodent species; and the third was an open country assemblage with no certain environmental signal except for the lack of forest-living species (Figure 8.4). These three mammal faunas were found close together in time and space, and they show that conditions changed rapidly during their accumulation and preservation.

We based our interpretations on the living relatives of the fossil (extinct) species, assuming that if the living species occurred in a particular environment,

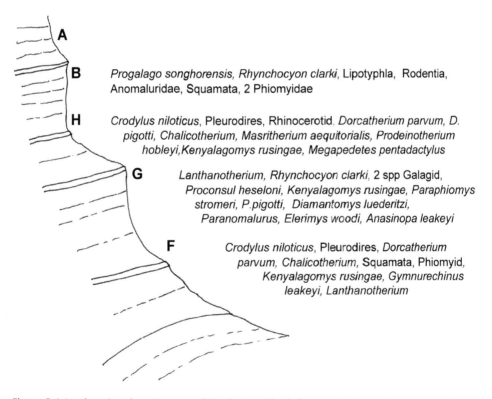

Figure 8.4 Local stratigraphy at Kaswanga Point, Rusinga Island, showing the five levels we excavated in 1971 and on the right their mammal communities. KG and KB had high diversity mammal faunas containing many forest-adapted species; KH was a waterside community of animals with many crocodiles; and KA and KF had open country mammals and no forest-adapted species. Amended from a section by John Van Couvering.

so too did its fossil relative. I have shown in Chapter 6 that this kind of assumption is highly suspect, for mammal species can and do change their habitats; for example, recent microwear texture analysis of the teeth of tragulids has shown that, unlike their living relatives in Africa, which live today in tropical forest, all three species present in the Rusinga fauna were mixed feeders, eating both grass and foliage. The presence of tragulids in the Rusinga fauna does not therefore support the presence of forest as has been supposed in the past. Another example of the hazards of this approach was mentioned above, that the common mouse in the Tana River forests is a species of *Acomys*, the spiny mouse typically an inhabitant of semi-arid bushland. As discussed above, the Tana forests are island forests in a sea of semi-arid bushland, and what seems to have happened is that the small forest rodents that would originally have been present in this environment died out and were replaced opportunistically by the common mouse in the surrounding land, the spiny mouse. Such an event would not be easily recognized in the fossil record.

The evidence from the mammals, therefore, indicates a high level of heterogeneity in the environment as do the soils and the gastropods, with discrete differences in the Miocene environment both in time and place. In other words, there was a mosaic of habitats, probably related to the presence of a river in the vicinity of the site, with wet conditions indicated by the presence of rushes and reeds, and patches of forest interspersed with areas of woodland. With the ongoing volcanic activity, it is likely that environments at that time were constantly changing, with woodland and even patches of forest growing up and local faunas moving into them, later to be displaced by the next volcanic activity. It is quite clear that the distribution of environments in the Miocene can only be properly understood once microstratigraphic excavations have taken place over a wide area.

After our 1971 excavation on Rusinga Island, I went on to excavate at other East Africa sites and did not return to continue the microstratigraphic excavations we had started. The work there was continued by Alan Walker, and in 1984 he went in search of a pothole described by Whitworth in 1953. We had looked for it in 1971 and failed to find it, but it was still there and far from being a pothole Walker found that it was the decayed remains of a tree trunk that had been half buried by advancing volcanic sediments (Figure 8.5). As the tree decayed it left a vertical hole in the sediment and this was filled in with other sediment and large numbers of fossil bones, including more parts of the *Proconsul heseloni* skeleton described by Napier (see Chapter 7). The animal fauna included numerous small mammal remains and some large mammals as well, and the remains of snakes and varanids (monitor lizards). Many articulated skeletons from juveniles were present, and even more significantly the bones from each one, were distinct and not mixed in with the bones from

Figure 8.5 Rusinga Island (Gumba) Whitworth's pothole being excavated in 1948. This is the site that the partial skeleton of *Proconsul heseloni* came from, and amazingly the pothole was located again when Alan Walker and Martin Pickford visited the site in the 1980s. Photo courtesy of the late Shirley Coryndon.

other skeletons. This shows that whole animal bodies were preserved at the site, they were undisturbed, and the skeletons remained in articulation when they were buried. This is direct evidence that carnivores did not dismember them and that the site was not a carnivore den. In other words they appear to represent natural deaths of animals, perhaps trapped inside the hollow tree trunk, but in the absence of taphonomic study no more can be said at present. The species present are typical of the indeterminate group of Rusinga fossils, with no indications on palaeoecology.

An even greater find made by Alan Walker was the discovery of nine partial skeletons of *Proconsul* in the Kaswanga site on Rusinga Island. This was by far the largest concentration of fossil ape skeletons ever found, and while he and his students have published many papers on the fossils, described in Chapter 7, much still needs to be done to truly understand all the features of this fossil ape. Perhaps the strangest things of all about the finds are, firstly, that only the fossil apes were present, and no other fossil animals, and secondly, that the fossil apes were mainly represented by legs and feet. There is clear taphonomic bias here, but what can have been the agent responsible for so many fossil apes and nothing else? Clearly a study of the taphonomy is needed, and in the absence of this nothing more can be said about the environment and conditions of preservation of this assemblage of fossil apes.

After my excavations at Rusinga Island, I moved over to Songhor, a slightly earlier *Proconsul* site in Kenya. This amazingly rich site has produced several faunas with forest affinities, richer than the Rusinga faunas and located in deeper palaeosols with a more distinct red colour, which means that they were more developed and iron in the soil had oxidized. Once the complex micro-stratigraphy was sorted out, as mentioned above, I was able to compile two mammal faunas from the two richest layers, and by analysing their ecological diversity I could show that they had the functional equivalence of forest faunas, with perhaps greater affinities with montane forest than with lowland forest. The gastropods associated with the mammals also have mainly forest affinities. The fossil apes *Proconsul africanus, P. major* and *Rangwapithecus gordoni* were associated with several ape-like species identified phylogenetically as stem catarrhines, that is, catarrhine primates preceding the divergence from the living families of apes and monkeys. As such they may provide an indication of the nature of early ape ancestors and their environment.

Later excavations with Martin Pickford at Koru produced similar faunas and the same fossil ape species. Again, the environment at Koru indicated (by indicator species) the presence of montane forest. The common ape species at these two sites contrast with the two common species of fossil ape on Rusinga Island, *Proconsul heseloni* and *P. nyanzae*, which are found at many different sites on Rusinga Island, together with *Nyanzapithecus* and *Dendropithecus macinnesi*. The latter was the most arboreal species found in the early Miocene, with its long slender limb bones, and although it had some suspensory adaptations, phylogenetically it is a stem ape.

Summary

- The sediments indicate high seasonality and moderate precipitation (~600 ml).
- On Rusinga Island, the sediments indicate a high water-table.
- Carbon isotope ratios of palaeosols indicate vegetation of C_3 plants, trees and shrubs.
- Isotope values indicate that the vegetation was water-stressed.
- Fossil leaf litter of twigs, leaves, fruits and buds indicate woodland.
- The patchiness of fruit and seed distribution indicates that the plant remains accumulated in places and reflect local floristic variability in the parent vegetation.
- The plant species preserved in the fruit and nut bed indicate broad-leaved deciduous woodland.

- There were very few twigs with thorns such as are found on more arid adapted species of *Acacia* or *Balanites*, and there was no evidence of forest trees.
- Forest tree fruits are present on Mfwangano Island, and on Rusinga Island the presence of forest is indicated by a flora of tree trunks and leaves.
- Land gastropods indicate mixed savanna and bush with gallery forest.
- Fossil mammals indicate at least six environments on Rusinga Island, Songhor and Koru:

  1. closed lowland forest, perhaps gallery forest on Mfwangano Island, and patches of forest on Rusinga Island interspersed with deciduous woodlands;

  2. montane forest at Songhor and Koru probably similar to the Tinderet forests close by the sites;

  3. waterside assemblage;

  4. open woodland;

  5. pothole assemblage of snakes, large and small mammals; and

  6. primate site with nine *Proconsul* individuals.

- General conclusions from this evidence are that *Proconsul heseloni* and *P. nyanzae* occupied a range of habitats, predominantly deciduous woodland but also a minor element of forest.
- Animals the size of the proconsulid species and living in single canopy woodlands must have spent some time on the ground, particularly when moving from one place to another, and they were adapted to seasonal habitats when fruit and leaves would become scarce.
- *Proconsul major*, *P. africanus* and *Rangwapithecus gordoni* are associated with forest environments, with reduced seasonality, *P. africanus* being more highly adapted for life in trees and *R. gordoni* being partly folivorous.

Chapter 9
The view from the middle Miocene

The proconsulids described in the previous chapter form a coherent group that had a limited geographical distribution in eastern Africa. They were succeeded by a number of genera and species with a greater range across East Africa, and for the first time apes are known outside Africa. The African apes are grouped in the Afropithecinae (Table 4.2), but none have yet received the monographic descriptions available for *Proconsul*. For this reason, full descriptions cannot be provided here, and it is more convenient to compare their morphologies with those present in *Proconsul*. The earliest apes found in Eurasia are similarly grouped with the afropithecines, mainly on the basis of shared primitive characters, and they are described together here for convenience.

African apes

The African afropithecines are represented by *Afropithecus turkanensis*, which gives its name to the subfamily and is represented by single skull and fragments of jaws and teeth. There is little information as to its context. More information is available from two partial skeletons: *Equatorius africanus* from Kipsaramon in the Tugen Hills and Maboko Island, and *Nacholapithecus kerioi* from Nachola in northern Kenya. Both have partial skeletons and both are from deposits approximately 15 million years old. The former species is now grouped with a specimen from Maboko Island that has had a rather chequered history since its discovery in 1948.

Wilfred Le Gros Clark and Louis Leakey attributed a single specimen of fossil ape from Kenya to *Sivapithecus africanus* because of its supposed similarities with the Indian species of *Sivapithecus* (Figure 9.1). It was recorded as coming from Rusinga Island and was thus coeval with *Proconsul*. However, it is also similar to the species of the middle Miocene genus *Kenyapithecus* from western Kenya, and in 1961 Louis Leakey renamed it *Kenyapithecus africanus* along with a number of other specimens from Rusinga, which together he was proposing as an early Miocene human ancestor. Its differences in morphology and preservation from the large sample of fossil apes from Rusinga remained a source of puzzlement for many years, and in 1978, Theya Molleson and I decided to test the provenance of the specimen. There were still traces of sediment

150

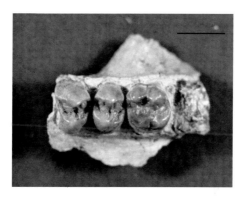

Figure 9.1 The type specimen of *Equatorius africanus*: maxilla with two premolars and one molar. This is the original maxilla from Maboko Island, originally thought to be from Rusinga Island. The scale bar is 1{ts}cm.

adhering to the maxilla, and we were able to get enough for analysis by X-ray fluorescence spectrometry. We compared the element distribution present in the sediment to samples of sediment from a range of East African sites, and although the results were not entirely conclusive, we concluded that there was a high level of probability that the specimen in fact came from Maboko Island, the deposits of which are about 3 million years younger than the Rusinga Island deposits. This conclusion is now generally accepted.

To know how this misidentification of the locality for the type specimen came about you have to know something of how the fossils were being collected in the mid-twentieth century. Maboko Island is half way along the Kavirondo Gulf, a deep embayment of Lake Victoria, and Rusinga Island lies just outside the entrance to the gulf, in Lake Victoria proper. Louis Leakey did not always visit the fossil sites himself, but he sent his crew on his boat, *Miocene Lady*, to visit the numerous sites and make collections of fossils. About once a week they would travel by boat back to Kisumu to meet him, sometimes stopping at Maboko Island on the way to collect fossils there. Larger fossils would make the journey wrapped in newspaper, but small ones were often stored in match-boxes, where incidentally they remained until I came to work on them many years later. It seems all too possible that the fragment of upper jaw that is the type specimen of 'Sivapithecus africanus' was placed for safe keeping in such a matchbox, perhaps along with other specimens collected earlier from Rusinga Island, and hence it came to be wrongly attributed to that site. A final change of name came about when it was associated with much better fossil remains from Kipsaramon in the Tugen Hills of the Kenya rift valley, and to demonstrate the link, and differences from *Kenyapithecus*, it was renamed *Equatorius africanus*.

The *Nacholapithecus kerioi* and *Equatorius africanus* partial skeletons provide the best evidence of afropithecine anatomy, and they will be described together. The only skull known for this group, however, is the specimen of *Afropithecus turkanensis*, and this will be included also. The key morphological features for the three afropithecine species are as follows: the skull has a strongly projecting face; low broad origin of the zygomatic root; greater robusticity of the jaws than is present in *Proconsul*; greater development of the inferior transverse torus of the mandible; relatively broad upper central incisors; lateral incisors highly asymmetrical with a broad but low lingual tubercle; lower crowned and relatively robust canines; enlarged premolars that are relatively long; molars with thick enamel and low dentine relief; lower molars with reduced cingulum, no upper molar cingulum; long flexible back as in *Proconsul*; cervical vertebrae large relative to presumed body mass; axis and atlas vertebrae are intermediate between monkeys and great apes, and suggest the beginnings of upright posture; lumbar vertebrae have long bodies with ventral keels but small body surface area relative to vertebral spine size and assumed body mass; neural spines of the lumbar vertebrae are caudally inclined, that is, towards the tail end of the vertebral column; thoracic vertebrae have heart-shaped bodies with a ventral keel and are small relative to presumed body mass; transverse processes arising from vertebral bodies as in *Proconsul*; clavicle is relatively long; head of the humerus is posteriorly directed; the greater tuberosity projects above the level of the head; the anatomy of the lower arm bones and wrist is strikingly similar to the condition in *Proconsul*; distal humerus at the elbow joint differs from that of *Proconsul* and is less ape-like than the early Miocene fossil apes; the medial epicondyle is long and bent backwards, unlike the condition in *Proconsul*; the olecranon fossa of the humerus is deep; the coronoid process is well developed and inclined distally; ulna has a long and projecting olecranon process; the head of the femur has a high neck angle and projects above the level of the greater trochanter (Figure 9.2); wide patellar surface; thick fibular shaft; metacarpal heads with well-developed transverse dorsal ridges and broad distal articular surfaces; hallux (big toe) is relatively long and stout; the terminal phalanx of the hallux is large and has a wide articular surface; and phalanges are lightly built and are not curved, but more robust in *Equatorius*.

In describing these species, Masato Nakatsukasa and Steve Ward separately concluded that the vertebrae of *Nacholapithecus kerioi* resemble those of *Proconsul* in many characters and that therefore the fossil apes had long flexible backs as in monkeys. The neural spines of the lumbar vertebrae are different from those of *Proconsul* and most other primates, however, as the vertebral spines are broader and project caudally (towards the tail end of the vertebral column). This limits the bending of the lower back, which is more similar to the condition in animals like koalas that are climbers and vertical clingers and indicates that they showed the beginnings of more upright posture (orthogrady). This condition is shared with the living apes, but because the morphology by which it is achieved differs from that of the living apes, it would appear to be convergent on the

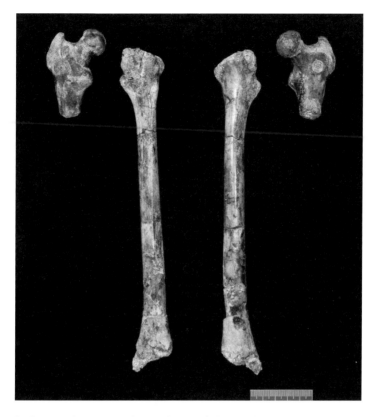

Figure 9.2 The femora of *Equatorius africanus* from Maboko Island.

living great apes, and not homologous. The forelimbs were adapted for both climbing and terrestrial locomotion and had a greater range of extension of the elbow than in *Proconsul*. The foot of *Nacholapithecus* was adapted for grasping and arboreal climbing to a greater extent than in *Proconsul*, although the differences in the forearm and the proportions of the metacarpals and phalanges suggest rather that they were both partly terrestrial. The fifth metacarpal and proximal phalanx are intermediate between those of arboreal and terrestrial living monkeys and are most similar to the bones of semi-terrestrial quadrupedal monkeys. The proportions of metacarpal and phalanx are also close to that of chimpanzees, but the closest comparison is with macaque-like adaptations.

Summary of African apes

- Middle Miocene apes from Africa include *Equatorius africanus* from Maboko Island and Kipsaramon, *Nacholapithecus kerioi* from Nachola, northern Kenya and *Afropithecus turkanensis* from northern Kenya, all dated to between 16 and 15 million years.

- Afropithecine skull with strong mid-face and alveolar prognathism.
- Robust jaws with large inferior torus, enlarged premolars and molars with loss of upper molar cingulum, molars with thick enamel and very high degree of sexual dimorphism.
- Trunk and limb bones show that they had a long curved back and forelimbs adapted for both climbing in trees and terrestrial locomotion.
- The vertebrae indicate stiff lower back analogous to but not homologous to the condition in living great apes.
- The hand proportions suggest adaptations to arboreal and terrestrial locomotion.
- The foot was adapted for powerful grasping.

The exit from Africa in the middle Miocene

At the same time as *Equatorius* and *Nacholapithecus* were present in Africa, there is evidence of fossil apes outside Africa for the first time. The earliest record is a single fossil ape molar described by Walter Heizmann and David Begun from the site of Engelswies in Germany. The deposits are dated to between 16 and 15 million years. I visited the site with Heizmann, and what I saw was an unimpressive small hole in the ground at the top of a hill covered with trees, although since I was quite ill at the time, maybe I missed something. At this time in the middle Miocene there was a land bridge connecting Africa with Europe, as discussed in Chapter 5, enabling migrations of mammals between the continents, and it is probable that apes took advantage of this, although as discussed below there is some doubt about the dating. During the subsequent rise in sea level, known as the Langhian transgression, the Tethys (Mediterranean) Sea was continuous with the Indian Ocean, so that Africa was once again cut off, and the possibilities of movement between continents greatly reduced (see Figure 5.2 in Chapter 5), and it may be that apes did not enter Eurasia until after this time. However, there are small mammals present at Engelswies that are attributable to the MN5 mammal stage, a stage that has been dated on other sites to about 16 million years. Similarly, the large mammals from a different depositional level at Engelswies are consistent with the small mammal stage, also indicating an age of at least 16 million years.

Slightly later in time is a fossil site in western Turkey called Paşalar, a site where I worked for many years during the 1980s. Over half the species identified at Engelswies are also found at Paşalar, although the Paşalar fauna is more than double the size of the Engelswies fauna (59 species compared with less than 30 at Engelswies). Some of the Paşalar faunal elements correlate with the same MN5 mammal stage as Engelswies, and some with the later stage, MN6, suggesting that the age of both sites is greater than 16 million years; however, it has also been proposed that the faunas from the Paşalar fossiliferous sediments are exclusively MN6, and based on correlation with the Global Polarity Timescale this gives an age range of about 14 million years. This issue has not yet been resolved, although I believe the earlier date is more likely. A third site is also known from Turkey, Çandır in central Anatolia to the north of the capital Ankara, and this appears to be slightly younger than the other sites.

Griphopithecus alpani from Çandır in Turkey (Figure 9.3) was first described by Ibrahim Tekkaya as *Sivapithecus alpani*. At that time it was the custom to attribute any fossil ape with robust jaws and thick-enamelled teeth to *Sivapithecus* if it was big or *Ramapithecus* if it was small, and I subsequently attributed this specimen to the species *Ramapithecus wickeri* in recognition of its similarities with the Kenyan fossil ape *Kenyapithecus wickeri* (which was then called *Ramapithecus wickeri*). The pros and cons of this will be discussed in Chapter 10, but suffice it to say that it was an intuitive guess, based as it was on a single specimen, but it was nonetheless wrong, for it is the similar but rare ape species from Paşalar that is now identified as a Eurasian species of *Kenyapithecus*. The Çandır ape is now called *Griphopithecus alpani*, and the numbers of specimens of this species have been greatly increased by excavations at Paşalar.

The fossiliferous sediments at both Paşalar and Çandır were discovered by a German team surveying for lignite deposits and led by Otto Sickenberg. Heinz Tobien was a member of the team in charge of palaeontological investigations, and he realized the potential of Paşalar, for it is almost unbelievably rich in fossils. It was exposed on the side of a road cutting leading up a beautiful forested valley on the lower slopes of the mountains. The German excavations

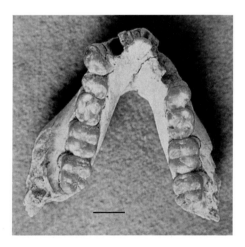

Figure 9.3 The mandible of *Griphopithecus alpani* described by Ibrahim Tekkaya from Çandir, Turkey. The scale bar is 1{ts}cm.

produced a collection of 86 isolated hominid teeth, and after Tobien and I published the teeth together, I resolved to find the site and start new excavations there. I was then working at some other middle Miocene sites in Turkey, and returning to Istanbul at the end of the excavation season I went searching for the site. The village of Paşalar was not shown on any map, and even after finding the village I only found the site after driving through several back gardens in the village to the general surprise and consternation of the villagers. The site is remarkable for its high concentrations of fossils, and I was resolved to find a way of working there. My then collaborators in Turkey were not interested, but by great good fortune I met up with Berna Alpagut when she was visiting the Natural History Museum on a study trip, and we began a long-standing collaboration in 1983. At that time Berna was more interested in the Mesolithic period, but I managed to persuade her to change to the Miocene.

There are other difficulties attendant on work in Turkey, and the archaeological authorities from whom we had to get excavation permits never really understood why we were investigating 15 million-year-old deposits. The fossils we were finding were obviously not human, and there were no human artefacts, and so they did not understand why we were using rigorous archaeological techniques to excavate and record the fossils. This is a view by no means restricted to Turkish archaeologists, for I have encountered similar attitudes from archaeologists in France, Spain and Hungary. It is also a view not uncommon in palaeontological fieldwork, where the preferred method is to walk the outcrops, surface-collecting fossils as they erode out of the sediments.

In the course of our excavations extending over 15 years, we have recovered about 20 jaws (Figure 9.4) and nearly 2000 teeth of *Griphopithecus alpani*, but unfortunately we have not so far found any intact skulls and only 21 postcranial bones. Most of the teeth are isolated, but the painstaking work of Turkish students has succeeded in reconstructing nearly 50 tooth rows by matching the wear facets on adjoining teeth where they contact each other. This was painstaking work, but it has greatly increased the value of the isolated teeth. Other students have described the milk teeth and postcranial remains, so that we can now calculate that there are at least 80 adult individuals and fourteen juveniles at the site.

The teeth of *Griphopithecus alpani* have high degrees of size variation but little morphological variation. Bivariate plots of length and breadth dimensions for most tooth types are grouped into two sets, which are completely separated for the canines and third premolars, for which there are no intermediates between the large and small specimens. These represent males and females, indicating considerable size dimorphism between the sexes (Figure 9.5). The central incisors are broader and more robust than *Proconsul*

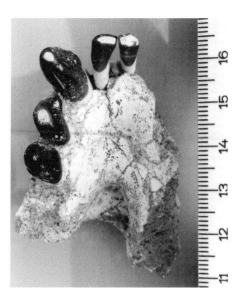

Figure 9.4 Mandibular symphysis of *Griphopithecus alpani*. Note the long sloping symphysis.

heseloni incisors, but like them they have a median pillar on the lingual side; the upper lateral incisors are asymmetrically conical and small, while the lower lateral incisors are asymmetrical and larger than the centrals; the lower canines are relatively low crowned and robust with a double distal ridge producing characteristic wear patterns on the apex and distal ridges of the crown; the upper canines are also low crowned and are mesiodistally symmetrical; the lower third premolars are single cusped but low crowned, and they lack continuous cingula but have a pronounced mesial beak which is almost certainly cingular in origin; the upper third premolars are asymmetrical, with the buccal cusp larger than the lingual one; the upper molars have low, rounded cusps, low dentine relief and thick enamel (Figure 9.6). Many of these characters are shared with *Equatorius africanus* from Africa and are probably primitive retentions from early Miocene apes such as *Proconsul*, and as such they provide an indication of geographical continuity between apes in Turkey and East Africa, but they do not indicate a cladistic relationship between them (but see further below). It may be that they should be included together in the subfamily Afropithecinae, but some workers prefer to assign them to a separate subfamily, Griphopithecinae.

Twenty-one phalanges of *Griphopithecus alpani* have been recovered so far from Paşalar. Most are from the hand, and they have expanded proximal articular surfaces that indicate that the apes moved quadrupedally like monkeys. The degree of curvature of the shafts, and the length indices between phalanges, are both intermediate between arboreal and terrestrial species of

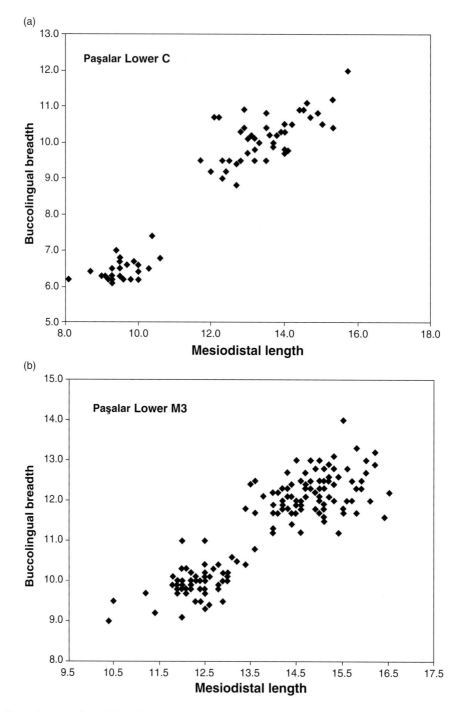

Figure 9.5 Lengths and breadths of two samples of teeth of *Griphopithecus alpani* from Paşalar. (a) The dimensions of the lower canine, the most dimorphic tooth in the tooth row, showing complete separation of large and small, assumed to be males and females; (b) the dimensions of one of the lower molars showing some overlap between males and females. Both teeth indicate that this fossil ape had a higher degree of sexual dimorphism than any of the proconsulids. Measurements are in millimetres.

(a)

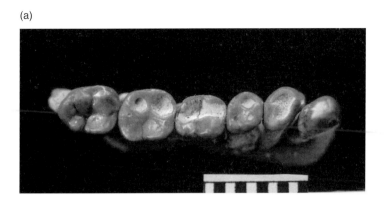

(b)

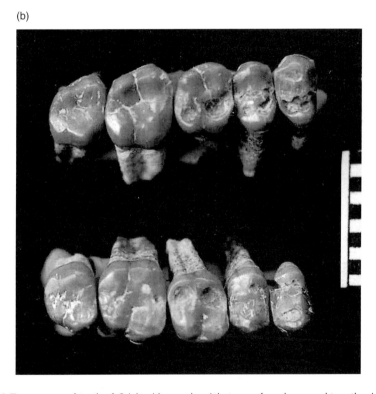

Figure 9.6 Two groups of teeth of *Griphopithecus alpani* that were found grouped together in the site. (a) The teeth in the mandibular tooth row were found lined up in place and facing downwards but with no trace of the body of the mandible. (b) Group of associated upper teeth belonging to both sides of the palate with no trace of bone left.

monkey, showing that the fossil apes were not exclusively arboreal but moved both in trees and on the ground, probably in a manner like that of macaques. Comparisons with other fossil apes also showed similarities with early and middle Miocene apes, supporting the conclusion that all of them were partly arboreal and partly terrestrial.

Summary

- Middle Miocene apes include *Equatorius africanus* from Maboko Island and Kipsaramon, *Nacholapithecus kerioi* from Nachola, northern Kenya and *Griphopithecus alpani* from Turkey.
- They are dentally similar, mainly as a result of shared primitive characters.
- They are dated to between 16 and 15 million years.
- Afropithecine skull with strong mid-face and alveolar prognathism.
- Robust jaws with large inferior torus.
- Enlarged premolars and molars with loss of upper molar cingulum.
- Molars with thick enamel.
- Very high degree of sexual dimorphism.

Chapter 10
Specialized apes from the middle Miocene

Living at the same time as the afropithecines was another group of fossil apes, the kenyapithecines. They are much less abundant in the fossil record and come from just two sites, Fort Ternan in Africa and Paşalar again in Turkey. The Turkish site is one of the very few sites in Europe and Asia that has two hominid species apparently coexisting, although it will be seen in the next chapter that although they were found together in the same fossil site, there is compelling evidence that they did not live together in the same environment. At least two fossil apes are also present in the Fort Ternan deposits, with a proconsulid apparently coexisting with the kenyapithecine, but again there is good evidence that they were not living together in the same environment but were transported to the site from different places (see Chapter 11).

The upper jaw of *Kenyapithecus wickeri* from Fort Ternan was first described in 1962 by Louis Leakey, who saw it as a fossil ape more advanced towards the human condition than other fossil apes. Elwyn Simons and David Pilbeam also recognized this, and in their 1965 synthesis they combined it with the Indian genus *Ramapithecus* as a putative human ancestor. For many years *Ramapithecus wickeri* in Africa and *Ramapithecus punjabicus* in India and Pakistan enjoyed a certain notoriety as the earliest evidence for human origins, and they were cited in all the textbooks of that period. *Ramapithecus wickeri*, however, did not long enjoy its position, for while I was working on my PhD in Nairobi I managed to get a look at a small mandible from Fort Ternan that for years had been locked away in Louis Leakey's safe. Louis had said for years that he had a specimen of dryopithecine from Fort Ternan that was like the fossil apes from Europe, but he kept it locked away and would not let anyone see it. One day when he was going off on one of his many trips overseas, he lent me the key to his safe because he wanted me to look at some other fossils that he kept there, and I took advantage of the privilege to take out the fragment of jaw and examine it. I saw at once that it was the lower jaw corresponding to the upper jaw of *Kenyapithecus wickeri*, and I showed this to Louis on his return. To his credit, Louis immediately accepted my findings, and he told me to send a short note to the prestigious journal *Nature*. I would have liked to have had his name on the paper with me, but I believe he felt embarrassed at his mistaken identification. The paper was duly published in 1971 and I still regret that we did not publish it together.

The mandible has two teeth preserved, the two lower premolars. The third premolar is a single cusped sectorial type of tooth, which is why Louis thought it was a fossil ape and which was not what was predicted for a human ancestor. If it belonged to the same species, or indeed the same individual, as the upper jaw of *Kenyapithecus wickeri*, the morphology of the lower premolars therefore seemed to exclude the possibility that it could be a human ancestor. This of course is a false premise, for as will be seen later, the earliest ancestors to the human lineage almost certainly retained sectorial premolars. In addition, I fitted an isolated upper canine, also in the collection from Fort Ternan, on to the part of the root socket exposed in the maxilla, and its wear facet fitted that of the lower third premolar in the mandible. This canine is typically ape-like, with its crown projecting beyond the level of the other teeth, and although this association is still not generally accepted, the morphology of the canine is consistent with the morphologies of the lower teeth against which it occluded (Figure 10.1).

As a consequence of linking the upper and lower jaws of *Kenyapithecus wickeri*, Alan Walker and I made a reconstruction of the lower face based on the fact that a portion of the front of the mandible was complete to beyond the midline. In point of fact, we originally failed to identify the midline on the

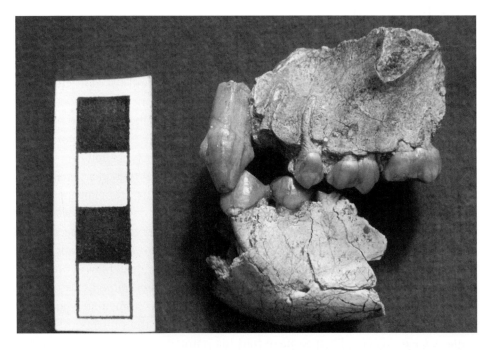

Figure 10.1 The upper and lower jaws of *Kenyapithecus wickeri* fitted together, with the disputed canine in place. The upper canine contacts the single cusped lower premolar, the mandible is robust and the body of the maxilla is deep and robust, with the zygomatic arch set high above the tooth row.

mandible, but trenchant criticism of the first draft of our article by Elwyn Simons, who like Leakey did not like the ape-like reconstruction we had produced, caused us to look again at the specimen, and at this stage we realized that the midline was preserved. This enabled us to reconstruct the dental arcade of the lower jaw, and by fitting the upper jaw to it, the upper dental arcade as well (Figure 10.2). The straight sided arcades were quite different from the rounded and human-like dental arches that Simons reconstructed for the Indian *Ramapithecus*, which showed both that it bore no relation to that fossil ape and that it could no longer be considered to be on the human lineage. The maxilla is extremely deep and robust, with an almost flattened surface of the floor of the maxillary sinus set well above the alveolar region so that there is no penetration of molar roots into the sinus. The root of the zygomatic process is anteriorly placed. This hyper robusticity is repeated in the mandible, which has a massively elongated mandibular symphysis and a low robust mandibular body. In addition to these two specimens, several isolated teeth from Fort Ternan are also attributed to *Kenyapithecus wickeri*, including an upper central incisor and two lower canines. These three teeth will be seen to be important in identifying the phylogenetic significance of *Kenyapithecus*.

A second species of *Kenyapithecus*, *K. kizili*, is based on fossils from Paşalar, and it is represented by two maxillae and 74 isolated teeth. Jay Kelley and I described this new species together with Berna Alpagut, and we made detailed comparisons between it and the much larger sample of *Griphopithecus alpani* from the same site. We also compared it with the *Kenyapithecus wickeri* specimens from Kenya, for there were some intriguing similarities. The maxilla of *Kenyapithecus kizili* from Paşalar is robust and with moderately deep maxillary alveolar processes, similar to the morphology of *Kenyapithecus wickeri*. In addition to being elevated, the floor of the maxillary sinus in the *Kenyapithecus* species is restricted in area and relatively flat, lacking the compartmentalization evident to varying degrees in many other taxa. The zygomatic process originates high above the alveolar margin. The incisive canal, which connects the nose and the mouth, is broad and long (Figure 10.3).

The anterior teeth of both species of *Kenyapithecus* show a series of highly derived morphologies distinct from all other fossil apes. The central incisors lack the lingual pillar but instead are broader and have prominent mesial and distal marginal ridges converging at the base of the crown in a V shape depression (Figure 10.4); the upper lateral incisors are relatively small and more symmetrical than in *Griphopithecus alpani*; the lower incisors also have distinct marginal ridges meeting cervically in a sharp V; the male upper canines bear a buccal cingulum; the lower canines are slender and high crowned and with a distinct lingual cingulum; the third lower premolar also has a continuous lingual cingulum; the upper and lower canines have

(a)

(b)

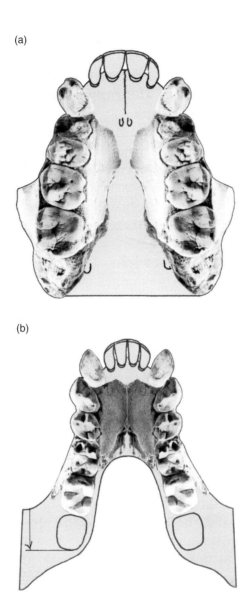

Figure 10.2 The reconstruction of the upper (a) and lower (b) jaws of *Kenyapithecus wickeri* showing the ape-like shape of the dental arcades, very different from the rounded arcade present in humans. The lower jaw is complete to the midline, which enabled us to reconstruct the shape of the mandibular tooth rows, and then by lining up the upper teeth with the lower, we could reconstruct the upper jaws as well, even though there was no part of the midline preserved.

relatively more slender and higher crowns; and the upper premolars have distinct and unbroken transverse crests (Figure 10.3).

In contrast to these differences in the anterior dentition, no definitive differences have yet been identified in molar morphology between the two species at Paşalar. Louise Humphrey showed that the molar distribution

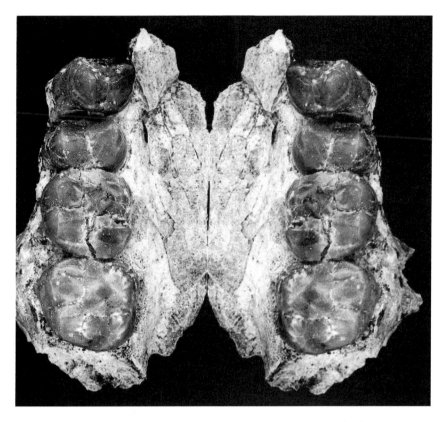

Figure 10.3 The upper jaw of *Kenyapithecus kizili*. Reconstructed palate: the left side is preserved to the midline, and the right side is a mirror image of the left. Note the large incisive fossa at the front end of the palate, which is a primitive feature compared with the great apes and humans. The two tooth rows converge posteriorly, which suggests large anterior teeth; the incisors are broad (Figure 10.4), but no canines were found with this specimen.

represents a heavily asymmetric assemblage of two species that are similar in size but not entirely overlapping in their size distributions. Both species have a very high degree of sexual dimorphism in their teeth (Figure 10.5), one of the highest of any fossil ape, and their similarity in size has made it difficult to distinguish them (see below). For the anterior teeth, which can be distinguished by morphology, the size distributions of the teeth show males and females falling into two distinct groups. The size distribution for the upper central incisor is shown in Figure 10.5, and this shows both the difference in proportion of the teeth in the two species at Paşalar, with the *Kenyapithecus* teeth being relatively longer and broader, and the difference in size for both species between males and females for both species. This degree of sexual dimorphism in the central incisor, one of the least dimorphic teeth, suggests that a similar degree of dimorphism may have existed for body size, and this suggests in turn that the social structure of both species may have included

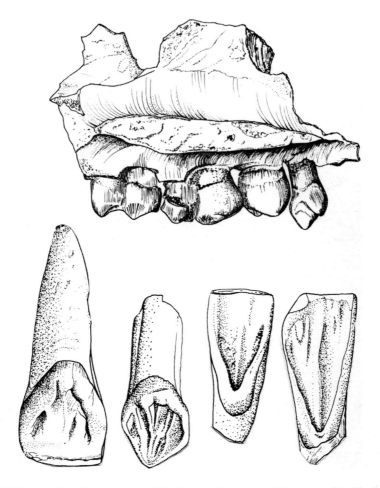

Figure 10.4 The maxilla of *Kenyapithecus kizili* at Paşalar. Below, the distinctive and highly derived anterior teeth of *Kenyapithecus kizili*. From left to right: I^1, broad and low crowned and prominent mesial and distal ridges depressed in the midline to form a deep V; I^2, symmetrical pointed crown bordered by mesial and distal ridges; I_1, prominent mesial and distal ridges forming deeply incised V; I_2, marginal ridges as for the central incisor. Drawings courtesy of Phi Rye.

some degree of male competition such as that seen in highly dimorphic gorillas and orang utans.

One indication of a possible difference in molar morphology between *Kenyapithecus* and *Griphopithecus* that Jay Kelley and I are considering is an apparent difference in development of lower molar cingulum. While most of the lower molars from Paşalar have cingula either weakly or strongly developed, 8% of the lower molars lack a buccal cingulum. We had earlier calculated that the 74 anterior teeth of *Kenyapithecus kizili* also constitute 8% of the total sample of anterior teeth from Paşalar, and this similarity in proportion suggests that the absence of a cingulum may be one character that

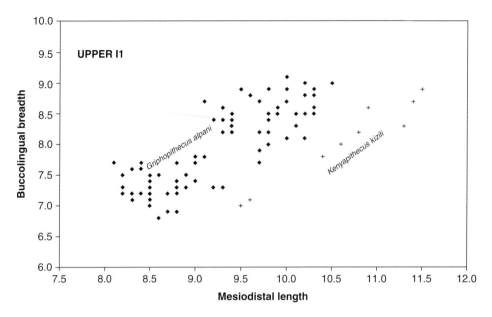

Figure 10.5 Lengths and breadths of the samples of the upper central incisor for *Kenyapithecus kizili* and *Griphopithecus alpani*. The specimens form two clusters, with the former species in the smaller cluster below the larger sample of *G. alpani*. They overlap extensively in size, but the incisors of *G. alpani* are narrower (and higher crowned), while those of *K. kizili* are broader.

distinguishes *Kenyapithecus kizili* molars. Because of the variability in development of the cingulum, however, we have so far hesitated to use it as a diagnostic character distinguishing the two species.

No postcrania that can be attributed to *Kenyapithecus kizili* are known from Paşalar. The 21 phalanges from this site described in Chapter 9 may have included one or two specimens from this species (by chance alone there could be 1.68 specimens of *K. kizili* – that is, 8% of the 21 phalanges), but there was nothing distinctive about any of them to suggest a second species was involved. We therefore have no evidence on the postcrania of this species. There is a single humerus from Fort Ternan that is attributed to *Kenyapithecus wickeri*. It is similar to the humerus of *Equatorius africanus* from Maboko Island, indicating that the Fort Ternan ape was also a quadruped with both arboreal and terrestrial adaptations. This evidence for some degree of ground living, however, continues the theme first encountered in the early Miocene apes.

Similarly, no differences were found in molar microwear within the Paşalar sample, although since we could not positively identify any molars belonging to *K. kizili* the significance of this observation is doubtful. The similarities in molar morphology between the species of *Kenyapithecus* and *Griphopithecus*, their shared incisor heteromorphy, enlarged premolars and massive inferior buttressing of the mandibular symphysis have all been linked with hard fruit diets, and this is consistent with the seasonal environments they occupied.

Summary

- *Kenyapithecus* species have distinct anterior tooth morphologies (incisors, canines and premolars) that are derived with respect to earlier and contemporaneous fossil apes.
- Molar morphology is not distinct from afropithecines except for the possibility that the lower molars lack buccal cingula.
- Upper and lower jaws are extremely robust and molar enamel is thick.
- No evidence is available on the postcranial adaptations of *Kenyapithecus kizili*, but a single limb bone of *Kenyapithecus wickeri* indicates quadrupedal locomotion similar to that of proconsulids.
- Sexual dimorphism is high in *Kenyapithecus kizili*, suggesting their social organization was based on single male social systems.

Chapter 11
The environment during the middle Miocene

Separate chapters have been given to afropithecines and kenyapithecines from Africa and Europe, both because they represent the first apes to leave Africa and because the latter group has strongly derived characters distinguishing it from earlier apes. The two groups will be treated together in the present chapter, however, for they also share many aspects of morphology, for example in the molars and jaws, and there is little difference in the environments associated with the two groups, not least when they are found together at one site. In other words, there does not seem to be a significant adaptive shift accompanying either the move into Europe or the morphological innovations seen in the kenyapithecines.

Environments in Europe

Ecological reconstruction of the site at Engelswies is based on several lines of evidence all indicating subtropical woodland where the earliest record of fossil hominids outside Africa is known. The evidence comes from several different stratigraphic levels, with small mammals at one level, large mammals from several metres below and plant remains from yet another level. The plant remains show the presence of an evergreen laurophyllous flora growing in a subtropical humid climate. This is a relic of the oak–laurel–palm forests that extended across southern Europe during the Paleogene and early Neogene supported by monsoonal climates with warm, wet summers and frost-free winters. Lower temperatures across Europe and the change to a pattern of winter rainfall have resulted in the replacement of laurel forests by schlerophyllous evergreen and broad-leaved deciduous forests over most of their range, but during the middle Miocene the floral evidence shows that subtropical conditions persisted, such as at Engelswies. The structure of these woodlands that still exist today is a single discontinuous upper canopy, often with conifers such as redwoods (*Sequoia* species) and a lower and denser evergreen canopy of laurels.

Analysis of the community structure of the mammal fauna from Engelswies is based on a composite fauna of large and small mammals, even though they are found in different levels. Even combining the two sets, the Engelswies fauna is small and only partially representative of the original fauna, and there is no information on the taphonomic bias affecting the fossil assemblages. Bearing these limitations in mind, terrestrial species have highest representation but only slightly higher than semi-arboreal species. Arboreal species are also relatively abundant, and browsing herbivores dominate, with few grazers, and frugivores are also well represented. Comparison of the Paşalar fossil fauna distribution with that of Engelswies is shown in Figure 11.1: both are intermediate but offset from the recent faunas; the high proportions of both terrestrial species and frugivores suggest something unlike any environment today. The ecological diversity distributions in Figure 11.1 indicate an environment at Paşalar with plentiful fruit and browse, limited opportunities for arboreal activity, but little grass for grazers. The vegetation was dominated by trees, but not multi-canopied as in tropical forest but a single canopy woodland, with movement of larger arboreal species probably being mainly along the ground. This is consistent with the evidence from the Engelswies flora for monsoonal (i.e. seasonal summer rainfall) woodlands.

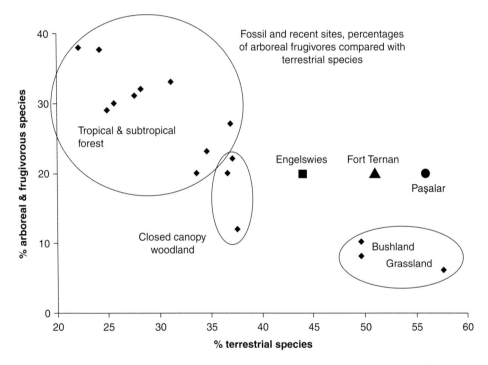

Figure 11.1 Ecological diversity plot comparing percentages of arboreal and frugivorous species with percentages of terrestrial species in recent and fossil faunas. Three main groups of recent faunas are tropical and subtropical forest faunas (top left), closed canopy woodland faunas (middle) and grassland and bushland faunas (bottom right). The three middle Miocene fossil faunas are from Engelswies, Fort Ternan and Paşalar, and all three have percentages of arboreal and frugivorous species similar to woodland and the lower limits forest faunas. Paşalar has the highest proportion of terrestrial species similar to open grassland faunas, but percentages for the other two sites are closer to woodland/bushland faunas.

Only a single hominid tooth has been recovered from Engelswies, but the available sample from Paşalar in Turkey is much larger. The fossiliferous sediments at Paşalar outcrop in a narrow valley cut through metamorphosed limestone. They form a small pocket probably no more than $50\,m^2$ on the edge of a long series of sediments that for the most part contain scattered middle Miocene fossils. The fossiliferous sediments consist of sands and gravels sandwiched between two calcareous palaeosols, greyish green in colour, with high clay content and with many calcareous nodules. Multiple soil formations occurred in both calcareous units as sediment built up and buried lower soils. The upper calcareous silt is poorly fossiliferous, but the faunal composition is the same as for the fossiliferous sands and gravels, which were deposited as a debris flow on top of the lower calcareous silt. This in turn developed immediately on top of the bedrock. Concentrations of gravel with many fossil bones occur in and above potholes (Figure 11.2), some of which formed as vertical fluid escape structures resembling the residues left after burning out of tree trunks but formed under very different conditions. Other potholes extend from the basement rock, up through the lower calcareous silt and into the sands and gravels, and these are spring deposits rising up from fissures in the underlying metamorphosed limestones (see Chapter 6, Figure 6.1). None of the spring or gravel pipes extend beyond the top of the fossiliferous sands. There was thus extensive reworking of the sediments after deposition by water flowing vertically through the sediments and producing in places a vertical stratigraphy, sorting and concentrating fossils into the vertical concentrations of gravels.

The morphology and abundance of the calcareous nodules in the calcareous silts is a feature of semi-arid soils with a mean annual rainfall of 450 to 650 mm.

 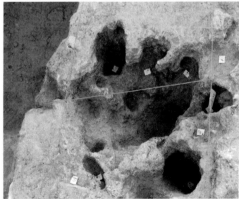

Figure 11.2 Two views of Paşalar showing the extensive system of potholes extending all through the fossiliferous sands and gravels. The potholes generally had coarser elements of the sediment, coarse sands and gravels, and some of them had many fossils, particularly of larger animals, while some were unfossiliferous.

Their presence indicates prolonged dry periods during the formation of the fossil soils as water evaporated from the soils and calcium carbonate precipitated out as calcareous nodules. In contrast to this, gleying is present in the calcareous silts, indicated by the greyish white colour produced in iron-reducing conditions, and this is caused by periods of high moisture content in the calcareous silts and periods of waterlogging of the soils during the wet seasons. This combination of gleying and calcareous nodule formation indicates strong seasonal changes, with long dry seasons when the soils dried out and calcareous nodules formed, succeeded by high precipitation during which the soils became waterlogged. It is evident, therefore, that the climate was strongly seasonal with pronounced wet and dry periods.

Our investigations of the geology have shown that the source material for the fossiliferous sands was close by the site. Most of the other sediments in the region were derived from the igneous rocks that outcrop further up the valley above the site, but the sediments making up the small pocket of fossiliferous deposits are largely composed of the local metamorphosed Mesozoic rocks within 2 to 3 km of the site. In other words, the fossiliferous sediments were not transported from far away but probably came from the neighbouring hillsides. The marbles exposed next to the fossil site dip strongly towards the fossil site, and since the deposits have the characteristics of a debris flow, similar to a massive mudslide down into the valley, the Paşalar sediments are taken to be essentially a single deposit representing a single moment of time, transported down from the side of the valley.

The debris flow would have picked up any and all bones lying about on the surface of the hillside above the present fossil site, but this leaves open the question of how the bones accumulated on the hills. The presence of all stages of weathering on many of the fossil bones, and some signs of carnivore ravaging on others, shows that before transport to the site (and before fossilization) the bones were exposed on the surface for a period of time. What that period is we do not know, for the evidence was destroyed in the debris flow that moved the bones to their present site, but the weathering profiles and root marks suggest a period of some hundreds of years.

The mammalian fossils from Paşalar are in general fragmentary with isolated teeth being the most abundant element. However, there are some mandibles and partial skulls, particularly of bovids and suids, and significantly there are numerous tooth rows more or less in place in the sediment, including several rows of fossil ape teeth (Chapter 9, Figure 9.6). In some cases, both left and right tooth rows are found together, without any bone, indicating that they were originally emplaced in the sediment as parts of upper or lower jaws, but the bone has decayed leaving the teeth still in the position they occupied in the jaws. This is clearly a secondary effect due to the water flow through the sediments, but the extreme fragmentation of the fossils is equally clearly the effect of being transported to the site as part of a debris flow, which has destroyed all but the strongest elements. These results provide a picture of bones accumulating in two phases; first, on a surface close to the fossil site, some becoming weathered, some buried, some brought in by carnivores; and second, the whole accumulation was then picked up and transported in a debris flow to the fossil site in a single catastrophic event. As noted above, there was also a post-depositional phase in which bones forming part of the sediment were destroyed by water movement through the sediments.

A wide range of mammals is preserved at Paşalar, from small insectivores to elephants and rhinos. Small mammals are under-represented both in species diversity and abundance of specimens, and by far the most common animals are small to medium-sized ungulates. We analysed the carbon isotopes on ten of the large herbivores from Paşalar, ranging from bovids and pigs to rhinos and proboscideans. Three carnivore species were also analysed. They indicate diets dominated by C_3 plants, with some species like the giraffe and the most common small bovid with depleted $\delta^{13}C$ values feeding only on C_3 plants, but some were mixed feeders inclining more towards enriched C_3 or C_4 plants. In either case, a more open environment is indicated, and the C4 signal may have been due to water stress in a highly seasonal environment. *Griphopithecus alpani* had an intermediate signal. The clustering of values for most taxa from Paşalar suggests that some mammals were consistently selecting their food from particular parts of the environment. Open grassland is not indicated by the isotopic results, but neither is forest, and some form of woodland with open areas is the general conclusion from the isotopes. This interpretation has been reinforced by recent comparisons of isotope values from a large population of chimpanzees from the Kibale Forest, Uganda, for in comparison with chimpanzees, *Griphopithecus alpani* is linked with the terrestrial part of the Paşalar fauna.

The most common species at Paşalar is the artiodactyl *Caprotragoides stehlini*, which constitutes nearly half of the specimens, so the evenness of the fauna is low. The fossil apes are next most abundant, while 33 species in the Paşalar fauna are represented by only one or two individuals. This highly asymmetric distribution is very distinctive, and I compared it with the expected distribution for a log series distribution. The statistical test (chi-squared value of 5.71 for 7 degrees of freedom) showed no significant difference from a log series distribution. This was a highly significant result, for log series ecological models apply to environments dominated by one or two factors, such as extreme aridity, monocultures or highly seasonal environments. However, the log series diversity index for the Paşalar fauna is relatively high (α = 14.016), showing departure from the log series distribution, perhaps due to small sample sizes of many of the mammal species. What this seems to show is that the environment at Paşalar was indeed highly seasonal, but it was not arid and was probably a form of monsoon woodland.

The Paşalar fauna is dominated by terrestrial species, but also with many arboreal species (Figure 11.1). Bovids, giraffids, rhinos and horses were also abundant and contribute to the high terrestrial component of the fauna. The distribution of dietary categories of the Paşalar fauna is similar to that of Engelswies, both dominated by browsing herbivores but with substantial numbers of frugivores as well. However, there were at least two species at Paşalar with hypsodont teeth. The adaptive profile of the Paşalar fauna is closest to present-day faunas from subtropical monsoon woodlands of India growing in highly seasonal climates (Figure 11.1), with intermediate levels of arboreal and frugivorous species. Taking the pattern as a whole, the ecological diversity spectra that I published for the Paşalar fauna are also similar to those of present-day tropical woodland faunas.

To examine more closely the evident bias against small mammals in the accumulation of the Paşalar fauna, I tested it against the patterns obtained from present-day faunas after selectively removing species from the modern faunas. The faunas that I used were 23 mammal communities representing habitats from specific times and places ranging from tropical rainforest to semi-desert. We have already seen in Figure 11.1 that the ecological diversity of the Paşalar fauna is intermediate between forest and woodland, and after removal of between 30 and 50% of the small species from the modern faunas, the pattern of the Paşalar fauna moved away from the forest pattern to become closer to that of tropical woodland. In other words, the reduced diversity of the Paşalar fauna, limited as it was by taphonomic bias, gives a slightly misleading picture of the environment present, and correcting for the known bias has produced a result that I believe is a more realistic one for the site.

The ecomorphology of the carnivores from Paşalar showed the presence of four carnivore guilds, hypercarnivores, main carnivores (including some bone crushers), omnivores and insectivores. The distribution of the four carnivore guilds, together with a measure of body mass, distinguishes between habitats at the present day. The Paşalar carnivore fauna, for example, includes high proportions of insectivorous carnivores in the small size category, which shows that it is not likely to derive from temperate woodlands; high proportions of omnivorous carnivores in the small- and medium-sized categories also exclude it from being derived from tropical forest; whereas on a positive note, the high proportions of hypercarnivores in the medium-sized category is most similar to tropical woodlands and subtropical forest/woodland. It is concluded therefore that the distribution of carnivore morphologies in the Paşalar fauna is closest to that of subtropical deciduous woodlands and seasonal woodlands of Africa.

The diet of *Griphopithecus alpani* was investigated by Tania King, who compared the microwear on the molars with that of chimpanzees, gorillas and orang utans. *Griphopithecus* has significantly higher microwear feature densities and higher percentages of pits than any of the great apes, and the high numbers of pits is most similar to that seen today in orang utans (Chapter 6, Figure 6.11). This suggests that the diet of *Griphopithecus* was similar to that of the orang utan, which consumes mainly fruit, and occasionally hard and unripe fruits and nuts, but the higher percentage of pits may indicate that it was ingesting harder fruits and/or objects. For example, over half of the microwear features on *Griphopithecus* were pits, whereas with extant hominoids only about one third were pits, which suggests that the fossil ape exploited a different kind of hard fruit. This is not surprising since it was associated with a habitat in which no living ape could survive.

The conclusion from these independent lines of inquiry, therefore, is that the environment in middle Miocene times at Paşalar, and associated with the abundant remains of *Griphopithecus alpani*, was most similar to deciduous subtropical woodland. The woodland would have had a single tree canopy with abundant ground vegetation but incorporating open areas, and it was set in a highly seasonal environment with summer rainfall (monsoon) and a long dry season. Open woodland or grassy woodland was also present. We cannot say at present if the vegetation was taxonomically similar to the laurel forests of Engelswies because of the absence of plant fossils at Paşalar, but structurally the types of vegetation were probably similar at the two sites. It may also be inferred that the availability of food would also have been similar, with the degree of seasonality restricting soft fruit availability to the wetter months, and fall-back foods consumed during the cooler dry season. Likewise, the mixture of substrates would have been similar at the two sites, with the single canopy restricting tree to tree movement for larger arboreal animals and the existence of more open areas making necessary some degree of movement on the ground.

The two ape species are represented by very different samples: there are nearly 100 individuals of *Griphopithecus alpani* based on a sample of just under 2000 specimens, while the nine individuals of *Kenyapithecus kizili* have 74 specimens. We cannot tell at present what the environment of *Kenyapithecus kizili* was like, since we believe that it was intrusive at the site and came from some distance away. The nine individuals attributed to this species, seven males and two females, are all young adult individuals at exactly the same stage of maturity, with just the beginnings of wear on their teeth. This age structure differs from that of *Griphopithecus alpani*, for which all age classes are represented, with many deciduous teeth from juveniles and heavily worn teeth from old adults. In a remarkable piece of detective work, Jay Kelley has shown additionally that the nine individuals all passed through precisely the same developmental stages. The evidence for this is based on the presence of two hypoplastic lines on each of the upper central incisors, showing that two traumatic events occurred at exactly the same stage of development for all nine individuals (Figure 11.3). Hypoplasias are interruptions in enamel growth on the teeth during infancy, such as shortage of food or during weaning, and it is seen on many fossil teeth, including the much more abundant incisors of *Griphopithecus alpani*. What is different about the hypoplasias on the *Kenyapithecus kizili* teeth, however, is that they are all in the same position on the crowns of the teeth, so that they occurred at the same stage of development on each individual, and on each tooth the two lines are separated by exactly the same interval of time as determined by counts of perikymata. The evidence of the hypoplasias indicates that the nine individuals were all born at more or less the same time and they were affected by identical traumatic events during their development. The chances of identical patterns of hypoplasia being repeated in different months or years are extremely small. When this is combined with the similarities in wear stage of the teeth, it appears that all nine individuals were also close to the same age when they died, and they also all died close together in time. What is even more striking is that the differences in developmental periods shown by the

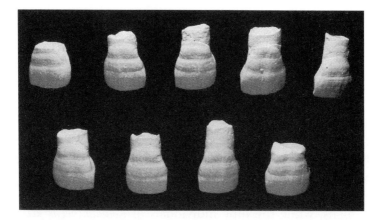

Figure 11.3 Nine upper incisors of *Kenyapithecus kizili* showing the double hypoplasias on each of the teeth. The intervals between the two hypoplastic episodes are close to identical for all the teeth, including specimens not shown here; the time intervals for the formation of the hypoplasias are based on counts of perikymata forming between the two episodes, so that the events that caused these growth anomalies were common to all nine individuals (four of the teeth, or two pairs, belong to two individuals). The likelihood of two such events producing near-identical hypoplasias and affecting seven individuals born in different years is extremely remote, and the conclusion is that these individuals were all born at approximately the same time and in the same place, that is, they form a birth cohort. Apparently they also died as they lived, for the teeth of all individuals of *K. kizili* are at equivalent wear stages indicating that they were similar aged young adults when they died. Photo courtesy of Jay Kelley.

hypoplasias on the teeth of *K. kizili* means that the nine individuals representing this species must have grown up in a place different from *G. alpani*, as none of the hypoplasias on the teeth of the latter match either one of the pair on the former.

The differences in abundance, nine young adult individuals of *K. kizili* compared with the 94 juveniles and adults of *Griphopithecus alpani*, suggests that the *K. kizili* individuals could have been an itinerant or immigrant population. They may have been part of a travelling group like those described for chimpanzees by Mitani in Kibale Forest, or even just a hunting party that was caught in the wrong place at the wrong time. How far they may have travelled, and from what type of environment, is not known.

Summary of environments in Europe

- Afropithecines are known from Europe at sites in Germany, the Czech Republic and Paşalar, Turkey.
- Fossil plants at Engelswies indicate an evergreen laurophyllous flora in a subtropical humid climate in the middle Miocene of Germany.
- The Engelswies mammal fauna has many terrestrial frugivores and browsers, indicating woodland.
- The Paşalar deposits accumulated rapidly in a debris flow and were affected post-depositionally by spring flow up from the bedrock below.
- Above and below the fossiliferous sands and clays are two calcareous silts, with gleying indicating waterlogged conditions and calcareous nodules indicating seasonal drying, with an estimated rainfall of 450 to 650 mm; together these indicate a highly seasonal habitat with enough rainfall to support woodland but not forest.
- Before transport to the site, some bones and teeth were exposed on the surface for a period of time, indicated by weathering alteration on the bones, and some were buried, indicated by root marks.
- Carbon isotopes of herbivore teeth from Paşalar show mainly C_3 diets but some indicate C_4 diets.
- The microwear on *Griphopithecus alpani* teeth indicates adaptation for hard object diets.
- The bones accumulated at a place within a few kilometres of the fossil site and were transported to the site at Paşalar in a debris flow.
- The carnivore guild structure of the Paşalar fauna identifies with those from tropical woodlands.
- Large mammals from Paşalar include many frugivores and terrestrial species, unlike the pattern seen in any recent habitat but equivalent to a closed canopy woodland.

177

- The woodland had a single tree canopy, abundant ground vegetation and incorporated open areas, and it was set in a highly seasonal environment with summer rainfall (monsoon) and a long dry season.
- Open woodland or grassy woodland was also present.

Environments in Africa

Afropithecines from the middle Miocene of Africa are known mainly from rift valley deposits and the Tugen Hills in Kenya. The carbon isotopes for a range of sites show that environments in the Tugen Hills were extremely varied from the middle Miocene onwards, as in fact they are today. Several independent analyses of the carbon isotopes have shown varying degrees of woody cover, from closed canopy woodland to open woodland. The published faunas associated with the fossil apes also indicate that probably non-forest environments were present.

When we excavated the Maboko Island sites, we were able to show that the bone assemblage was accumulated in and around a shallow lake or flood plain, with many of the bones having been trampled into the soft mud so that they were lying nearly vertically in the mud (Figure 11.4). Many aquatic animals were present, including fish, frogs, salamanders, varanid lizards and crocodiles. We also found monkey fossils at this level, but no fossil apes; these were present at another site on the island of approximately the same age but with the fauna indicating slightly drier conditions. The mammals present, however,

Figure 11.4 A photo of the author excavating in the shallow lake beds on Maboko Island. We were able to reconstruct the environment with some degree of precision by careful excavation and measuring the way the fossils were located in the sediments, particularly the angle they were lying at in the fine silty clays.

were similar for all three sites that we investigated, and they were dominated by bovids, rhinos and proboscideans, with the common rodents being generalized non-forest species, and our conclusion from this was that the environment at Maboko Island consisted of woodlands bordering a shallow lake or flood plain.

Louis Leakey excavated Fort Ternan for many years, and his excavations had cut deeply into the hillside, following a richly fossiliferous layer into the hill. When Alan Walker and I made plans to extend the excavation, there was some uncertainty about whether it could be done because of the amount of over-burden that would have to be removed before we could get access to the fossiliferous levels. I spent several months working with a large team of local workers digging out about $60\,m^3$ of solid rock so as to uncover the fossil horizons. Several palaeosols were formed throughout the long sequence, but only two have proved to be fossiliferous. Mica flakes in the upper palaeosol have been dated to just under 14 million years, and phonolite lavas above and below the fossil soils further constrain the dating (Figure 11.5). The fossiliferous palaeosols are Chogo and Onuria palaeosols, soil types that we know from present-day examples form beneath tropical grassland. Three species of grass have been preserved in another palaeosol higher up the section, and they have been identified as belonging to the families Panicoideae and Chlorideae, the modern species of which follow the C_4 photosynthetic pathway at low to intermediate altitudes but C_3 at high altitude. It is not likely that the setting at Fort Ternan could have been alpine meadow, and there is no evidence of the sediments having accumulated in a wetland setting, which also could have altered the isotopic setting to C_3. During the clearing of the site in 1973 I noted a fine grass horizon in a palaeosol above the fossiliferous Chogo palaeosol. Regrettably I did not photograph this horizon, expecting to find it on my next visit, but so fast did the site clearing proceed that by the time I returned the grass horizon had vanished. What it showed was a continuous grass sward, with the tops of the grass bent over and buried by the sediments above, and there is no doubt that it showed the presence of an area of open grassland present at the site. Open areas of grass may form in woodlands and forest, particularly in an area subject to continued disturbance by volcanic eruptions, and two pieces of information are needed to interpret this finding. One is that the area exposed for examination is big enough to show the landscape setting rather than the limited area exposed at Fort Ternan; and the other is the element of time, for the grass horizon was in a later palaeosol, probably laid down many thousands of years after the fossiliferous palaeosols, and it may have been an ephemeral area of grass resulting from habitat disturbance. Grass can colonize an area quickly, and just as quickly disappear when trees regenerate, without the episode being recorded by the isotopic signal of the soils.

(a)

(b)

Figure 11.5 Two views of Fort Ternan. (a) The site as discovered in 1960 when it was exposed on the surface of the hillside, so that initial excavations were on the surface of the hill; fossils were exposed in great abundance on the surface in fossil soils. (b) Subsequent excavations required deep cuts into the hill. Both photos by the late Shirley Coryndon, who worked at the site when it was first discovered, and who is shown on the left.

The carbon isotopes from three of the palaeosols, including the Chogo palaeosol from which *Kenyapithecus wickeri* was recovered, show that the $\delta^{13}C$ values for the Fort Ternan fossil soils are at the negative end of the values both for soil organic matter and for soil carbonates, indicating vegetation with C_3 photosynthetic pathways. Closed canopy tree cover is indicated by these results, either woodland or forest. Similarly, the carbon isotopes on the teeth of nine herbivores from Fort Ternan, including the two bovids that constitute a large proportion of the fauna, also show the C_3 photosynthetic pathway, which indicates diets of browse on leaves of trees and bushes rather than grass. A question to be raised here is what kinds of grass were present in African habitats before the spread of C_4 grasses, which according to the more recent publication by Cerling did not take place until 7 to 8 million years ago. Were there open country C_3 grasses present in the middle Miocene that were replaced by C_4 grasses?

The fossil fauna from Fort Ternan (Figure 11.5) appears to have been derived from two or more sources. The common animals that make up by far the greatest proportion of the fauna are well preserved and are relatively intact, with many skulls and limb bones. This indicates that the animal remains were not transported any great distance to the site prior to fossilization, and they consisted therefore of a local fauna, that is, of animals living and dying in close proximity to the site. They were probably transported to the site by surface sheet wash rather than river or stream action, and such channels as occur in this situation are shallow and poorly defined. In both fossiliferous palaeosols, the fossils are aggregated both horizontally and vertically, with concentrations of fossils in some areas surrounded by barren deposits. The vertical distribution is particularly interesting, for it suggests limited periods of deposition and erosion while the bones were being brought together and deposited in small channels or gullies extending across the site. The fossils are oriented randomly in these gullies, which indicates that they were not laid down all at once but accumulated as a result of episodic events, which both brought in new bones and disturbed the orientations of previously deposited bones. The duration of these episodes is hard to determine, but it was probably in the region of many hundreds of years. The fossil specimens are relatively complete and well preserved and had not been weathered. They also showed little sign of abrasion, which indicates that most of them were transported quickly to the site from a short distance away and buried in the sediments before they were weathered. The *K. wickeri* specimens formed part of this assemblage.

In contrast to this assemblage, a second group of fossils is made up of fragmentary teeth and bones. More than half the fossils in this group were abraded during transport to the site, and many of them are heavily weathered. The highest degrees of weathering are present on the most abraded bones, and the two types of modification appear to be highly correlated, both features suggesting that the bones were exposed for longer periods of time and were transported to the site from further away. This fossil assemblage includes the faunal elements that appear to indicate the presence of forest, for example the flying squirrel and prosimian primates, and it is evident from the taphonomic modifications that it was transported to the site at Fort Ternan from some distance away. The specimens of proconsulid are also part of this assemblage.

Less than one quarter of the fossils overall showed signs of carnivore activity, and it is not likely that carnivores were significant contributors to either the main fossil assemblage or the more fragmentary assemblage. Three of the nine specimens of *Kenyapithecus wickeri* have chewing marks from carnivores, a proportion comparable to that of similar sized animals like the gazelles and tragulids. In all other respects, the state of preservation of the *Kenyapithecus* specimens indicates that they were part of the main faunal assemblage at the site.

The fossil fauna from Fort Ternan has 57 species recorded. The fossil bovid *Oioceros* is the most common, and its sample of 87 individuals is a large enough sample to be able to analyse the age structure of the species. Highest mortality occurred in the young and old individuals, with mature adults having low mortality. This is similar to the pattern observed today for animals dying as a result of attritional mortality (i.e. highest death rates in the young and old) and low mortality in mature adults. This is the common pattern found when animals die 'naturally' through processes such as accident, predation and starvation, and it provides a good representation of the animals present in the Miocene community. Taken together with the evidence that *Oioceros* is a prominent part of the proximal assemblage it is probable that this assemblage can provide a good indication of the local environment.

We know from work on ecomorphology that the bovids have adaptations that are neither indicators of open grassland nor forest. For example, we have seen in Chapter 6 that the head of the femur at the hip joint is functionally related to habitat type in modern bovids. The Fort Ternan bovids have an intermediate morphology in their hip joints, the head of the femur being neither rounded nor cylindrical, which compares today with bovids living in closed cover bushland and woodland habitats such as impala or bushbuck. The microwear of the teeth of the bovid *Oioceros* showed that it was a habitual grazer, while the other common bovid species was an intermediate feeder, eating both grass and browse. This suggests that the environment included both open areas of grass and closed cover woodland, but perhaps the area was more open than closed, for grass is the common vegetation type growing under open woodland. Combining this evidence with that from the sediments, palaeosols and isotopes, the general conclusions are that: both open grassland and closed canopy woodland were present at or close to the fossil site; there was also forest in the vicinity (indicated by the minor, transported element of the fauna); and *Kenya-pithecus wickeri* was associated with the more open parts of the habitat. Its apparent association with another ape species at Fort Ternan turns out to be false, since the two ape species belonged to different faunal associations and came from different environments.

Summary of environments in Africa

- The environments associated with afropithecines at the African sites are poorly known, but indicate woodland vegetation. The better documented sites from Europe indicate subtropical woodland.
- The environment on Maboko Island was lakeside or shallow water flood plain with no evidence of forest, although the abundance of monkeys indicates some form of tree vegetation.
- The environments at Nachola and Kipsaramon are taken to indicate woodland, but the evidence is poor.
- Kenyapithecines are known from two sites, Fort Ternan in Kenya and Paşalar again in Turkey.
- The fossil soils at Fort Ternan indicate the presence of grassland or wooded grassland during the middle Miocene.
- The carbon isotopes at Fort Ternan indicate the presence of closed canopy woodland.
- Different modes of preservation at Fort Ternan show that most of the fauna was transported to the site from a short distance away and represents the local fauna living close to the site.
- The second mode of preservation is present on a small element of the fauna, indicating exposure of the bones on the surface and transport from further away from a forest habitat.
- The *Kenyapithecus wickeri* specimens were part of the local assemblage, which included mainly open country grazers.
- There is little evidence of carnivore activity except on intermediate–small mammals the size of *Kenyapithecus* and gazelles.
- It is concluded that both closed and open woodland was present at Fort Ternan, with forest nearby, and that *Kenyapithecus wickeri* was associated with the more open parts of the habitat.

Chapter 12
A second view from Europe

During the second half of the middle Miocene and extending into the late Miocene, there was a proliferation of fossil apes in Europe and Asia, postdating the early arrivals described in Chapters 9 and 10 by several million years. There are also a small number of genera and species known in Africa, as mentioned in Chapter 4, and they will be discussed again later, but here I am going to describe the place of the dryopithecines in human ancestry. The genus *Dryopithecus* has passed through several stages in its history, from the time when it included almost all known fossil apes, after the 1965 revision by Elwyn Simons and David Pilbeam, to the later part of the twentieth century when almost everything except *Dryopithecus* itself had been removed. The Dryopithecinae now is split into six genera and species, one species to each genus (Table 4.3). This situation will certainly change in the future, with some of the species and genera perhaps being combined and new ones found. For the purposes of this book, I have retained the names currently in use, but to avoid overloading the reader with too many names I will be using mainly the genus names.

No monographic treatment has yet been attempted on the dryopithecines, although Johannes Hürzeler was planning to prepare a monograph on European dryopithecines similar to his one on pliopithecids. At the time when I was touring Europe examining and measuring fossil apes, Hürzeler had collected most of the known dryopithecine fossils at his office in Basel, and he was most generous in sharing the specimens and his thoughts about them with me. Meeting him was one of the highlights of my European tour, but it was frustrating that his work was not completed at the time of his death. My descriptions of dryopithecine morphology has followed his methodology, as has all my taxonomic work on fossil apes, and it is a tribute to him and his far-sighted approach that, at a time when most anthropologists concentrated on naming new species (as they still do today), he was attempting to synthesize and analyse all that was available in the fossil record. In this chapter, I will concentrate on the species with the best-preserved specimens, *Hispanopithecus laietanus* from Spain. The type specimen is shown here (Figure 12.1) compared with a species of *Dryopithecus*, and differences between some of the species will be noted as we go along.

(a)   (b)

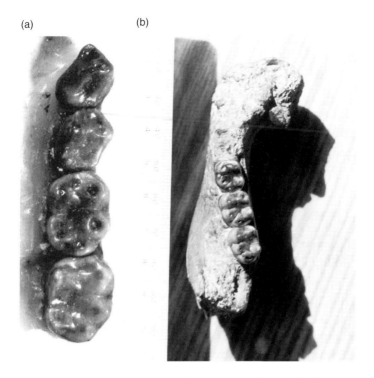

Figure 12.1 (a) Type specimen of *Hispanopithecus laietanus*, a tooth row with the crowns of P_3 to M_2. The length of the tooth row is 33.4 mm, which gives an idea of just how small this fossil ape was (Villalta & Crusafont 1964). (b) the three molars from the mandible of *Dryopithecus crusafonti* from Seo d'Urgell (tooth row length 32.7 mm).

Villalta and Miquel Crusafont first described *Hispanopithecus laietanus* in 1944 from the site of La Tarumba 1 (Villadecaballs, Barcelona) (Figure 12.1). They found many specimens of jaws and teeth at a site that Crusafont first came upon when he had joined a geological excursion in northwest Spain. The site is Can Llobateres, and the result of his endeavours has left a big cut out of the hillside, which he showed me when I first visited Spain in the summer of 1968. Crusafont was a charming man and took me and my wife on a tour of all the then known Miocene sites in northeastern Spain. I visited him again with Lawrence Martin in 1981 when he was suffering terribly from throat cancer, and despite his illness he was still as charming and helpful as he could be. His efforts produced the first extensive collection of fossil apes in Europe and he is now remembered from the institute he founded, *Palaeontology Institute "Miquel Crusafont"*. After his death the site at Can Llobateres was abandoned, for it appeared to be all worked out. However, one of his successors at the institute, Salvador Moyà-Solà, started searching the area again, and just along the hillside from Crusafont's pit, and at a slightly higher level, Moyà-Solà and Meike Köhler found a partial skull which they attributed to *Dryopithecus laietanus*.

They extended their search the following year, and from the same level as the skull, but scattered over 900 m², they found a large part of the skeleton, almost certainly from the same individual as the skull. The level from which this fossil ape came is slightly later in time than the fossils from Crusafont's excavation, with a date of 10 to 9 million years. More recently, Moyà-Solà and Köhler have reinstated *Hispanopithecus* as the generic name for *H. laietanus*. Because of the potential confusion about the site and the naming of this fossil ape, I have figured here the type specimen (Figure 12.1), which I do not believe has been illustrated since it was first described in 1964.

The skull and dentition of great ape-like fossils

The skull of *Hispanopithecus laietanus* is lightly built, as in other fossil apes, with fairly well-developed brow ridges. The nose is narrow and the distance between the eyes is broad (Figure 12.2). In these features it resembles earlier fossil apes such as *Proconsul*, but unlike these the cheek region is flatter and directed more forwards, in some cases similar to the condition in orang utans. This is also a feature of *Sivapithecus* and (probably) of *Kenyapithecus*, and it differs from the muzzle-like shape of the lower face of *Proconsul* and *Afropithecus*. The anatomy of the floor of the nose and the incisive fossa in the palate retains the primitive condition and differs little from *Proconsul* and *Griphopithecus* but differs greatly from the derived region in the great apes and especially from the orang utan. Its cheek teeth are primitively small and have relatively thin enamel, unlike other fossil apes from the same period. In fact, most dryopithecine teeth differ from the primitive pattern seen in *Proconsul* only in minor details, such as loss of the upper molar lingual cingulum.

In all these features, the skull of *Hispanopithecus* is similar to the partial skull of *Rudapithecus* from Rudabánya in Hungary (Figure 12.2). The Rudabánya sediments are about the same age as Can Llobateres, but the depositional setting is different, as will be described below. The mining geologist Gabor Hernyak discovered the site when he found a partial lower jaw in Miocene sediments, and he gave it to Miklos Kretzoi to identify. Kretzoi named it *Rudapithecus hungaricus*, and so it is called today after passing through a number of other species and genus names over the ensuing years. I contacted Kretzoi in 1978 and asked to come and see his new fossils, which at that time he kept at his home in Budapest. Budapest in those days was a different place from the way it is now; hotels were few and far between, and so Kretzoi said he would arrange accommodation for when Libby and I arrived there. With great difficulty we located the apartment block where he lived, rang the bell and waited. We could hear noises inside the flat, so rang the bell again, and again. Still no answer, and with

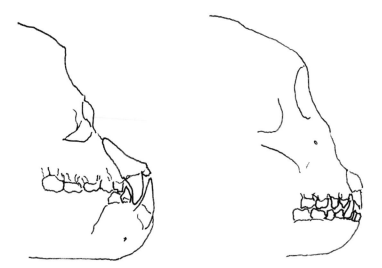

Figure 12.2 The skulls of *H. laietanus* (left) and *R. hungaricus* (right) compared.

nowhere else to go we camped out in the lobby of his apartment block, and there we waylaid him several hours later as he was on his way out. He seemed surprised to see us, but set to right away to find us accommodation. This he eventually did, in a Soviet-style apartment block in a wilderness of land on the outskirts of Budapest with what seemed like hundreds of regimented apartment blocks extending as far as the eye could see. The apartment was rented by a soldier in the Hungarian army, a friendly man but whose remit did not include providing food or speaking any language that we could understand. The area did not run to restaurants, and it was now too late to find any shops open, and so we had to wait until the following day before getting any food.

After these minor mishaps, we had a delightful stay in Budapest and Kretzoi was generous with information and photographs of his fossil apes, all of which he habitually kept locked in a cupboard at his home. It was quite common at this time for elder statesmen of the academic world to keep the fossils they found at their homes, sometimes in cupboards, sometimes under their bed, and it always involved patient negotiation for foreign visitors to arrange to see them. In Kretzoi's case I was lucky, for whereas he could be persuaded to show his fossils to an English student, he refused absolutely to show them to his fellow countrymen and particularly his students.

My second trip to Hungary took place when Ray Bernor invited me to direct new excavations at Rudabánya 2, the site from which much of Kretzoi's dryopithecine material had come. Lazslo Kordos had also found a partial skull from the same site, and it was clearly the most prolific of the Rudabánya sites. The sedimentary sequence is too short to tie into the geomagnetic timescale, and there are no volcanics that could be used for dating, and so dating the site relies on comparing its mammalian fauna with those of other, better dated sites. On the basis of the evolutionary stage of the fauna, Rudabánya 2 fits into the MN9 land mammal stage, similar in faunal composition to the late Miocene faunas from the Sinap Formation (late Miocene of Turkey, see Chapter 14) that has a palaeomagnetic date of older than 9.5 million years.

The characters of the teeth of *Rudapithecus hungaricus* have only minor differences from *Hispanopithecus laietanus* (see Figure 12.3, which shows the type specimen of this species): the incisors are narrow and high crowned, the canines are relatively small, the premolars lack some of the honing function present in earlier apes and monkeys, the molars have no or reduced cingula, the lower molars are elongated with broad central basins and the third lower molar is reduced in size. The characters of the nose, palate and face of the skull are all similar to the condition in *Hispanopithecus*. This is a mixture of primitive characters also present in early Miocene apes and a few derived characters, some of which are seen also in *Griphopithecus*.

There is a very active group of palaeontologists based at the Crusafont Institute in Sabadell, Spain, headed by Salvador Moyà-Solà. They have already been mentioned above as the discoverers of the skull of *Hispanopithecus,* and they have found also many of the newly available fossils in northeast Spain. More recently they have found another partial skull, which they have attributed to *Dryopithecus fontani* (Figure 12.4c). This was a bold step, for the type specimen of *D. fontani* is a lower jaw, whereas the new specimen has the upper jaw. The partial skull of *Dryopithecus fontani* comes from Can Mata, Hostalets de Pierola, from a site well dated by magnetostratigraphy to just over 12 million years (Table 4.3). It consists of the lower face and dentition and its morphology is more primitive than that of *Hispanopithecus* and *Rudapithecus*. The face has a large triangular nose and a wide palate; it has moderately strong prognathism, that is, the front of the face is strongly sloping, so that the nose projects forwards in front of the eyes, but the alveolar prognathism, the

Figure 12.3 Type specimen of *Rudapithecus hungaricus,* a mandible with the crowns of P_4 to M_3. The specimen is very weathered and has little morphological detail, and much better specimens are now available described by Kordos (1991) and Kordos & Begun (1997). The scale bar equals 1{ts}cm.

188

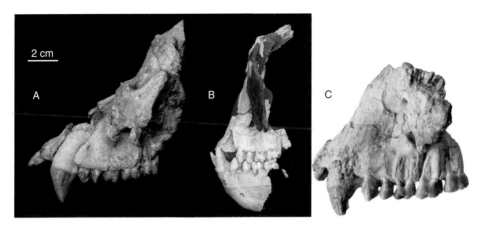

Figure 12.4 Side views of the skulls of (a) *Pierolapithecus catalaunicus,* (b) *Anoiapithecus brevirostris* and (c) *Dryopithecus fontani*. Photos courtesy of Salvador Moyà-Solà and David Alba (Moyà-Solà et al. 2009 a&b, 2004).

projection of the alveolar margin in front of the nose, is low. This combination of mid-facial prognathism but low alveolar prognathism is characteristic of early Miocene apes and differs from the great apes, where alveolar prognathism is very great, especially in the orang utan. The face is also more muzzle-like in that the nose projects in front of the cheekbones, which is similar to the condition in proconsulids and afropithecines and also the great apes, but this is probably a primitive character retained in *Dryopithecus*. The orbits of the eyes are placed well above the top of the nose, again as in proconsulids and African great apes. The canines are high crowned and robust, with a distinct honing facet where they occlude against the lower premolars. The premolars are relatively broad, and the molars are moderately broader than long, both of which are primitive characters. The third molar, however, is reduced in size, which is an unusual character not present in proconsulids, afropithecines or, for that matter, living great apes, where the third molar is approximately the same size as the second. The molars of *D. fontani* have thinner enamel than other dryopithecines.

A partial skeleton from Can Vila (Hostalets de Pierola) is named *Pierolapithecus catalaunicus* (Figure 12.5). This site is about the same age as St Gaudens, the type site of *Dryopithecus fontani*, between 12 and 13 million years. The skull appears to differ from *Dryopithecus* in the more strongly sloping face that is low and broad, unlike the straighter and narrower faces of the other dryopithecines (Figure 12.4). The skull has suffered some degree of crushing during preservation, compressing the supraorbital region, and this may have had the effect of shortening the face and broadening the eye, nose and cheek region. The front of the face is flat from side to side, with the cheekbones in

189

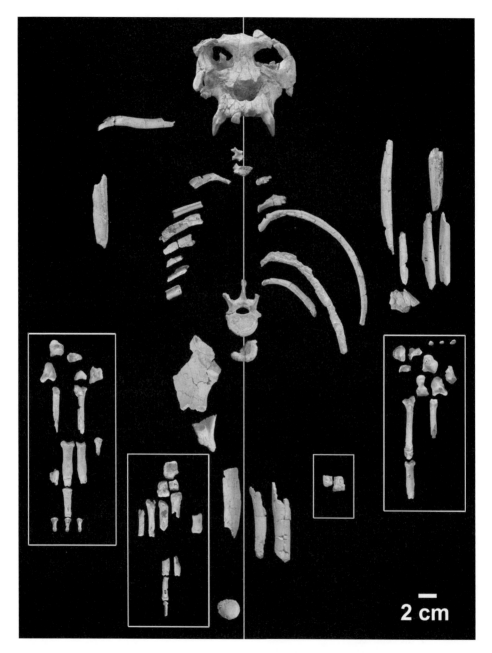

Figure 12.5 The skeleton of *Pierolapithecus catalaunicus*. Photo courtesy of Salvador Moyà-Solà and David Alba (Moyà-Solà et al. 2004).

the same plane as the nose (Figure 12.5). In this regard it is similar to orang utans and later Miocene apes like *Sivapithecus* and *Ankarapithecus*. The orbits are also low relative to the nose, although there is little difference from the condition in *Dryopithecus*. The molars and premolars of *Pierolapithecus* have thick enamel similar to that of *Sivapithecus*, *Kenyapithecus* and afropithecines, but they differ from all these in being more elongated, with the molars almost as long as broad. Both these are significant differences from *Dryopithecus*, but the third upper molar is reduced in size as it is in *Dryopithecus*. The canines are laterally compressed, more blade-like than in *Dryopithecus*, so that it is likely that the lower third premolar will be found to be high crowned with honing function. The upper central incisor is procumbent (sticking forward in line with the strongly sloping face).

The overall appearance of the face of *Pierolapithecus* is great ape-like, but there are some characters that link it with the orang utan, for example the flattened face mentioned above. The maxillary sinus is restricted anteriorly but extends posteriorly towards the ethmoid and this together with the lack of a frontal sinus are both orang utan characters. In other respects the skull either retains primitive characters, for example the large size of the incisive canal, or shares characters with the hominid clade.

The other species to be considered here is *Anoiapithecus brevirostris*, also from middle Miocene deposits at Can Mata, Hostalets de Pierola. This site is similar in age to Can Vila, about 12 million years, and a skull and mandible have been found. Remarkably, the skull combines a nearly vertical face (very reduced prognathism) with projecting narrow canines and a well-developed canine-premolar honing mechanism. It shares a number of characters with *Kenyapithecus*, as Moyà-Solà points out, including the high zygomatic root, reduced maxillary sinus set high above the roots of the upper teeth and a massive inferior torus on the mandibular symphysis. The palate is short, wide and deep and alveolar prognathism is reduced. The lower canines and third premolars are slender and high crowned, the lower molars retain traces of buccal cingula and the upper third molar is reduced in size. The molars have thick enamel, similar to the values in *Pierolapithecus* and thicker than in *Dryopithecus*. The nose is relatively narrow, widest at the base and with slightly projecting nasal bones, and the face is high and narrow. The incisive fossa is reduced compared with proconsulids but is still large and similar to the condition in *Kenyapithecus* and the later dryopithecines. Although Can Mata is 2 million years later than the latest kenyapithecine, it may be that *Anoiapithecus* should be grouped in the Kenyapithecinae.

Summary of the skull and dentition

- **Later Miocene taxa** with skulls having lightly built crania with relatively prominent brow ridges:
  moderate mid-facial prognathism but low alveolar prognathism in *D. fontani*, *H. laietanus* and *R. hungaricus*;

strong angle between face and skull (klinorhynchy) in *H. laietanus*;

primitive teeth in *D. fontani*, molars with broad basins between cusps around the periphery of the crowns, reduced/no cingulum, thin enamel, traces of lower molar cingulum; incisors with lingual pillars in *D. crusafonti*.

- **Middle Miocene taxa** with strong mid-facial prognathism but low alveolar prognathism in *Pierolapithecus*:

  nearly vertical face in *Anoiapithecus* and low alveolar prognathism;

  muzzle-like mid-face in *D. fontani*;

  flat face in *Pierolapithecus*;

  ethmoid connection in *Pierolapithecus*;

  reduced maxillary sinus;

  broad triangular nose;

  broad palate;

  high zygomatic root;

  elongated molars and premolars in *Pierolapithecus*, teeth with thick enamel;

  teeth with thick enamel in *Anoiapithecus* and *Pierolapithecus*;

  reduced M^3 in the three earlier species but not in *H. laietanus* and *R. hungaricus*.

- All five dryopithecine species share some characters with the living great apes, but some characters are shared only with the African great apes and others only with the orang utan. None are shared exclusively with humans, and it does not seem possible at this stage to link dryopithecines with one or other hominid group.

- The mosaic nature of evolutionary change depicted by the dryopithecines suggests that many of the cranial and dental similarities shared by the great apes evolved independently and should not be expected to be present in their common ancestor.

Postcranial anatomy of great ape-like fossils

Several of the dryopithecines possess postcranial features of the forelimb, hind limb and axial skeleton that are functionally related to suspensory and arboreal climbing behaviours seen in extant apes. Based on this, David Begun has proposed that *Hispanopithecus* is part of the great ape clade, that is to say, it is more closely related to the great apes than is any other fossil ape, and even more specifically he relates it to the African apes. The first specimen found was the shaft of a humerus from Saint Gaudens (Table 4.3), the same site from which the type specimens of *Dryopithecus fontani* were recovered. It is similar to the humerus of the bonobo in overall size and robusticity. Although the head of the humerus is missing, it is apparent that the head has some degree of medial torsion, unlike the arm bones of earlier fossil apes. The flattened and broad distal end of the humerus is also like that of chimpanzees and unlike monkeys, although in this case the ape-like distal humerus of *Proconsul heseloni* described in Chapter 7 foreshadowed this morphology. Two other limb bones from Klein Hadersdorf provide little additional evidence, but all three indicate that for the first time in the fossil record we have evidence of definitely great ape-like postcranial morphologies as opposed to the monkey-like morphologies prevalent in the early and middle Miocene of Africa and Europe.

The proximal end of a femur was found at the same site as the lower face at Can Mata. The head is large relative to the neck, and it is situated at a level with the greater trochanter. The neck is relatively short and at a low angle to the shaft (123° compared with 130° for the *Equatorius* femur from Maboko Island and 132–136° for *Hispanopithecus*). Moyà-Solà and colleagues point out that this indicates more quadrupedal locomotor behaviour for *Dryopithecus*, which contrasts with the high neck angle seen in *Hispanopithecus* (Figure 12.6), which is interpreted as an orang utan-like adaptation to life in trees in the latter species. Both differ from afropithecine morphology, however, for the head of the femur of the Maboko specimen is placed well below the level of the greater trochanter (Chapter 9, Figure 9.2), another character which limits movement at the hip joint and which was a feature of early Miocene monkey-like fossil apes. Although the Can Mata specimen is attributed to *Dryopithecus*, there is also the possibility that the femur could be attributed to *Pierolapithecus* found in another part of the site and from similar aged deposits.

The partial skeleton of *Pierolapithecus* includes parts of the ribs and vertebrae (Figure 12.5). It has been shown by Moyà-Solà and colleagues that, contrary to the narrow deep chest present in early Miocene apes (and most quadrupedal animals), the curvature of the ribs indicates that this fossil ape had a broad chest; this is also indicated by the length of the clavicle, which places the shoulder on the back rather than the side of the rib cage. The single lumbar vertebra known for *Pierolapithecus* is similar to great ape vertebrae in its robustness and reduced wedging angle, both of which indicate this fossil ape had a relatively rigid lower back. The transverse processes are placed on the interval between the pedicle and the vertebral body, as they are on the Moroto vertebra (Chapter 7, Figure 7.9). This differs from both the early Miocene apes, where they are placed on the vertebral body, and the living great apes, where they are placed on the pedicle. Nearly all the wrist bones are preserved in the *Pierolapithecus* skeleton, showing that the wrist is similar to that of the great apes, but the phalanges are shorter and less curved than in the *H. laietanus* skeleton. These two fossil apes are assumed to be about the same overall size, and it is suggested by Almécija and colleagues that the shorter hand may indicate that *Pierolapithecus*

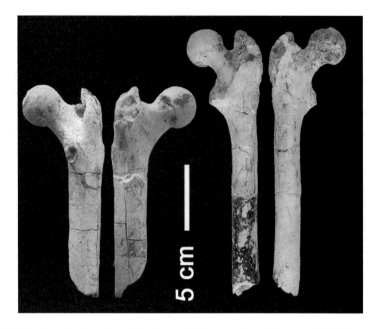

Figure 12.6 The dryopithecine femur. The femur of *Hispanopithecus laietanus* (right) is compared with *Dryopithecus fontani* (left). Photo courtesy of Salvador Moyà-Solà and David Alba (Alba 2012, Moyà-Solà et al. 2009a,b).

supported itself on the palms of its hands rather than having the suspensory locomotor repertoire characteristic of living apes. In particular they raise the point that this monkey-like hand was part of the skeleton of a fossil ape that in other respects showed that it had developed key great ape characters indicating more upright posture. In the great apes, this posture is sometimes linked with suspensory behaviour, but this does not appear to be the case in *Pierolapithecus*, indicating that what is now viewed as a composite set of suspensory characters may in fact have evolved piecemeal or have been related more to upright posture. However, this does not rule out the possibility that this fossil ape had developed some part at least of suspensory locomotion.

The two later Miocene dryopithecines from Can Llobateres and Rudabánya also have postcrania associated with the skulls and teeth. From the same site in Hungary that the skull of *Rudapithecus hungaricus* came from, a number of postcranial fossils have also been found. Nothing is known about the stratigraphic level from which most of these early finds at Rudabánya were recovered, but recent excavations by a team led by Ray Bernor have shown that most of the dryopithecines came from one level (what we called the black mud – see below) and most specimens of the pliopithecid primate came from a different level. These differences were documented by Miranda Armour-Chelu together with Ray and me, but only a few specimens could be located in this way. Most specimens come from unknown levels, for example the distal end of a humerus described initially by Kretzoi (Figure 12.7), and in more detail by Mary Ellen Morbeck. This specimen has a wide trochlea for articulation with the ulna and a prominent trochlear ridge, both providing stability to the elbow joint, and a rounded capitulum for articulation with the radius which gives mobility to the elbow joint. These adaptations are present to a lesser extent in proconsulids, but in the case of *Rudapithecus* we see an elbow joint that provides enhanced elbow joint movement, with full extension of the arm and increased rotation of the lower arm at the joint.

Several wrist and finger bones have also been recovered from Rudabánya, and while some can be attributed to *Rudapithecus*, others have uncertain affinities. The wrist bones show enhanced mobility at the wrist joint, as is the case in the great apes and in particular with the orang utan. The scaphoid is not fused to the os centrale, which is a primitive character present in most primates and the orang utan, but the two bones are fused in the African apes and humans. These characters indicate suspensory and climbing activities to a greater degree than is seen in monkeys and the earlier Miocene apes. Four phalanges are attributed to *Rudapithecus* by Begun, who shows that they are longer and more slender than equivalent phalanges in chimpanzees. They are thus not adapted for weight support such as is present in quadrupedal

Figure 12.7 Distal end of a humerus from early collections from Rudabánya. The broad trochlea with prominent trochlear ridge provides stability of the elbow joint with the ulna when the arm is fully extended, and the rounded capitulum provides mobility with the radius.

movement or knuckle-walking and indicate suspensory locomotion in trees. The thumb is stoutly built, and although the distal end is broken it does not appear to be reduced in length as it is in chimpanzees. This is also not a feature of suspensory movement in trees, and it is probably more related to arboreal climbing.

Moyà-Solà and Meike Köhler described the most complete dryopithecine fossil and indeed one of the three most complete specimens of fossil ape so far known. The bones of this skeleton were recovered from Can Lobateres, and while not directly associated with the skull of *Hispanopithecus*, they are from the same stratigraphic horizon and there is no duplication of skeletal elements, and so it is presumed that they come from the same individual. The distribution of the skeleton shows that the bones were scattered, probably by taphonomic processes, although that has yet to be demonstrated. Many of the bones of the skeleton of *Hispanopithecus* show that it had adopted more upright posture: the lumbar vertebrae are short and robust; the transverse processes originate above the vertebral body, although not as high on the pedicle as in living great apes, indicating reduced mobility in the lumbar region (stiffer back); the thoracic vertebrae indicate a broad chest; and similarly the clavicle is proportionately long. The clavicle is relatively longer than in African apes and is more similar to the orang utan clavicle, and this suggests that the scapula was situated on the back of the thorax rather than on the sides as in early Miocene apes. The arm bones indicate that the arms were powerful with a wide range of movement and the hands are very large relative to body size. The phalanges in particular are long, and are longer relative to the rest of the hand than in any of the great apes: the phalanges of *Hispanopithecus* are nearly as long as the metacarpals (Figure 12.8), whereas in chimpanzees they are two thirds the length of the metacarpals and in the orang utan three quarters the length. In addition, the phalanges are curved with strong insertion markings for the flexor muscles. The large head of the femur extends beyond the greater trochanter and the neck has a high angle with the femoral shaft as in the orang utan (Figure 12.6). These features in the orang utan are adaptations for extreme mobility at the hip joint, where the legs are almost as mobile as the arms and in fact function as a second set of arms, but these features are not as well developed in *Hispanopithecus*. The distal tibia also differs from the condition in orang utans, combining adaptations for above-branch quadrupedalism with adaptations for vertical climbing. Together this mixture of characters indicates a form of locomotion different from any living primate.

Comparisons of leg length against arm length give some indication that the former was reduced in *Hispanopithecus*. Leslie Aiello has shown that arm and leg length varies with body size in monkeys and apes, such that larger species have relatively and absolutely longer limbs. The major exceptions to

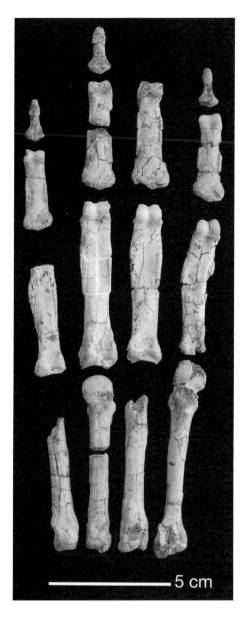

Figure 12.8 The hand from Can Llobateres attributed to *Hispanopithecus laietanus*. Note the great length of the proximal row of phalanges, nearly as long as the metacarpals. Photo courtesy of Sergio Almécija (Moyà-Solà & Köhler 1996).

this size relationship in monkeys and apes are seen firstly in humans, which have slightly longer legs compared with body size than other primates; secondly in the great apes and *Hispanopithecus*, which have reduced legs relative to body weight; and thirdly in gibbons, which have relatively long arms. Arm length in the African great apes is no different from that of other primates, including humans, when compared with body weight. *Hispanopithecus* may have shared longer forearms relative to estimated body weight with the orang utan, so that even though the humerus is not elongated in either, the overall length of the arms is greater than expected for their body size. These proportions and the morphology of the femur are characters similar to the orang utan, and they may be evidence of a relationship between *Hispanopithecus* and the orang utan, but in all cases these features are not as well developed as they are on the orang utan. They may be characters on their way to the orang condition, or they may be independent adaptations for powerful suspensory climbing in trees convergent on the orang utan. The African great apes by contrast appear to have long arms because their legs are short, and they are not long relative to body weight.

Much of the same suite of dryopithecine characters is also present in the enigmatic fossil ape *Oreopithecus bambolii*. This fossil ape from the late Miocene of Italy and Sardinia is known from a nearly complete skeleton and a large number of isolated and associated postcranial remains, jaws and teeth, and while it represents one of the best-known Miocene hominoids, it is also one of the hardest to understand. Hürzeler was the first to point out its human-like qualities, with small canines, lack of canine-premolar honing, short and relatively vertical face; however, Eric Delson has pointed out its affinities with monkeys rather than apes. Terry Harrison and Lorenzo Rook show that with its long arms, broad thorax, short trunk, mobile hind limbs, and powerful grasping hands and feet, it was like *Hispanopithecus* in being adapted for forelimb suspension and arboreal climbing. It also may have had precision grip in the hand. It is possible that these apparent similarities to humans and the great apes were adaptations for climbing and bipedalism in an arboreal setting and were convergent on the similar conditions in the great apes and humans. The unique specializations of its teeth, which are unlike those of any other fossil ape, would seem to preclude it being in any way ancestral to any of the living apes, but it does not exclude it from relationship with the dryopithecines, and at present it is not clear if this suite of postcranial characters evolved independently or if it is evidence of relationship with dryopithecines.

Summary of the postcranial skeleton

Great ape-like features of the postcrania in dryopithecines:

- orthograde (upright) posture;
- broad chest region;
- long clavicle;

- scapula shifted on to back;
- stiff lumbar region;
- mobile elbow joint, stable at full extension;
- mobile wrist;
- long slender hand phalanges;
- femur head above greater trochanter;
- femur neck steeply angled in *Hispanopithecus*.

Monkey-like quadrupedal features:

- short phalanges in *Pierolapithecus* and less curved shafts;
- short metacarpals;
- low angle of the neck of femur in *Dryopithecus;*
- keeled distal tibia.

Not all these characters are known for all species (no postcrania are known for *Anoiapithecus*), but where they are known for two or more species the characters are consistent with the conclusion that upright posture, broad chests and stiff lower backs had evolved in some species of dryopithecines. Some but not all of these species were adapted for suspensory locomotion; however, some of the features associated with orthograde posture occurred independently and in the absence of some suspensory characters and may not have been associated with suspensory locomotion.

Chapter 13
The environment in Europe

The dryopithecines have been shown in Chapter 12 to have had a distribution across southern Europe, from Spain to Italy (if we accept *Oreopithecus* as a dryopithecine). They are also known from several sites in Germany across to Georgia, which suggests that they had pretty eclectic environmental requirements. Generally speaking, they are the only fossil ape present at any of the sites, although at several sites they appear to coexist with pliopithecids, which are primitive catarrhines that appear to be strongly arboreal. More than one dryopithecine species may occur at some sites, for example Hostalets de Pierola in Spain, but it is not clear if they come from the same fossiliferous horizon or even the same site within that region.

There is little information about the environment at Saint Gaudens. Regional floras not directly associated with the fossil site suggest warm temperate conditions, with pine, chestnut and oak forming mainly deciduous woodlands similar to the region today. Whether this was anything like the environment occupied by *D. fontani* must be doubtful for the teeth of this fossil ape have thin enamel, based on measured tooth sections and on the rapid appearance of dentine pits at cusp apices. Thin enamel has been shown earlier to be associated with soft fruit diets, and while soft fruit is seasonally plentiful in temperate woodlands, it is in short supply during the winter.

Rudabánya

One site with abundant dryopithecine fossils is Rudabánya 2 in Hungary. There are a number of other fossiliferous localities within the Rudabánya Basin, including a site with well-preserved fossil leaves. The sites were formed on gently sloping land incised by valleys draining into a large lake that now forms the Pannonian Plain in northern Hungary. The fossil sites were located in some of these valleys. Here I am describing the excavations at Rudabánya 2, but the depositional setting of the other sites is broadly equivalent and they will be mentioned briefly when reconstructing the landscape ecology of the region during the Miocene.

The Rudabánya 2 deposits were laid down in a shallow valley running approximately east to west into the ancient Pannonian Lake. The Pannonian

Basin in the late Miocene was enclosed by the Carpathians to the north and east and by the Alps to the west. The regional land surface has been reconstructed in detail by Kordos, showing the presence of a line of low hills about 300 m in altitude, with valleys dissected between them. The deposition of sediments within these valleys was largely controlled by rise and fall of the lake level during development of the Pannonian Basin and by regional tectonic movements, resulting in cyclical sedimentation. Palaeoenvironments shifted up and down the valley as their depositional position in the palaeo-valley changed with respect to rises and falls of lake level. In relation to this regional palaeotopography, the Rudabánya locality 2 sediments can be described in terms of two cyclical events. The earliest was the formation of a swampy fossil soil topped by lignite on the surface of alluvial deposits. The area was then flooded and covered by the palaeolake, and a thick deposit of grey marls accumulated; after an erosional period during which red silts derived from the eroded lake deposits were redeposited, the second event mirrors the first, with a palaeosol topped by another lignite. In both cases, roots from the vegetation growing on and contributing to the lignite formation penetrate down into the underlying inorganic horizons. To understand this it is necessary to briefly document the sediments.

The earlier of the two cyclical events is a palaeosol with four horizons which are, from top to bottom, a thick lignite horizon grading sharply down into black clay, which changes slowly into a lighter coloured grey clay, which grades into the underlying alluvial deposits. This sequence accumulated in waterlogged anoxic conditions with abundant remains of wood forming the bulk of the lignite deposits. No fossil bones were found.

The second event is also a palaeosol with two horizons preserved, a thick lignite on top of a black mud (see Figures 13.2 and 13.3). The soil developed on the surface of a red marl, which consists of reworked silts from the eroded surface of a massive grey marl. Fossil bone is most abundant in the black mud, including *Rudapithecus* specimens, but there were few fossils in the red marl, which was lightly oxidized, and all were exposed to desiccation and erosion. The massive grey marl formed when the area was under the lake; fossil bone is abundant at this level, but it is scattered, heavily broken and abraded. The marl deposition was interrupted at least once with a temporary drop in lake level and the accumulation of a thin layer of black clay from localized ponding on the exposed surface of the grey marl. The black clay had many fossils, including the pliopithecid *Anapithecus*.

Seeds or endocarps are common throughout the deposits, without any apparent pattern of distribution, but the most abundant biotic remains were fragments of wood, either plant stems or roots, with many set vertically in the sediment and still in growth position. These originated in the soil at the top of the sequence, the black mud and lignite, and it includes bases of tree trunks still in growth position, the aerial roots of trees (Figure 13.1) such as swamp cypress (Taxodiaceae) that were growing in the permanently wet or water-logged conditions, and abundant root traces. Taphonomic analysis of the roots by David Cameron showed that they take on the colour of the sediment through which they pass, so that the colour of the roots change from black to red to dark grey to black as they pass through the black mud, red marl, grey marl and black clay. Their continuity through the different layers and the colour change indicate that they penetrated the sediments after deposition, and since many of them can be traced to root stumps in the overlying black mud and lignite it is evident that they derive from trees growing in place at this later stage of sediment accumulation (Figure 13.2).

The subtropical flora from a series of sites in the Rudabánya region have been described by Kretizoi, so far only in Hungarian and none of them associated with fossil mammals. Based on the list of plants, there is a great abundance of tree species, both temperate and subtropical, conifers and angio-sperms. No information is given on relative abundances, and so it is difficult to assess the nature of the environment just from the list of species, but Taxo-diaceae pollen is ubiquitous, and aerial roots from the swamp cypress are abundant in the lignite deposits of Rudabánya 2. The swamp cypress is the key species in warm temperate to subtropical swamp forests such as occur today along the eastern seaboard of the United States. A significant feature of present-day species of swamp cypress is that their seeds cannot germinate under water; they grow in seasonally wet environments, and the seeds germin-ate during dry periods when water levels recede to below the ground surface. Warm-loving species such as *Zelkova, Celtis, Diospyros* and *Engelhardtia* are also present at two or more levels, and *Pterocarya* pollen is also common. It may be concluded from this list that a rich and varied form of subtropical woodland was present in the Rudabánya area during the middle to late Miocene, and it would have been warm temperate to subtropical in nature, and with a highly seasonal climate. Since this level is associated with many of the fossils of *Rudapithecus* it strongly suggests that this was the environment associated with the fossil ape.

The mesowear and microwear on the mammal teeth from Rudabánya show that the cervid species was a mixed feeder, engaging in both browsing and grazing. *Micromeryx* is generally thought of as a browsing herbivore, and the microwear on its teeth indicates it was eating fruits and seeds, but the meso-wear indicates that it was also eating abrasive food such as grass. The equid *Hippotherium* was probably a mixed feeder, with wear patterns indicating intermediate patterns between grazing and browsing, but the ecomorphology of its elongated limbs indicate that it was adapted for running in open

(a)

(c)

(b)

(d)

Figure 13.1 Excavation at Rudabánya. (a) View of the surface of the black mud overlain by the upper lignite seen in the side walls of the trench. There were many vertical roots still in place, which are identified as the aerial roots of the swamp cypress growing in waterlogged conditions. (b) Close-up of one of these aerial roots. (c) General view of the excavation area. At the back of the picture, two people are excavating the black mud, and in the foreground five people are working at a lower level in the red marl. (d) Aerial roots of swamp cypress growing today.

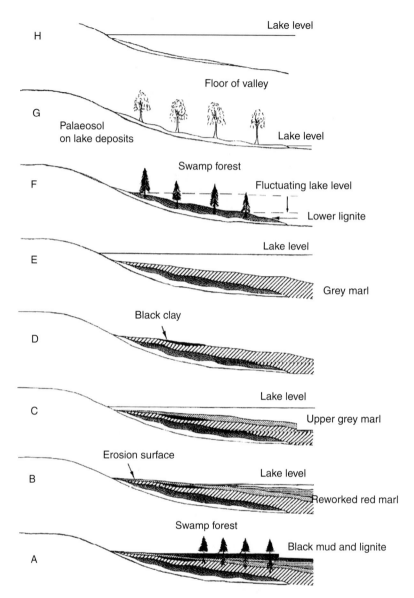

Figure 13.2 Eight stages in the formation of two cyclical events during accumulation of sediments at Rudabánya 2, from the top (earliest) to bottom (latest): H Lake level high, drowning the valley leading down to the Pannonian Lake; G Drop in lake level, with woodland developed on the lake deposits along the valley; F Fluctuating lake level with further sedimentation and lignite formation (lower lignite); fossil wood abundant, but no mammals; E High lake level, drowning the lignite and deposition of the grey marls on top of the lower lignite; fossil mammals dispersed in the lake deposits; D Drop in lake level, with black clays deposited in ephemeral ponds on the surface of the grey marls; many fossil mammals; C High lake level, with the upper grey marls being deposited on top of the black clay; B Drop in lake level: the grey marls were exposed on the surface at the head of the valley, oxidized to reddish colour, eroded and redeposited lower down the valley to form the red marl; some fossils from the eroded grey marl may have been reworked into the red marl; A Slight rise in lake level with the formation of the upper lignite and black mud on the surface of the red marl; many fossils, both mammals and plant, including decayed tree trunks, roots and aerial roots; the tree roots from this level penetrate down into the grey marl. This figure was compiled by Douglas Ekart, David Cameron and the author. Andrews & Cameron 2010.

(a)

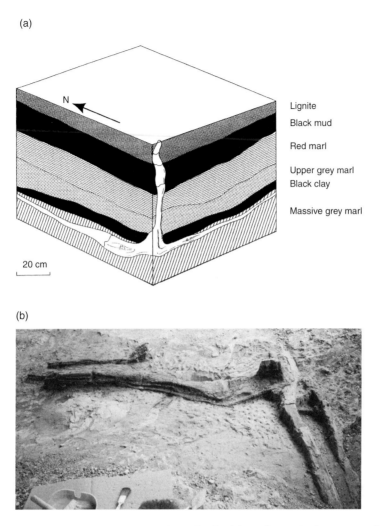

Lignite

Black mud

Red marl

Upper grey marl
Black clay

Massive grey marl

20 cm

(b)

Figure 13.3 (a) Block diagram of four accumulation levels of the sediments in the upper cyclical event at Rudabánya, showing a buried tree stump exposed at the top of the section in the upper lignite as a projecting root. Within the grey marl, just below the black clay, the roots spread out laterally. The vertical section is 50 cm from the lignite surface to the upper surface of the grey marl. (b) The excavation of the lateral roots in the grey marl. The upper part of the vertical root has been removed during excavation.

environments rather than moving through thick cover. Apart from this, most evidence points to the presence of subtropical woodland in the Rudabánya area, which is also consistent with the palaeobotanical results, suggesting a mixture of swamp forest with a few open areas, the latter indicated by the elongated limbs of *Hippotherium* species.

The fossil ape *Rudapithecus hungaricus* has been found associated with a second primate species (*Anapithecus*) at Rudabánya, but they are present in differing proportions at different levels. Analysis of their distributions by

Miranda Armour-Chelu has shown that *Rudapithecus* is most abundant in the swamp forest environment dominated by swamp cypress (*Taxodium*), whereas *Anapithecus* is most abundant in lakeshore environments. Both were predominantly frugivorous, but there is some evidence that *Anapithecus* had more leaf foliage in its diet and *Rudapithecus* had adaptations of its incisors for breaking into the tough outer skin of hard fruits. In both cases these alternative adaptations may have been to use fall-back resources when their regular fruit diet was scarce, and this niche partitioning may have allowed them to coexist in the same environment.

Summary of the environment at Rudabánya

- The fossil ape *Rudapithecus hungaricus* from Rudabánya is associated with subtropical swamp forest dominated by the swamp cypress *Taxodium distichum*.
- Swamp forest in the warm temperate and subtropical regions of Miocene Europe combined conifers like the swamp cypress with mesophytic broad-leaved trees such as maple, oak and ash occurring in drier areas.
- This type of forest has now been replaced in southern Europe by deciduous broad-leaved forest, and the best present-day examples of *Taxodium* forest are along the eastern seaboard of the United States and in the Florida wetlands.
- A significant feature of the life cycle of living *Taxodium* species is that their seeds cannot germinate under water, so that for the trees to regenerate there have to be fluctuations in water level.
- The forests are deciduous, with the swamp cypress forming a monotype in the wetter areas and broad-leaved trees and cypress in the drier areas.
- The forests are open but with single canopy structure as in tropical deciduous woodlands, and the cypresses may be emergents rising above the level of the broad-leaved trees.
- Vines are abundant because of the open canopy structure (Figure 13.4).

The Iberian Peninsula

Palaeobotanical evidence from the Iberian Peninsula indicates that while central Spain had dry deciduous woodland during the later part of the middle Miocene, the northeastern region of Spain, close to the dryopithecine localities of the Vallès-Penedès region, had warm temperate evergreen woodland and

(a)   (b)

Figure 13.4 Two views of swamp forest in warm temperate/subtropical climate zone. (a) In the wet areas, swamp cypress is the only tree species able to survive. Aerial roots can be seen in the right foreground (black arrow). (b) A slightly drier area, still with swamp cypress but with broad-leaved trees as well.

forest. This type of forest was common across southern Europe at that time, while broad-leaved deciduous woodland occupied more northerly areas of Europe. The evergreen forests appear to be a remnant of the once extensive sclerophyllous evergreen forests described by Axelrod that once extended across southern Europe into China, present today only in Yunnan Province in China but with remnants on the Canary Islands.

The site of Can Llobateres is situated in a narrow basin bounded by mountains formed by tectonic movements. The sediments are alluvial fan deposits washing off the pre-littoral range of mountains and consist of mudstones, breccias and conglomerates composed of the Palaeozoic rocks that form the mountains. Fossils are associated with the finer sediment grades, and fossil soils had formed on the surfaces of the sediment. I mentioned earlier that fossil apes have been recovered from two levels at Can Llobateres, the original level at the bottom of the stratigraphic sequence and a new level higher up the sequence. The lower level was accumulated in a poorly drained alluvial plain between two channels, with ponding and impeded drainage shown by the dark, almost black

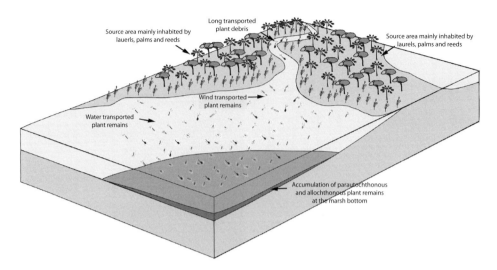

Figure 13.5 Reconstruction of the depositional setting and environment at Can Llobateres based on the palaeobotanical remains. Reproduced with permission from Marmí et al. 2012.

sediments. The upper level was better drained, lighter in colour, with the formation of calcareous nodules indicating seasonality in precipitation.

Josep Marmi has provided a detailed stratigraphic description of the lower unit at Can Llobateres. Some stratigraphic levels have no fossils, while others include small mammals, or large mammals, or fossil plants, but only one level has an association of fossil mammals and *Hispanopithecus laietanus*. The plant fossils include few species, and they were preserved in shallow water such as a marshy area in the alluvial fan. Leaves, twigs, fruits and seeds are all represented, ranging from large palm leaves to small seeds. Monocots such as palms are the most abundant trees, and also present are reeds such as *Phragmites*. They are all mixed up in the deposit, and while some are heavily damaged by water transport, laurel leaves are present and almost all are undamaged and even showing signs of insect feeding marks The laurel leaves are similar to the species of *Cinnamomum*, which was common during the Miocene in the Vallès-Penedès region, and laurels were an important understorey component of the ubiquitous sclerophyllous forests during the Miocene. In addition, seven morphotypes of angiosperms, so far unidentified, were present. Fig fruits had been found, but from a different excavation.

The fossil plants were transported to the site at Can Llobateres by water, but because of their good preservation they could not have been moved from a great distance and some species do not appear to have been transported at all (Figure 13.5). This is consistent with the regional geography, where drainage was local, coming off the slopes of the surrounding mountains. Reeds were probably growing close to the site, and so also were the laurels, for even though they have tough leaves they would not survive long water transport. Some of the unidentified angiosperms are also well preserved, suggesting that there was evergreen forest bordering the depositional environment. It is unlikely that any of the plants were growing actually at the site because there are no roots or root marks in the sediments, and the random orientations of the fossil plants makes it unlikely that they were preserved in running water. These observations are all consistent with the sedimentary evidence, which shows that the depositional environments at Can Llobateres were swamps interspersed with more active water movement.

Similarly the figs from lower in the section could also have been growing in riparian forests. It is hard to say how far the forests may have extended away from the wetland area, but as we have seen for Rudabánya, even a small area of subtropical forest could have harboured populations of fossil apes. This conclusion is contrasted with another dryopithecine site, Seo d'Urgell, from which a single mandible of *Dryopithecus* has been recovered and for which the environment has been interpreted, on rather slender evidence, as a humid mixed mesophytic forest with a high diversity of evergreen laurels and many deciduous species.

The mammal fauna from Can Llobateres has many aquatic species such as otters and beavers. The small mammals include species like flying squirrels and several species of arboreal dormice, and the large mammals include many species with supposed forest affinities, although there are some indicating more open conditions. The fossil ape *Hispanopithecus* is probably another indicator of wooded conditions, and analyses of the microwear on its teeth show that it was adapted to a soft fruit diet like that of *Rudapithecus* from Rudabánya. The habitat reconstructed by Meike Köhler based on strong eco-morphological data for the mammal fauna was one of swampy woodlands in humid warm conditions.

It was mentioned above that the formation of calcareous nodules in the Can Llobateres sediments is an indicator of seasonality. This was particularly marked in the sediments at Paşalar and it is only to be expected at the latitude of these sites, even if temperatures were higher than they are today. As for *Kenyapithecus* and *Griphopithecus* at Paşalar, the teeth of *Hispanopithecus* also indicate a possible seasonal environment. Nearly half the specimens of *Hispanopithecus* have one or more hypoplasias, and these are common in living apes as well, which may be attributed in part to their extended maturation, compared, for instance, with monkeys, for which hypoplasia is rare, or to periodic traumas due to diseases such as malaria, which is a disease common to all living great apes but not present in monkeys.

The environment at Can Vila where *Pierolapithecus* was found is situated in another broad basin between two mountain ranges. The sediments consist mainly of alluvial fan deposits with a high rate of sedimentation. Within this context the fossil assemblages accumulated from at least three different sources: the large mammal fossils were scattered through the site, and isolated bones were weathered and abraded and transported to the site; the *Pierolapithecus* bones were mostly concentrated in one place with little weathering or abrasion but with evidence of carnivore damage; and the small mammals were the prey assemblage of an unknown predator. The large mammals indicate the presence of a warm humid evergreen forest based on the relative contributions the mammal species make to the fossil fauna compared with modern faunas. The small mammals also indicate wooded environments based on the presence of several arboreal species. These conclusions are consistent with the palaeobotanical evidence, and it should be noted that similarities of the Can Mata fauna with that of La Grive in southern France, from which *Dryopithecus fontani* is known, suggest a similar environment for that species as well.

Summary of dryopithecine environments

- The environment associated with *Hispanopithecus* in the late Miocene of the Vallès-Penedès region of Spain has strong similarities with, and some differences from, that recorded from Rudabánya. Like that site, some at least of the Iberian deposits were formed as wetlands.
- Palms and laurels dominated the woodlands at Can Llobateres, with figs at another level, indicating warm temperate to subtropical evergreen forest.
- Laurel forests today have dense canopy structure, usually with an overstorey above, and they grow in areas that are frost-free, of high humidity or on wetlands. They were once extensive across southern Europe and on the shores of the Tethys during the Eocene and into the early Miocene, and it may be that the middle Miocene sites of Can Mata and Can Vila and the other Spanish sites have had similar environments, but the evidence is slim.
- Within this environment, the dryopithecines adopted an orthograde, suspensory mode of life, living in trees and eating soft fruits.
- Their skulls and postcrania share many characters in common with the great apes and humans and show that this group, Hominidae, was present in Europe during the period 12 to 9 million years ago, associated with deciduous swamp forest (*Rudapithecus*), evergreen laurel forest (*Hispanopithecus*) and even mesophytic deciduous broad-leaved forest (*Dryopithecus*).
- These forests as noted earlier all had canopy structures intermediate between those of African tropical woodlands and tropical forests.

Chapter 14
Late Miocene to Pleistocene apes

Up to this point, we have had the advantage of dealing with relatively well-preserved fossil apes. In the early Miocene we had the partial skeletons of proconsulids, and in the middle Miocene we had either partial skeletons of afropithecines in Africa or very large samples of teeth and jaws with fascinating environmental contexts in Turkey. The later middle Miocene and late Miocene fossil dryopithecines in Europe are equally well preserved, with several skulls and partial skeletons. Late Miocene apes in Africa, by contrast, are poorly represented in the fossil record, but because they are the only fossil apes known in Africa during the late Miocene, they are of some importance. Most apes disappeared from the fossil record by about 8 million years ago, including those previously living in Europe and Asia, although we can mention the giant fossil ape *Gigantopithecus blacki,* which survived well into the Pleistocene in China and Vietnam. The teeth of this fossil ape has some parallels with human teeth, for example the small incisors and canines, and bicuspid premolars completely lacking any premolar honing, but there is little doubt that these similarities were due to convergence and do not indicate significant evolutionary relationship with humans.

Late Miocene apes in Africa

The three fossil apes in Africa during the period 9 to 10 million years ago are too incomplete to be able to assign them either with each other or to any living or fossil ape. They share few similarities with the great ape and human clade, and in the absence of cranial, dental and postcranial characters such as are present for the dryopithecines, and which link them with the great apes, it is impossible at this stage to assign them to this or any other clade.

In 2007, a fossil ape named *Chororapithecus abyssinicus* was named from 10 million-year-old deposits at Beticha in the Chorora Formation in Ethiopia. There are only nine isolated teeth, but they showed that it had gorilla-sized dentition and combined a degree of shearing crest formation on the molars with thickened enamel and relatively flat dentine surfaces, an unusual combination not seen in any living or fossil ape. In combination with the thickened enamel, this suggests a functional adaptation to hard and/or abrasive food items.

A second late Miocene ape was found in deposits in the Nakali valley in northern Kenya. In the last years of his life, Louis Leakey had set his heart on visiting the Nakali valley, as he was convinced it had late Miocene and Pliocene deposits, and he considered it likely that early human remains would be found there. He was prevented from undertaking this work, and so far just the one hominid species has been found, a fossil ape named *Nakalipithecus nakayamai* which is represented by a lower jaw and eleven isolated teeth that are dated to just under 10 million years ago. It is similar in size to gorillas and orang utans, but the canine is low crowned, the upper incisor is broad and the premolars are mesiodistally long, all conditions similar to *Kenyapithecus*.

At a third site in the Samburu Hills, also in northern Kenya, *Samburupithecus kiptalami* has a single fragment of upper jaw. The site is slightly younger than that of *Chororapithecus*, which it greatly resembles. It is also similar to *Nakalipithecus* in its elongated molars and large premolars, but it is difficult to compare the two fossils at present, for *Samburupithecus* is known only from five upper teeth and *Nakalipithecus* mainly from lower teeth. The palate is deeply arched, as in dryopithecines, and the zygomatic root is low, again as in dryopithecines but unlike kenyapithecines and great apes. The cusps of the molars are greatly inflated, and the third molar is the largest of the upper molars. This is an unusual condition, for in most fossil apes the second molar is the largest tooth and the third is slightly smaller, symbolized by M1<M2>M3. We have seen that the dryopithecines conform to this pattern, but many have the third molar greatly reduced. The general pattern for kenyapithecines, afropithecines and proconsulids (except for *Rangawapithecus gordoni*) is that the third upper molar is slightly smaller than the second.

Four isolated teeth from the late Miocene of East Africa (Ngorora, Lukeino, Kapsomin and Cheboit) appear to be fossil apes, and they are important in that they show that apes were present over a wide area and probably in a variety of environments, but they are too fragmentary to provide any information on the origin of the extant African apes.

Late Miocene apes in Europe and Asia

The lack of good fossil evidence in Africa during the later part of the Miocene contrasts with the situation in southern Europe and Asia. The species of dryopithecine were described in Chapter 12, but contemporaneous with them were a number of other species of fossil ape both in Europe and in Asia, ranging from Italy and Greece to Pakistan and Southeast Asia. Often grouped in the genus *Sivapithecus*, at least on their initial descriptions, these are all similar in having relatively large molar teeth with thick enamel and rounded cusps, broad spatulate incisors, large premolars, lower crowned canines and reduced honing, and relatively large lower jaws (Figure 14.1). These characters are all present in the species of *Sivapithecus*, but there is no consensus about how the other species relate to this genus.

One group of sivapithecines, including *Sivapithecus* itself and *Ankarapithecus meteai* from Turkey (Figure 14.2), has orang utan-like skulls, sharing a number of characters with the orang utan skull such as a concave mid-face contour, broad flat cheek regions, narrow distance between the eyes and a reduced incisive canal. The face of *Sivapithecus indicus* in particular is set at a very low angle to the base of the skull as it is in the orang utan (airorhynch condition) and differing from the African great apes and most other monkeys and apes. The other group lacks the orang utan-like characters of the skull. This is *Ouranopithecus macedoniensis* from Greece described in 1977 but is almost identical to *Graecopithecus freybergi,* which was described earlier by Ralph von Koenigswald. *Graecopithecus* is known only from a single mandible (Figure 14.3), the front end of which is missing and only one tooth is intact. Because of its poor preservation, many scientists prefer to use the name *Ouranopithecus macedoniensis*, which includes several upper and lower jaws, a skull and some phalanges. There are some minor

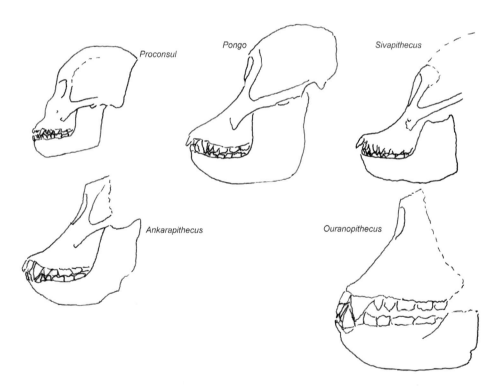

Figure 14.1 Specimens of Miocene apes showing the side view profiles of the face. Notice the dished faces of *Sivapithecus* and *Ankarapithecus* compared with the straight faces of *Proconsul* and *Ouranopithecus*. This is one of the similarities of the former fossil apes with the orang utan.

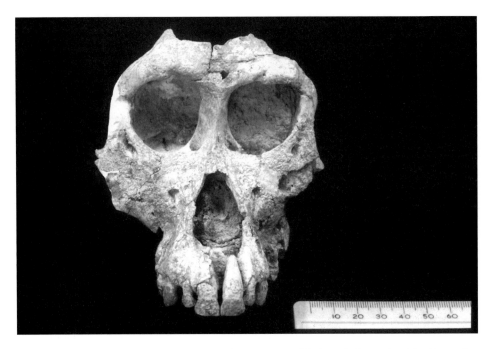

Figure 14.2 The face of *Ankarapithecus meteai*, late Miocene of Turkey, similar to the dished face of *Sivapithecus*.

differences between it and *Graecopithecus*. The skull of *Ouranopithecus* is broad and robust, with broad nose and eye sockets, superficially similar to the condition in the African apes, and it may have similarities with the African apes in the angle of the face. The condition is not certain in *Ouranopithecus*, however, because the upper face was crushed during preservation, making the face broader than it probably was. The mandible is relatively deep and gracile in contrast to the large thick-enamelled molars. The two phalanges are similar to those of quadrupedal terrestrial primates, and this is consistent with the savanna-like environment predicted for this fossil ape.

There are two specimens of humerus recovered from the same deposits as *Sivapithecus indicus*, and the shape of the shafts indicates pronograde posture, although there is some indication that this was acquired independently of the earlier pronograde apes, for the elbow joint has functional similarities with the morphology of great apes and unlike the earlier fossil apes. In addition, a *Sivapithecus* femur shows that the fossil ape had a flexible hip joint, with the leg capable of medial rotation, and with a relatively mobile ankle. These are characters that indicate flexible hind limbs for agile climbing in trees. The hand phalanges are more robust than those of the hands of early Miocene apes, which are rather gracile, and the thumb is long and well developed and capable of opposing the other fingers to a greater extent than in any of the

(a)   (b)

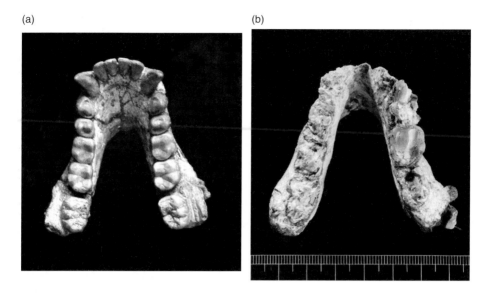

Figure 14.3 (a) One of the large mandibles of *Ouranopithecus macedoniensis* with all its teeth intact compared with (b) the fragmentary mandible of *Graecopithecus freybergi* which is missing the front of the mandible and most teeth except for the crown of the second molar and the broken remains of the first molar and fourth premolar.

living hominids except humans (and the fossil ape *Oreopithecus*, which will be discussed below). This contrasts with the hands of the great apes whose thumbs are short relative to the lengths of the hands. The foot bones were also robust, and overall the bones of the skeleton indicate that *Sivapithecus* was pronograde like the monkeys. Similarly, the two wrist bones known so far are robust and similar in morphology to those of the great apes. The single leg bone (tibia) has a unique combination of characters, some monkey-like (the distal articular surface), some indicating mobile ankles with a tendency towards upright orthograde posture.

In terms of postcrania, therefore, *Sivapithecus* combined powerful grasping hands and mobile legs and ankles, a combination that differs from earlier Miocene apes and monkeys but also differs from the great apes at a time when some great ape morphologies were already present in the dryopithecines. However, David Begun has suggested that the robust carpal bones indicate a degree of knuckle-walking in this fossil ape.

Carbon and oxygen isotope values indicate that this fossil ape fed in tree canopies but inhabited more open forest environments than do orang utans today. All this presents a problem, for if indeed they are on the lineage leading to orang utans, as suggested by their skull morphology, the postcranial adaptations which this great ape shares with the African great apes, and which have been generally assumed to be homologous in the great apes, must have

215

evolved independently in the orang utan. Conversely, if *Sivapithecus* and *Ankarapithecus* are not on the lineage leading to the orang utan, the many characters of the skull and face shared with it are not shared derived characters but must themselves have evolved independently in the orang utan and the fossil apes.

Disregarding phyletic relationship, however, David Begun summarizes the position in the late Miocene of Europe very well: "Diversity in European Miocene hominines parallels that of Pliocene to recent hominines, with a range of ecological preferences from suspensory, highly arboreal soft fruit frugivores living in closed forests, to hard object feeders, possibly much more terrestrial, living in more open settings." This ecological dichotomy may prove to have been present in Africa as well as in Europe, but at present there is insufficient fossil evidence to show it. The question will be raised in Chapters 15 and 16 as to which part of this diversity the last common ancestor of apes and humans arose from, but we shall see that the late Miocene and early Pliocene hominins have combinations of characters unlike either of the two groups of fossil ape defined above. They differ from the dryopithecines in lack of suspensory adaptations in their postcrania and they differ from the *Ouranopithecus* group in lacking enlarged teeth.

Orang utan ancestry

It has been mentioned in Chapter 4 that numerous fossil orang utans are known from Pleistocene deposits, but so far their late Miocene ancestry eludes us. *Lufengpithecus lufengensis* has been proposed as an orang utan ancestor; it comes from late Miocene deposits at Lufeng in Yunnan Province, China. It was described originally as *Ramapithecus*, and most of the teeth are very like those of this defunct genus, but a few teeth appear to have the uniquely specialized wrinkling on the occlusal surfaces that are like those of the orang utan. Several skulls are known for this species, but unfortunately they are so crushed by sediment pressure that little can be discerned of their morphology. A juvenile skull recently described from Shuitangha has also been attributed to *Lufeng-pithecus*, but it shows none of the facial characters that distinguish the orang utan, which seems to exclude it from orang utan ancestry. To me it looks a good candidate for gibbon ancestry, especially as there is some indication that the gibbons are descended from larger sized ancestors. It is dated to between 7 and 5 million years.

Rather more convincing evidence of orang utan ancestry is seen in fossil apes from the late Miocene of Thailand described by J.J. Jaeger and assigned to the genus *Khoratpithecus*. The teeth have no characters linking it with the orang utan, but the mandible lacks a scar for the insertion of the anterior digastric muscle, which signifies that the muscle was also lacking, and this is a unique character of orang utans. On the basis of this one character alone it is possible to say with some confidence that *Khoratpithecus* was related to orang utans.

One other fossil specimen with links to the orang utan is a skeleton from the Pleistocene of Vietnam. The significance of this specimen, which is undated but much more recent than any of the forgoing specimens, is that it was found on the mainland of Southeast Asia whereas orang utans today are restricted to the islands Sumatra and Borneo. Pleistocene orang utans have been recovered all over the Far East and Java, as mentioned in Chapter 4.

Summary

- One group of fossil apes from Europe and Asia have skulls similar to that of the orang utan but with postcrania distinct from both monkeys and great apes: quadrupedal, pronograde, arboreal (*Sivapithecus, Ankarapithecus*). Their skull has many orang utan-like characters, with robust jaws, broad central incisors, low crowned canines and enlarged molar teeth with thick enamel.
- A second group of fossil apes from Europe has skulls more similar to those of African apes but with postcrania distinct from the great apes, showing that they were quadrupedal, pronograde and terrestrial (*Ouranopithecus, Graecopithecus*). They have relatively slender jaws, broad central incisors, low crowned canines and enlarged molar teeth with thick enamel.
- A third group of fossil apes has teeth and mandibular morphology similar to those of the orang utan (*Lufengpithecus, Khoratpithecus*).
- Whether hominids evolved in Europe and migrated back to Africa or whether they evolved in Africa and emigrated to Europe is not known for certain yet. There are some 'shared derived characters' linking dryopithecines with the African apes, and other 'shared derived characters' linking them with the orang utan; there are yet other 'shared derived characters' linking sivapithecines with the orang utan, but obviously not all of these can be correct, for it is not clear at present which are homoplasies and which homologous.
- Characters were evolving in mosaic fashion before the divergence of the species of great ape.
- What can be concluded, based in part on absence of evidence from Africa, is that the separation between the orang utan on the one hand, and the African apes and humans on the other, could have taken place in southern Europe 12 to 9 million years ago. David Pilbeam put it succinctly in his

commentary in 1996 when he said: "Few of us asked ourselves whether the known record was adequate to answer the questions we posed. As I noted recently (1996), we were like the drunk looking for his keys under the lamppost where it was light rather than where he had dropped them, working with what we had rather than asking whether or not that was adequate."

Chapter 15

Apes, hominins and environment in the late Miocene

I am attempting several things in this chapter. In the first place we must consider the environments associated with the fossil apes described in the previous chapter, although for some of them there is little information. I am then going to go straight on to investigate both the morphology and the environment of a group of hominids that have been published as early human ancestors but which have only been mentioned in passing so far in this account. I am making no judgement about whether or not they are on the human lineage, but they are included in this chapter to produce a measure of continuity between them and their fossil ape precursors. They are all important in the tracing of the common ancestor of apes and humans, and the one thing that all can agree on is that they are close to the ape/human common ancestor, either as descendants or as precursors. The only disagreement comes when a decision has to be made as to which side of the common ancestor they fall: on the human or hominin lineage after it has split off from the apes; or on the hominid lineage preceding the split. Before discussing the environments associated with them, it is necessary to consider some of the morphologies present on these fossils, both to show how they were adapted to the environment and to extract characters that may have been important in the common ancestry of apes and humans.

The environment in the late Miocene

The site at Beticha from which *Chororapithecus abyssinicus* was found occurs relatively late in the Chorora Formation and has a rather different animal fauna from that present in the lower deposits. The sediments formed in a braided river system with palaeosol formation, and the sparse fauna includes a monkey species as well as the fossil ape. There is, however, almost no information on the likely palaeoenvironment present at that time. Similarly, the site at Nakali with fragmentary remains of *Nakalipithecus nakayamai* has little information on environment. The deposits come from a volcanic mudflow in the upper member of the Nakali Formation, suggesting rapid sediment accumulation. The animal fauna is similar to that of the Samburu Hills site (see below), and it includes several other primate species. It is said to resemble the southern Eurasian faunas linked with evergreen woodland. Stable isotope distribution shows the presence of mainly C_3 plants, again indicating some form of closed woodland or forest.

The environment of the *Sivapithecines* appears to have been distinct from that associated with the dryopithecines. Depositional environments for *Sivapithecus* in the Siwaliks of Pakistan indicate a wide range of fluvial to flood plain environments, but the fossil ape was a minor constituent of faunas in the early part of the sedimentary succession which was dominated by bovids and equids, most of which were browsing forms. The predominance of browsing herbivores and their wide range of body size suggests that leafy forage was present through a considerable vertical range, but whether woodland or forest is not clear. The variety of depositional environments suggests that the habitats were heterogeneous, changing rapidly across river valleys and flood plains as the rivers changed their course, and in this situation it is likely there would have been a variety of vegetation associations. There was constant low-level faunal change, and body sizes of rodents and artiodactyls (mainly giraffes) gradually increased during the period 10 to 9 million years ago. In parallel with this was an increase of species with more hypsodont teeth in both groups of mammals.

Stable isotope analyses for the Siwalik succession show that the early sites had C_3 vegetation, and there was a transition to C_4 grasses starting at just over 8 million years. Sivapithecines are present in the fauna associated with browsing herbivores and C_3 plants indicating the presence of wooded environments. The exact nature of the woodlands is not known, but the nature of the sedimentary conditions suggests that at best they were subject to rapid change as the river systems periodically changed course. It is also likely that *Sivapithecus* made use of many parts of the environment, much as chimpanzees do today, and given its body size it is likely that the fossil ape was at least as terrestrial in its behaviour as chimpanzees are today. However, isotope values for the teeth of this fossil ape indicate that it fed in tree canopies, perhaps on leaves to a certain extent or in open canopy forest. The loss of fossil apes at the end of this period is linked with the replacement of C_3 by C_4 plants and the increasing hypsodonty of herbivores. Both are strong indicators of changes in habitat to which fossil apes could not adapt.

The sites from which *Ouranopithecus* fossils have been found in Greece also consist of fluviatile gravels. Bovids make up nearly three quarters of the fauna, and faunal resemblance and size indices show that the faunas are most similar to present-day African savanna faunas. Some form of seasonal climate is indicated, and this could range from seasonal forests to more open environments. Stable isotopes of bovids associated with the fossil ape show them to have had C_3 diets, indicating browsing adaptations, but at the latitude of northern Greece, where the fossil sites are located, grasses growing in winter rainfall areas are mostly C_3, and so this finding does not exclude the possibility of grasses being present. Analyses of pollen and phytoiths show the presence of abundant C_3 grasses, and combined with the microwear and mesowear present on their teeth indicate the probable environment as open woodland with grass ground vegetation.

The same may be said for the *Ankarapithecus* localities. The long sequence of the Sinap Formation in central Turkey has a succession of faunas that could provide good evidence on the environment, but little work has been done despite a major monograph having been produced on the site. Small bovids dominate the oldest localities, and the hipparion horses had low crowned teeth, both indicating the widespread presence of vegetation for browsing herbivores. There was a change through the sequence, however, with later species developing higher crowned teeth, indicating increase in grazing, and limb morphology adapted for running in open spaces. It appears from this that the faunal change along the Sinap sequence documents habitat change from closed cover environments, with abundant trees and shrubs, to more open woodland environments. The specimens of *Ankarapithecus meteai* were found in the later deposits, associated with hipparions with cursorial limb adaptations and higher crowned teeth, indicating association with more open environments. In such an environment it must have been largely terrestrial even if there were still patches of forest or woodland present, for in such broken environments, movement on the ground is necessary to get from one patch of trees to the next.

The fossil fauna from Lufeng has been correlated with later parts of the finely documented Siwalik sequence which is about 8 million years old, although the environment indicated at Lufeng is very different from that of the Siwaliks succession. The fossils were accumulated in swamp deposits in an upland valley in a part of China that now has a subtropical to tropical climate. The sediments consist of five alternating lignites and clays, similar to the depositional environment described earlier for Rudabánya in Hungary, and the pollen flora from the site is dominated by arboreal pollen. The trees were probably growing in place in the lignite swamps, as at Rudabánya, with tree ferns, understorey ferns and epiphytes all present, indicating moist to moderately dry habitats. Several of the mammals present at Lufeng are related to present-day forest dwellers, like flying squirrels and tragulids, and aquatic mammals are also present. Approximately one third of the faunal assemblage consists of the fossil ape *Lufengpithecus lufengensis*, and although there appears to have been a climatic shift up through the section, passing from warm and humid to cool and humid, this fossil ape was present throughout these changes. These lines of evidence suggest strongly both that the environment was a forested swamp with thickly vegetated margins, and that this environment was the one occupied by *Lufengpithecus*. It is interesting that this fossil ape persisted into cooler conditions, but it is likely that the area was a refuge forest area like that of Rudabánya in Eastern Europe.

Summary of late Miocene environments

- African fossil ape environments in the late Miocene were woodland with patches of forest, although evidence is poor.
- *Ouranopithecus* is associated with seasonal woodland environments with some degree of terrestrial behaviour.
- *Sivapithecus* species are mainly arboreal, associated with seasonal woodland environments and with some degree of terrestrial behaviour.
- *Lufengpithecus* with similarities to the orang utan is associated with subtropical to tropical swamp forest.
- *Khorapithecus* is said to be associated with a tropical flora, but no details are available.
- The restriction of fossil apes to the southern fringes of Europe and Asia suggests that they were restricted to climates with summer rainfall, for example like those of the monsoon climates of India and southern Africa.
- The woodlands in such conditions would have had many structural similarities with woodland environments in Africa.

Proposed hominin ancestors

More and more publications are proposing that the early evolution of humans up to the emergence of the genus *Homo* took place in woodland or even forest conditions. Even though we have seen earlier that C_4 plants did not enter the environment in Africa until about 7 million years ago, isotope evidence shows that they were not a major component of hominin environments until after about 1.7 million years ago. This suggests that early hominins preferred woody C_3 habitats, perhaps riparian woodlands in particular, because of availability of plant foods, scavenging opportunities and trees for shade, predator refuge and sleeping platforms. Associated animal faunas show a similar thing; for example the ecomorphology of pigs shows that they were adapted for closed and intermediate habitats at later stages of human evolution. This work was published in the proceedings of a conference on biogeography, climate change and human evolution held in exotic surroundings on the shores of Lake Malawi, and my conclusions in the same volume stated

The earliest hominins in the Pliocene are associated with closed woodland ecosystems, in some cases approaching forest ecosystems in terms of community richness but not actually overlapping with them. The earliest hominins appear to have been medium-sized frugivores that were still at least partly arboreal, so that the niche space occupied by them overlapped the range of habitats associated with Miocene apes. The change to complete terrestriality, more varied diets, and from woodland environments to more open ones would then have occurred at a later stage of hominin evolution.

So what can we say about those late Miocene fossils assigned to the human lineage? The earliest proposed fossil hominin ancestor is a crushed skull and mandible and a number of isolated teeth from Toros-Menalla, Chad, in north-Central Africa named *Sahelanthropus tchadensis*. The skull has a short lower face, a broad interorbital region, a strong and continuous supraorbital torus, a small braincase with a low posteriorly placed sagittal crest and well-developed nuchal crest, small canines and relatively small cheek teeth with moderately thick enamel. There are similarities between *Sahelanthropus* and gorillas and also with *Ouranopithecus macedoniensis*, particularly in the form of the orbits, wide inter-orbital distance and the shape of the nose. Characters shared with later hominins include small canines with wear concentrated at the tips of the canine, and a short base of the skull with an anteriorly placed foramen magnum. It is possible, however, that the canine was small because the fossil came from a female individual, as is the case for some species of fossil ape, for the sex of the single individual is not known; in addition, the roots of the lower third premolar indicate that the crown would have been elongated and obliquely set to hone against the upper canine, as in apes. The morphology of the base of the skull indicates that the body position of *Sahelanthropus* was upright (orthograde), although Milford Wolpoff points out in his critique of the species that the anterior edge of the foramen magnum is set well posterior to the level of the third molar, and so the degree of orthogrady may have been no greater than that of chimpanzees and gorillas. In addition, orthograde posture does not necessarily indicate bipedal walking, and it should be considered that there is a general trend in ape evolution, both living and fossil, towards greater upright posture, which may or may not be combined with bipedal locomotion. As Wolpoff points out, it is premature to assess the significance of this character without further evidence.

Another late Miocene fossil is *Orrorin tugenensis* from the Lukeino Formation of northern Kenya. It comes from slightly younger deposits than *Sahelanthropus*, dated to about 6 million years. The molars are relatively small and have thick enamel, as in the Chad individual, a combination of characters not seen either in later hominins or in middle to late Miocene thick-enamelled apes, in both of which the thick-enamelled molars and premolars are enlarged. The canine in *Orrorin* is large and pointed like those of apes, both conditions unlike that seen in *Sahelanthropus tchadensis* unless of course it represents a male individual to the female of that species. The femur resembles that of Pliocene hominins in several respects that may be derived traits associated with bipedalism, for example the morphology of the femoral neck (Figure 15.1), but the functional significance of these traits has yet to be established. CT scans of the femoral neck of *Orrorin* show that the thickness of the cortical bone is greater inferiorly than superiorly, a feature present in the femur of bipedal hominins, but comparisons have not been made with the cortical bone distribution in fossil apes such as *Equatorius africanus*. That such a comparison is essential is brought out by the work of Kathy Rafferty, who has shown that quadrupedal Old World monkeys also have a relatively thicker inferior cortex compared with superior cortex in the femoral neck. The functional significance of this character in both monkeys and humans may have more to do with weight bearing than specifically with bipedal locomotion, and while this tells us something of the gait of *Orrorin*, it does not necessarily tell us that it was bipedal. There are several fossil ape femora that are complete enough for investigation of this trait, and this needs to be done before its significance can be determined.

Slightly later in time again are two species of *Ardipithecus*, *A. ramidus* from Pliocene deposits at Aramis and Gona (4 to 5 million years) and *A. kadabba* from the Middle Awash region (5 to 6 million years), all three sites being in Ethiopia. The geological context of the sites and descriptions of the fossil hominids are described in a series of papers published in 2009 in the journal *Science*, and following is a brief summary of their main anatomical features.

The skull of *Ardipithecus ramidus* is small, particularly relative to body size, and it lacks lower face prognathism in common with several of the middle and

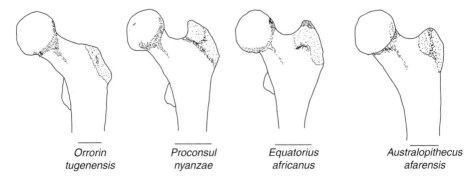

| *Orrorin* tugenensis | *Proconsul* nyanzae | *Equatorius* africanus | *Australopithecus* afarensis |

Figure 15.1 The femur of *Orrorin tugenensis* (left) compared with those of *Proconsul nyanzae*, *Equatorius africanus* and *Australopithecus afarensis*. The scale bars represent 2 cm.

late Miocene fossil apes both from Africa and Europe and in contrast to the skulls of living African great apes (Figure 15.2). Brain size is estimated at between 300 and 350 cm^3, which is within the range of the great apes and twice the size of the much smaller fossil ape *Proconsul heseloni* (which was probably only about one quarter the body mass of *A. ramidus*). The foramen magnum is relatively anteriorly placed on the base of the skull, reflecting a shortened base of the skull, which probably reflects a more upright posture than is present in the great apes and *Sahelanthropus*. The cranial base differs from that of the great apes, and is therefore said to be more human-like, but it is possible that it is similar to that of Miocene apes and therefore a primitive retention. We do not know at present if that is the case, for the cranial base is not preserved in any Miocene ape. It is possible, therefore, that it is the great apes that are derived in this respect. Reduced premolar honing is present in *A. ramidus*, and canine size is small, not just the tooth present in the skull but the isolated canines from the same sites and attributed to this species. The earlier species *Ardipithecus kadabba* has high crowned ape-like canines and a third lower premolar with a mesial wear facet (Figure 15.2), implying at least some degree of functional honing. The postcanine teeth are relatively small with thick enamel, similar to those of *A. ramidus* and *Orrorin* and not enlarged as in other later Miocene hominids such as *Ouranopithecus* and *Sivapithecus* (Chapter 14, Figure 14.3).

The head of the humerus in the *A. ramidus* skeleton is not strongly rotated medially and the deltoid crest is well developed, as it is in *Proconsul* and *Sivapithecus*. The elbow joint lacks the upwards facing ulnar trochlear articular surface present in African apes, and the contact of the radius with the

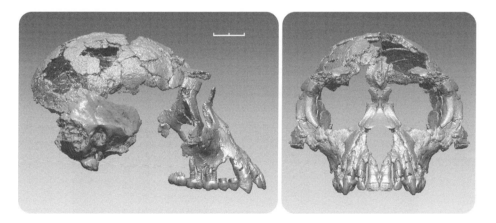

Figure 15.2 The skull of *Ardipithecus ramidus*, side view left and face right. Micro-CT renders by, (c), and courtesy of Gen Suwa, The University of Tokyo.

wrist bones (scaphoid) is primitive. The bones of the hand are relatively short, unlike the elongated hands of living great apes, and they have similar proportions to the hands of *Proconsul* and *Equatorius* (Figure 15.3). The articulations with the wrist bones are also narrow as in *Proconsul*, and the bones of the thumb are relatively large and robust, similar to the proportions in *Proconsul*, *Equatorius* and *Sivapithecus*. The thumb in particular is robust as it is in humans, and in some respects the hand of *A. ramidus* is less like that of the great apes than is the hand of *Hispanopithecus laietanus* from the late Miocene of Spain, which has the greatly elongated finger bones described in Chapter 12 (Figure 12.8). Thus there are few similarities with African apes and humans in the forelimb of *A. ramidus*, and as Owen Lovejoy points out, "these known Late Miocene to Early Pliocene hominids probably all lacked the numerous, apparently derived, forelimb features of extant African apes".

The pelvis has features indicating early adaptation to bipedal locomotion and also to life in trees. The ilium (upper part of the hip bone) is expanded laterally as it is in humans and some fossil apes, and it is also shortened to some extent, although not as much as in humans (Figure 15.4). The lower part of the hip joint (ischium) is elongated as it is in the great apes (not known for Miocene apes), and the morphology of the proximal femur suggests that the gluteal muscles, so essential for bipedal walking, had not been modified in

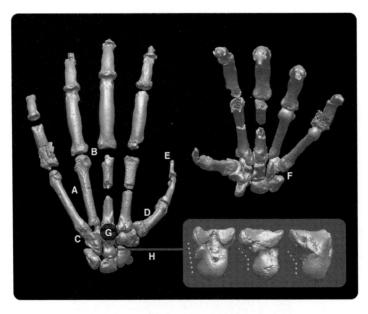

Figure 15.3 The hand bones of *Ardipithecus ramidus*. Photographs by, (c), and courtesy of Tim White, UC Berkeley.

Figure 15.4 The pelvis of *Ardipithecus ramidus*. Micro-CT renders by, (c), and courtesy of Gen Suwa, The University of Tokyo.

A. ramidus and were still similar to their disposition in the great apes and in *Proconsul* species. However, more fragmentary fossils from the Maka Sands and Dikika, both in Ethiopia, indicate that some aspects of the hip joint in fossils of approximately the same age as *A. ramidus* shared derived morphologies with humans, but other characters of this species also show that it differed in many respects from later hominins, for example the gorilla-like scapula of the juvenile individual from Dikika, and the long and curved finger bones. In other words, there had been major changes in the hip joint between *A. ramidus* and Miocene apes in the direction of later hominins, but not all of the characters for bipedal walking had yet evolved.

Most of the bones of the foot are preserved as part of the *A. ramidus* skeleton, and they display a remarkable mix of characters. The most obvious feature is the divergent big toe, which has the grasping function present in one form or another in most primates (Figure 15.5), and it is similar in particular to the morphology in the African apes. However, the mid-tarsal region of the foot, that is, the part of the foot between the heel and the main body of the foot, is elongated as it is in humans and monkeys, but the elongated cuboid, and the tendons associated with it, lack the modifications present in the arched foot of humans and retain the primitive morphology present in monkeys. The lateral side of the foot is more robust than in African apes and monkeys and approaches the range seen in the human foot, and the foot was not inverted during locomotion as it is in the African apes. This may be an adaptation for terrestrial locomotion, and specifically an incipient form of bipedal locomotion. The angle of the proximal joint surface on an isolated phalanx has been put forward as a hominin character, but this morphology is present also in pronograde quadrupeds, not just bipeds, and it is present also in the fossil ape *Sivapithecus*, which was an arboreal pronograde quadruped.

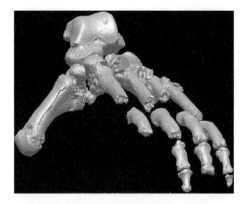

Figure 15.5 The foot of *Ardipithecus ramidus*. Lovejoy et al. 2009, Walker 2005. Micro-CT renders by, (c), and courtesy of Gen Suwa, The University of Tokyo.

The lengths of the major limb elements and the proportions of arm length and leg length, as well as proportions within the bones of the leg and arm, are similar to those of the early Miocene ape *Proconsul* and most living Old World monkeys, and they are different from those of both living apes and humans. In other words, there has been no shortening of the legs that is a feature of the living great apes (although not of gibbons), and no leg lengthening characteristic of humans.

Shortening of the legs is seen in the Pleistocene australopithecines, starting with *Australopithecus afarensis* in the Pliocene, although the condition is unknown for the earliest of the australopithecines, *A. anamensis*. The latter species comes from Kanapoi and Allia Bay in Kenya and the former from Laetoli in Tanzania. All these sites are a little later in time than Aramis, and *Australopithecus anamensis* combines a unique blend of primitive characters of the skull and teeth with advanced morphological features of the postcrania. The teeth in particular are markedly ape-like, with relatively large canines, parallel tooth rows and asymmetrical premolars. These are all characters of Miocene apes[1] and are probably primitively retained characters, and the shallow palate is another primitive feature also shared with *Australopithecus afarensis*. Tooth enamel is thick, and molars are buccolingually expanded, broader mesially than distally. The postcrania, however, show that *A. anamensis* was probably bipedal, perhaps to a greater extent than was *A. afarensis* nearly half a million years later in time, for the elbow and ankle joints are more like those of species of *Homo*. While there is little doubt that *Australopithecus anamensis* is on the hominin lineage, many similarities with fossil apes should be expected.

In terms of hominin origins, *Ardipithecus ramidus* retains many characters present in Miocene apes (but notably few characters with chimpanzees), with the addition of some characters linking it with bipedal hominins. It was not, however, as accomplished a biped as either *Australopithecus anamensis* or *A. afarensis*, and with its divergent big toe, and the conformation of the gluteal muscles as shown by the elongated lower ischium, it may have been more at home in trees than on the ground. There is no evidence of ancestral-descendant relationship with these three hominins, and with so little time separating them it could well be that more than one lineage of ape-like hominin was trying out this new form of locomotion independently. Still earlier fossils cannot at present be accepted as being bipedal without further evidence. *Orrorin tugenensis*, for

---

[1] In my News and Views comment in *Nature* on the publication of *A. anamensis*, I said: "At this early stage of human evolution, however, it is to be expected that there will be many similarities with fossil apes ... Rather than questioning which hominid lineage the Kanapoi species may be on, therefore, I would like to raise the question of how it differs from fossil apes." The rather ascerbic response from one of the authors was: "If Andrews wants to compare it to Miocene apes, let him do it, but personally I can't be bothered."

example, may have had an upright body posture, as shown by the internal structure of the proximal femur, and *Sahelanthropus tchadensis* may also have been more upright, as indicated by the position of the foramen magnum on the base of the skull, but neither morphology says anything direct about these fossil hominids being bipedal, since orthograde posture is present in several fossil apes that are demonstrably not bipeds. It is evident that some characteristics associated with bipedalism, as well as the modifications of the canine–premolar complex discussed above, occurred independently in different lineages of later Miocene hominids, and by themselves they are not diagnostic of the human lineage.

Two points need to be emphasized here in the light of these descriptions. One is that absence of hominin characters does not exclude these early fossils from the hominin lineage so long as at least one character is shared between them. The earlier species of *Ardipithecus*, *A. kadabba*, does not appear to share any hominin characters, but *A. ramidus* (characters of the skull, pelvis and foot) and *Australopithecus anamensis* (characters of the elbow and ankle) share derived characters with later hominins. The second point is that none of these hominin fossils share characters exclusively with African apes. The morphology present today in the African apes is highly derived while on the contrary *Ororrin tugenensis* and *Ardipithecus kadabba* share many primitive characters with Miocene fossil apes that appear to be primitive retentions from earlier ape ancestry. They do not show that these two fossils were apes, but they may have been closer to the common ancestor of apes and humans than the fossil apes discussed so far. As such, they can provide crucial information about the common ancestor of apes and humans, and whether they are already on the human lineage, or precede the split with the apes, is not important for the identification of the characters of the last common ancestor.

Summary of late Miocene hominids

Late Miocene hominids have a mix of characters that are shared with Miocene apes, with at least one species sharing some characters with hominins. The similarities and differences are listed below:

- Cranial capacity small – similar to Miocene apes.
- Broad central incisors – common in fossil apes: primitive for Hominidae.
- Low crowned canine – present in at least two genera of fossil apes; may be shared derived character with hominins or convergent; *A. kadabba* retains large canines.
- Reduced P_3 honing – also present in at least two genera of fossil apes; may be shared derived character with hominins or convergent; *A. kadabba* still has premolar honing.

- Small molars and premolars – shared with dryopithecines and earlier Miocene apes: primitive for Homininae.
- Enamel thickness variable.
- Short base of skull – present in gibbons, some short-faced monkeys not necessarily related to bipedal locomotion.
- Shoulder joint – similar to *Proconsul heseloni*: primitive for Hominoidea.
- Elbow joint – similar to *Proconsul heseloni*: primitive for Hominoidea.
- Hand proportions – metacarpals are short as in *Proconsul heseloni*, phalanges are relatively longer but not as long as in *Hispanopithecus laietanus*: primitive for Hominidae.
- Thumb – adapted for grasping and long relative to the hand: present in Miocene apes and primitively retained in humans.
- Pelvis – broad ilium, but gluteal muscles not yet repositioned: derived character shared with later hominins.
- Ischium – long and ape-like: primitive for Hominidae.
- Femoral neck features – present in monkeys, not known for fossil apes, function not known: probably convergent on humans.
- Divergent big toe as in African apes and most other primates.
- Elongated mid-tarsal region of the foot – present in monkeys and humans but differs from African apes: primitive for Hominoidea.
- Phalanges are short and robust as in gorillas and unlike the elongated toe bones in chimpanzees and other apes.
- Leg length relatively long – present in Miocene apes, gibbons and monkeys: primitive for Hominoidea; the shortening of the legs in australopithecines and the great apes may be convergent.

Environments of late Miocene and Pliocene hominids

The environment in the Lukeino Formation associated with *Orrorin tugenensis* is interpreted as open woodland with patches of forest. The palaeoecology has not yet been studied, but there are 38 species of mammal in the associated fauna, dominated by impala but including some possible woodland/forest indicators such as colobus monkeys and bushbabies. Non-forest equids, rhinos and some bovids are also present, and the presence of crocodiles, hippos and freshwater mussels (*Iridina* species) in the fauna show that there was permanent fresh water nearby. A very similar habitat has been proposed for *Sahelanthropus*, again based on the fauna and in the absence of palaeoecological analysis. There are many fish, crocodiles and aquatic mammals, all suggesting the nearby presence of permanent bodies of water. The lower sediments have cross-bedded and sorted sands characteristic of wind-blown deposits or sandy dunes, and these indicate desert conditions in the vicinity of the site. The middle part of the section, which includes the mammal fauna and *Sahelanthropus*, consists of water-deposited sediments, the random nature of the direction of water flow apparently being due to water drainage between the still-existing sand dunes. Patchy woodlands would have formed wherever drainage conditions made it possible.

The geology and plant remains from the Middle Awash area show that in the southeast of the area there were deltaic and lake margin deposits, but the centre of the basin near Aramis, where *A. ramidus* and most fossils came from, was a low relief flood plain with springs and occasional channels running through it. Calcareous palaeosols were developed on areas of low relief and could have had impeded drainage, and the deposits between the two dated tuffs indicate stable conditions. This is in contrast to the same aged deposits at Gona, where similar faunas were recovered from what has been interpreted as mixed habitats. Analysis of carbon isotopes indicates intermediate values between the C_3 and C_4 photosynthetic pathways, with up to 70% C_4 plants present in the eastern part of the region. This is taken to indicate a range of vegetation types from woodland to wooded grassland. Fossil wood is abundant throughout the Aramis deposits but little pollen. Phytoliths were found, however, and they show the presence of palms, woody plants and grass. The abundance of grass phytoliths in the east of the region is taken to indicate grassland with less than 40% tree cover, but further west the tree cover increased to over 60%. The land gastropods do not seem to have had high diversity, but the species identified are similar to those found today in ground water forests, that is, forests like those bordering Lake Manyara which grow in an arid climate but which are plentifully supplied with water by streams and ground water flowing off the adjoining rift valley escarpment.

The large mammals from Aramis are directly associated with the fossils of *Ardipithecus ramidus*. The two most common animal species are tragelaphine antelopes, which are browsing herbivores, and colobine monkeys, which are arboreal leaf-eaters. Together these make up more than half the recorded mammal specimens, with the tragelaphines making up the great majority of the bovid assemblage. This is an unusual combination of animals and it is obviously highly selective. The fossils from the large mammals show many signs of carnivore action, which accounts for their fragmentary nature but which does not necessarily account for the taxonomic imbalance. Supposing the assemblage to be the product of a single predator species, only leopards are big enough to tackle most tragelaphines, which are at least gazelle-sized or bigger, and colobine monkeys, which might have fallen prey to leopards at night or when they came to the ground, as some of the larger fossil colobines probably did (some species have mixed terrestrial/arboreal adaptations). The other alternative is that the large mammal assemblage is not the product of a single predator species, in which case the different hunting preferences of the predators has to be taken into account. For example, leopards may have killed and eaten the tragelaphines and other antelopes in the fauna, while eagles may have killed the monkeys, in which case the question has to be asked, were the two sets of animals killed actually living in the same place or may some have been carried in by the predators? And if this is the case, to which part of the assemblage did *Ardipithecus* belong? Another speculation is to wonder if the tragelaphines, of which bushbucks are the most common representative, were juvenile individuals. If so, could this be a prey assemblage of *Ardipithecus* itself, like the prey of common chimpanzees today consisting of juvenile antelopes and monkeys?

The carbon isotope values of herbivore teeth from Aramis show a range of $\delta^{13}C$ values, with *Ardipithecus ramidus* linked with the tragelaphines, neotragines and giraffes with C_3 photosynthetic pathway. There is only a relatively small number of species showing the C_4 pattern. Recent comparisons of carbon and oxygen isotopes with those of a large chimpanzee population in the Kibale Forest indicate that this fossil hominin inhabited a more open habitat than living chimpanzees and fed both in trees and on the ground. Small mammals are abundant and they are identified as the product of owl pellets by Antoine Louchart. The lack of digestion on the teeth suggests that the owl accumulating the assemblage was a barn owl (*Tyto alba*), which is also the only owl species recorded at Aramis, although it should be pointed out that some of the African eagle owls also produce little digestion on the bones of their prey. Since they have different hunting preferences from barn owls, their prey assemblages are different even when occupying the same habitat. For example eagle owls hunt by perch-pounce in woodland and waterside environments, quite different from hunting by slow quartering flight over open ground characteristic of barn owls. The large rodent and bird assemblages indicate the presence of mesic woodland at Aramis, which would be an unusual hunting habitat of barn owls.

At Gona, about 70 km to the north of Aramis, the mammal assemblage of 27 species includes many primates and pigs associated with *A. kadabba*. The primate fauna is divided into approximately two thirds baboon and one third colobus monkeys. Combined with evidence from the sediments and carbon isotopes discussed in Chapter 6, and the presence of *Celtis* seeds, the environment at Gona is reconstructed as woodland with moderate rainfall. The mollusc fauna of bivalves and gastropods indicates in addition the presence of a permanent water source consisting of both slow moving water and interconnected lakes. The isotope analysis of herbivore teeth indicates greater numbers of C_4 feeders, although the soil isotopes indicate C_3 vegetation. This suggests woodland was present actually at the site, that is, at the depositional environment where the sediments and the fossils accumulated, but the presence of more open country nearby is indicated by the C_4 feeders, perhaps transported in from some distance. This possibility has yet to be investigated. The ecomorphology of the primate foot bones shows that most of them have the morphology of animals giving a 'forest' signal, which means in effect heavy wooded cover. Similarly, the limb bones of the colobine monkey appear to have been adapted for life in trees, with no good evidence for terrestriality. The mesowear of the bovids indicates that most have browsing adaptations, while grazing bovids like alcelaphines are rare at Aramis.

In a paper I published with Louise Humphrey on the early collection from Aramis, based on only 10% of the present fauna, we used a taxon-free approach which showed that the Aramis fauna was dominated by browsing herbivores and frugivores, and we concluded from this that the environment represented by the large mammals was woodland or dry forest. The results published on a more extensive fauna by Tim White and the Berkeley team are in broad agreement with this conclusion. They "suggest its (*Ardipithecus ramidus*) persistent occupation of a woodland with patches of forest across the paleolandscape" and stress in particular the varied nature of the habitat occupied by this fossil hominin.

To finish off this review, brief mention can be made of the Pliocene localities of the earliest australopithecines. Little has been published on the palaeoecology or taphonomy of *Australopithecus anamensis* from just over 4 million years ago at Kanapoi and Allia Bay, but the slightly later site at Laetoli in Tanzania is well documented. The Laetolil Beds have remains of *Australopithecus afarensis* and, more importantly, footprints of this fossil hominin are preserved in the sediments. Both these and the later remains of the same species from Hadar in Ethiopia demonstrate unequivocally that *A. afarensis* walked upright on two legs. At both sites there is strong taphonomic and ecomorphological evidence that the fossil hominin was associated with deciduous woodland environments, probably dry woodland at Laetoli and moist woodland at Hadar. Later deposits at Laetoli, the Ndolanya Beds, have been shown by Kris Kovarovic to have a fauna representing more open environments, so that there was a transition from closed to open woodland during this period and this coincided with a change from the gracile *A. afarensis* to the heavily robust *Paranthropus blacki*. Much of this evidence, from the fauna, flora, ecomorphology, geomorphology and carbon isotopes, was documented in Chapter 6 and reference can be made to it there.

Summary of late Miocene environments

- Late Miocene apes *Chororapithecus*, *Nakalipithecus* and *Samburupithecus* have no clear phylogenetic or ecological affinities.

- Late Miocene *Sahelanthropus, Orrorin* and *Ardipithecus kababba* have small teeth, thick enamel, canine/premolar honing, equivocal evidence for canine reduction (small in females?), some indications of more upright posture.
- Late Miocene environments associated with the hominin ancestors were woodland next to water.
- *Ardipithecus kadabba* environment was woodland with moderate rainfall near lakes or rivers.
- *Ardipithecus ramidus* has a mixture of ape-like characters in the foot, humerus, aspect of pelvis, hand and thumb, phalanges, hominin-like characters in the small canine and reduced premolar honing, and some adaptations for bipedal locomotion in the pelvis and foot.
- The *A. ramidus* environment was woodland with patches of forest, nearby presence of water.
- In general, late Miocene environments associated with the hominin ancestors were woodland next to water, similar in most respects to those of later Miocene apes.

Part IV
Last common ancestor

Chapter 16
Putting together the evidence

The evidence from fossil apes

We have seen in Chapters 7 to 14 that fossil apes span the period from before 20 million years ago in the early Miocene to about 8 million years ago in the late Miocene. In the early Miocene, apes were locally abundant but only known from East Africa. They were arboreal monkey-like primates, quadrupedal (moving on all four legs) with pronograde posture (the body parallel with the ground). One possible exception to this is *Morotopithecus,* which appears to have had incipient stages of upright posture. Their skulls were lightly built, with narrow noses, broad orbits and a muzzle-like lower face with moderate lower and mid-face prognathism. They had relatively narrow incisors, projecting canines, variable canine/premolar honing, and relatively small molars and premolars with variable enamel thickness. They had narrow chests, limited mobility of the hind legs but greater mobility at their shoulders and elbows, and their hands and feet were adapted for gripping but not for load bearing. Their thumbs were not reduced in length as in great apes, but were slightly shorter relative to the thumb in human hands. The thumb in the *Proconsul* hand (Chapter 7) had a hinge joint rather than the rotatory joint present in the human hand, but it is likely that they had a precision grip, and with the greater thumb length they probably had greater manipulative abilities than chimpanzees today. The species ranged in size from 10 to 80{ts}kg, the weight of male chimpanzees. They had relatively large brains for their size, and they were associated with tropical forest and deciduous woodland environments, the latter with single tree canopies growing in seasonal (wet−dry) climates. They had primarily arboreal adaptations, but the body size of the larger species would have necessitated some degree of terrestrial locomotion in their woodland habitats, particularly if any distance had to be covered from one part of the woodland to another, as the small branch contact between woodland trees limits movement from one tree to another for all but small mammals. For the most part they had soft fruit diets, although one group at least was more folivorous (leaf-eating *Rangwapithecus*).

Middle Miocene apes had similar locomotor capabilities to the early Miocene apes. They were all still pronograde arboreal quadrupeds, again with one possible exception (*Nacholapithecus* may have been suspensory but in a form unlike any other suspensory primate). There is some evidence of orthograde posture (for example *Morotopithecus*) and some for terrestriality, but for the most part the fossil apes in the middle to late Miocene demonstrate a mixture of arboreal and terrestrial adaptations, and they have mostly been found associated with woodland habitats. Sixteen million years ago, some species of fossil ape were present in Europe and Asia associated with subtropical summer rainfall woodland habitats (*Griphopithecus, Kenyapithecus*), some with savanna habitats (*Ouranopithecus*) and some with subtropical forest (many of the Dryopithecinae).

Both summer rainfall woodland and subtropical woodland are structurally analogous with single canopy tropical woodlands and differ from multi-canopy tropical forest in having lighter tree canopies and therefore more abundant ground vegetation. They are all associated with highly seasonal climates, whether having warm−cold variation or wet−dry, and the shortage of food supplies during the cold or dry seasons would have been a limiting factor for ape survival. The functional complex of powerful mastication, with relatively large molars and premolars, thicker enamel on the molar teeth, crowns with more rounded cusps and more robust jaws, is found in terrestrial or semi-terrestrial fossil apes associated with woodland or savanna habitats; while the functional adaptation of relatively smaller molars with thinner enamel and more gracile jaws is found on arboreal apes living in subtropical forest: for example late Miocene *Hispanopithecus laietanus* combines elongated hands with the high angle of the head of the femur (which means that the leg functions more like an arm, as can be seen in the orang utan). These are good indicators of suspensory locomotion (at least in the form taken by orang utans).

For many years it was thought, including by me, that thick enamel was a significant character of the human lineage, as it was believed that African great apes have relatively thin enamel and humans have thick enamel, so that fossil apes with thick enamel could be ancestral to humans. This was one of the characters which was earlier thought to link 'Ramapithecus' with the human lineage, but it is now known that enamel thickness is variable in living apes, with some having enamel almost as thick as in humans. It is also variable in fossil apes, but it seems to be linked more with diet than with phylogeny. There is some indication, however, that middle and late Miocene apes differ from early Miocene species in having thicker enamel with less pointed and lower cusps. They also have relatively larger molars (known as megadonty) and both characters are also characteristic of Pleistocene species of australopithecines (and to a lesser extent to later species of *Homo*). The variation seen in this character will be evident from the discussion below.

Towards the end of the middle Miocene and the late Miocene, groups of pronograde quadrupedal apes still persisted in Europe and Asia, living in sub-tropical summer rainfall woodlands more open than those of the middle Miocene described above. They still had relatively large thick-enamelled molars and premolars and robust jaws, and upper incisors very broad and low crowned, but they fall into two distinct groups based on their skull morphology: one group had characters similar to those of the orang utan (facial characters in *Sivapithecus, Ankarapithecus,* and lower jaw and teeth in *Khoratpithecus, Lufeng-pithecus*) while retaining large projecting canines; and the other group had characters more similar to the African apes, with broader, more robust skulls, broad noses, broad orbits, very thick enamel of their molars, relatively smaller canines and reduction in canine–premolar honing (*Ouranopithecus, Graeco-pithecus*). These characters continue the trend seen in the middle Miocene of adaptations for powerful chewing. David Begun puts it most recently that "These features leave an overwhelming impression on facial and dental morph-ology, though they are all closely interrelated and essentially constitute a single trait complex that results from selection for more powerful mastication." In their postcranial skeletons, *Sivapithecus* had a mobile ankle, distinguishing it from monkeys, and bones of the forearm indicating generalized pronograde arboreality, but with perhaps a tendency towards orthograde posture.

Both these groups with robust jaws and large teeth persisted through the late Miocene, and they were contemporaneous with a third group, the dryo-pithecines. These have relatively small molars and premolars for their body size and projecting canines with premolar honing contrasting with rather deep mandibles. The dryopithecines as presently recognized form a disparate group. Skull form is variable, with some having broad noses and orbits, similar to the *Ouranopithecus* skull, some having features similar to the orang utan (and *Sivapithecus*), some with narrow projecting muzzles, some with almost vertical faces and some with strong lower face prognathism (but little alveolar prognathism). Their postcrania are also variable, with some differing markedly from the pronograde fossil apes considered so far in having numerous adapta-tions for orthograde (upright) posture, such as their broad chest region and stiff lumbar region. One of these combines orthograde posture with short fingers (*Pierolapithecus catalsaunicus*) so that it seems to have had a more baboon-like form of locomotion, and at least two dryopithecine species have adaptations for suspensory locomotion with mobile elbow joint, stable at full extension, long slender hand phalanges and femur neck steeply angled (*Hispanopithecus laietanus*).

The late Miocene ape from Italy, *Oreopithecus bambolii,* appears to have developed a similar suite of postcranial adaptations for orthograde posture and suspensory locomotion to *Hispanopithecus*. Like *Rudapithecus*, it is associated with subtropical swamp forest environments, with perennially wet, evergreen or semi-evergreen forest dominated by swamp cypress and laurels, in both cases supported by the edaphic features of the environment. It seems likely that the shared suspensory adaptations in the two fossil ape species are linked with this type of environment, in contrast to the woodlands associated with other late Miocene apes. Mention has also been made of possible ortho-grade adaptations of the early Miocene ape *Morotopithecus bishopi*, and although little is known of the environment of this species, it does indicate that orthograde postural adaptations evolved independently at least three times in the Miocene apes.

Unfortunately, little is known of the postcranial skeletons of the African late Miocene apes. By the early Pliocene, however, it is evident that *Ardipithecus ramidus* had upright (orthograde) posture but had neither suspensory nor knuckle-walking adaptations, and it was probably incipiently bipedal. What is important here is to distinguish between characters that are primarily adapted for suspensory locomotion and those that are primarily adapted for upright orthograde posture. The latter may be a pre-adaptation for suspensory activity, for example the convergence between gibbons and spider monkeys, but it may exist independently of this activity, for example in the largely terrestrial chimpanzees and gorillas. It was certainly a pre-adaptation for upright bipedalism.

Summary of the evidence from fossil apes

- The common adaptation of fossil apes throughout the Miocene was as pronograde arboreal monkey-like apes.
- Associated environments were tropical and subtropical woodland.
- The fossil apes must have been partly terrestrial because of their relatively large body size (up to 80{ts}kg), and the type of environment they were living in (closed to open woodland) since tree to tree canopy contact is limited to small branches even in closed canopy woodland.
- In the middle Miocene in Africa, two branches of fossil ape developed thick enamel on the teeth and robust jaws, both associated with wood-land environments.
- In the middle to late Miocene, a second group of species in Europe and Asia developed robust skulls and jaws and enlarged molars and premolars with thick enamel and retained quadrupedal pronograde locomotion.
- This group of fossil apes is associated with deciduous woodland or open woodland habitats.
- A third group retained primitively small teeth with thinner enamel but developed orthograde posture (*Pierolapithecus catalaunicus*, at about

12 million years) and in some cases additional suspensory adaptations for life in trees (*Hispanopithecus laietanus* and *Rudapithecus hungaricus* at about 10 million years).

- Most of the species in this third group are associated with subtropical woodlands, a vegetation type having similar canopy structure to tropical woodlands but probably evergreen in part.
- Independent evolution of orthograde posture has been shown once in the early Miocene (*Morotopithecus bishopi*) and once in the late Miocene (*Oreopithecus bambolii*) where it was combined with suspensory adaptations.

The evidence from fossil hominins

Characters present in early human ancestors after the divergence from the last common ancestor with the apes must either be primitive retentions from the common ancestor or uniquely derived characters present only in humans. Examples of the latter include large brains, reduced sexual dimorphism, fully upright posture, bipedalism, reduced canine size and canine/premolar honing, and the development of the precision grip in the hand; probable primitive retentions are thick molar enamel, enlarged cheek teeth and robust jaws, and hand proportions. Some of the derived characters, however, are absent in the earliest hominins; they appear later in human evolution, some not until the appearance of species of the genus *Homo*, and since they are absent in earlier fossil hominins they also cannot have been present in the ape/human common ancestor. An example of this is the increase in brain size: from the time of *Proconsul heseloni* in the early Miocene, brain size (relative to body mass) in apes remained about the same as it is in the great apes, and it was still the same in the early hominins such as the species of *Ardipithecus* and *Australopithecus*. Clearly, therefore, increase in brain size is not a basal hominin character.

No fossil apes show any evidence for bipedalism, the earliest definitive evidence for which comes from *Australopithecus afarensis,* both in the form of footprints at Laetoli just under 4 million years ago, and from the leg bones from the slightly later fossils from Kenya and Ethiopia. There is also a case to be made for a degree of bipedalism in *Ardipithecus ramidus* from Aramis and *Australopithecus anamensis* from Kanapoi, both just over 4 million years ago. The evidence for the first is in the lateral development of the foot bones and the relatively broad upper part of the pelvis (ilium) from Aramis; and the evidence for the second is in the morphology of the partial tibia from Kanapoi. Upright posture, however, while present in the earliest fossil hominins so far discovered, may have featured in the last common ancestor, at least to the extent that chimpanzees are partially upright, but it is far from certain that this is the case, for the great majority of fossil apes were pronograde.

Mark Teaford and Peter Ungar suggest that a trend in hominin evolution was towards harder and tougher diets, as shown by some Pliocene hominins. This is seen in the increase in size of the molars and premolars and decrease in size of the anterior teeth, and it is linked with the buttressing of the face and increase in enamel thickness. However, this trend does not start with hominins but is a feature of some fossil apes, several lineages of which also had enlarged teeth and thick enamel beginning in the early middle Miocene. Middle Miocene apes such as *Kenyapithecus* and *Equatorius* both have enlarged molars with thickened enamel, and this trend is magnified in the late Miocene with *Ouranopithecus*, *Ankarapithecus* and *Sivapithecus*. With the possible exception of some later australopithecines, *Ouranopithecus* has the thickest enamel of any hominid. In all cases, thick enamel is associated with thickened or buttressed upper and lower jaws of similar dimensions to early hominins such as *Ardipithecus ramidus* and *Australopithecus anamensis*. These trends are followed by the massive increase in molar and premolar size and enamel thickness in Pleistocene australopithecines.

It is very likely that the extreme adaptations of the teeth may be linked with a diet of hard objects, hard fruits, nuts and seeds as suggested above, for they are associated with increasing seasonality in climate and increasingly impoverished woodlands between 2 and 3 million years ago. The causes of this during the earlier stages of these trends in the Miocene are not so clear, for even in the early Miocene fossil apes are associated with tropical woodlands as well as forest, and by the middle Miocene there is no evidence of association between fossil apes and forest environments.

Body size dimorphism is difficult to estimate in fossil assemblages, partly because samples of fossil species are often too small for the statistical procedures necessary to measure it, but also because it can only be estimated from skeletal proxies such as size variation in canines or the diameter of the limb bone shafts. Fossil assemblages are often derived from more than one source and may be accumulated over a period of time. Either of these factors could introduce errors in estimating body size, which could change with time or with geographical location. In addition, some sites have more than one species of fossil ape present, and where they are difficult to differentiate, as at Paşalar, special measures have to be employed to estimate dimorphism. Taking all these factors into account, it appears that sexual dimorphism was generally high in fossil apes; for example it was moderate to high in *Proconsul* species during the early Miocene, higher in *Griphopithecus* and *Kenyapithecus* during the middle Miocene and higher still in *Lufengpithecus* and *Sivapithecus* in the late Miocene. It was probably high in the dryopithecines as well, although since a different species has been attributed to each site where they are found, it is impossible to measure the degree of size variation. However, another indicator of size dimorphism, the ratio of the second to the fourth digits, has been shown to covary with intra-sexual competition in living hominids, and hence with social system, and the low ratio for two of the dryopithecines, *Pierolapithecus* and *Hispanopithecus*, may be evidence of polygynous social systems in these two fossil apes, and by reverse argument, high sexual dimorphism.

Reduction in canine size and canine/premolar honing in fossil hominins also followed a trend in ape evolution, but it was probably not a characteristic of the last common ancestor. Based on high canine dimorphism and low digit ratios, later Miocene apes had high degrees of sexual dimorphism. There is a low digit ratio also for the early Pliocene *Ardipithecus ramidus*, similar in value to that of the two fossil apes, and it appears that this fossil hominin also retained high levels of dimorphism. *Australopithecus anamensis* and *Ardipithecus kadabba* have relatively large ape-like canines and elongated third lower premolars. Despite having two cusps on the premolar, they also have a wear facet on the mesial (front) surface, implying at least some degree of functional honing. This could well be a transitional stage from the single cusped honing action of the lower premolar in apes to the bicuspid non-honing premolar in later hominins, and it may well have been present in the last common ancestor of apes and humans, but we cannot be certain because it is evident that loss of honing has evolved in different ways in fossil apes and hominins and probably more than once.

Reduction in sexual dimorphism within hominins may have appeared quickly, for *Australopithecus afarensis* had high digit ratios and low canine dimorphism. However, body size dimorphism appears to be high in this fossil hominin based on variations in size of the postcranial skeleton, and the reduction in canine dimorphism may not have been associated with lowered sexual dimorphism. It is possible that reduction in sexual dimorphism in hominin evolution did not occur until the emergence of species of *Homo*, and that monogamy evolved at this time, but there is no indication that it was present in the last common ancestor. The putative condition in the last common ancestor is most likely therefore to have retained high degrees of sexual dimorphism, shared primitively with Miocene apes and *Ardipithecus*.

Distinguishing basal hominin characters would be more straightforward if we had evidence of fossil chimpanzees comparable to that of hominins. The only fossil chimpanzees, however, are late in time, and no fossil bonobos are known at all. We cannot therefore plot the acquisition of derived chimpanzee characters in the way that we can for hominins. Chimpanzee evolution is made even more complicated by the fact that some of the highly derived characters present in the two living species, for example the many adaptations for knuckle-walking, are present also in gorillas, and their elongated hands and short thumbs are also present in gorillas and orang utans. So far none of these characters are present in the earliest hominins; however, the short legs present in chimpanzees, gorillas and orang utans are also a feature of later australopithecines, so that this could be a shared primitive character of chimpanzees and early hominins.

The evolution of the human hand is more problematic. The development of prehensile hands is an ancient primate adaptation probably related to life in trees, particularly the small branch niche, but both humans and great apes today have highly specialized hands. In the case of humans, the joints of the thumb are modified to allow rotatory movement at the joints, so that the thumb can be placed against the other fingers in a very precise way, the so-called precision grip. John Napier defined this many years ago, and it entails in addition relatively long thumbs and the ability to apply power to the precision grip. The great apes all have relatively short thumbs as a result of their greatly elongated hand lengths, so they lack the manual dexterity of humans. This makes tool use a rather clumsy affair in chimpanzees, as can be seen when they are fishing for termites while holding a thin stick. However, they are able to manipulate small objects, changing their grip to achieve the desired alignment. This dexterity is learned behaviour, and adult chimpanzees have a more varied repertoire of hand movements than juveniles, including precision grips, working with two hands and with differentiation between fingers. Gorillas similarly have a surprisingly large repertoire of hand movements, with 72 functionally distinct actions recorded for the mountain gorilla, again with two-handed actions and with the two hands taking on different but synchronized actions and differentiation between fingers.

Susman has shown that the morphology of the thumb in *Australopithecus afarensis* differed from that of all known later hominins in the narrow metacarpal head of the thumb, as in the chimpanzee hand, but when the size of the thumb metacarpal is compared with that of the chimpanzee, it is longer and more robust despite the fact that *A. afarensis* was smaller in size than chimpanzees. The thumbs in the fossil apes *Proconsul heseloni, Equatorius africanus* and *Oreopithecus* also were long and narrow, as in *A. afarensis* and humans. The thumb of *Proconsul* was opposable, and its greater length compared with the chimpanzee thumb suggests that *Proconsul* had a stronger grip, although the cylindrical articular surface of the thumb joint shows that it lacked the rotatory movement of the thumb seen in the human hand and therefore lacked a human-like precision grip. *Oreopithecus* probably did have a precision grip, as seen for example in the specialized orientation of the carpometacarpal joint and the thumb–index finger proportions, and it shares with *Australopith-ecus africanus* a well-developed long flexor muscle on the thumb. The first of these is present also in *Proconsul*, and the resemblance to the australopithecine pattern is probably the result of convergence. It is likely that the long thumb in *A. afarensis* is a primitively retained character from earlier ape ancestry, and it is the living apes that have modified hands, reducing the lengths of their thumbs while extending the rest of the hand.

The similar hand proportions in the early to middle Miocene apes to those of the human hand suggest that the elongation of the hand in great apes is a derived character. In contradiction to this, the most parsimonious interpret-ation based on comparisons of humans with living apes suggests rather that the ancestral condition is the ape one, indicated by the elongated hands of all the great apes, and much of the discussion on hand evolution stems from this assumption, which by strict cladistic principles is valid. However, I suggest that in this case parsimony is giving a misleading result, one that is unsupported by any fossil evidence for hominins and directly contradicted by the evidence of Miocene apes. If this be the case, the evolution of the human hand is the reverse of what is generally assumed, and the ancestral condition is that found in several fossil apes (the ones for which there is evidence), namely human-like hand proportions, with short fingers and a long thumb. These were primitively retained in the early hominins such as *Australopithecus afarensis*, and they were as good or bad for making tools as in any of the fossil apes. Whether they used or made tools is not known, for stone industries did not come into being until the end of the Pliocene, two and a half million years ago, but there is every reason to believe that prior to the manufacture of stone tools, simpler tools would have been made by early hominins out of wood and leaves, as done by chimpanzees today. These materials are perishable and would not be preserved as fossils.

We can speculate further that it is more likely that the hominin hand evolved in fossil apes that were pronograde and partly terrestrial, such as *Proconsul* and *Equatorius*. They are known to have supported themselves on the fingers of the hand, as do baboons and macaques, and like these semi-terrestrial living species, their hand proportions were similar to those of early hominins and modern humans, that is, relatively short fingers and long thumbs capable of hinge-joint opposability. As such they had equivalent or even superior manipulative ability to the living great apes, and it is a reason-able speculation that they were in fact tool users. The manufacture of tools, however, is shared uniquely by humans and chimpanzees, and not by gorillas and orang utans (as far as we know at present), and parsimony suggests that while the last common ancestor of chimpanzees and humans uniquely made and used tools, tool manufacture goes back no further in ape ancestry.

Summary of the evidence from fossil hominins

- Characters denoting bipedalism appear in the fossil record between 4 and 5 million years ago, incipient in *Ardipithecus ramidus* and more developed in *Australopithecus anamensis* and *A. afarensis*.
- Loss of canine/premolar honing in the transition from *Ardipithecus kadabba* to *A. ramidus* at about 5 million years.
- Greater upright posture occurred earlier in the Miocene, as demonstrated for *Morotopithecus*, *Nacholapithecus* and *Hispanopithecus*, and it may have been primitively retained in *Sahelanthropus tchadensis* and *Orrorin tugenensis*.
- The partially human-like hand proportions in *A. ramidus* may have been primitively retained from Miocene apes, with the lengthened great ape hands being derived. The distinctive human hand morphology probably coincided with the later development of stone tool technologies.

The evidence from living apes

There have been a number of detailed morphological studies of living apes and humans to identify characters held in common and to distinguish characters by which they differ. The literature is too large to review here, and I have concentrated on two major scenarios in Chapter 2 that have dominated investigations into human origins: the presence of suspensory adaptations in apes and humans on the one hand, and the significance of knuckle-walking adaptations in human evolution on the other. At issue here is how these two behaviours, and their adaptations, relate to upright posture and the evolution of bipedal locomotion (Figure 16.1). I have taken the position that in some respects this is asking the wrong question, for the primary adaptation in ape evolution is the extent to which they have developed some degree of upright posture, and acquired the shared suite of characters relating to that. These characters may have been pre-adaptive both for knuckle-walking and suspension, and the prevalence of upright posture in all living apes and humans is a strong indication that it would have been present in the common ancestor of apes and humans. We have seen that it was present to some degree in fossil apes from before the divergence of orang utans to the time of the last common ancestor of chimpanzees and humans, but fossil evidence for this being the case is tenuous, for the common morphology for apes throughout much of their fossil history shows that they were pronograde quadrupeds.

A number of aspects of the biology of the last common ancestor have been proposed by Duda and Zrzavy based on patterns observed in living apes. These include slow postnatal growth, postponing female age of first reproduction,

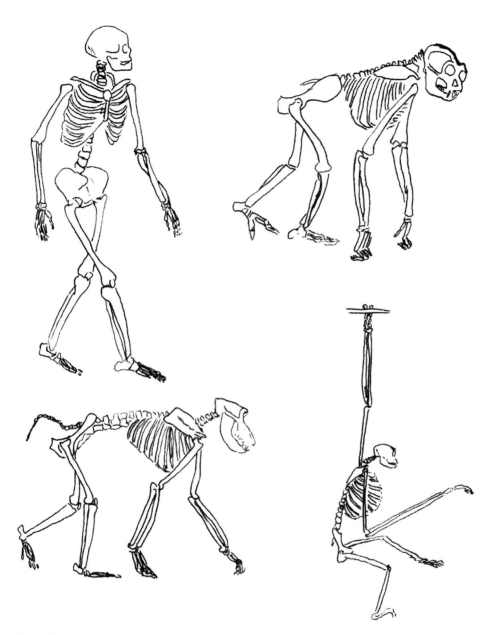

Figure 16.1 Development of upright posture. Clockwise from top right, gorilla skeleton showing knuckle-walking posture, semi-upright because of its short legs and relatively long arms; gibbon skeleton in upright brachiating posture, hanging by its extremely elongated arms, but note also its legs are also relatively long; baboon skeleton in pronograde quadrupedal posture, arms and legs about the same length and back bone parallel to the ground; human skeleton in upright posture.

short interbirth interval, non-seasonal breeding, loss of sexual skin swelling, flexible copulatory position, paternal care and cultural diversity. Some of these are difficult to verify, but they may be ancestral retentions in the common ancestor. Other features such as delayed onset of puberty, delayed eruption of the first molar and tooth row, and extended life span are probably unique to humans and were not present in the common ancestor.

Isotopic studies in chimpanzees have shown little variation in stable carbon isotopes between chimpanzees living in rainforests and those from woodland environments. This suggests that chimpanzee diets are isotopically homogeneous, and by extension may also be nutritionally homogeneous. In addition, Catherine Smith also found little difference in nitrogen isotope values between male and female chimpanzees despite the fact that males consume much more meat than females. This contrasts with baboon populations, which feed in more open and variable habitats, and for example have more variable carbon isotope values. It remains to be seen which of these two results applies more to early human populations.

Many authors propose that tooth reduction in hominins has come about because of reduction in size of the upper and lower jaws. Sam Cobb has suggested the exact opposite, that because bone is:

> phenotypically more plastic than dental tissues, it is not unreasonable to suggest that the causal relationship could be the other way around, such that the dentition influences the development of the bone. This version of the spatial model would predict that a selection pressure to reduce the canine size and or postcanine size, as is the case in hominins, *P. paniscus* and *Oreopithecus*, would result in a correlated reduction in palatal length and or width.

In other words, dental reduction possibly arising from changes in behaviour took place first and the reduction in size of the jaws followed after. Reduction in palatal length would lead in turn to reduction in prognathism. We may predict, therefore, that canine size was reduced in the last common ancestor of chimpanzees and humans, but not necessarily robusticity of the jaws. On the contrary, the evidence from the Miocene apes shows that the last common ancestor probably had robust jaws as part of a trend towards enlarged molars and premolars.

Sexual dimorphism is moderate to high in the great apes, being least in chimpanzees and greater in gorillas and orang utans. It is loosely linked with great ape social structure, with the greatest dimorphism in gorillas associated with single male polygynous societies, and the lower dimorphism in chimpanzees associated with multi-male fusion-fission groups. In polygynous species, males are up to twice the body weight of females, and the larger male size comes about through delayed maturity and therefore prolonged growth. Because the canine teeth are the last to erupt in primates, the delayed maturation results in relatively larger canines in male individuals, and this results in canine size dimorphism which is commonly used to estimate sexual dimorphism. Hominoids with the least degrees of sexual dimorphism, gibbons and humans, also have the smallest body size and canine dimorphism, and they are both monogamous.

Chimpanzees and gorillas have high degrees of flexion of the face relative to the base of the skull. This is known as klinorhynchy, which is seen at its most extreme in modern humans. On the basis of outgroup comparison, extending back to gibbons and monkeys, it is likely that this condition was primitively retained in hominoids, hominids and hominins. The alternative condition in orang utans (airorhynchy) and *Sivapithecus* and *Ankarapithecus* was independently assumed by David Pilbeam and me to be evidence linking these two fossil apes with orang utan ancestry (see Chapter 14). There is some indication of klinorhynchy being present in the dryopithecine skull (see Chapter 12) but for most fossil apes the polarity of this character is unknown. Developmentally, there is some indication that airorhynchy is primitive and was the ancestral condition for hominoids, but it is present only in orang utans and is almost unknown for non-hominoid primates, with one or two unrelated exceptions. In addition, indications from the *Proconsul heseloni* skull (see Chapter 7), the dryopithecine skulls (see Chapter 12) and even the fragmentary *Kenyapithecus* reconstruction made by Alan Walker and me and described in Chapter 11, all preserve enough of the skulls to show that they probably have the klinorhynch condition like most other primates.

Some aspects of behaviour shared by humans and chimpanzees are more speculative, based as they are on assumptions about common ancestry. For example, meat-eating is common to chimpanzees and humans, as described in Chapter 2. It occurs sporadically in other primates as well, and it is probable that it was a feature of the last common ancestor. Hunting of other primates and small antelopes was probably a major source of meat, since scavenging does not feature large in chimpanzee behaviour, but it has been documented for early hominins and might have been a factor in the last common ancestor with humans. In addition, chimpanzees kill other chimpanzees during inter-group rivalries, and this was initially characterized as warfare, which includes the killing and sometimes eating of individuals from rival groups. Warfare is a very human attribute, and it also puts in mind the group of young adults of *Kenyapithecus kizili* from Paşalar during the middle Miocene of Turkey. This group was described in Chapter 11 and was shown to have been a birth cohort of seven males and two females that was intrusive into the territory of the much more abundant *Griphopithecus alpani*. Their great similarities in development, size and age (all different from the resident population) suggest that they were indeed a cohesive travelling group of possibly related individuals. There is no evidence, however, that it was a predatory group, and indeed there does not seem to be much difference between chimpanzees killing other chimpanzees in defence of their territory and the many examples of carnivorous mammals such as lions doing likewise. It is unlikely also that meat formed a very high proportion of the diet of the last common ancestor as it was seen in Chapter 2 that age of weaning in chimpanzees follows the herbivore pattern, not the carnivore one, and isotope analyses fail to pick up any sign of meat-eating even when it is known to have occurred.

As a basis for understanding fossil ape societies, it has been noted that living ape species do not associate with each other, even when living in the same environment. Where chimpanzees and gorillas are sympatric, they tend to occupy different parts of the environment; for example, in areas of moderate relief, chimpanzees occupy the high ridges and gorillas remain in the valley bottoms. Even in times of food shortage, chimpanzees seek to maintain their mainly fruit diet while gorillas have green herbiage as a fall-back food. Chimpanzees have larger home ranges in which to look for food, and in general, the more open the habitat the larger are their home ranges, but it is not actually known if fruiting trees are more widely dispersed in savanna habitats compared with forest. Tropical forests are characterized by high species diversity, and species with suitable fruits, that is, species with fleshy fruits or berries, may be widely dispersed in forest environments. Savannas may even have greater concentrations of fruiting trees where there are watercourses and abundant fig trees (see Chapter 2 and Figure 2.1).

In a comparison of savanna habitats at Fongoli, Senegal, Jill Pruetz found 27 fruiting trees compared with 34 in the Kibale Forest. In both cases, the chimpanzee populations relied heavily on fig fruits throughout the year, and the significant factor here is that a sufficient number of fig trees (which have asynchronous fruiting based on life cycles of the fig wasps) should be present in the environment to ensure all year availability of figs. In competition with gorillas, chimpanzees may be excluded from parts of their areas. Arboreal monkeys, however, may congregate in multispecies groups, and it is likely that the smaller and more monkey-like fossil apes behaved more like monkeys than apes, although we have seen that many of them were more terrestrial than most living monkeys.

Bill McGrew has recently summarized the behaviour of chimpanzees to investigate what this shows about the behaviour of the last common ancestor with humans. In Chapter 17 I have combined his conclusions with my summary of the preceding sections to show the shared adaptations and behaviour of the last common ancestor with chimpanzees and humans. As shared characters in their common ancestor, all are primitively retained in both chimpanzees and humans, so while this tells us a great deal about the life style and behaviour of the ancestor, it does not help in identifying how the earliest hominin differentiated from the ancestor.

Chapter 17
An ape's view of human evolution

In this last chapter, I am going to consider the evidence for when the last common ancestor might have lived, what kind of environment it lived in and what its major characteristics were.

The date of the last common ancestor

There is no direct evidence on the date of the common ancestor. I have shown in Chapter 3 how the 'molecular clock' has to be calibrated from the fossil record, and the two most reliable calibration points are the divergence of monkeys and apes and the divergence of the orang utan. Nothing is known about gibbon ancestry or the divergence date of gibbons from other apes, and the evidence for the timing of gorilla divergence is no better than that for humans and chimpanzees. The earliest fossil records for both monkeys and apes are in the early Miocene of East Africa, and both occur about 20 million years ago, for I am not convinced by the apparent monkey and ape species recorded from the Oligocene of Tanzania (see discussion in Chapter 3). How much earlier the actual split occurred is of course not known, and based on the high diversity of fossil ape species by 18 million years, it might be up to 6 million years earlier.

The second divergence date often used for calibrating the 'molecular clock' is that for the orang utan. In Chapter 3, I have discussed some of the difficulties in setting a date for this event. It was proposed that the Indian ape *Sivapithecus indicus* was on the orang utan lineage, and since the earliest record for this fossil ape is about 12 million years, this gives a minimum age for the origin of the orang utan lineage. However, the postcranial skeleton of this fossil ape is nothing like that of the orang utan, whereas the skeleton and some aspects of the skull of *Hispanopithecus laietanus* from 9 million-year-old deposits in Spain, and the lower jaw of *Khoratpithecus* from Thailand slightly later in time, have stronger similarities with the orang utan. The earliest dryopithecines known in Europe also date from about 12 million years, and it seems possible that there were at least two evolving lineages within this group, one ancestral to Ponginae and the other ancestral to African apes, as suggested by David Begun. There is little likelihood that *Sivapithecus indicus* and *Hispanopithecus laietanus* are closely related, in which case it is evidence that one or the other was converging on the orang utan morphology. We are left, therefore, with a range of dates for the divergence of the orang utan, between 9 and 12 million years ago (or earlier), and for the divergence date of apes and monkeys 20 to 26 million years ago. Calibration from these dates supports divergence of humans and chimpanzees between 4 and 8 million years ago.

The environment of the last common ancestor

The present distribution of living apes in the tropical forests of Africa and Asia has long been taken as evidence of the apes as forest dwellers. On the contrary, the evidence of most fossil apes known at present is that they were associated with non-forest environments in seasonal climates, and the evidence of many of them as having terrestrial adaptations indicates that the apes as a whole may have originated and lived for most of their evolutionary past in woodland habitats. This is based on present evidence, and it may be that future discoveries of fossil apes in forest environments may lead to differing conclusions, but for the present this is what the fossil evidence is showing.

Woodland environments of a similar nature are also associated with early hominins, and the similarities in postcranial adaptations between the fossil apes and the earliest hominins indicate a similar way of life in these woodland environments. In other words, the development of upright bipedal walking took place in woodland environments without any major change in environment. The climatic cooling in the later part of the Miocene and the Pliocene is known to have led to great expansion of woodlands in Africa, and this may have led in turn to the expansion of opportunities for an increasingly terrestrial and tool using lineage such as the hominins. There were probably subtle differences in habitat that our methods of analysis cannot pick up, but the general picture for most apes and early hominins is that they shared deciduous woodland habitats in a strongly seasonal climate and that the last common ancestor of chimpanzees and humans lived in a woodland environment, probably deciduous and certainly strongly seasonal.

The significance of fig trees in woodland and savanna environments has been stressed in Chapter 2. Fig trees may occur wherever there is sufficient water to support their growth, and their unique relationship with fig wasps results in fruit production by African figs throughout the year, each tree fruiting independently of other fig trees. In a large enough expanse of woodland, savanna or forest, or even in semi-desert if a local water supply is available, there are always some fruiting figs throughout the year, and it is this more than anything that allows fruit-eating animals such as chimpanzees to survive even in apparently hostile environments.

The morphology of the last common ancestor

We have seen that the last common ancestor shared characters with Miocene apes and extant great apes. It lived in Africa 4 to 8 million years ago in tropical woodlands, similar to the deciduous woodland environments common to most fossil evidence known at present. Following now is a brief summary of what we can say about the morphology and behaviour of this last common ancestor.

Dental evidence

Large and projecting canines and canine-premolar honing were present to various degrees in most fossil apes, the living apes and in the earliest of the proposed hominins (*Orrorin*, *Ardipithecus kadabba*). They were probably primitively present in the last common ancestor and lost in the earliest hominins, but since some fossil apes had small canines and greatly reduced or absent premolar honing, these are characters that evolved independently in at least three hominid lineages. As such, these characters cannot be categorically stated to be uniquely hominin characters. At least in *Australopithecus afarensis*, the reduction in size of the canines is not associated with reduced body size dimorphism.

Small incisors are sometimes listed as hominin characters because of their presence in australopithecines, but this seems to be a unique character to these early hominins that is not seen in any Miocene or Pliocene hominids with the exception of *Gigantopithecus*. The last common ancestor of apes and humans probably lacked small incisors.

Enlarged molars with thick enamel were present in many middle and late Miocene hominids and in Pleistocene hominins, but some late Miocene and Pliocene hominids proposed as hominins do not have enlarged molars although they have thick enamel (*Sahelanthropus tchadensis, Orrorin tugenensis*). It is likely that the last common ancestor of apes and humans had molars with thick enamel, but there is no evidence that it also had enlarged molars and premolars as seen in later Pleistocene hominins.

Cranial evidence

Most apes for which the condition is known had faces strongly angled with respect to the base of the skull (known as klinorhynchy). It is likely that this is the primitive ape condition retained in the African apes and humans but derived in orang utans and some fossil apes (*Sivapithecus indicus*), and if this is the case it would have been primitively retained in the last common ancestor of apes and humans.

Most fossil apes have relatively shallow palates, with parallel tooth rows. At least one late Miocene ape (*Samburupithecus kiptalami*) and early hominins (*Ardipithecus ramidus*) have more deeply arched palates, present also in the living great apes. Outgroup comparisons with the living apes suggests that the last common ancestor of apes and humans had deep palates, but the fossil evidence of the Miocene apes suggests otherwise, indicating independent development of deep palates in great apes and humans.

Most fossil apes had moderate mid-facial prognathism but low alveolar prognathism (*Proconsul, Kenyapithecus*), and this condition is present also in early hominins but not in the living great apes. The orang utan and possible fossil relatives (*Sivapithecus indicus*) have prominent alveolar prognathism, but this is reduced in the African apes. This character is associated with incisor and canine size, and the relatively small size of these teeth in hominins and most fossil apes suggests that the last common ancestor of apes and humans probably retained the primitive fossil ape condition, with moderate mid-facial prognathism and low alveolar prognathism. The living great apes are derived.

Most fossil apes had moderate to low buttressing of the face (zygomatic and frontal regions), present also in early hominins. Later australopithecines developed unique buttressing of the face, described by Yoel Rak, and the orang utan has massive expansion of the zygomatic region (present also in *Ankarapithecus* and *Sivapithecus*). The last common ancestor of apes and humans probably retained the primitive fossil ape condition.

Robust mandibles with inferior tori of the symphysis were present on many middle Miocene apes and early hominins, usually associated with enlarged molars with thick enamel (*Kenyapithecus, Griphopithecus, Sivapithecus, Ouranopithecus*). One fossil ape at least combined relatively lightly built mandibles with thick-enamelled molars (*Ouranopithecus macedoniensis*), showing that these characters do not always go together. The last common ancestor probably had robust jaws with strong inferior torus, and thick enamel.

The foramen magnum is placed forward on the base of the skull in species with greater upright posture, such as gibbons, humans and some New World monkeys. It is associated with upright bipedalism in early hominins, but it is not by itself evidence of bipedalism since in gibbons and monkeys upright posture is associated with suspension below branches. The morphology of Miocene apes is unknown in this respect, although their limb morphology, which indicates pronograde quadrupedalism like that of most monkeys, would seem to exclude it. Some fossil apes have a certain degree of uprightness (*Hispanopithecus*), in some cases associated with suspensory locomotion but not in others (*Pierolapithecus*). The retention of a posterior position of the foramen magnum in the living great apes, despite greater upright posture (compared with monkeys), makes it hard to interpret this character in the last common ancestor.

Postcranial evidence

The feet in all apes have divergent big toes with the long axis of the foot running through the third phalanx. The divergent big toe was retained in *Ardipithecus ramidus* but with increased rigidity and strengthened lateral margin of the foot as in humans. The last common ancestor almost certainly retained the primitive morphology of the foot.

The hand in fossil apes had monkey-like proportions, with long thumbs and moderately long metacarpals and phalanges (*Proconsul, Equatorius*), similar also to the human hand. These proportions are retained in some late Miocene apes (*Pierolapithecus catalaunicus*) and Pliocene hominins (*Ardipithecus ramidus*). The living great apes differ in having elongated hands and relatively short thumbs. It is likely that the last common ancestor of apes and humans would have had proportions like that of monkeys and humans. Outgroup comparison with great apes would necessitate two evolutionary reversals.

The phalanges of the hand of most fossil apes are curved with varying degrees of development of the flexor ridges, both adaptations for grasping branches. These features are retained in the living great apes, with the addition of elongation of the phalanges, also present in *Hispanopithecus laietanus*, and they are retained without the elongation in early hominins (*Ardipithecus ramidus, Australopithecus afarensis*). Short curved phalanges were probably present in the last common ancestor.

The head and neck of the femur is set at a high angle to the femur shaft in most fossil apes, and it does not project above the greater trochanter. It is angled more upwards in living African great apes and fossil apes (*Equatorius, Dryopithecus*) and angled strongly upwards in the orang utan and in some fossil apes (*Hispanopithecus*). This is an adaptation for suspensory locomotion, most strongly developed in the orang utan, and it was probably not present in the last common ancestor. The condition of the last common ancestor was likely to have been like the African ape condition.

The pelvis is elongated in the fossil ape *Proconsul nyanzae* as in monkeys, associated with its long flexible back and six lumbar vertebrae. The upper part of the pelvis (ilium) is broader in great apes and broader still in earliest hominins (*Ardipithecus ramidus*), but the lower part (ischium) remains narrow and long in the great apes and the fossil hominin. The condition in the last common ancestor of apes and humans was probably like that of African great apes.

None of the fossil apes so far known have a complete vertebral column: humans have five lumbar vertebrae, while the great apes have four and gibbons six. The long flexible backs of most Miocene apes indicates non-reduction of the lumbar region, and the presence of six lumbar vertebrae in gibbons and early Miocene apes (*Proconsul nyanzae*), and six also in early fossil hominins

(*Australopithecus africanus*) suggests the ancestral number of six lumbars was retained in the last common ancestor and reduced independently in the great apes and humans.

By outgroup comparison, the ancestral state for the chimpanzee/human clade would have been a knuckle-walker, because this adaptation is present in the gorilla, and by outgroup comparison this would involve least change. There is no evidence for this adaptation, however, in any fossil ape or in early hominins, while on the contrary there is an indication that some at least of the knuckle-walking morphologies arose independently in chimpanzees and gorillas. It is likely, therefore, that the last common ancestor of chimpanzees and humans was not a knuckle-walker.

Several characters in living apes and humans are adaptations for upright (orthograde) posture, such as the broad thorax, long clavicle, medial rotation of the humeral head, rounded humeral shaft, more superiorly directed femur head, more robust lumbar vertebrae, short lumbar region, elongated hands with curved phalanges, shortened thumbs, mobile ball-and-socket mid-carpal joints and ball-and-socket joint between the first metacarpal-carpal joint (in gibbons only). These may also be adaptations (or pre-adaptations) for suspensory locomotion and/or vertical climbing; most are absent in fossil apes (except for dryopithecines and *Oreopithecus*) and the earliest hominins, which indicates that the last common ancestor of chimpanzees and humans was only incipiently orthograde and not suspensory.

Behavioural evidence

All apes, both fossil and living, are arboreal to a certain extent, but most also have some degree of terrestrial behaviour. This is greatest in chimpanzees and gorillas, and for the fossil apes in the middle to late Miocene it is greatest in species such as the afropithecines and kenyapithecines. It is likely therefore that a high degree of terrestrial behaviour was present in the last common ancestor of chimpanzees and humans.

Sexual dimorphism in most early and middle Miocene fossil apes was moderate to high, increasing in degree from early to late Miocene. Some later Miocene apes had high degrees of sexual dimorphism, as great or greater than is present in gorillas and orang utans. The last common ancestor of apes and humans had high sexual dimorphism, primitively retained in the great apes and early hominins (*Australopithecus afarensis*) and lost in later hominins.

The shared presence of several behaviours in humans and chimpanzees, such as tool use, provides much information on aspects of behaviour that were probably present in the last common ancestor of humans and chimpanzees. These are listed below, based in part on work by Bill McGrew.

The diet of the last common ancestor of chimpanzees and humans included fruits but also a low proportion of meat.

Probable low reproductive rate as in living apes.

Tool making for food acquisition and processing, self-maintenance and providing shelter, and social and sexual life.

Regional differences in tool cultures despite the common presence of both prey and raw materials.

Re-use of artefacts depending on availability of raw materials.

Evolution of stone technology may be foreshadowed (and possibly identified) in the last common ancestor by use of stone hammer and anvil technology.

Absence of compound artefacts other than possibly nest building.

Probable absence of use of tools to make other tools.

Transport of tools, or raw material for tools, over short distances but probably not over long distances.

Greater manipulative abilities than are current in chimpanzees, because it retained hand proportions similar to those of baboons and humans.

Opportunistic omnivory, but presence of meat undetectable isotopically.

Wide-ranging foraging from evergreen forest to open woodland savanna.

Sharing meat important in social interactions but probably not a significant contributor to dietary needs.

Probable absence of scavenging.

Nest building in trees for night time protection.

Distribution of nests share complex patterns, and their non-random distribution may presage establishment of home bases.

Nomadic over large areas, but minimum requirements are trees for nest building at night, water (and presence of fig trees – see Chapter 2).

Extent of ranges partly determined by distribution of fig trees and their seasonal differences in fruiting

This interpretation of the last common ancestor of apes and humans differs from previous interpretations that rely almost entirely on morphological analyses of fossil hominins. It shows the ancestor to have evolved from an already partly terrestrial ape living in tropical woodland in Africa. It did not come down from the trees in tropical forest, and it was already probably a tool user and perhaps a tool maker with high degrees of hand manipulation. The earliest hominins differed little from this ancestor, still relying on trees for their food and shelter, and the main changes this early in human evolution were probably increasing terrestriality, shift to bipedal locomotion, and increasing freeing of the hands, increasing tool use. Only later did hominins leave the shelter of the woodlands, later still develop stone technology and last but not least undergo an increase in brain size.

References and further reading

References are not actually cited in most cases, but many authors are named and the reference lists per chapter are relatively short, making it easy to identify sources.

Preface

Andrews, P. 1995. Ecological apes and ancestors. *Nature* 376, 555–556.

Andrews, P. & Harrison, T. 2005. The last common ancestor of apes and humans. In D.E. Lieberman, R.J. Smith & J. Kelley, Editors, *Interpreting the Past: Essays on Human, Primate, and Mammal Evolution in Honor of David Pilbeam*, 103–21. Boston, Brill Academic Publishers, Inc.

Clark Howell, F. 1965. *Early Man*. New York, Time/Life Books.

Clark Howell, F. & Bourliere, F. 1963. *African Ecology and Human Evolution*. Chicago, Aldine.

Groves, C.P. 2001. *Primate Taxonomy*. Washington, The Smithsonian Institution.

Hartwig, W.C. (Editor) 2002. *The Primate Fossil Record*. Cambridge, Cambridge University Press.

Stringer, C. & Andrews, P. 1988. Genetic and fossil evidence for the origin of modern humans. *Science* 239, 1263–1268, and 241, 772–774.

Washburn, S.L. 1951. The new physical anthropology. *Transactions of the New York Academy of Sciences* 13, 298–304.

Washburn, S.L. 1968. Speculations on the problem of man's coming to the ground. In B. Rothblatt, Editor, *Changing Perspectives on Man*, 191–206. Chicago, University of Chicago Press.

Werdelin, L. & Sanders, W.J. (Editors) 2010. *Cenozoic Mammals of Africa*. Berkeley, University of California Press.

Chapter 1 How can we recognize common ancestors?

There have been many books on the last common ancestor of apes and humans, notable among them T.H. Huxley's *Man's Place in Nature,* Robert Broom's *Finding the Missing Link,* Bjorn Kurten's *Not from the Apes,* Louis Leakey's *Adam's Ancestors,* Raymond Dart's *Adventures with the Missing Link* and Jonathan Kingdon's *Lowly Origin.* Charles Darwin in *Descent of Man* followed Huxley in placing human ancestry with the African apes, while Jeffery Schwartz in *The Red Ape* put forward the case for common ancestry with the orang utan. Good general books on human ancestors are Pat Shipman's biography of Eugene Dubois, *The Man Who Found the Missing Link, Darwin's Island* by Steve Jones, *Demonic Males* by Richard Wrangham and Dale Peterson and *The Blind Watchmaker* by Richard Dawkins. These and other works cited in this chapter are as follows:

Andrews, P. 1973. The vegetation of Rusinga Island. *Journal of the East African Natural History Society* 142, 1–8.

Andrews, P., Groves, C.P. & Horne, J.F.M. 1975. The ecology of the Lower Tana River Flood Plain. *Journal of the East African Natural History Society* 151, 1–31.

Andrews, P. & Harrison, T. 2005. The last common ancestor of apes and humans. In D.E. Lieberman, R.J. Smith & J. Kelley, Editors, *Interpreting the Past: Essays on Human, Primate, and Mammal Evolution in Honor of David Pilbeam*, 103–121. Boston, Brill Academic Publishers, Inc.

Broom, R. 1950. *Finding the Missing Link*. London, Watts & Co.

Broom, R. & Schepers, G.W.H. 1946. The South African fossil ape-men. The Australopithecinae. *Transvaal Museum Memoir, Pretoria 2*.

Dart, R.A. with Craig, D. 1959. *Adventures with the Missing Link*. London, Hamish Hamilton.

Darwin, C. 1859. *The Origin of Species*. London, John Murray.

Darwin, C. 1872. *Descent of Man*. London, John Murray.

Dawkins, R. 1986. *The Blind Watchmaker*. London, Longman.

Gregory, W.K. 1916. Studies on the evolution of the primates, Part II – phylogeny of recent and extinct anthropoids with special reference to the origin of man. *Bulletin of the American Museum of Natural History* 35, 239–355.

Grehan, J.R. 2006. Mona Lisa smile: the morphological enigma of human and great ape evolution. *The Anatomical Record* 289B, 139–157.

Haeckel, E. 1876. *The History of Creation*. London, D. Appleton & Co.

Haeckel, E. 1903. *The Evolution of Man*. London, Watts & Co.

Harrison, T. 2012. Apes among the tangled branches of human origins. *Science* 327, 532–534.

Huxley, T.H. 1863. *Man's Place in Nature*. Reprinted in 1906 in the Eversley Series. London, MacMillan and Co.

Jones, S. 2008. *Darwin's Island*. London, Little Brown.

King, W. 1863. On the Neanderthal skull. *Proceedings of the British 33rd Meeting of the British Association*, page 81.

King, W. 1864 The reputed fossil man of the Neanderthal. *Quarterly Journal of the Geological Society* 1, 88–97.

Kingdon, J. 2002. *Lowly Origin*. Princeton, Princeton University Press.

Kurten, B. 1972. *Not from the Apes*. London, Victor Gollancz.

Lartet, E. 1856. Note sur un grand singe fossile qui se rattache au groupe des singes superieur. *Compte Rendu de l'Academie de Science, Paris* 43, 210–223.

Leakey, L.S.B. 1953. *Adam's Ancestors, an Up-to-date Outline of the Old Stone Age (Palaeolithic) and What is Known about Man's Origin and Evolution*. London, Methuen.

Mayr, E. 1969. *Principles of Systematic Zoology*. New York, McGraw-Hill.

Oakley, K. 1957. Tools makyth man. *Antiquity* 31, 199–209.

Rose, M.D. 1997. Functional and phylogenetic features of the forelimb in Miocene hominoids. In D.R. Begun, C.V. Ward & M.D. Rose, Editors, *Function, Phylogeny and Fossils: Miocene Hominoid Evolution and Adaptations*, 79–100. New York, Plenum Press.

Schwartz, J. 1987. *The Red Ape*. London, Elm Tree Books.

Schwartz, J. & Maresca, B. 2006. Do molecular clocks run at all? A critique of molecular systematics. *Biological Theory* 1, 357–371.

Shipman, P. 2001. *The Man Who Found the Missing Link: The Extraordinary Life of Eugene Dubois*. London, Weidenfeld and Nicolson.

Simpson, G.G. 1961. *Principles of Animal Taxonomy*. New York, Columbia University Press.

Tudge, C. 2005. *The Secret Life of Trees*. London, Penguin Books.

Von Koenigswald, G.H.R. 1956. *Meeting Prehistoric Man*. London, Thames and Hudson.

Wood, B. & Harrison, T. 2011. The evolutionary context of the first hominins. *Nature* 470, 347–352.

Wrangham, R. & Peterson, D. 1997. *Demonic Males: Apes and the Origins of Human Violence*. London, Bloomsbury Press.

Chapter 2 Morphology and behaviour of living apes

The extant apes are described briefly from a range of sources listed below, including their morphology, distribution and behaviour. Particular stress is placed on evidence of tool use and tool making first described by Jane Goodall and an important paper on ape locomotion has been published by Robin Crompton. Material culture in chimpanzees is described in several books and papers by Bill McGrew and by C. Boesch, the importance of meat-eating in apes and humans described by Psouni and by Smith et al. and chimpanzee cannibalism by Aaracadi et al., Newton-Fisher and Nishida. Comparisons between chimpanzee and human behaviours have been described by Pobiner, Stanford, White and Fernández-Jalvo.

Aiello, L.C. 1981. Locomotion in the Miocene Hominoidea. In C.B. Stringer, Editor, *Aspects of Human Evolution*, 63–98. London, Taylor and Francis.

Aiello, L.C. 1981. The allometry of primate body proportions. *Symposium of the Zoological Society of London* 48, 331–358.

Aiello, L. & Dean, C. 1990. *An Introduction to Human Evolutionary Anatomy*. New York, Academic Press.

Aiello, L.C. & Wheeler, P. 1995. The expensive tissue hypothesis. *Current Anthropology* 36, 199–221.

Andrews, P. & Fernández-Jalvo, Y. 2003. Cannibalism in Britiain: taphonomy of the Cresswellian (Pleistocene) faunal and human remains from Gough's Cave, Somerset, England. *Bulletin of the Natural History Museum, London* 58, 59–81.

Arcadi, A.C. & Wrangham, R.W. 1999. Infanticide in chimpanzees: review of cases and a new within-group observation from the Kanyawara study group in Kibale National Park. *Primates* 40, 337–351.

Blumenschine, R.J. 1987. Characteristics of an early hominid scavenging niche. *Current Anthropology* 28, 383–407.

Blumenschine, R.J. & Cavallo, J.A. 1988. Scavenging and human evolution. *Scientific American* 267, 90–96.

Boesch, C. 1996. Three approaches for assessing chimpanzee culture. In A. Russon, K. Bard & S. Parker, Editors, *Reaching Into Thought*, 404–429. Cambridge, Cambridge University Press.

Boesch, C. & Boesch, H. 1990. Tool use and tool making in wild chimpanzees. *Folia Primatologica* 54, 86–99.

Boesch, C. & Boesch-Achermann, H. 2000. *The Chimpanzees of the Tai Forest: Behavioural Ecology and Evolution*. Oxford, Oxford University Press.

Boesch, C., Head, J. & Robbins, M.M. 2009. Complex tool sets for honey extraction among chimpanzees in the Loango National Park, Gabon. *Journal of Human Evolution* 56, 560–569.

Byrne, R.W., Corp, N. & Byrne, J.M.E. 2001. Manual dexterity in the gorilla: bimanual and digit role differentiation in a natural task. *Animal Cognition* 4, 347–361.

Carbone, L. Harris, R.A., Gnerre, S. et al. 2014. Gibbon genome and the fast karyotype evolution of small apes. *Nature* 513, 195–206.

Chaimanee, Y., Suteethorn, V., Jintasakul, P. et al. 2004. A new orang-utan relative from the late Miocene of Thailand. *Nature* 427, 439–441.

Cobb, S.J. 2008. The facial skeleton of the chimpanzee-human last common ancestor. *Journal of Anatomy* 212, 469–485.

Corp, N. & Byrne, R.W. 2002. The ontogeny of manual skill in wild chimpanzees: evidence from feeding on the fruit of *Faba florida*. *Behaviour* 139, 137–168.

Crompton, R.H., Vereeke, E.E. & Kalb, J.E. 2008. Locomotion and posture from the common hominoid ancestor to fully modern hominins, with special reference to the common panin/hominin ancestor. *Journal of Anatomy* 212, 501–543.

Dainton, M. & Macho, G.A. 1999. Did knuckle walking evolve twice? *Journal of Human Evolution* 36, 171–194.

Derex, M., Beugen, M.-P., Godelle, P. & Raymond, M. 2013. Experimental evidence for the influence of group size on cultural complexity. *Nature* 503, 389–391.

Diogo, R. & Wood, B. 2011. Soft-tissue anatomy of the primates: phylogenetic analyses based on the muscles of the head, neck, pectoral region and upper limb, with notes on the evolution of these muscles. *Journal of Anatomy* 219, 273–359.

Fernández-Jalvo, Y. & Andrews, P. 2011. When humans chew bones. *Journal of Human Evolution* 60, 117–123.

Foley, R.A. 2001. The evolutionary consequences of increased carnivory in hominids. In C.B. Stanford & H.T. Bunn, Editors, *Meat-Eating & Human Evolution*, 305–331. Oxford, Oxford University Press.

Gibbs, S., Collard, M. & Wood, B. 2002. Soft tissue anatomy of the extant hominoids: a review and phylogenetic analysis. *Journal of Anatomy* 200, 3–49.

Goodall, J. 1986. *The Chimpanzees of Gombe: Patterns of Behavior*. Cambridge, Harvard University Press.

Gregory, W.K. 1916. Studies on the evolution of primates. *Bulletin of the American Museum of Natural History* 35, 258–355.

Gregory, W.K. 1929. Were the ancestors of man primitive brachiators? *Proceedings of the American Philosophical Society* 67, 129–150.

Grehan, J.R. 2006. Mona Lisa smile: the morphological enigma of human and great ape evolution. *The Anatomical Record* 289B, 139–157.

Groves, C.P. 2001. *Primate Taxonomy*. Washington, The Smithsonian Institution.

Hernandez-Aguilar, R.A. 2009. Chimpanzee nest distribution and site reuse in a dry habitat: implications for early hominin ranging. *Journal of Human Evolution* 57, 350–364.

Hockings, K.J., Anderson, A.R. & Matsuzawa, T. 2010. Flexible feeding on cultivated underground storage organs by rainforest-dwelling chimpanzees at Bossou, West Africa. *Journal of Human Evolution* 58, 227–233.

Johnson, R.J. & Andrews, P. 2010. Fructose, uricase, and the back to Africa hypothesis. *Evolutionary Anthropology* 19, 250–257.

Keith, A. 1899. On the chimpanzees and their relationship to the gorilla. *Proceedings of the Zoological Society* 1899, 296–312.

Kennedy, G.E. 2005. From the ape's dilemma to the weanling's dilemma: early weaning and its evolutionary context. *Journal of Human Evolution* 48, 123–145.

Kingdon, J. 2002. *Lowly Origin*. Princeton, Princeton University Press.

Larsen, C.S. 2003. Equality for the sexes in human evolution? Early hominid sexual dimorphism and implications for mating systems and social behavior. *Proceedings of the National Academy of Sciences* 100, 9103–9104.

Larson, S.G. 1998. Parallel evolution in the hominoid trunk and forelimb. *Evolutionary Anthropology* 6, 87–99.

Leakey, L.S.B. 1953. *Adam's Ancestors, an Up-to-date Outline of the Old Stone Age (Palaeolithic) and What is Known about Man's Origin and Evolution.* London, Methuen.

Marean, C. 1989. Sabertooth cats and their relevance for early hominid diet and evolution. *Journal of Human Evolution* 18, 559–582.

McGrew, W.C. 1992. *Chimpanzee Material Culture.* Cambridge, Cambridge University Press.

McGrew, W.C. 2010. In search of the last common ancestor: new findings on wild chimpanzees. *Philosophical Transactions of the Royal Society of London* 365, 3267–3276.

McGrew, W.C. 2014. The 'other faunivory' revisited: insectivory in human and non-human primates and the evolution of human diet. *Journal of Human Evolution* 71, 4–11.

McGrew, W.C., Baldwin, P.J. & Tutin, C.E.G. 1981. Chimpanzees in a hot, dry and open habitat: Mt. Assirik, Senegal, West Africa. *Journal of Human Evolution* 10, 227–244.

McGrew, W.C., Marchant, L.F. & Nishida, T. 1996. *Great Ape Societies.* Cambridge, Cambridge University Press.

McNulty, K.P., Begun, D., Kelley, J., Manthi, F.K. & Mbua, E.N. 2015. A systematic revision of *Proconsul* with the description of a new genus of early Miocene hominoid. *Journal of Human Evolution* 84, 42–61.

Napier, J.R. 1960. Studies of the hands of living primates. *Proceedings of the Zoological Society of London* 134, 647–657.

Napier, J.R. 1963. Brachiation and brachiators. *Symposium of the Zoological Society* 10, 183–195.

Napier, J.R. 1964. The evolution of bipedal walking in the hominids. *Archives de Biologie Liege* 75, 673–708.

Napier, J.R. & Davis, P.R. 1959. The forelimb skeleton and associated remains of *Proconsul africanus. Fossil Mammals of Africa* 16, 1–83.

Nelson, S.V. 2013. Chimpanzee fauna isotopes provide new interpretations of fossil ape and hominin ecologies. *Proceedings of the Royal Society* 280, 2013–2324.

Newton-Fisher, N. 1999. Infant killers of Budongo. *Folia Primatologica* 70, 167–169.

Nishida, T. & Kawanaka, K. 1985. Within-group cannibalism by adult male chimpanzees. *Primates* 26, 274–284.

Oakley, K. 1957. Tools makyth man. *Antiquity* 31, 199–209.

O'Malley, R.C. & McGrew, W.C. 2014. Primates, insects and insect resources. *Journal of Human Evolution* 71, 1–3.

Owen, R. 1859. *On the Classification and Geographic Distribution of the Mammalia.* London, Parker.

Patel, B.A., Ruff, C.B., Simons, E.L.R. & Organ, J.M. 2013. Humeral cross-sectional shape in suspensory primates and sloths. *The Anatomical Record* 296, 545–556.

Plummer, T.W. & Stanford, C.B. 2000. Analysis of a bone assemblage made by chimpanzees at Gombe National Park, Tanzania. *Journal of Human Evolution* 39, 345–365.

Pobiner, B.L., DeSilva, J., Sanders, W.J. & Mitani, J.C. 2007. Taphonomic analysis of skeletal remains from chimpanzee hunts at Ngogo, Kibale National Park, Uganda. *Journal of Human Evolution* 52, 614–636.

Psouni, E., Jankes, A. & Garrwiz, M. 2012. Impact of carnivory on human development and evolution revealed by a new unifying model of weaning in mammals. *PLOS One* 7, 1–8.

Rein, T. 2010. Locomotor function and phylogeny: implications for interpreting the hominoid fossil record. PhD thesis, New York University.

Richmond, B.G., Begun, D.R. & Strait, D.S. 2001. Origin of human bipedalism: the knuckle-walking hypothesis revisited. *Yearbook of Physical Anthropology* 44, 70–105.

Richmond, B.G. & Strait, D.S. 2000. Evidence that humans evolved from a knuckle-walking ancestor. *Nature* 404, 382–385.

Rose, M.D. 1994. Quadrupedalism in some Miocene catarrhines. *Journal of Human Evolution* 26, 387–411.

Sarringhaus, L.A., MacLatchy, L.M. & Mitani, J.A. 2014. Locomotor and postural development of wild chimpanzees. *Journal of Human Evolution* 66, 29–38.

Smith, C.C., Morgan, M.E. & Pilbeam, D. 2010. Isotopic ecology and dietary profiles of Liberian chimpanzees. *Journal of Human Evolution* 58, 43–55.

Stanford, C.B. & Bunn, H.T. 2001. (Editors). *Meat-Eating & Human Evolution*, 305–331. Oxford, Oxford University Press.

Tuttle, R.H. 1969. Knuckle-walking and the problem of human origins. *Science* 166, 953–961.

Villa, P. & Mahieu, E. 1991. Breakage pattern of human long bones. *Journal of Human Evolution* 21, 27–48.

Washburn, S.L. 1978. The evolution of man. *Scientific American* 239, 194–208.

Watts, D.P. 2008. Scavenging by chimpanzees at Ngogo and the relevance of chimpanzee scavenging to early hominin behavioural ecology. *Journal of Human Evolution* 54, 125–133.

White, T.D. & Toth, N. 2007. Carnivora and Carnivori: assessing hominid toothmarks in zooarchaeology. In T.R. Pickering, K. Schick & N. Toth. (Editors), *Breathing Life into Fossils: Taphonomic Studies in Honor of C.K. (Bob) Brain*, 281–296. Gosport, IN, Stone Age Institute Press.

Whiten, A., McGrew, W.C., Aaiello, L.C. et al. 2010. Studying extant species to model our past. *Science* 327, 410.

Williams, S.A. 2010. Morphological integration and the evolution of knuckle-walking. *Journal of Human Evolution* 58, 432–440.

Wood, B. & Harrison, T. 2011. The evolutionary context of the first hominins. *Nature* 470, 347–352.

Wrangham, R. & Peterson, D. 1997. *Demonic Males: Apes and the Origins of Human Violence.* London, Bloomsbury Press.

Chapter 3 Human and ape phylogenies

I try to avoid taxonomic controversies by using presently accepted classifications of fossil and living apes by Terry Harrison, but a basic understanding of ape phylogeny is essential to the purpose of this book. Morris Goodman pioneered molecular methods of phylogenetic reconstruction, followed by many papers by Bradley, Disotell, King and Wilson, Langergraber, Miyamoto, Prüfer, Raaum, Sarich, Yand and Yoder. They review the molecular and morphological evidence for the relationships of living apes and humans, and problems with calibrating dating from the fossil record. The chapter ends with the classification of living species used in this book based on my recent publication with Terry Harrison.

Aiello, L. & Dean, C. 1990. *An Introduction to Human Evolutionary Anatomy*. Academic Press, New York.

Andrews, P. 1986. Fossil evidence on human origins and dispersal. In J.D. Watson, Editor. *Molecular Biology of Homo sapiens*, 419–428. Cold Spring Harbor Symposia on Quantitative Biology.

Andrews, P. 1987. Aspects of hominoid phylogeny. In C. Patterson, Editor, *Molecules and Morphology in Evolution: Conflict or Compromise*, 23–53. Cambridge, Cambridge University Press.

Andrews, P. & Harrison, T. 2005. The last common ancestor of apes and humans. In D.E. Lieberman, R.J. Smith & J. Kelley, Editors, *Interpreting the Past: Essays on Human, Primate, and Mammal Evolution in Honor of David Pilbeam*, 103–121. Boston, Brill Academic Publishers, Inc.

Anon. 2005. The Chimpanzee Sequencing and Analysis Consortium 2005. *Nature* 437, 69–87.

Bradley, B.J. 2008. Reconstructing phylogenies and phenotypes: a molecular view of human evolution. *Journal of Anatomy* 212, 337–353.

Caccone, A. & Powell, J.R. 1989. DNA divergence among hominoids. *Evolution* 43, 925–942.

Caswell, J.L., Mallick, S., Richter, D.J. et al. 2008. Analysis of chimpanzee history based on genome sequence alignments. *PLoS Genetics* 4, 1–14.

Disotell, T.R. 2006. 'Chumanzee' evolution: the urge to diverge and merge. *Genome Biology* 7, 240.

Dubois, E. 1894. *Pithecanthropus erectus, eine menschenähnliche übergangsform aus Java*. Landsdrukkerij, Batavia, Batavuam Kabdesdrycjereu.

Endicott, P., Ho, S.Y.W., Metspalu, M. & Stringer, C. 2009. Evaluating the mitochondrial timescale of human evolution. *Trends in Ecology and Evolution* 24, 515–521.

Figueirido, B., Janis, C., Pérez-Claros, J.A., Renzi, M. & Palmqvist, P. 2012. Cenozoic climate change influences mammalian evolutionary dynamics. *Proceedings of the National Academy of Sciences* 109, 722–727.

Goodman, M. 1963. Man's place in the phylogeny of the primates as reflected in serum proteins. In S.L. Washburn, Editor, *Classification and Human Evolution*, 204–234. Chicago, Aldine.

Goodman, M. 1975. Protein sequence and immunological specificity: their role in phylogenetic studies of primates. In W.P. Luckett & F.S. Szalay, Editors, *Phylogeny of the Primates: A Multidisciplinary Approach*, 219–248. New York, Plenum Press.

Goodman, M., Porter, C. A., Czelusniak, J. et al. 1998. Toward a phylogenetic classification of primates based on DNA evidence complemented by fossil evidence. *Molecular Phylogenetics and Evolution* 9, 585–598.

Goodman, M., Tagle, D.A, Fitch, H.A. et al. 1990. Primate evolution at the DNA level and a classification of the hominoids. *Journal of Molecular Evolution* 30, 260–266.

Goodman, M. & Tashian, R.E. (Editors) 1976. *Molecular Anthropology*. New York: Plenum Press.

Harrison, T. 2002. Late Oligocene to middle Miocene catarrhines from Afro-Arabia. In W.C. Hartwig, Editor, *The Primate Fossil Record*, 311–338. Cambridge, Cambridge University Press.

Hartwig, W.C. (Editor) 2002. *The Primate Fossil Record*. Cambridge, Cambridge University Press.

Hughes, J.F., Skaletsky, H., Pyntikova, T. et al. 2010. Chimpanzee and human Y chromosomes are remarkably divergent in structure and gene content. *Nature* 463, 536–539.

Jones, S. 2008. *Darwin's Island*. London, Little Brown.

Kaessmann, H., Hellig, F., Haeseler, A. & Pääbo, S. 2001. Great ape DNA sequences reveal a reduced diversity and an expansion in humans. *Nature Genetics* 27, 78–81.

Kaessmann, H. Wiebe, V. & Paabo, S. 1999. Extensive nuclear DNA sequence diversity among chimpanzees. *Science* 286, 1159–1162.

Kaessmann, H., Wiebe, V., Weiss, G. & Pääbo, S. 1999. DNA sequence variation in a non-coding region of low recombination on the human X chromosome. *Nature Genetics* 22, 778–781.

King, M.-C. & Wilson, A.C. 1975. Evolution at two levels in humans and chimpanzees. *Science* 188, 107–116.

Langergraber, K.E., Prufer, K., Rowney, C. et al. 2012. Generation times in wild chimpanzees and gorillas suggest earlier divergence times in great ape and human evolution. *Proceedings of the National Academy of Sciences* 109, 15716–15721.

Locke, D.P., Hillier, L.W., Warren, W.C. et al. 2011. Comparative and demographic analysis of orang-utan genomes. *Nature* 469, 529–533.

Miyamoto, M.M. & Goodman, M. 1990. DNA systematics and evolution of primates. *Annual Review of Ecology and Systematics* 2, 197–220.

Miyamoto, M.M., Slightom, J.L. & Goodman, M. 1987. Phylogenetic relationships of humans and African apes from DNA sequences in the ψη-globin region. *Science* 238, 369–373.

Orlando, L., Ginolhac, A., Zhang, G. et al. 2013. Recalibrating *Equus* evolution using the genome sequence of an early Middle Pleistocene horse. Nature online, 499(7456), 74–78.

Patterson, C. (Editor) 1987. *Molecules and Morphology in Evolution: Conflict or Compromise.* Cambridge, Cambridge University Press.

Patterson, N., Richter, D.J., Gnerre, S., Lander, E.S. & Reich, D. 2006. Genetic evidence for complex speciation of humans and chimpanzees. *Nature* 441, 1103–1108.

Pozzi, L, Hodgson, J.A., Burrell, A.S. & Disotell, T.R. 2011. The stem catarrhine *Saadanius* does not inform the timing of the origin of the Crown Catarrhines. *Journal of Human Evolution* 61, 209–210.

Prüfer, K., Kelso, J., Paabo, S. et al. 2012. The bonobo genome compared with the chimpanzee and human genomes. *Nature*, 486(7404), 527–531.

Raaum, R., Sterner, K.N., Noviello, C.M., Stewart, C.-B. & Disotell, T.R. 2005 Catarrhine primate divergence dates estimated from complete mitochondrial genomes: concordance with fossil and nuclear DNA evidence. *Journal of Human Evolution* 48, 237–257.

Sarich, V.M. & Wilson, A.C. 1967. Immunological time scale for hominid evolution. *Science* 158, 1200–1203.

Scally, A. & Durbin, R. 2012. Revising the human mutation rate: implications for understanding human evolution. *Nature Reviews Genetics* 13, 745–753.

Schwartz, J. 1990. *Lufengpithecus* and its potential relationship to an orang-utan clade. *Journal of Human Evolution* 519, 591–605.

Sibley, C.G. & Ahlquist, J.E. 1984. The phylogeny of the hominoid primates, as indicated by DNA-DNA hybridization. *Journal of Molecular Evolution* 20, 2–15.

Smith, C.C., Morgan, M.E. & Pilbeam, D. 2010. Isotopic ecology and dietary profiles of Liberian chimpanzees. *Journal of Human Evolution* 58, 43–55.

Stanford, C.B. & Bunn, H.T. (Editors) 2001. *Meat-Eating & Human Evolution*, 305 331 Oxford, Oxford University Press.

Stevens, N.J., Seiffert, E.R., O'Connor, P.M. et al. 2013. Palaeontological evidence for an Olidgocene divergence between Old World monkeys and apes. *Nature* 497, 611–614.

Takahata, N., Satta, Y. & Klein, J. 1995. Divergence time and population size in the lineage leading to modern humans. *Theoretical Population Biology* 48, 198–221.

Tavaré, S., Marchall, C.R., Will, O., Soligo, C. & Martin, R.D. 2002. Using the fossil record to estimate the age of the last common ancestor of extant primates. *Nature* 416, 726–729.

Werdelin, L. & Sanders, W.J. (Editors) 2010. *Cenozoic Mammals of Africa*. Berkeley, CA: University of California Press.

White, F. 1983. *The Vegetation of Africa. A Descriptive Memoir to Accompany the UNESCO/ AETFAT/UNSO Vegetation Map of Africa*. Paris, UNESCO.

Wilson, A.C. 1985. The molecular basis of evolution. *Scientific American* 253, 164–173.

Wilson, A.C. & Sarich, V.M. 1969. A molecular time scale for human evolution. *Proceedings of the National Academy of Sciences* 63, 1088–1093.

Wu, R. & Xu, Q. 1986. Relationship between Lufeng *Sivapithecus* and *Ramapithecus* and their phylogenetic position. *Acta Anthropologia* 5, 26–30.

Xiao, M. 1981. Discovery of a fossil hominoid scapula at Lufeng. In *Collected Papers of the 30th Anniversary of the Yunnan Provincial Museum*, 41–44. Yunnan Provincial Museum.

Yang, Z. & Yoder, A.D. 2003. Comparison of likelihood and Bayesian methods for estimating divergence times using multiple gene loci and calibration points, with application to a radiation of cute-looking mouse Lemur species. *Systematic Biology* 52, 705–716.

Yoder, A.D. & Yang, Z. 2000. Estimation of primate speciation dates using local molecular clocks. *Molecular Biology and Evolution* 17, 1081–1090.

Chapter 4 Review of fossil apes

This chapter provides a quick review of the fossil apes based on chapters in Walter Hartwig's book *The Primate Fossil Record*, and they will be described in more detail in the following chapters with full references. The possibility that most fossil ape lineages were adapted to woodland rather than forest is again discussed, the effects of the environment enabling dispersal and a mutation of the uricase gene in the middle Miocene is put forward as a possible adaptation for seasonal habitats.

Andrews, P. 1981. Species diversity and diet in monkeys and apes during the Miocene. In C.B. Stringer, Editor, *Aspects of Human Evolution*. London, Taylor and Francis.

Andrews, P. & Cameron, D. 2010. Rudabanya: taphonomic analysis of a fossil hominid site from Hungary. *Palaeogeography, Palaeoclimatology, Palaeoecology* 297, 311–329.

Andrews, P. & Van Couvering, J.A.H. 1975. Environments in the East African Miocene. In F.S. Szalay, Editor, *Contributions to Primatology*, Vol. 5, 62–103. Basel, Karger.

Armour-Chelu, M., Andrews, P. & Bernor, R.L. 2005. Further observations on the primate community at Rudbànya II (late Miocene, early Vallesian age), Hungary. *Journal of Human Evolution* 49, 88–98.

Begun, D.R. 1992. Miocene fossil hominids and the chimp-human clade. *Science* 257, 1929–1933.

Deane, A.S., Nargolwalla, M.C., Kordos, L. & Begun, D.R. 2013. New evidence for diet and niche partitioning in *Rudapithecus* and *Anapithecus* from Rudabánya, Hungary. *Journal of Human Evolution* 65, 704–714.

Harrison, T. & Andrews, P. 2009. The anatomy and systematic position of the early Miocene proconsulid from Meswa Bridge, Kenya. *Journal of Human Evolution* 56, 479–496.

Hartwig, W.C. (Editor) 2002. *The Primate Fossil Record*. Cambridge, Cambridge University Press.

Hürzeler, J. 1954. Contribution à l'odontologie et à la phylogénès du genre *Pliopithecus* Gervais. *Annales de Paléontologie* 40, 1–63.

Ibrahim, Y.Kh., Tshen, L.T., Westaway, K.E. et al. 2013. First discovery of Pleistocene orangutan (*Pongo* sp.) fossils in Peninsular Malaysia: biogeographic and paleoenvironmental implications. *Journal of Human Evolution* 65, 770–797.

Jacobs, B.F. 1992. Taphonomy of a middle Miocene authochthonous forest assemblage, Ngorora Formation, central Kenya. *Palaeogeography, Palaeoclimatology, Palaeoecology* 99, 31–40.

Johnson, R.J. & Andrews, P. 2010. Fructose, uricase, and the back to Africa hypothesis. *Evolutionary Anthropology* 19, 250–257.

McBrearty, S. & Jablonsky, N.G. 2005. First fossil chimpanzee. *Nature* 437, 105–108.

Moyà-Solà, S., Alba, D.M., Almecija, S. et al. 2009. A unique middle Miocene European hominoid and the origins of the great ape and human clade. *Proceedings of the National Academy of Sciences* 106, 1–6.

Moyà-Solà, S. & Köhler, M. 1993. Recent discoveries of *Dryopithecus* shed new light on evolution of great apes. *Nature* 365, 543–545.

Moyà-Solà, S. & Köhler, M. 1995. New partial cranium of *Dryopithecus* Lartet, 1863 (Hominoidea, Primates) from the upper Miocene of Can Llobateres, Barcelona, Spain. *Journal of Human Evolution* 29, 101–139.

Moyà-Solà, S. & Köhler, M. 1996. The first *Dryopithecus* skeleton: origins of great ape locomotion. *Nature* 379, 156–159.

Retallack, G.J., Dugas, D.P. & Bestland, E.A. 1990. Fossil soils and grasses of a middle Miocene East African grassland. *Science* 247, 1325–1328.

Simons, E.L. & Pilbeam, D.R. 1965. A preliminary revision of the Dryopithecinae. *Folia Primatologica* 3, 81–152.

Werdelin, L. & Sanders, W.J. (Editors) 2010. *Cenozoic Mammals of Africa*. Berkeley, University of California Press.

Wren, C.D., Xue, J.Z., Costopoulos, A. & Burke, A. 2014. The role of spatial foresight in models of hominin dispersal. *Journal of Human Evolution* 69, 70–78.

Chapter 5 Structure and composition of ape environments

Since the present is the key to the past, a classification of present-day environments is first provided based in part on my classifications and in part on the adaptation that Thure Cerling made from Frank White's seminal book on African vegetation. The brief review of the history of vegetation change during the Neogene, Miocene environments is based in part on publications by Axelrod, Suc and Kovar-Eder. I make the new proposal that the primary habitat of most Miocene apes was woodland rather than forest.

Anderson, G.D. & Talbot, L.M. 1965. Soil factors affecting the distribution of grassland types and their utilization by wild animals on the Serengeti plains, Tanganyika. *Journal of Ecology* 53, 33–55.

Andrews, P. & Bamford, M. 2008. Past and present vegetation ecology of Laetoli, Tanzania. *Journal of Human Evolution* 54, 78–98.

Andrews, P., Bamford, M., Njau, F. & Leliyo, G. 2011. The ecology and biogeography of the Endulen-Laetoli area in northern Tanzania. In T. Harrison, Editor, *Palaeontology and Geology of Laetoli, Tanzania*, 167–200. New York, Springer.

Andrews, P. & O'Brien, E. 2000. Climate, vegetation, and predictable gradients in mammal species richness in southern Africa. *Journal of Zoology* 251, 205–231.

Andrews, P. & O'Brien, E. 2010. Mammal species richness in Africa. In L. Werdelin & W. Sanders, Editors, *Cenozoic Mammals of Africa*, 929–947. Berkeley, University of California Press.

Andrews, P. & Van Couvering, J.H. 1975. Palaeoenvironments in the East African Miocene. In F.S. Szalay, Editor, *Approaches to Primate Paleobiology*, 62–103. Basel, Karger.

Axelrod, D.I. 1975. Evolution and biogeography of the Madrean-Tethyan sclerophyll vegetation. *Annals of the Missouri Botanical Garden* 62, 280–334.

Axelrod, D.I. & Raven, P.H. 1978. Cretaceous and Tertiary vegetation history in Africa. In M.J.A. Werger, Editor, *Biogeography and Ecology of Southern Africa*, 77–130. The Hague, W. Junk.

Cerling, T.E., Wynn, J.G., Andanje, S.A. et al. 2011. Woody cover and hominin environments in the past 6 million years. *Nature* 476, 51–56.

De Wit, H.A. 1978. Soils and grassland types of the Serengeti Plain (Tanzania): their distribution and interrelations. PhD thesis, Agricultural University of Wageningen.

Denton, G. 1999. Cenozoic climate change. In T. Bromage & F. Schrenk, Editors, *African Biogeography, Climate Change, and Early Hominid Evolution*, 94–114. Oxford, Oxford University Press.

Elton, C.S. 1966. *The Pattern of Animal Communities*. London, Methuen.

Eronen, J.T., Puolamaki, K., Liu, L. et al. 2010a. Precipitation and large herbivorous mammals II: applications to fossil data. *Evolutionary Ecology Research* 12, 235–248.

Eronen, J.T., Puolamaki, K., Liu, L. et al. 2010b. Precipitation and large herbivorous mammals I: estimates from present-day communities. *Evolutionary Ecology Research* 12, 217–233.

Figueirido, B., Janis, C., Pérez-Claros, J.A. et al. 2012. Cenozoic climate change influences mammalian evolutionary dynamics. *Proceedings of the National Academy of Sciences* 109, 722–727.

Fortelius, M., Eronen, J., Jenvall, J. et al. 2002. Fossil mammals resolve regional patterns of Eurasian climate change over 20 million years. *Evolutionary Ecology Research* 4, 1005–1016.

Greenway, P.J. 1943. *Second Draft Report on Vegetation Classification*. Nairobi, East African Pasture Research Conference

Griffiths, J.F. 1976. *Climate and the Environment*. Boulder, Westview Press.

Hamilton, A. 1981. *A Field Guide to the Trees of Uganda*. Kampala: Makerere University Press.

Jacobs, B.F. 1992. Taphonomy of a middle Miocene authochthonous forest assemblage, Ngorora Formation, central Kenya. *Palaeogeography, Palaeoclimatology, Palaeoecology* 99, 31–40.

Jager, T.J. 1982. *Soils of the Serengeti Woodlands, Tanzania: Agricultural Research Reports* 912. Wageningen, Centre for Agricultural Publishing and Documentation.

Jarman, P.J. 1974. The social organization of antelope in relation to their ecology. *Behaviour* 48, 215–266.

Kennet, J. 1995. A review of polar climatic evolution during the Neogene based on the marine sediment record. In E.S. Vrba, G.H. Denton, T.C. Partridge & L.H. Burckle, Editors, *Paleoclimate and Evolution with Emphasis on Human Origins*, 49–64. New Haven, Yale University Press.

Kingdon, J. 1971–1982. *East African Mammals*. London, Academic Press.

Kingston, J.D., Jacobs, B.F., Hill, A. & Deino, A. 2002. Stratigraphy, age and environments of the late Miocene Mpesida Beds, Tugen Hills, Kenya. *Journal of Human Evolution* 42, 95–116.

Kovar-Eder, J. 2003. Vegetation dynamics in Europe during the Neogene. *Deinsea* 10, 373–392.

Kovarovic, K. Andrews, P. & Aiello, L. 2002. The palaeoecology of the Upper Ndolanya Beds at Laetoli, Tanzania. *Journal of Human Evololution* 43, 395–418.

Marmí, J., Casanovas-Vilar, I., Robles, J.M., Moyá-Sola, S. & Alba, D.M. 2012. The paleo-environment of *Hispanopithecus laietanus* as revealed by paleobotanical evidence from the late Miocene of Can Llobateres 1 (Catalonia, Spain). *Journal of Human Evolution* 62, 412–423.

Michelmore, A.P.G. 1939. Observations on tropical African grasslands. *Journal of Ecology* 27, 282–312.

Milne, G. 1935. Some suggested units of classification and mapping, particularly for East African soils. *Soil Research* 4, 183–198.

Milne, G. 1947. A soil reconnaissance journey through parts of Tanganyika Territory December 1935 to February 1936. *Journal of Ecology* 35, 192–265.

Morison, C.G.T., Boyle, A.C. & Hope-Simpson, J.F. 1948. Tropical soil-vegetation catenas and mosaics. *Journal of Ecology* 36, 1–84.

Pickford, M. 1995. Fossil land snails of East Africa and their palaeoecological significance. *Journal of African Earth Sciences* 20, 167–226.

Plummer, T.W. & Stanford, C.B. 2000. Analysis of a bone assemblage made by chimpanzees at Gombe National Park, Tanzania. *Journal of Human Evolution* 39, 345–365.

Pobiner, B.L., DeSilva, J., Sanders, W.J. & Mitani, J.C. 2007. Taphonomic analysis of skeletal remains from chimpanzee hunts at Ngogo, Kibale National Park, Uganda. *Journal of Human Evolution* 52, 614–636.

Richards, P.W. 1952. *The Tropical Rain Forest*. Cambridge, Cambridge University Press.

Rogl, F. 1999. Mediterranean and Paratethys palaeogeography during the Oligocene and Miocene. In J. Agusti, L. Rook & P. Andrews, Editors, *The Evolution of Neogene Terrestrial Ecosystems in Europe*, 8–22. Cambridge, Cambridge University Press.

Sinclair, A.R.E. 1979. Dynamics of the Serengeti ecosystem. In A.R.E. Sinclair & M. Norton-Griffiths, Editors, *Serengeti, Dynamics of an Ecosystem*, 1–30. Chicago, University of Chicago Press.

Sinclair, A.R.E. 1979. The eruption of the ruminants. In A.R.E. Sinclair & M. Norton-Griffiths, Editors, *Serengeti, Dynamics of an Ecosystem*, 82–103. Chicago, University of Chicago Press.

Stanford, C.B. & Bunn, H.T. (Editors). 2001. *Meat-Eating & Human Evolution*, 305–331. Oxford, Oxford University Press.

Strömberg, C.A.E. 2011. Evolution of grasses and grassland ecosystems. *Annual Review of Earth Planetary Science* 39, 517–544.

Suc, J.P. 1999. Neogene vegetation change in West European and West circum-Mediterranean areas. In J. Agusti, L. Rook & P. Andrews, Editors, *The Evolution of Neogene Terrestrial Ecosystems in Europe*, 378–388. Cambridge, Cambridge University Press.

White, F. 1983. *The Vegetation of Africa. A Descriptive Memoir to Accompany the UNESCO/AETFAT/UNSO Vegetation Map of Africa*. UNESCO.

White, T.D., Suwa, G. & Asfaw, B. 1994. *Australopithecus ramidus*: a new species of early hominid from Aramis, Ethiopia. *Nature* 371, 306–312.

WoldeGabriel, G., Ambrose, S.H., Barboni, D. et al. 2009. The geological, isotopic, botanical, invertebrate, and lower vertebrate surroundings of *Ardipithecus ramidus*. *Science* 326, 65e1–5.

Wood, B. 2014. Welcome to the family. *Scientific American* 311, 27–31.

Wood, B. & Harrison, T. 2011. The evolutionary context of the first hominins. *Nature* 470, 347–352.

Wrangham, R. & Peterson, D. 1997. *Demonic Males: Apes and the Origins of Human Violence.* London, Bloomsbury Press.

Wren, C.D., Xue, J.Z., Costopoulos, A. & Burke, A. 2014. The role of spatial foresight in models of hominin dispersal. *Journal of Human Evolution* 69, 70–78.

Chapter 6 Environmental indicators

This review of palaeoecology is in part an update of my 1996 review, with additions from recent papers by Kaye Reed and Andrews and Hixson. Evidence is reviewed for sedimentary structures, soil analysis and isotopic studies; trace fossils and taphonomy; taxonomic evidence from plants; and the use of indicator species. Recent reviews on the importance, and limitations, of ecomorphology have been published by Kaye Reed and by Sylvia Hixson and me, and an important monograph has been published by Meike Köhler. Evidence for the ecomorphology of mammals is based on postcrania, crania, tooth hypsodonty, macrowear, mesowear and microwear of teeth, and the publications describing these ecomorphologies are cited below. The final sections on palaeoecology combines evidence from many sources on community ecology. It also draws on my 1996 publication, updated from my recent work with Bonnie O'Brien, Sylvia Hixson and Sally Reynolds. Two particular issues concern the differences between point collecting localities and regional ones, and extinct (or fossilized) ecosystems.

Andrews, P. 1990. *Owls, Caves and Fossils.* London, Natural History Museum.

Andrews, P. 1996. Palaeoecology and hominoid palaeoenvironments. *Biological Reviews* 71, 257–300.

Andrews, P. 2006. Taphonomic effects of faunal impoverishment and faunal mixing. *Palaeogeography, Palaeoclimatology, Palaeoecology* 241, 572–589.

Andrews, P. & Alpagut, B. 1990. Description of the fossiliferous units at Paşalar, Turkey. *Journal of Human Evolution* 19, 343–361.

Andrews, P. & Bamford, M. 2007. Past and present vegetation ecology of Laetoli, Tanzania. *Journal of Human Evolution* 58, 78–98.

Andrews, P., Groves, C.P. & Horne, J. 1975. Ecology of the Tana River flood plain. *Journal of the East African Natural History Society* 151, 1–31.

Andrews, P. & Hixson, S. 2013. Taxon-free methods of palaeoecology. *Annales Zoologici Fennici* 51, 269–284.

Andrews, P., Lord, J.M. & Evans, E.M.N. 1979. Patterns of ecological diversity in fossil and modern mammalian faunas. *Biological Journal of the Linnean Society* 11, 177–205.

Andrews, P. & O'Brien, E. 2000. Climate, vegetation, and predictable gradients in mammal species richness in southern Africa. *Journal of Zoology* 251, 205–231.

Andrews, P. & O'Brien, E. 2010. Mammal species richness in Africa. In L. Werdelin & W. Sanders, Editors, *Cenozoic Mammals of Africa*, 929–947. New York, Columbia University Press.

Andrews, P. & Van Couvering, J.A.H. 1975. Environments in the East African Miocene. In F.S. Szalay, Editor, *Contributions to Primatology*, Vol. 5, 62–103. Basel, Karger.

Avery, D.M. 1987. Micromammalian evidence for natural vegetation and the introduction of farming during the Holocene in the Magaliesberg, Transvaal. *South African Journal of Science* 83, 221–225.

Avery, D.M. 1990. Holocene climatic change in Southern Africa: the contribution of micro-mammals to its study. *South African Journal of Science* 86, 407–412.

Avery, D.M. 1991. Micromammals, owls and vegetation change in the Eastern Cape Midlands, South Africa, during the last millennium. *Journal of Arid Environments* 20, 357–369.

Bamford, M. 2011a. Fossil wood. In T. Harrison, Editor, *Palaeontology and Geology of Laetoli: Human Evolution Context*, 217–234. New York, Springer.

Bamford, M. 2011b. Fossil leaves, fruits and seeds. In T. Harrison, Editor, *Palaeontology and Geology of Laetoli: Human Evolution Context*, 235–252. New York, Springer.

Bamford, M., Albert, R.M. & Cabanes, D. 2006. Plio-Pleistocene macroplant fossil remains and phytoliths from lowermost Bed II in the eastern palaeolake margin of Olduvai Gorge, Tanzania. *Quaternary International* 148, 95–112.

Bamford, M., Stannistreet, I.G., Stollhofen, H. & Albert, R.M. 2008. Late Pliocene grassland from Olduvai gorge, Tanzania. *Palaeogeography, Palaeoclimatology, Palaeoecology* 257, 280–293.

Barry, J.C., Morgan, M.E., Flynn, L.J. et al. 2002. Faunal and environmental change in the late Miocene Siwaliks of northern Pakistan. *Paleobiology* 28, 1–71.

Bedaso, Z.K., Wynn, J.G., Alemseged, Z. & Geraads, D. 2013. Dietary and paleoenvironmental reconstruction using stable isotopes of herbivore tooth enamel from middle Pliocene Dikika, Ethiopia: implication for *Australopithecus afarensis* habitat and food resources. *Journal of Human Evolution* 64, 21–38.

Bishop, L.C. 1999. Suid paleoecology and habitat preferences at African Pliocene and Pleistocene hominid localities. In T. Bromage & F. Schrenk, Editors, *African Biogeography, Climate Change, and Early Hominid Evolution*, 216–225. Oxford, Oxford University Press.

Blumenschine, R.J., Stannistreet, I.G., Njau, J.K. et al. 2012. Environments and hominin activities across the FLK Peninsula during Zinjanthropus times (1.84 Ma), Olduvai Gorge, Tanzania. *Journal of Human Evolution* 63, 363–383.

Bobe, R., Behrensmeyer, A.K. & Chapman, R.E. 2002. Faunal change, environmental variability and late Pliocene hominin evolution. *Journal of Human Evolution* 42, 475–497.

Bocherens, H., Fizet, M. & Mariotti, A. 1994. Diet, physiology and ecology of fossil mammals as inferred from stable carbon and nitrogen isotope biogeochemistry: implications for Pleistocene bears. *Palaeogeography, Palaeoclimatology, Palaeoecology* 107, 213–225.

Bonnefille, R. 1984. Cenozoic vegetation and environments of early hominids in East Africa. In R.O. White, Editor, *The Evolution of the East Asian Environment*, 579–612. Hong Kong, University of Hong Kong.

Brain, C.K. 1981. *The Hunters or the Hunted*. Chicago, University of Chicago Press.

Butler, P. 1952. The milk molars of Perissodactyla, with remarks on molar occlusion. *Proceedings of the Zoological Society of London* 121, 777–817.

Cerling, T.E. 1992. Development of grasslands and savannas in East Africa during the Neogene. *Palaeogeography, Palaeoclimatology, Palaeoecology* 97, 241–247.

Collinson, M.E. & Hooker, J.J. 1987. Vegetational and mammalian changes in the early Tertiary of southern England. In E.M. Friis, W.G. Chaloner & P.R. Crane, Editors, *The Origins of Angiosperms and their Biological Consequences*, 259–304. Cambridge, Cambridge University Press.

Collinson, M.E. & Hooker, J.J. 1991. Fossil evidence of interactions between plants and plant-eating mammals. *Philosophical Transactions of the Royal Society of London* 333, 197–208.

Collinson, M.E. & Hooker, J.J. 2003. Paleogene vegetation of Eurasia: framework for mammalian faunas. *Deinsea* 10, 41–83.

Currie, D.J. 1991. Energy and large-scale patterns of animal- and plant-species richness. *American Naturalist* 137, 27–49.

Currie, D.J. & Paquin, V. 1987. Large scale biogeographic patterns of species richness in trees. *Nature* 329, 326–327.

Damuth, J. & Janis, C. 2011. On the relationship between hypsodonty and feeding ecology in ungulate mammals, and its utility in palaeoecology. *Biological Reviews* 86, 733–758.

Darwin, C. 1859. *On the Origin of Species by means of Natural Selection*. London, John Murray.

Dawkins, R. 1986. *The Blind Watchmaker*. London, Longman.

Deane, A.S. 2009. Early Miocene catarrhine dietary behaviour: the influence of the Red Queen effect on incisor shape and curvature. *Journal of Human Evolution* 56, 275–285.

Dolphin, A.E., Naftel, S.J., Nelson, A.J., Martin, R.R. & White, C.D. 2013. Bromine in teeth and bone as an indicator of marine diet. *Journal of Archaeological Science* 40, 1778–1786.

Eronen, J.T & Rook, L. 2004. The Mio-Pliocene European primate fossil record: dynamics and habitat tracking. *Journal of Human Evolution* 47, 323–341.

Evans, E.M.N., Van Couvering, J.H. & Andrews, P. 1981. Palaeoecology of Miocene sites in Western Kenya. *Journal of Human Evolution* 10, 35–48.

Fernandez-Jalvo, Y., Denys, C., Andrews, P. et al. 1998. Taphonomy and palaeoecology of Olduvai Bed-I (Pleistocene, Tanzania). *Journal of Human Evolution* 34, 137–172.

Fleming, T.H. 1973. Numbers of mammal species in north and central American forest communities. *Ecology* 54, 555–563.

Fortelius, M., Eronen, J., Jenvall, J. et al. 2002. Fossil mammals resolve regional patterns of Eurasian climate change over 20 million years. *Evolutionary Ecology Research* 4, 1005–1016.

Fortelius, M. & Solounias, N. 2000. Functional characterization of ungulate molars using the abrasion-attrition wear gradient: a new method of reconstructing paleodiets. *American Museum Novitates* 3301, 1–36.

Geraads, D. 1994. Evolution of bovid diversity in the Plio-Pleistocene of Africa. *Historical Biology* 7, 227–237.

Gordon, K.D. 1982. A study of microwear on chimpanzee molars: implications for dental microwear analysis. *American Journal of Physical Anthropology* 59,195–215.

Gordon, K.D. 1988. A review of methodology and quantification in dental microwear analysis. *Scanning Microscopy* 2, 1139–1147.

Griffiths, J.F. 1976. *Climate and the Environment*. Boulder, Westview Press.

Grine, F.E. 1981. Trophic differences between gracile and robust australopithecines: a scanning electron microscope analysis of occlusal events. *South African Journal of Science* 77, 203–230.

Grine, F.E., Ungar, P.S. & Teaford, M.F. 2002. Error rates in dental microwear quantification using scanning electron microscopy. *Scanning Microscopy* 24,144–153.

Harrison, J.L. 1962. The distribution of feeding habits among animals in a tropical rain forest. *Journal of Animal Ecology* 31, 53–64.

Harrison, T. 2010. Coprolites: taphonomic and palaeoecological implications. In T. Harrison, Editor, *Palaeontology and Geology of Laetoli, Tanzania*, 279–292. New York, Springer.

Harvey, P.H. & Pagel, M.D. 1991. *The Comparative Method in Evolutionary Biology*. Oxford, Oxford University Press.

Hay, R.L. 1987. The geology of the Laetoli area. In M.D. Leakey & J.M. Harris, Editors, *Laetoli, a Pliocene Site in Northern Tanzania*, 23–47. Oxford, Clarendon Press.

Hunter, J.P. & Fortelius, M. 1994. Comparative dental occlusal morphology, facet development and microwear in two sympatric species of *Listriodon* (Mammalia, Suidae) from the middle Miocene of western Anatolia (Turkey). *Journal of Vertebrate Paleontology* 14, 105–126.

Jacobs, B.F. 1999. Estimation of rainfall variables from leaf characters in tropical Africa. *Palaeogeography, Palaeoclimatology, Palaeoecology* 145, 231–250.

Jacobs, B.F. 2001. Estimation of low-latitude paleoclimates using fossil angiosperm leaves: examples from the Miocene Tugen Hills, Kenya. *Paleobiology* 28, 399–421.

Janis, C.M. 1988. An estimation of tooth volume and hypsodonty indices in ungulate mammals, and the correlation of these factors with dietary preference. *Memoires du Musée National d'histoire naturele, Paris* 53, 367–387.

Janis, C.M. 1989. A climatic explanation for patterns of evolutionary diversity in ungulate mammals. *Palaeontology* 32, 463–481.

Janis, C.M. & Fortelius, M. 1988. On the means whereby mammals achieve increased functional durability of their dentitions, with special reference to limiting factors. *Biological Reviews* 63, 197–230.

Jernvall, J. & Fortelius, M. 2002. Common mammals drive the evolutionary increase of hypsodonty in the Neogene. *Nature* 417, 538–540.

Kaiser, T.M. & Fortelius, M. 2003. Differential mesowear in occluding upper and lower molars: opening mesowear analysis for lower molars and premolars in hypsodont horses. *Journal of Morphology* 258, 67–83.

Kappelman, J. 1988. Morphology and locomotor adaptations of the bovid femur in relation to habitat. *Journal of Morphology* 198, 119–130.

Kappelman, J. 1991. The paleoenvironment of *Kenyapithecus* at Fort Ternan. *Journal of Human Evolution* 20, 95–129.

Kay, R.F. 1975. The functional adaptations of primate molar teeth. *American Journal of Physical Anthropology* 43, 195–216.

Kay, R.F. & Hiiemae, K.M. 1974. Jaw movement and tooth use in recent and fossil primates. *American Journal of Physical Anthropology* 40, 227–256.

Kerr, J.T. & Packer, L. 1997. Habitat heterogeneity as a determinant of mammal species richness in high-energy regions. *Nature* 385, 252–254.

King, T., Aiello, L. & Andrews, P. 1999. Dental microwear of *Griphopithecus alpani*. *Journal of Human Evolution* 36, 3–31.

Kingston, J.D. 2010. Stable isotope analyses of Laetoli fossil herbivores. In T. Harrison, Editor, *Palaeontology and Geology of Laetoli, Tanzania*, 367–380. New York, Springer.

Kingston, J.D. & Harrison, T. 2007. Isotopic dietary reconstructions of Pliocene herbivores at Laetoli: implications for early hominin paleoecology. *Palaeogeography, Palaeoclimatology, Palaeoecology* 243, 272–306.

Köhler, M. 1993. Skeleton and habitat of recent and fossil ruminants. *Munchner Geowissenschaftliche Abhandlungen* 25, 1–88.

Kovar-Eder, J. 2003. Vegetation dynamics in Europe during the Neogene. *Deinsea* 10, 373–392.

Kovar-Eder, J., Kvacek, Z., Zastawniak, E. et al. 1996. Floristic trends in the vegetation of the Paratethys surrounding areas during Neogene times. In R.L. Bernor, V. Fahlbusch & H.-W. Mitmann, Editors, *The Evolution of Western Eurasian Neogene Mammal Faunas*, 395–413. New York, Columbia University Press.

Kovarovic, K. & Andrews, P. 2011. Environmental change within the Laetoli fossiliferous sequence: vegetation catenas and bovid ecomorphology. In T. Harrison, Editor, *Palaeontology and Geology of Laetoli, Tanzania*, 367–380. New York, Springer.

Kovarovic, K., Andrews, P. & Aiello, L. 2002. The palaeoecology of the Upper Ndolanya Beds at Laetoli, Tanzania. *Journal of Human Evololution* 43, 395–418.

Kovarovic, K., Stepkov, R. & McNulty, K.P. 2013. Ecological continuity between Lower and Upper Bed II, Olduvai Gorge, Tanzania. *Journal of Human Evolution* 64, 538–555.

Krigbaum, J., Berger, M.H., Daegling, D.J. & McGraw, W.S. 2013. Stable isotope canopy effects for sympatric monkeys at Tai Forest, Cote d'Ivoire. *Biology Letters* 9, 20130466.

Leakey, M.D. & Harris, J.M. 1987. *Laetoli: A Pliocene Site in Northern Tanzania*. Oxford, Clarendon Press.

Lehmann, T., Manthi, F.K. & McNulty, K.P. 2012. Early Neogene environents in East Africa: evidence from dental microwear of tragulids. *Palaeogeography, Palaeoclimatology, Palaeoecology* 342, 84–96.

Lucas, P.W., Omar, R., Al-Fadhalah, K. et al. 2013. Mechanisms and causes of wear in tooth enamel: implications for hominin diets. *Journal of the Royal Society Interface* 10, 20120923.

Lyell, C. 1830–1833. *Principles of Geology*. London, John Murray.

Marean, C. 1989. Sabertooth cats and their relevance for early hominid diet and evolution. *Journal of Human Evolution* 18, 559–582.

Mares, M.A. 1992. Neotropical mammals and the myth of Amazonian biodiversity. *Science* 255, 976–979.

Matson, S.D. & Fox, D.L. 2010. Stable isotopic evidence for terrestrial latitudinal climate gradients in the late Miocene of the Iberian Peninsula. *Palaeogeography, Palaeoclimatology, Palaeoecology* 287, 28–44.

Maxbauer, D.P., Peppe, D.J., Bamford, M. et al. 2013. A morphotype catalog and paleoenvironmental interpretations of early Miocene fossil leaves from the Hiwegi Formation, Rusinga Island, Lake Victoria, Kenya. *Palaeontologia Electronica* 16.3.28A.

O'Brien, E.M. 1993. Climatic gradients in woody plant species richness: towards an explanation based on an analysis of southern Africa's woody flora. *Journal of Biogeography* 20, 181–198.

O'Brien, E.M. 1998. Water-energy dynamics, climate and prediction of woody plant species richness: an interim general model. *Journal of Biogeography* 25, 379–398.

Palmqvist, P., Pérez-Claros, J.A., Janis, C.M. & Gröcke, D.R. 2008. Tracing the ecophysiology of ungulates and predaro-prey relationships in an early Pleistocene large mammal community. *Palaeogeography, Palaeoclimatology, Palaeoecology* 266, 95–111.

Pilbeam, D.R. 1996. Comments on the last decades of research on Miocene hominoids and hominid origins. In D. Begun, C. Ward & M.D. Rose, Editors, *Miocene Hominoid Fossils: Functional and Phylogenetic Implications*. New York, Plenum Press.

Plummer, T., Bishop, L., Kingston, J. et al. 1999. Reconstructing Oldowan hominid paleoecology. *Journal of Human Evolution* 36, A18.

Quade, J., Cerling, T.E., Andrews, P. & Alpagut, B. 1995. Palaeodietary reconstruction of Miocene fauna from Paşalar, Turkey, using stable carbon and oxygen isotopes of fossil tooth enamel. *Journal of Human Evolution* 28, 373–384.

Raunkiær, C. 1934. *The Life Forms of Plants and Statistical Plant Geography, being the Collected Papers of C. Raunkiær.* Oxford, Oxford University Press. Reprinted 1978 (ed. by Frank N. Egerton), Ayer Co. Pub.

Reed, K.E. 2013. Multiproxy palaeoecology: reconstructing evolutionary context in paleo-anthropology. In D.R. Begun, Editor, *A Companion to Paleoanthropology*, 204–225. Oxford, Wiley-Blackwell.

Rein, T. 2010. Locomotor function and phylogeny: implications for interpreting the hominoid fossil record. PhD thesis, New York University.

Retallack, G.J. 1991. *Miocene Paleosols and Ape Habitats of Pakistan and Kenya.* New York, Oxford University Press.

Retallack, G.J., Bestland, E.A. & Dugas, D.P. 1995. Miocene paleosols and habitats of *Proconsul* on Rusinga Island, Kenya. *Journal of Human Evolution* 29, 53–91.

Rossouw, L. & Scott, L. 2010. Phytoliths and pollen, the microscopic plant remains in Pliocene volcanic sediments around Laetoli, Tanzania. In T. Harrison, Editor, *Palaeontology and Geology of Laetoli, Tanzania*, 201–216. New York, Springer.

Saarinen, J., Oikarinen, E., Fortelius, M. & Mannila, H. 2010. The living and the fossilized: how well do unevenly distributed points capture the faunal information in a grid? *Evolutionary Ecology Research* 12, 263–376.

Scott, R.S., Teaford, M.F. & Ungar, P.S. 2012. Dental microwear texture and anthropoid diets. *American Journal of Physical Anthropology* 147, 551–579.

Sikes, N.E. 1999. PlioPleistocene floral context and habitat preferences of sympatric hominid species in East Africa. In T. Bromage & F. Schrenk, Editors, *African Biogeography, Climate Change, and Early Hominid Evolution*, 301–315. Oxford, Oxford University Press.

Sikes, N.E. & Ashley, G.M. 2007. Stable isotopes of pedogenic carbonates as indicators of paleoecology in the Plio-Pleistocene (upper Bed I), western margin of the Olduvai Basin, Tanzania. *Journal of Human Evolution* 53, 574–594.

Simpson, G.G. 1964. Species diversity of North American recent mammals. *Systematic Zoology* 13, 57–73.

Smith, C.C., Morgan, M.E. & Pilbeam, D. 2010. Isotopic ecology and dietary profiles of Liberian chimpanzees. *Journal of Human Evolution* 58, 43–55.

Soligo, C. & Andrews, P. 2005. Taphonomic bias, taxonomic bias and historical non-equivalence of faunal structure in early hominin localities. *Journal of Human Evolution* 49, 206–229.

Steininger, F.F. 1999. Chronostratigraphy, geochronology and biochronology of the Miocene European Land Mammal zones (MN zones). In G.E. Rossner & K. Heissig, Editors, *The Miocene Land Mammals of Europe*, 9‒24. Munich, Dr Friedrich Pfeil.

Strait, D.S., Weber, G.W., Constantino, P. et al. 2012. Microwear, mechanics and the feeding adaptations of *Australopithecus africanus*. *Journal of Human Evolution* 62, 165–168.

Su, D. 2010. Large mammal evidence for the paleoenvironment of the Upper Laetolil and Upper Ndolanya Beds of Laetoli, Tanzania. In T. Harrison, Editor, *Palaeontology and Geology of Laetoli, Tanzania*, 381–392. New York, Springer.

Su, D. & Harrison, T. 2008. Ecological implications of the relative rarity of fossil hominins in Laetoli. *Journal of Human Evolution* 55, 672–681.

Teaford, M.F. 1988. A review of dental microwear and diet in modern mammals. *Scanning Microscopy* 2, 1149–1166.

Teaford, M.F. 1991. Dental microwear: what can it tell us about diet and dental function? In J. Else & P. Lee, Editors, *Advances in Dental Anthropology*, 341–356. New York, Wiley-Liss Inc.

Teaford, M.F. 1994. Dental microwear and dental function. *Evolutionary Anthropology* 3, 17–30.

Ungar, P.S. 1994. Incisor microwear of Sumatran anthropoid primates. *American Journal of Physical Anthropology* 94, 339–363.

Ungar, P.S. 2005. Dental evidence for the diets of fossil primates from Rudabánya, North-eastern Hungary with comments on extant primate analogs and 'noncompetitive' sympatry. *Palaeontologia Italia* 90, 97–112.

Ungar, P.S. (Editor) 2007. *Evolution of the Human Diet*. Oxford, Oxford University Press.

Ungar, P.S. 2009. Tooth form and function: insights into adaptation through the analysis of dental microwear. *Frontiers of Oral Biology* 13, 38–43.

Ungar, P.S. & Kay, R.F. 1995. The dietary adaptations of European Miocene catarrhines. *Proceedings of the National Academy of Sciences* 93, 5479–5481.

Van Couvering, J.A.H. 1980. Community evolution in East Africa during the late Cenozoic. In A.K. Behrensmeyer & A.P. Hill, Editors, *Fossils in the Making*, 272–298. Chicago, University of Chicago Press.

Van der Meulen, A.J. & Daams, R. 1992. Evolution of early-middle Miocene rodent faunas in relation to long-term palaeoenvironmental changes. *Palaeogeography, Palaeoclimatology, Palaeoecology* 93, 227–253.

Van Valkenburgh, B. 1987. Skeletal indicators of locomotor behaviour in living and extinct carnivores. *Journal of Vertebrate Paleontology* 7, 162–182.

Verdcourt, B. 1963. The Miocene non-marine Mollusca of Rusinga Island, Lake Victoria and other localities in Kenya. *Palaeontographica* 121,1–37.

Vrba, E.S. 1980. The significance of bovid remains as indicators of environment and predation patterns. In A.K. Behrensmeyer & A.P. Hill, Editors, *Fossils in the Making*, 247–271. Chicago, University of Chicago Press.

Walker, A. 1981. Dietary hypotheses and human evolution. *Philosophical Transactions of the Royal Society of London* 292, 57–64.

Walker, A. & Teaford, M. 1988. The hunt for *Proconsul*. *Scientific American* 260, 76–82.

Werdelin, L. & Lewis, M.E. 2013. Temporal change in functional richness and evenness in the eastern African Plio-Pleistocene carnivoranguild. *PLOS One* 8 (8), 1–11.

Chapter 7 The view from the early Miocene

Most of the descriptions of skull and skeletal morphology of *Proconsul* are based on descriptions of this species by John Napier in 1959, Le Gros Clark and Leakey in 1951, my work in 1978 and Alan Walker's book *The Ape in the Tree*. The history of work on Miocene deposits in East Africa is given in my 1981 publication and Alan Walker's book. The account of our fieldwork at Meswa Bridge is in Andrews (2000) – 'The day of a thousand fossils'. Later additions include the publications of new species and descriptions of the postcranial anatomy of proconsulids.

Andrews, P. 1978. A revision of the Miocene Hominoidea of East Africa. *Bulletin of the British Museum of Natural History (Geology)* 30, 85–224.

Andrews, P. 1981. A short history of Miocene field palaeontology in Western Kenya. *Journal of Human Evolution* 10, 3–9.

Andrews, P. 2000. The day of a thousand fossils. In P.J. Whybrow, Editor, *Travels with the Fossil Hunters*, 160–175. Cambridge, Cambridge University Press.

Beard, K.C., Teaford, M.F. & Walker, A. 1986. New wrist bones of *Proconsul africanus* and *P. nyanzae* from Rusinga Island, Kenya. *Folia Primatologia* 47, 97–118.

Begun, D.R., Teaford, M.F. & Walker, A. 1994. Comparative and functional anatomy of *Proconsul* phalanges from the Kaswanga primate site, Rusinga Island, Kenya. *Journal of Human Evolution* 26, 89–165.

Beynon, A.D., Dean, M.C., Leakey, M.G., Reid, D.J. & Walker, Q. 1998. Comparative dental development and microstructure of *Proconsul* teeth from Rusinga Island, Kenya. *Journal of Human Evolution* 35, 163–209.

Boschetto, H.B., Brown, F.H. & McDougall, I. 1992. Stratigraphy of the Lothidok Range, northern Kenya, and K-Ar ages of its Miocene primates. *Journal of Human Evolution* 22, 47–71.

Deane, A.S. 2009. Early Miocene catarrhine dietary behaviour: the influence of the Red Queen effect on incisor shape and curvature. *Journal of Human Evolution* 56, 275–285.

Gebo, D.L. 1989. Locomotor and phylogenetic considerations in anthropoid evolution. *Journal of Human Evolution* 18, 201–233.

Gebo, D.L., Beard, K.C., Teaford, M.F. et al. 1988. A hominoid proximal humerus from the early Miocene of Rusinga Island, Kenya. *Journal of Human Evolution* 17, 393–401.

Gebo, D.L., Malit, N.R. & Nengo, I.O. 2009. New proconsuloid postcranials from the early Miocene of Kenya. *Primates* 50, 311–319.

Harrison, T. & Andrews, P. 2009. The anatomy and systematic position of the early Miocene proconsulid from Meswa Bridge, Kenya. *Journal of Human Evolution* 56, 479–496.

Hill, A., Odhiambo Nengo, I. & Rossie, J.B. 2013. A *Rangwapithecus gordoni* mandible from the early Miocene site of Songhor, Kenya. *Journal of Human Evolution* 65, 490–500.

Hopwood, A.T. 1933. Miocene primates from Kenya. *Zoological Journal of the Linnean Society* 37, 437–464.

Johnson, R.J. & Andrews, P. 2010. Fructose, uricase, and the back to Africa hypothesis. *Evolutionary Anthropology* 19, 250–257.

Kay, R.F. 1977. Diet of early Miocene African hominoids. *Nature* 268, 628–630.

Le Bas, M.J. 1977. *Carbonatite-Nephelinite Volcanism*. London, John Wiley and Sons.

Le Gros Clark, W.E. & Leakey, L.S.B. 1950. Diagnoses of East African Miocene Hominoidea. *Quarterly Journal of the Geological Society* 105, 260–262.

Le Gros Clark, W.E. & Leakey, L.S.B. 1951. *The Miocene Hominoidea of East Africa*. London, British Museum (Natural History).

Lewis, O.J. 1989. *Functional Morphology of the Evolving Hand and Foot*. Oxford, Clarendon Press.

MacInnes, D. 1943. Notes on the East African Miocene primates. *Journal of the East African Natural History Society* 17, 141–181.

MacLatchy, L. 2004. The oldest ape. *Evolutionary Anthropology* 13, 90–103.

MacLatchy, L. & Bossert, W.H. 1996. An analysis of the articular surface distribution of the femoral head and acetabulum in anthropoids, with implications for hip function in Miocene hominoids. *Journal of Human Evolution* 31, 425–453.

Marzke, M.W. 1997. Precision grips, hand morphology and tools. *American Journal of Physical Anthropology* 102, 91–110.

McNulty, K.P., Begun, D., Kelley, J., Manthi, F.K. & Mbua, E.N. 2015. A systematic revision of *Proconsul* with the description of a new genus of early Miocene hominoid. *Journal of Human Evolution* 84, 42–61.

Nakatsukasa, M. 2008. Comparative study of Moroto vertebral specimens. *Journal of Human Evolution* 55, 581–588.

Napier, J.R. 1960. Studies of the hands of living primates. *Proceedings of the Zoological Society of London* 134, 647–657.

Napier, J.R. 1964. The evolution of bipedal walking in the hominids. *Archives de Biologie Liege* 75, 673–708.

Napier, J.R. & Davis, P.R. 1959. *The Fore-limb Skeleton and Associated Remains of Proconsul africanus*. London, British Museum (Natural History).

Pickford, M. & Andrews, P. 1981. The Tinderet Miocene sequence in Kenya. *Journal of Human Evolution* 10, 11–33.

Rafferty, K.L. 1998. Structural design of the femoral neck in primates. *Journal of Human Evolution* 34, 361–383.

Rafferty, K., Walker, A., Ruff, C., Rose, M. & Andrews, P. 1995. Postcranial estimates of body weight in *Proconsul*, with a note on a distal tibia of *P. major* from Napak, Uganda. *American Journal of Physical Anthropology* 97, 391–402.

Rein, T.R., Harrison, T. & Zollikofer, P.E. 2012. Skeletal correlates of quadrupedalism and climbing in the anthropoid forelimb: implications for inferring locomotion in Miocene catarrhines. *Journal of Human Evolution* 61, 564–574.

Rose, M.D. 1983 Miocene hominoid postcranial morphology: monkey-like ape-like, neither, or both? In R.L. Ciochon & R.S. Corruccini, Editors, *New Interpretations of Ape and Human Ancestry*, 405–417. New York, Plenum Press.

Ungar, P.S. (Editor) 2007. *Evolution of the Human Diet*. Oxford, Oxford University Press.

Ungar, P.S. 2009. Tooth form and function: insights into adaptation through the analysis of dental microwear. *Frontiers of Oral Biology* 13, 38–43.

Walker, A.C., Falk, D., Smith, R. & Pickford, M. 1983. The skull of *Proconsul africanus*: reconstruction and cranial capacity. *Nature* 305, 525–527.

Walker, A. & Pickford, M. 1983. New postcranial fossils of *Proconsul africanus* and *Proconsul nyanzae*. In R.L. Ciochon & R.S. Corruccini, Editors, *New Interpretations of Ape and Human Ancestry*, 325–351. New York, Plenum Press.

Walker, A. & Shipman, P. 2005. *The Ape in the Tree*. Cambridge, Harvard University Press.

Walker, A., Teaford, M., Martin, L. & Andrews, P. (1993). A new species of *Proconsul* from the early Miocene of Rusinga/Mwangano Islands, Kenya. *Journal of Human Evolution* 25, 43–56.

Ward, C.V. 1993. Torso morphology and locomotion in *Proconsul nyanzae*. *American Journal of Physical Anthropology* 92, 291–328.

Ward, C.V., Ruff, C.B., Walker, A. et al. 1995. Functional morphology of *Proconsul* patellas from Rusinga Island, Kenya, with implications for other Miocene-Pliocene catarrhines. *Journal of Human Evolution* 29, 1–19.

Ward, C.V., Walker, A. & Teaford, M.F. 1991. *Proconsul* did not have a tail. *Journal of Human Evolution* 21, 215–220.

Ward, C.V., Walker, A., Teaford, M.F. & Odhiambo, I. 1993. Partial skeleton of *Proconsul nyanzae* from Mfangano Island, Kenya. *American Journal of Physical Anthropology* 90, 77–111.

Whybrow, P.J. & Andrews, P. 1978. Restoration of the holotype of *Proconsul nyanzae*. *Folia Primatologica* 30, 115–125.

Zingeser, M.R. 1969. Cercopithecoid canine tooth honing mechanisms. *American Journal of Physical Anthropology* 31, 205–214.

Chapter 8 The environment in the early Miocene

Many of the early Miocene apes are associated both with forest and non-forest environments based on my work and that of my collaborators. There is no overall review, but recent work has shown the presence of forest at some sites.

Andrews, P., Groves, C.P. & Horne, J.F.M. 1975. The ecology of the Lower Tana River Flood Plain. *Journal of the East African Natural History Society* 151, 1–31.

Andrews, P., Lord, J.M. & Evans, E.M.N. 1979. Patterns of ecological diversity in fossil and modern mammalian faunas. *Biological Journal of the Linnean Society* 11,177–205.

Andrews, P. & Van Couvering, J.H. 1975. Palaeoenvironments in the East African Miocene. In F.S. Szalay, Editor, *Approaches to Primate Paleobiology*, 62–103. Basel, Karger.

Bestland, E. 1990. Sedimentology and paleopedology of Miocene alluvial deposits at the Paşalar hominoid site, western Turkey. *Journal of Human Evolution* 19, 363–377.

Bestland, E.A. & Retallack, G.I. 1993. Volcanically influenced calcareous palaeosols from the Miocene Kiahera Formation, Rusinga Island, Kenya. *Journal of the Geological Society of London* 150, 293–310.

Chesters, K.I.M. 1957. The Miocene flora of Rusinga Island, Lake Victoria, Kenya. *Palaeontographica* 101, 30–71.

Collinson, M.E. 1983. *Fossil Plants of the London Clay*. London, Palaeontological Association Field Guide.

Collinson, M.E., Andrews, P. & Bamford, M. 2009. Taphonomy of the early Miocene flora, Hiwegi Formation, Rusinga Island, Kenya. *Journal of Human Evolution* 57, 149–162.

Drake, R., Van Couvering, J.A., Pickford, M., Curtis, G. & Harris, J.A. 1988. New chronology for the early Miocene mammalian faunas of Kisingiri, western Kenya. *Journal of the Geological Society of London* 145, 479–491.

Harrison, T. 2002. Late Oligocene to middle Miocene catarrhines from Afro-Arabia. In W.C. Hartwig, Editor, *The Primate Fossil Record*, 311–338. Cambridge, Cambridge University Press.

Le Bas, M.J. 1977. *Carbonatite-nephelinite Volcanism: An African Case History*. London, Wiley.

Lehmann, T., Manthi, F.K. & McNulty, K.P. 2012. Early Neogene environents in East Africa: evidence from dental microwear of tragulids. *Palaeogeography, Palaeoclimatology, Palaeoecology* 342, 84–96.

Maxbauer, D.P., Peppe, D.J., Bamford, M. et al. 2013. A morphotype catalog and paleoenvironmental interpretations of early Miocene fossil leaves from the Hiwegi Formation, Rusinga Island, Lake Victoria, Kenya. *Palaeontologia Electronica* 16.3.28A.

McCall, G.J.H. 1958. *Geology of the Gwasi Area. Geological Survey of Kenya,* Report No. 48.

Michel, L.A., Peppe, D.J., Lutz, J.A. et al. 2014. Remnants of an ancient forest provide ecological context for early Miocene fossil apes. *Nature Communications* 5, 3236. DOI10:1038.

Pickford, M. & Andrews, P. 1981. The Tinderet Miocene sequence in Kenya. *Journal of Human Evolution* 10, 11–33.

Raunkiær, C. 1934. *The Life Forms of Plants and Statistical Plant Geography, being the collected papers of C. Raunkiær*. Oxford, Oxford University Press. Reprinted 1978 (ed. by Frank N. Egerton), Ayer Co. Pub.

Retallack, G.J. 1990. *Soils of the Past: An Introduction to Paleopedology*. Boston, Unwin Hyman.

Richards, P.W. 1952. *The Tropical Rain Forest*. Cambridge, Cambridge University Press.

Van Couvering, J.A. & Miller, J.A. 1969. Miocene stratigraphy and age determinations, Rusinga Island, Kenya. *Nature* 221, 628–633.

Verdcourt, B. 1963. The Miocene non-marine Mollusca of Rusinga Island, Lake Victoria, and other localities in Kenya. *Palaeontographica* 121, 1–37.

Walker, A. & Shipman, P. 2005.*The Ape in the Tree*. Cambridge, Harvard University Press.

Walker, A. & Teaford, M. 1988. The hunt for *Proconsul*. *Scientific American* 260, 76–82.

Walker, A. & Teaford, M. 1989. The Kaswanga primate site: an early Miocene hominoid site on Rusinga Island, Kenya. *Journal of Human Evolution* 17, 539–544.

Whitworth, T. 1953. A contribution to the geology of Rusinga Island, Kenya. *Quarterly Journal of the Geological Society* 109, 75–92.

Chapter 9 The view from the middle Miocene

There is some disagreement about the taxonomic status of African and Eurasian middle Miocene apes (see Begun 2002; Harrison 2002) but there is no final resolution of differences; and there are some differences of interpretation in the dating of the Eurasian middle Miocene sites. Alba dated the deposits at Engelswies and Paşalar to after the Langhian transgression so are younger than 15 million years ago. A summary of correlations for each major taxonomic group at Paşalar is given by Bernor and Tobien as part of three special issues of the *Journal of Human Evolution* devoted exclusively to this site. The site at Çandır has been published in a monograph edited by Erksin Guleç.

Alba, D.M., Fortuny, J. & Moyà-Solà, S. 2010. Enamel thickness in the middle Miocene great apes *Anoiapithecus, Pierolapithecus* and *Dryopithecus*. *Proceedings of the Royal Society* 277, 2237–2245.

Alpagut, B., Andrews, P. & Martin, L. 1990. New hominoid specimens from the middle Miocene site at Paşalar, Turkey. *Journal of Human Evolution* 19, 397–422.

Andrews, P. 1995. Time resolution of the Miocene fauna from Paşalar. *Journal of Human Evolution* 28, 343–358.

Andrews, P. & Alpagut, B. 1990. Description of the fossiliferous units at Paşalar, Turkey. *Journal of Human Evolution* 19, 343–361.

Andrews, P. & Ersoy, A. 1990. Taphonomy of the Miocene bone accumulations at Paşalar, Turkey. *Journal of Human Evolution* 19, 379–396.

Andrews, P. & Humphrey, L. 1999. African Miocene environments and the transition to early hominines. In T. Bromage & F. Schrenk, Editors, *African Biogeography, Climate Change, and Early Hominid Evolution*, 282–300. Oxford, Oxford University Press.

Andrews, P., Meyer, G.E., Pilbeam, D.R., Van Couvering, J.A. & Van Couvering, J.A.H. 1981. The Miocene fossil beds of Maboko Island, Kenya: geology, age, taphonomy and palaeontology. *Journal of Human Evolution* 10, 35–48.

Andrews, P. & Molleson, T.I. 1978. The provenance of *Sivapithecus africanus*. *Bulletin of the British Museum of Natural History (Geology)* 32, 19–23.

Andrews, P. & Tobien, H. 1977. New Miocene locality in Turkey with evidence on the origins of *Ramapithecus* and *Sivapithecus*. *Nature* 268, 699–701.

Becker-Platen, J.D., Sickenberg, O. & Tobien, H. 1975. Die Gliderung der Kanozoischen sedimente der Turkei nach vertebraten-faunengruppen. *Geologische Jahrbuch* 15, 19–45.

Begun, D.R. 2002. European hominoids. In W.C. Hartwig, Editor, *The Primate Fossil Record*, 339–368. Cambridge, Cambridge University Press.

Begun, D.R., Geraads, D. & Guleç, E. 2003. The Çandır hominoid locality: implications for the timing and pattern of hominoid dispersal events. *Courier Forschungsinsitut Senckenberg* 240, 251–265.

Casanovas-Vilar, I., Alba, D.M., Moyà-Solà, S. et al. 2008. Biochronological, taphonomical and paleoenvironmental background of the fossil great ape *Pierolapithecus catalaunicus* (Primates, Hominidae). *Journal of Human Evolution* 55, 589–603.

Ersoy, A., Kelley, J., Andrews, P. & Alpagut, B. 2008. Hominoid phalanges from the middle Miocene site of Paşalar, Turkey. *Journal of Human Evolution* 54, 518–529.

Fortelius, M. & Bernor, R. 1990. A provisional systematic assessment of the Miocene Suoidea from Pasalar, Turkey. *Journal of Human Evolution* 19, 509–528.

Gençturk, I., Alpagut, B. & Andrews, P. 2008. Interproximal wear facets and tooth associations in the Paşalar hominoid sample. *Journal of Human Evolution* 54, 480–493.

Guleç, E., Begun, D.R. & Geraads, D. 2003. Geology and vertebrate paleontology of the middle Miocene hominoid locality Çandır. *Courier Forschungsinstitut Senckenberg* 240, 1–265.

Harrison, T. 2002. Late Oligocene to middle Miocene catarrhines from Afro-Arabia. In W.C. Hartwig, Editor, *The Primate Fossil Record*. Cambridge, Cambridge University Press.

Heizmann, E. & Begun, D. 2001. The oldest Eurasian hominoid. *Journal of Human Evolution* 41, 463–481.

Ishida, H., Kunimatsu, Y., Nakatsukasa, M. & Nakano, Y. 1999. New hominoid genus from the middle Miocene of Nachola. *Anthropological Science* 107, 189–191.

Ishida, H., Kunimatsu, Y., Takano, T., Nakano, Y. & Nakatsukasa, M. 2004. *Nacholapithecus* skeleton from the Middle Miocene of Kenya. *Journal of Human Evolution* 46, 69–103.

Kelley, J. 2002. The hominoid radiation in Asia. In W.C. Hartwig, Editor, *The Primate Fossil Record*, 339–368. Cambridge, Cambridge University Press.

Kelley, J., Ward, S., Brown, B., Hill, A. & Downs, W. 2000. Middle Miocene hominoid origins: response. *Science* 287, 2375a.

Kelley, J., Ward, S., Brown, B., Hill, A. & Duren, D.L. 2002. Dental remains of *Equatorius africanus* from Kipsaramon, Tugen Hills, Baringo District, Kenya. *Journal of Human Evolution* 42, 39–62.

Kikuchi, Y., Nakano, Y., Nakatsukasa, M. et al. 2012. Functional morphology and anatomy of cervical vertebrae in *Nacholapithecus kerioi,* a middle Miocene hominoid from Kenya. *Journal of Human Evolution* 62, 677–695.

King, T., Aiello, L. & Andrews, P. 1999. Dental microwear of *Griphopithecus alpani*. *Journal of Human Evolution* 36, 3–31.

Kunimatsu, Y., Ishida, H., Nakatsukasa, M., Nakano, Y., Sawada Y. & Nakayama, K. 2004. Maxillae and associated gnathodental specimens of *Nacholapithecus kerioi*, a large-bodied hominoid from Nachola, northern Kenya. *Journal of Human Evolution* 46, 365–400.

Le Gros Clark, W.E. & Leakey, L.S.B. 1950. Diagnoses of East African Miocene Hominoidea. *Quarterly Journal of the Geological Society* 105, 260–262.

Leakey, L.S.B. 1967. An early Miocene member of Hominidae. *Nature* 213, 155–163.

Leakey, L.S.B. 1968. Lower dentition of *Kenyapithecus africanus*. *Nature* 217, 827–830.

McCrossin, M.L. & Benefit, B.R. 1997. On the relationships and adaptations of *Kenypithecus*, a large-bodied hominoid from the middle Miocene of eastern Africa. In D.R. Begun, C.V. Ward & M.D Rose, Editors, *Function, Phylogeny and Fossils: Miocene Hominoid Evolution and Adaptations*, 241–267. New York, Plenum Press.

McCrossin, M.L., Benefit, B.R., Gitau, S.N., Palmer, A.K. & Blue, K.T. 1998. Fossil evidence for the origin of terrestriality among Old World higher primates. In E. Strasser, J. Fleagle, A. Rosenberger & H. McHenry, Editors, *Primate Locomotion: Recent Advances*, 353–396. New York, Plenum Press.

Mortzou, G. & Andrews, P. 2008. The deciduous dentition of *Griphopithecus alpani* from Paşalar. Turkey. *Journal of Human Evolution* 54, 494–502.

Nakatsukasa, M., Kunimatsu, Y., Nakano, Y. & Ishida, H. 2007. Vertebral morphology of *Nacholapithecus kerioi* based on KNM-BG 35250. *Journal of Human Evolution* 52, 347–369.

Nakatsukasa, M., Yamanaka, A., Kunimatsu, Y., Shimizu, D. & Ishida, H. 1998. A newly discovered *Kenyapithecus* skeleton and its implications for the evolution of positional behaviour in Miocene East African hominoids. *Journal of Human Evolution* 34, 657–664.

Patel, B.A., Susman, R.L., Rossie, J.B. & Hill, A. 2009. Terrestrial adaptations in the hands of *Equatorius africanus* revisited. *Journal of Human Evolution* 57, 763–772.

Rossie, J.B. & MacLatchy, L. 2013. Dentognathic remains of an *Afropithecus* individual from Kalodirr. *Journal of Human Evolution* 65, 199–208.

Sickenberg, O. 1975. Die Gliederung des hoheren Jungtertiars und Altquartiars in der Türkei nach Vertebraten und ihre Bedeutung für die internationale Neogen-stratigraphie. *Geologische Jahrbuch* 15, 1–167.

Tekkaya, I. 1974. A new species of anthropoid (Primates, Mammalia) from Anatolia. *Bulletin of the Mineralogical Exploration Institute, Ankara (MTA)* 83, 148–165.

Ward, S.C., Brown, B., Hill, A., Kelley, J. & Downs, W. (1999). *Equatorius*: a new hominoid genus from the middle Miocene of Kenya. *Science* 285, 1382–1386.

Ward, S.C. & Pilbeam, D.R. 1983. Maxillofacial morphology of Miocene hominoids from Africa and Indo-Pakistan. In R.L. Ciochon & R.S. Corruccini, Editors, *New Interpretations of Ape and Human Ancestry*, 211–238. New York, Plenum Press.

Chapter 10 Specialized apes from the middle Miocene

The kenyapithecines are the most controversial group of fossil apes. McCrossin and Benefit group them with *Equatorius africanus*, but Kelley and Andrews distinguish the two species at subfamily level. It is also the only genus of ape, living or dead, that has an intercontinental distribution, species of the genus being identified in both Eurasia and Africa. The Eurasian species is described by Alpagut and Andrews, and by Kelley and Andrews, while the African species is described by Louis Leakey and by me.

Alpagut, B., Andrews, P. & Martin, L. (1990). New hominoid specimens from the middle Miocene site at Paşalar, Turkey. *Journal of Human Evolution* 19, 397–422.

Andrews, P. 1971. *Ramapithecus wickeri* mandible from Fort Ternan, Kenya. *Nature* 231, 192–194.

Andrews, P. J. & Tekkaya, I. 1980 A revision of the Turkish Miocene hominoid *Sivapithecus meteai*. *Paleontology* 23, 85–95.

Andrews, P.J. & Tobien, H. 1977. New Miocene locality in Turkey with evidence on the origin of *Ramapithecus and Sivapithecus*. *Nature* 268, 699–701.

Gentry, A.W. 1970. The Bovidae (Mammalia) of the Fort Ternan fossil faunas. *Fossil Vertebrates of Africa* 2, 243–323.

Humphrey, L. & Andrews, P. 2008. Metric variation in the postcanine teeth from Paşalar, Turkey. *Journal of Human Evolution* 54, 503–507.

Kelley, J. 2008. Identification of a single birth cohort in *Kenyapithecus kizili* and the nature of sympatry between *K. kizili* and *Griphopithecus alpani* at Paşalar. *Journal of Human Evolution* 54, 530–537.

Kelley, J., Andrews, P. & Alpagut, B. 2008. A new hominoid species from the middle Miocene site of Paşalar, Turkey. *Journal of Human Evolution* 54, 455–479.

King, T., Aiello, L. & Andrews, P. 1999. Dental microwear of *Griphopithecus alpani*. *Journal of Human Evolution* 36, 3–31.

Leakey, L.S.B. 1962. A new lower Pliocene hominoid from Kenya. *Annals and Magazine of Natural History* 4, 689–696.

Lehmann, T., Manthi, F.K. & McNulty, K.P. 2012. Early Neogene environments in East Africa: evidence from dental microwear of tragulids. *Palaeogeography, Palaeoclimatology, Palaeoecology* 342, 84–96.

Makishima, H. 2005. Flora and vegetation of Nachola, Samburu District, northern Kenya: a study of vegetation in an arid land. *African Study Monographs Supplement* 32, 63–78.

McCrossin, M.L. & Benefit, B.R. 1997. On the relationships and adaptations of *Kenypithecus*, a large-bodied hominoid from the middle Miocene of eastern Africa. In D.R. Begun, C.V. Ward & M.D. Rose, Editors, *Function, Phylogeny and Fossils: Miocene Hominoid Evolution and Adaptations*, 241–267. New York, Plenum Press.

Retallack, G.J. 1990. *Soils of the Past: An Introduction to Paleopedology*. Boston, Unwin Hyman.

Shipman, P. 1982. Reconstructing the paleoecology and taphonomic history of *Ramapithecus wickeri* at Fort Ternan, Kenya. *Museum Briefs* 26, Museum of Anthropology, Columbia.

Shipman, P. 1986 Paleoecology of Fort Ternan reconsidered. *Journal of Human Evolution* 15,193–204.

Simons, E.L. & Pilbeam, D.R. 1965. A preliminary revision of the Dryopithecinae. *Folia Primatologica* 3, 81–152.

Walker, A. & Andrews, P. 1973. Reconstruction of the dental arcades of *Ramapithecus wickeri*. *Nature* 244, 313–314.

Chapter 11 The environment during the middle Miocene

There is no monographic treatment of Miocene environments. The two principal kenyapithecine sites have been described by Pat Shipman and her collaborators for Fort Ternan and by me and my collaborators for Paşalar. John Kingston and Bonnie Jacobs have described the environment of the Tugen Hills; Judy Van Couvering and I described the environment at Maboko Island, the type site of *Equatorius africanus*.

Andrews, P. 1990. Palaeoecology of the Miocene fauna from Paşalar, Turkey. *Journal of Human Evolution* 19, 569–582.

Andrews, P. 1995. Time resolution of the Miocene fauna from Paşalar. *Journal of Human Evolution* 28, 343–358.

Andrews, P. 1996. Palaeoecology and hominoid palaeoenvironments. *Biological Reviews* 1996, 257–300.

Andrews, P. 2006. Taphonomic effects of faunal impoverishment and faunal mixing. *Palaeogeography, Palaeoclimatology, Palaeoecology* 241, 572–589.

Andrews, P. & Alpagut, B. 1990. Description of the fossiliferous units at Paşalar, Turkey. *Journal of Human Evolution* 19, 343–361.

Andrews, P., Meyer, G.E., Pilbeam, D.R., Van Couvering, J.A. & Van Couvering, J.A.H. 1981. The Miocene fossil beds of Maboko Island, Kenya: geology, age, taphonomy, and palaeontology. *Journal of Human Evolution* 10, 35–48.

Axelrod, D.I. 1975. Evolution and biogeography of the Madrean-Tethyan sclerophyll vegetation. *Annals of the Missouri Botanical Garden* 62, 280–334.

Begun, D.R. 2002. European hominoids. In W.C Hartig, Editor, *The Primate Fossil Record*, 339–368. Cambridge, Cambridge University Press.

Bernor, R.L. & Tobien, H. 1990. The mammalian geochronology and biogeography of Paşalar (middle Miocene, Turkey). *Journal of Human Evolution* 19, 551–568.

Bestland, E. 1990. Sedimentology and paleopedology of Miocene alluvial deposits at the Paşalar hominoid site, western Turkey. *Journal of Human Evolution* 19, 363–377.

Cerling, T.E., Harris, J.M., Ambrose, S.H., Leakey, M.G. & Solounias, N. 1997. Dietary and environmental reconstruction with stable isotope analyses of herbivore tooth enamel from the Miocene locality of Fort Ternan, Kenya. *Journal of Human Evolution* 33, 635–650.

Cerling, T.E, Quade, J., Ambrose, S.H. & Sikes, N.E. 1991. Fossil soils from Fort Ternan, Kenya: grassland or woodland. *Journal of Human Evolution* 21, 295–306.

Galdikas, B.M. & Wood, J.W. 1990. Birth spacing patterns in humans and apes. *American Journal of Physical Anthropology* 83, 185–191.

Gentry, A.W. 1970. The Bovidae (Mammalia) of the Fort Ternan fossil fauna. In L.S.B. Leakey & R.J.G. Savage, Editors, *Fossil Vertebrates of Africa*, 243–324. London, Academic Press.

Harrison, T. 1992. A reassessment of the taxonomic and phylogenetic affinities of the fossil catarrhines from Fort Ternan, Kenya. *Primates* 33, 501–522.

Harrison, T. 2002. Late Oligocene to middle Miocene catarrhines from Afro-Arabia. In W.C. Hartwig, Editor, *The Primate Fossil Record*, 311–338. Cambridge, Cambridge University Press.

Kappelman, J. 1991. The paleoenvironment of *Kenyapithecus* at Fort Ternan. *Journal of Human Evolution* 20, 95–129.

Kelley, J. 2008. Identification of a single birth cohort in *Kenyapithecus kizili* and the nature of sympatry between *K. kizili* and *Griphopithecus alpani* at Paşalar. *Journal of Human Evolution* 54, 530–537.

King, T., Aiello, L. & Andrews, P. 1999. Dental microwear of *Griphopithecus alpani*. *Journal of Human Evolution* 36, 3–31.

Kingston, J.D., Jacobs, B.F., Hill, A. & Deino, A. 2002. Stratigraphy, age and environments of the late Miocene Mpesida Beds, Tugen Hills, Kenya. *Journal of Human Evolution* 42, 95–116.

Leakey, L.S.B. 1962. A new lower Pliocene fossil primate from Kenya. *Annals and Magazine of Natural History* 4, 689–696.

Leakey, L.S.B. 1967. An early Miocene member of Hominidae. *Nature* 213, 155–163.

Nelson, S.V. 2013. Chimpanzee fauna isotopes provide new interpretations of fossil ape and hominin ecologies. *Proceedings of the Royal Society* 280, 2013–2324.

Quade, J., Cerling, T.E., Andrews, P. and Alpagut, B. 1995. Palaeodietary reconstruction of Miocene fauna from Paşalar, Turkey, using stable carbon and oxygen isotopes of fossil tooth enamel. *Journal of Human Evolution* 28, 373–384.

Retallack, G.J., Dugas, D.P. & Bestland, E.A. 1990. Fossil soils and grasses of a middle Miocene East African grassland. *Science* 247, 1325–1328.

Shipman, P. 1982. Reconstructing the paleoecology and taphonomic history of *Ramapithecus wickeri* at Fort Ternan, Kenya. *Museum Briefs* 26. Museum of Anthropology, Columbia.

Shipman, P. 1986 Paleoecology of Fort Ternan reconsidered. *Journal of Human Evolution* 15,193–204.

Shipman, P., Walker, A., Van Couvering, J.A., Hooker, P.J. & Miller, J.A. 1981. The Fort Ternan hominoid site, Kenya: geology, age, taphonomy and paleoecology. *Journal of Human Evolution* 10, 49–72.

Viranta, S. & Andrews, P. 1995. Carnivore guild structure in the Paşalar Miocene fauna. *Journal of Human Evolution* 28, 359–372.

Chapter 12 A second view from Europe

There is no monographic teatment of the dryopithecines. The two groups most active in the field at present are the Canadian team led by David Begun and the Spanish team led by Salvador Moyà-Solà. Between them they have described nearly all of the recent fossil discoveries, and there are many of these from Hungary and Spain. There is a large literature on older discoveries of dryopithecines, for example Miguel Crusafont-Pairó and Johannes Hürzeler, and references can be found in the book by Walter Hartwig.

Agustí, J., Köhler, M., Moyà-Solà, S., Cabrera, L., Garcés, M. & Parés, J.M. 1996. Can Lobateres: the pattern and timing of the Vallesian hominoid radiation reconsidered. *Journal of Human Evolution* 31, 143–155.

Alba, D.M. 2012. Fossil apes from the Vallès-Penedès. *Evolutionary Anthropology* 21, 254–269.

Alba, D.M., Fortuny, J. & Moyà-Solà, S. 2010. Enamel thickness in the middle Miocene great apes *Anoiapithecus, Pierolapithecus* and *Dryopithecus*. *Proceedings of the Royal Society* 277, 2237–2245.

Alba, D.M., Fortuny, J., Perez de los Rios, M. et al. 2010. New dental remains of *Anoiapithecus* and the first appearance datum of hominoids in the Iberian Peninsula. *Journal of Human Evolution* 65, 573–584.

Almécija, S., Alba, D.M., Moyà-Solà, S. & Köhler, M. 2007. Orang-like manusal adaptations in the fossil hominoid *Hispanopithecus laietanus*: first steps towards great ape suspensory behaviours. *Proceedings of the Royal Society B* 274, 2375–2384.

Almécija, S., Alba, D.M. & Moyà-Solà, S. 2009. *Pierolapithecus* and the functional morphology of Miocene ape hand phalanges: paleobiological and evolutionary implications. *Journal of Human Evolution* 57, 284–297.

Begun, D.R. 1992. Miocene fossil hominids and the chimp-human clade. *Science* 257, 1929–1933.

Begun, D.R. 1992. Phyletic diversity and locomotion in primitive European hominids. *American Journal of Physical Anthropology* 87, 311–340.

Begun, D.R. 1993. New catarrhine phalanges from Rudabánya (Northeastern Hungary) and the problem of parallelism and convergence in hominoid postcranial morphology. *Journal of Human Evolution* 24, 373–402.

Begun, D.R. 1994. Relations among the great apes and humans: new interpretations based on the fossil great ape *Dryopithecus*. *Yearbook of Physical Anthropology* 37, 11–63.

Begun, D.R. 2000. Middle Miocene hominoid origins. *Science* 287, 31.

Begun, D.R. 2002. European hominoids. In W.C Hartig, Editor, *The Primate Fossil Record*, 339–368. Cambridge, Cambridge University Press.

Begun, D.R. 2004. The earliest hominins – is less more? *Science* 303, 1478–1480.

Begun, D.R. 2009. Dryopithecins, Darwin, de bonis and the European origin of the African apes and human clade. *Geodiversitas* 31, 789–816.

Begun, D.R. & Kordos, L. 1993. Revision of *Dryopithecus brancoi* Schlosser, 1910, based on the fossil hominid material from Rudabanya. *Journal of Human Evolution* 25, 271–286.

Begun, D.R., Moyá-Sola, S. & Köhler, M. 1990. New Miocene hominoid specimens from Can Llobateres (Valles Penedes, Spain) and their geological and paleoecological context. *Journal of Human Evolution* 9, 255–268.

Begun, D.R., Nargolwalla, M.C. & Kordos, L. 2012 European Miocene hominids and the origin of the African ape and human clade. *Evolutionary Anthropology* 21, 10–23.

Bernor, R.L., Armour-Chelu, M., Kaiser, T.M. & Scott, R.S. 2003. An evaluation of the late MN9 (late Miocene, Vallesian age) Hipparion assemblage from Rudabánya (Hungary): systematic background, functional anatomy, paleoecology. *Colloquios de Palaeontología Volumen Extraordinario* 1, 35–45.

Crusafont-Pairó, M. 1978. El Gabón fosil (*Pliopithecus*) del Vindobonense terminal del Vallès. *Paleontologia y Evolución* 13, 11–12.

Crusafont-Pairó, M. & Golpe-Posse, J.M. 1981. Estudio de la denticion inferior del primer Pliopithécido hallado en España (Vindobonensis terminal de Castell de Barbera, Cataluña, España). *Bolletin de Informaciones de la Institut de Palentologia, Sabadell* 13, 25–38.

Crusafont-Pairó, M. & Hürzeler, J. 1961. Les pongidés fossilles d'Espagne. *Comptes Rendus bebdomadaires d l'Academie des Sciences Paris* 254, 582–584.

Hammond, A.S., Alba, D.M., Almécija, S. & Moyà-Solà, S. 2013. Middle Miocene *Pierolapithecus* provides a first glimpse into early hominid pelvic morphology. *Journal of Human Evolution* 64, 658–666.

Harrison, T. 1987. A reassessment of the phylogenetic relationships of *Oreopithecus bambolii* Gervais. *Journal of Human Evolution* 15, 541–583.

Harrison, T. 1991. The implications of *Oreopithecus* for the origins of bipedalism. In Y. Coppens & B. Senut, Editors, *Origine(s) de la Bipédie Chez les Hominidés*, 235–244. Paris, Cahiers de Paléoanthropologie, CNRS.

Harrison, T.S. & Harrison, T. 1989. Palynology of the late Miocene *Oreopithecus*-bearing lignite from Baccinello, Italy. *Palaeogeography, Palaeoclimatology, Palaeoecology* 76, 45–65.

Harrison, T. & Rook, L. 1997. Enigmatic anthropoid or misunderstood ape? The phylogenetic status of *Oreopithecus bambolii* reconsidered. In D.R. Begun, C.V. Ward & M.D. Rose, Editors, *Function, Phylogeny, and Fossils: Miocene Hominoid Evolution and Adaptations*, 327–362. New York, Plenum Press.

Hartwig, W.C. (Editor) 2002. *The Primate Fossil Record*. Cambridge, Cambridge University Press.

Kivell, T.L. & Begun, D.R. 2009. New primate carpal bones from Rudabánya (late Miocene, Hungary): taxonomic and functional implications. *Journal of Human Evolution* 57, 697–709.

Köhler, M., Moyà-Solà, S. & Andrews, P. 1999. Order Primates. In G. Rossner & K. Heissig, Editors, *Land Mammals of Europe*, 91–104. Munich, Verlag Fridrich Pfeil.

Kordos, L. 1985. Environmental reconstruction for prehominids of Rudabànya, NE Hungary. *Akademie der Wissenschaftern der DDR Zentralinstitut fur alte Geschichte und Archaologie* 41, 82–85.

Kordos, L. 1991. Le *Rudapithecus hungaricus* de Rudabànya (Hongrie). *L'Anthropologie* 95, 343–362.

Kordos, L. & Begun, D.R. 1997. A new reconstruction of RUD 77, a partial cranium of *Dryopithecus brancoi* from Rudabánya, Hungary. *American Journal of Physical Anthropology* 103, 277–294.

Kretzoi, M. 1975. New ramapithecines and *Pliopithecus* from the lower Pliocene of Rudabànya in northeastern Hungary. *Nature* 257, 578–581.

Morbeck, M.E. 1983. Miocene hominoid discoveries from Rudabánya: implications from the postcranial skeleton. In R.L. Ciochon & R.S. Corruccini, Editors, *New Interpretations of Ape and Human Ancestry*, 369–404. New York, Plenum Press.

Moyà-Solà, S., Alba, D.M., Almecija, S. et al. 2009a. A unique middle Miocene European hominoid and the origins of the great ape and human clade. *Proceedings of the National Academy of Sciences* 106, 1–6.

Moyà-Solà, S. & Köhler, M. 1993. Recent discoveries of *Dryopithecus* shed new light on evolution of great apes. *Nature* 365, 543–545.

Moyà-Solà, S. & Köhler, M. 1995. New partial cranium of *Dryopithecus* Lartet, 1863 (Hominoidea, Primates) from the upper Miocene of Can Llobateres, Barcelona, Spain. *Journal of Human Evolution* 29, 101–139.

Moyà-Solà, S. & Köhler, M. 1996. The first *Dryopithecus* skeleton: origins of great ape locomotion. *Nature* 379, 156–159.

Moyà-Solà, S. & Köhler, M. 1997. The phylogenetic relationships of *Oreopithecus bambolii* Gervais, 1872. *Comptes Rendus de l'Académie des Sciences de Paris* 324, 141–148.

Moyà-Solà, S., Köhler, M., Alba, D.M., Casanovas-Vilar, I. & Galindo, J. 2004. *Pierolapithecus catalaunicus*, a new middle Miocene great ape from Spain. *Science* 306, 1339–1344.

Moyà-Solà, S., Köhler, M., Alba, D.M. et al. 2009b. First partial face and upper dentition of the middle Miocene hominoid *Dryopithecus fontani* from Abocador de Can Mata (Valles-Penedes Basin, Catalonia, NE Spain): taxonomic and phylogenetic implications. *American Journal of Physical Anthropology* 139, 126–145.

Moyà-Solà, S., Köhler, M. & Rook, L. 1999. Evidence of hominid-like precision grip capability in the hand of the Miocene ape *Oreopithecus*. *Proceedings of the National Academy of Sciences* 96, 313–317.

Pérez de los Ríos, M., Moyà-Solà, S. & Alba, D.M. 2012. The nasal and parnasal architecture of the middle Miocene ape *Pierolapithecus catalaunicus* (Primates: Hominidae): phylogenetic implications. *Journal of Human Evolution* 63, 497–506.

Pilbeam, D.R. & Simons, E.L. 1971. Humerus of *Dryopithecus* from Saint Gaudens, France. *Nature* 229, 406–407.

Skinner, M.F., Dupras, T.L. & Moyà-Solà, S. 1995. Periodicity of linear enamel hypoplasia among Miocene *Dryopithecus* from Spain. *Journal of Paleopathology* 7, 195–222.

Smith-Woodward, A. 1914. On the lower jaw of an anthropoid ape (*Dryopithecus*) from the upper Miocene of Lerida, Spain. *Quarterly Journal of the Geological Society* 70, 316–320.

Tallman, M., Almecija, S., Reber, S.L., Alba, D.M. & Moyà-Solà, S. 2013. The distal tibia of *Hispanopithecus laietanus*: more evidence for mosaic evolution in Miocene apes. *Journal of Human Evolution* 64, 319–327.

Villalta, J.F. & Crusafont, M. 1964. Dos nuevos antropomorfos de Mioceno español y su situación de la moderno sistemática de los simidos. *Notas de Comision de investigationes geologicas mineralogicas* 13, 91–139.

Chapter 13 The environment in Europe

The environment of *Rudapithecus hungaricus* has been described in some detail by G. Merceron, David Begun, and Andrews and Cameron, as subtropical swamp forest/ woodland; the environment of *Hispanopithecus laietanus* has also been well described, with definitive papers by David Alba, Marmí and Merceron: subtropical seasonal evergreen forest with palms and laurels.

Agustí, J., Köhler, M., Moyà-Solà, S., Cabrera, L., Garcés, M. & Parés, J.M. 1996. Can Loba-teres: the pattern and timing of the Vallesian hominoid radiation reconsidered. *Journal of Human Evolution* 31, 143–155.

Alba, D.M., Fortuny, J. & Moyà-Solà, S. 2010. Enamel thickness in the middle Miocene great apes *Anoiapithecus, Pierolapithecus* and *Dryopithecus*. *Proceedings of the Royal Society* 277, 2237–2245.

Almécija, S., Alba, D.M. & Moyà-Solà, S. 2009. *Pierolapithecus* and the functional morphology of Miocene ape hand phalanges: paleobiological and evolutionary implications. *Journal of Human Evolution* 57, 284–297.

Andrews, P. & Cameron, D. 2010. Rudabanya: taphonomic analysis of a fossil hominid site from Hungary. *Palaeogeography, Palaeoclimatology, Palaeoecology* 297, 311–329.

Andrews, P. & Cronin, J. 1982. The relationships of *Sivapithecus* and *Ramapithecus* and the evolution of the orang utan. *Nature* 297, 541–546.

Armour-Chelu, M., Andrews, P. & Bernor, R.L. 2005. Further observations on the primate community at Rudbànya II (late Miocene, early Vallesian age), Hungary. *Journal of Human Evolution* 49, 88–98.

Axelrod, D.I. 1975. Evolution and biogeography of the Madrean-Tethyan sclerophyll vege-tation. *Annals of the Missouri Botanical Garden* 62, 280–334.

Casanovas-Vilar, I., Alba, D.M., Moyà-Solà, S. et al. 2008. Biochronological, taphonomical and paleoenvironmental background of the fossil great ape *Pierolapithecus catalaunicus* (Primates, Hominidae). *Journal of Human Evolution* 55, 589–603.

Deane, A.S., Nargolwalla, M.C., Kordos, L. & Begun, D.R. 2013. New evidence for diet and niche partitioning in *Rudapithecus* and *Anapithecus* from Rudabánya, Hungary. *Journal of Human Evolution* 65, 704–714.

Fortelius, M. & Solounias, N. 2000. Functional characterization of ungulate molars using the abrasion-attrition wear gradient: a new method of reconstructing paleodiets. *American Museum Novitates* 3301, 1–36.

Kordos, L. 1985. Environmental reconstruction for prehominids of Rudabànya, NE Hungary. *Akademie der Wissenschaftern der DDR Zentralinstitut fur alte Geschichte und Archaologie* 41, 82–85.

Kordos, L. & Begun, D.R. 2002. Rudabánya: a late Miocene subtropical swamp deposit with evidence of the origin of the African apes and humans. *Evolutionary Anthropology* 11, 45–57.

Kovar-Eder, J. 2003. Vegetation dynamics in Europe during the Neogene. *Deinsea* 10, 373–392.

Kovar-Eder, J., Kvacek, J., Zastawniak, E., Givulescu, R. et al. 1996. Floristic trends in the vegetation of the Paratethys surrounding areas during Neogene times. In R.L. Bernor, V. Fahlbusch & H.-W. Mitmann, Editors, *The Evolution of Western Eurasian Neogene Mammal Faunas*, 395–413. New York, Columbia University Press.

Kretzoi, M., Krolopp, E., Lorincz, H. & Palfalvy, I. 1974. A Rudabanyai Alsopannonai prehominidas lelohely floraja, faunaja es retegtani helyzete. *M. All. Foldtani Intezet Evi Jelentezi* 1974, 365–394.

Marmí, J., Casanovas-Vilar, I., Robles, J.M., Moyá-Sola, S. & Alba, D.M. 2012. The paleoenvironment of *Hispanopithecus laietanus* as revealed by paleobotanical evidence from the late Miocene of Can Llobateres 1 (Catalonia, Spain). *Journal of Human Evolution* 62, 412–423.

Merceron, G., Schulz, E., Kordos, L. & Kaiser, T.M. 2007. Paleoenvironment of *Dryopithecus brancoi* at Rudabánya, Hungary: evidence from dental meso- and micro-wear analyses of large vegetarian mammals. *Journal of Human Evolution* 53, 331–349.

Myers, R.L. & Ewel, J.J. 1990. *Ecosystems of Florida*. Gainesville, University of Central Florida Press.

Odum, E.P. 1983. *Basic Ecology*. Philadelphia, Holt-Saunders.

Suc, J.-P. 1999. Neogene vegetation change in West European and West circum-Mediterranean areas. In J. Agusti, L. Rook & P. Andrews, Editors, *The Evolution of Neogene Terrestrial Ecosystems in Europe*, 378–388. Cambridge, Cambridge University Press.

Ungar, P.S. 2005. Dental evidence for the diets of fossil primates from Rudabánya, Northeastern Hungary with comments on extant primate analogs and 'noncompetitive' sympatry. *Palaeontologia Italia* 90, 97–112.

Ungar, P.S. (Editor) 2007. *Evolution of the Human Diet*. Oxford, Oxford University Press.

Ungar, P.S. 2009. Tooth form and function: insights into adaptation through the analysis of dental microwear. *Frontiers of Oral Biology* 13, 38–43.

Ungar, P.S. & Kay, R.F. 1995. The dietary adaptations of European Miocene catarrhines. *Proceedings of the National Academy of Sciences* 93, 5479–5481.

Villalta, J.F. & Crusafont, M. 1964. Dos nuevos antropomorfos de Mioceno español y su situación de la moderno sistemática de los simidos. *Notas de Comision de investigationes geologicas mineralogicas* 13, 91–139.

Chapter 14 Late Miocene to Pleistocene apes

The late Miocene apes from Africa have each been described piecemeal by their discoverers, and the best summary is in Harrison (2002). The Asian megadont apes are best summarized in the edited volume by Hartwig (2002). Of particular note is the series of papers on postcrania of sivapithecines by Mike Rose, the description of fossil chimpanzee teeth by Sally McBrearty and the Pleistocene orang utan skull by Anne-Marie Bacon.

Alpagut, B., Andrews, P., Fortelius, M. et al. 1996. A new specimen of *Ankarapithecus meteai* from the Sinap Formation of central Anatolia. *Nature* 382, 349–351.

Andrews, P.J. & Tekkaya, I. 1980. A revision of the Turkish Miocene hominoid *Sivapithecus meteai*. *Paleontology* 23, 85–95.

Bacon, A.-M. & Long, V.T. 2001. The first discovery of a complete skeleton of a fossil orang-utan in a cave of the Hoa Binh Province, Vietnam. *Journal of Human Evolution* 41, 227–241.

Badgley, C. 1984. The palaeoenvironment of South Asian Miocene hominoids. In R.D. White, Editor, *The Evolution of East Asian Environments*, 796–811. Hong Kong, Centre for Asian Studies.

Badgley, C. 1989. Community analysis of Siwalik mammals from Pakistan. *Journal of Vertebrate Paleontology* 9, 11A.

Begun, D.R. & Güleç, E. 1998. Restoration of the type and palate of *Ankarapithecus meteai*: taxonomic and phylogenetic implications. *American Journal of Physical Anthropology* 105, 279–314.

Begun, D.R. & Kivell, T.L. 2011. Knuckle-walking in *Sivapithecus*? The combined effects of homology and homoplasy with possible implications for pongine dispersals. *Journal of Human Evolution* 60, 158–170.

Bonis, L. de, Bouvrain, G., Geraads, D. & Koufos, G. 1992. Diversity and palaeoecology of Greek late Miocene mammalian faunas. *Palaeogeography, Palaeoclimatology, Palaeoecology* 91, 99–121.

Bonis, L. de & Koufos, G.D. 2014. First discovery of postcranial bones of *Ouranopithecus macedoniensis* (Primates, Hominoidea) from the late Miocene of Macedonia (Greece). *Journal of Human Evolution* 74, 21–36.

Bonis, L. de & Melentis, J. 1977. Un nouveau genre de primate hominoide dans leVallesien (Miocène supérieur) de Macédoine. *Comptes Rendues de l'Academie des Sciences de Paris* 284, 1393–1396.

Bonis, L. de & Melentis, J. 1978. Les primates hominoides du Miocène supérieur de Macédoine. *Annales de Paléontologie* 64, 185–202.

Brown, B. & Ward, S.C. 1988. Basicranial and facial topography in *Pongo* and *Sivapithecus*. In J. Schwartz, Editor, *Orang utan Biology*, 247–260. New York, Plenum Press.

Chaimanee, Y., Jolly, D., Benanmml, M. et al. 2003. A middle Miocene hominoid from Thailand and orangutan origins. *Nature* 422, 61–65.

Chaimanee, Y., Suteethorn, V., Jintsakul, P. et al. 2004. A new orang-utan relative from the late Miocene of Thailand. *Nature* 427, 439–441.

Cerling, T.E., Quade, J., Wang, Y. & Bowman, J.R. 1989. Carbon isotopes in soils and palaeosols as ecology and palaeoecology indicators. *Nature* 341, 138–139.

Costeur, L. 2005. Cenogram analysis of the Rudabánya mammalian community: palaeo-environmental interpretations. *Palaeontologia Italia* 90, 303–309.

DeSilva, J.M., Morgan, M.E., Barry, J.C. & Pilbeam, D. 2010. A hominoid distal tibia from the Miocene of Pakistan. *Journal of Human Evolution* 58, 147–154.

Harrison, T. 2002. Late Oligocene to middle Miocene catarrhines from Afro-Arabia. In W.C. Hartwig, Editor, *The Primate Fossil Record*, 311–338. Cambridge, Cambridge University Press.

Hartwig, W.C. (Editor) 2002. *The Primate Fossil Record*. Cambridge, Cambridge University Press.

Ibrahim, Y.Kh., Tshen, L.T., Westaway, K.E. et al. 2013. First discovery of Pleistocene orangutan (*Pongo* sp.) fossils in Peninsular Malaysia: biogeographic and paleoenvironmental implications. *Journal of Human Evolution* 65, 770–797.

Ishida, H., Kunimatsu, Y., Takano, T., Nakano, Y. & Nakatsukasa, M. 2004. *Nacholapithecus* skeleton from the middle Miocene of Kenya. *Journal of Human Evolution* 46, 69–103.

Jacobs, B.F. 1992. Taphonomy of a middle Miocene authochthonous forest assemblage, Ngorora Formation, central Kenya. *Palaeogeography, Palaeoclimatology, Palaeoecology* 99, 31–40.

Jaeger, J.-J., Soe, A.N., Chavasseau, O. et al. 2011. First hominoid from the late Miocene of the Irrawaddy Formation (Myanmar). *PLOS One* 6(4), 1–14.

Kappelman, J., Richmond, B.G., Seiffert, E.R., Maga, A.M. & Ryan, T.M. 2003. Hominoidea (Primates). In M. Fortelius & J. Kappelman, Editors, *Geology and Paleontology of the Miocene Sinap Formation, Turkey*, 90–124. New York, Columbia University Press.

Koenigswald, G.H.R. von 1972. Ein Unterkiefer eines fossilen Hominoiden aus dem Unterpliozän Griechenlands. *Koninklijke Nederlandse Akademie van Wetenschappen, Amsterdam* 75, 385–394.

Kunimatsu, Y., Nakatsukasa, M., Sawada, Y. et al. 2007. A new late Miocene great ape from Kenya and its implications for the origins of African great apes and humans. *Proceedings of the National Academy of Sciences* 104, 19220–19225.

Maden, S.L., Rose, M.D., Kelley, J., MacLatchy, L. & Pilbeam, D. 2002. New *Sivapithecus* postcranial specimens from the Siwaliks of Pakistan. *Journal of Human Evolution* 42, 705–752.

McBrearty, S. & Jablonsky, N.G. 2005. First fossil chimpanzee. *Nature* 437, 105–108.

Nelson, S.V. 2013. Chimpanzee fauna isotopes provide new interpretations of fossil ape and hominin ecologies. *Proceedings of the Royal Society* 280, 2013–2324.

Nevell, L. & Wood, B. 2008. Cranial base evolution within the hominin clade. *Journal of Anatomy* 212, 455–468.

Pickford, M., Coppens, Y., Senut, B., Morales, J. & Braga, J. 2009. Late Miocene hominoid from Niger. *Comptes Rendus Paleoevolution* 8, 413–425.

Pickford, M. & Senut, B. 2001. The geological and faunal context of late Miocene hominid remains from Lukeino, Kenya. *Comptes Rendus de l'Academie des Sciences de Paris* 332, 145–152.

Pickford, M. & Senut, B. 2005. Hominoid teeth with chimpanzee- and gorilla-like features from the Miocene of Kenya: implications for the chronology of ape-human divergence and biogeography of Miocene hominoids. *Anthropological Science* 113, 95–102.

Pilbeam, D.R. 1982. New hominoid skull material from the Miocene of Pakistan. *Nature* 295, 232–234.

Preuss, T.M. 1982. The face of *Sivapithecus indicus*: description of a new, relatively complete specimen from the Siwaliks of Pakistan. *Folia Primatologica* 38, 141–157.

Rein, T.R., Harrison, T. & Zollikofer, P.E. 2012. Skeletal correlates of quadrupedalism and climbing in the anthropoid forelimb: implications for inferring locomotion in Miocene catarrhines. *Journal of Human Evolution* 61, 564–574.

Rose, M.D. 1984 Hominoid postcranial specimens from the middle Miocene Chinji Formation, Pakistan, *Journal of Human Evolution* 13, 503–516.

Rose, M.D. 1986. Further hominoid postcranial specimens from the late Miocene Nagri Formation of Pakistan. *Journal of Human Evolution* 15, 333–367.

Rose, M.D. 1988 Another look at the anthropoid elbow. *Journal of Human Evolution* 17, 193–224.

Rose, M.D. 1989. New postcranial specimens of catarrhines from the middle Miocene Chinji Formation, Pakistan: descriptions and a discussion of proximal humeral functional morphology in anthropoids. *Journal of Human Evolution* 18, 131–162.

Rose, M.D. 1994. Quadrupedalism in some Miocene catarrhines. *Journal of Human Evolution* 26, 387–411.

Schwartz, J. 1990 *Lufengpithecus* and its potential relationship to an orang-utan clade. *Journal of Human Evolution* 519, 591–605.

Shea, B.T. 1985. On aspects of skull form in African apes and orangutans, with implications for hominoid evolution. *American Journal of Physical Anthropology* 68, 329–342.

Smith, T.M., Martin, L.B., Reid, D.J., de Bonis, L. & Koufos, G.D. 2004. An examination of dental development in *Graecopithecus freybergi* (= *Ouranopithecus macedoniensis*). *Journal of Human Evolution* 46, 551–577.

Spoor, C.F., Sondaar, P.Y. & Hussain, S.T. 1991. A new hominoid hamate and first metacarpal from the late Miocene Nagri Formation of Pakistan. *Journal of Human Evolution* 21, 413–422.

Suc, J.-P. 1999. Neogene vegetation change in West European and West circum-Mediterranean areas. In J. Agusti, L. Rook & P. Andrews, Editors, *The Evolution of Neogene Terrestrial Ecosystems in Europe*, 378–388. Cambridge, Cambridge University Press.

Suwa, G., Kono, R.T., Katoh, S., Asfaw, B. & Beyene, Y. 2007. A new species of great ape from the late Miocene epoch in Ethiopia. *Nature* 448, 921–924.

XuePing, J.I., Jablonski, N.G., Su, D.F. et al. 2013. Juvenile hominoid cranium from the terminal Miocene of Yunnan, China. *Chinese Science Bulletin* 55, 2–9.

Zhang, X. 1987. New materials of *Ramapithecus* from Kaiyuan, Yunnan. *Acta Anthropologica Sinica* 6, 81–86.

Zhang, X., Lin, Y., Jiang, C. & Xaio, L. 1987. A new species of *Ramapithecus* from Yuanmou, Yunnan. *Journal of Yunnan University* 3, 54–56.

Chapter 15 Apes, hominins and environment in the late Miocene

The palaeoecology of the sivapithecines is best summarized in the mongraph by the Harvard Pakistan group (John Barry and others). There is also a monograph on the Sinap deposits, although there is next to nothing on the palaeoecology (Fortelius). There is also little information on the environment of *Ouranopithecus*, but what there is is best described in the work of G. Merceron and Louis de Bonis. Environments during the late Miocene and Pliocene have been the subjects of two books, *Paleoclimate and Evolution*, edited by Elizabeth Vrba and others, and *African Biogeography, Climate Change, and Early Hominid Evolution* edited by Tim Bromage and Friedemann Schrenk, while the hominid remains have been described by their discoverers in a large number of unconnected papers. Of special note is the series of papers on *Ardipithecus* by Tim White, WoldeGabriel and others, published in a special issue of the journal *Science*.

Aiello, L. & Dean, C. 1990 *An Introduction to Human Evolutionary Anatomy*. New York, Academic Press.

Alemsedged, Z., Spoor, F., Kimbel, W.H. et al. 2006. A juvenile early hominin skeleton from Dikika, Ethiopia. *Nature* 443, 296–301.

Almécija, S., Tallman, M., Alba, D.M. et al. 2007. *Nature Communications*. DOI: 10.1038/ncomms 3888.

Andrews, P. 1995. Ecological apes and ancestors. *Nature* 376, 555–556.

Andrews, P. & Humphrey, L. 1999. African Miocene environments and the transition to early hominines. In T. Bromage & F. Schrenk, Editors, *African Biogeography, Climate Change, and Early Hominid Evolution*, 282–300. Oxford, Oxford University Press.

Badgley, C. 1984. The palaeoenvironment of South Asian Miocene hominoids. In R.D. White, Editor, *The Evolution of East Asian Environments*, 796–811. Hong Kong, Centre for Asian Studies.

Badgley, C. 1989. Community analysis of Siwalik mammals from Pakistan. *Journal of Vertebrate Paleontology* 9, 11A.

Barry, J.C., Morgan, M.E., Flynn, L.J. et al. 2002. Fauna and environmental change in the late Miocene Siwaliks of northern Pakistan. *Paleobiology Memoirs* 3, 1–70.

Begun, D.R. & Kivell, T.L. 2011. Knuckle-walking in *Sivapithecus*? The combined effects of homology and homoplasy with possible implications for pongine dispersals. *Journal of Human Evolution* 60, 158–170.

Behrensmeyer, A.K. 1978. Taphonomic and ecologic information from bone weathering. *Paleobiology* 4, 150–162.

Behrensmeyer, A.K. 1988. Vertebrate preservation in fluvial channels. *Palaeogeography, Palaeoclimatology, Palaeoecology* 63, 183–199.

Behrensmeyer, A.K., Deino, A.L., Hill, A., Kingston, J.D. & Saunders, J.J. 2002. Geology and geochronology of the middle Miocene Kipsaraman site complex, Muruyur, Tugen Hills, Kenya. *Journal of Human Evolution* 42, 11–38.

Bernor, R.L., Scott, R., Fortelius, M. Kappelman, J. & Sen, S. 2003. Equidae (Peissocactyla). In M. Fortelius, J. Kappelman, S. Sen & R.L. Bernor, Editors, *Geology and Palaeontology of the Miocene Sinap Formation, Turkey*, 220–271. New York, Columbia University Press.

Bishop, L.C. 1999. Suid paleoecology and habitat preferences at African Pliocene and Pleistocene hominid localities. In T. Bromage & F. Schrenk, Editors, *African Biogeography, Climate Change, and Early Hominid Evolution*, 216–225. Oxford, Oxford University Press.

Bobe, R., Behrensmeyer, A.K. & Chapman, R.E. 2002. Faunal change, environmental variability and late Pliocene hominin evolution. *Journal of Human Evolution* 42, 475–497.

Bromage, T. & Schrenk, F. (Editors) 1999. *African Biogeography, Climate Change, and Early Hominid Evolution*. Oxford, Oxford University Press.

Brunet, M. 2002. Reply. *Nature* 419, 582.

Brunet, M., Guy, F., Pilbeam, D. et al. A new hominid from the Upper Miocene of Chad, Central Africa. *Nature* 418, 145–151.

Duda, P. & Zrzavy, J. 2013. Evolution of life history and behavior in Hominidae: towards phylogenetic reconstruction of the chimpanzee-human last common ancestor. *Journal of Human Evolution* 65, 424–446.

Flynn, L.J. & Guo-qin, Q. 1982. Age of the Lufeng, China, hominoid locality. *Nature* 298, 746–747.

Fortelius, M., Kappelman, J., Sen, S. & Bernor, R.L. (Editors) 2003. *Geology and Palaeontology of the Miocene Sinap Formation Turkey*. New York, Columbia University Press.

Galik, K., Senut, B., Pickford, M. et al. 2004. External and internal morphology of the BAR 1002′00 *Orrorin tugenensis* femur. *Science* 305, 1450–1453.

Guo-qin, Q. 1993. The environmental ecology of the Lufeng hominoids. *Journal of Human Evolution* 24, 3–11.

Haile-Selassie, Y. 2001. Late Miocene hominids from the Middle Awash. *Nature* 412,178–181.

Haile-Selassie, Y. 2004. Late Miocene teeth from Middle Awash, Ethiopia, and early hominid dental evolution. *Science* 303, 1503–1505.

Harrison, T. 1987. A reassessment of the phylogenetic relationships of *Oreopithecus bambolii* Gervais. *Journal of Human Evolution* 15, 541–583.

Harrison, T. 1991. The implications of *Oreopithecus* for the origins of bipedalism. In Y. Coppens & B. Senut, Editors, *Origine(s) de la Bipédie Chez les Hominidés*, 235–244. Paris, Cahiers de Paléoanthropologie, CNRS.

Harrison, T.S. & Harrison, T. 1989. Palynology of the late Miocene *Oreopithecus*-bearing lignite from Baccinello, Italy. *Palaeogeography, Palaeoclimatology, Palaeoecology* 76, 45–65.

Harrison, T. & Rook, L. 1997. Enigmatic anthropoid or misunderstood ape? The phylogenetic status of *Oreopithecus bambolii* reconsidered. In D.R. Begun, C.V. Ward &

M.D. Rose, Editors, *Function, Phylogeny, and Fossils: Miocene Hominoid Evolution and Adaptations*, 327–362. New York, Plenum Press.

Hartwig, W.C. (Editor) 2002. *The Primate Fossil Record*. Cambridge, Cambridge University Press.

Hürzeler, J. 1958. *Oreopithecus bambolii* Gervais: a preliminary report. *Verhandlungen der naturforschenden Gesellschaft, Basel* 69, 1–47.

Hürzeler, J. 1968. Questions et réflexions sur l'histoire des anthropomorphes. *Annales de Paléontologie* 44, 13–233.

Hürzeler, J. & Engesser, B. 1976. Les faunes de mammiferes néogènes du basin de Baccinello (Grosseto, Italie). *Comptes Rendus de l'Académie des Sciences de Paris* 283, 333–336.

Johanson, D.C., Taieb, M. & Coppens, Y. 1982. Pliocene hominids from Hadar, Ethiopia. *American Journal of Physical Anthropology* 57, 373–719.

Johanson, D.C., White, T.D. & Coppens, Y. 1978. A new species of the genus *Australopithecus* (Primates, Hominidae) from the Pliocene of eastern Africa. *Kirtlandia* 28, 1–14.

Kovar-Eder, J. 2003. Vegetation dynamics in Europe during the Neogene. *Deinsea* 10, 373–392.

Kovarovic, K., Andrews, P. & Aiello, L. 2002. The palaeoecology of the Upper Ndolanya Beds at Laetoli, Tanzania. *Journal of Human Evolution* 43, 395–418.

Leakey, M.G., Feibel, C.S., MacDougall, I. & Walker, A. 1995. New 4 million year old hominid species from Kanapoi and Allia Bay, Kenya. *Nature* 376, 565–571.

Leakey, M.G., Feibel, C.S., MacDougall, I. & Walker, A. 1998. New specimens and confirmation of an early age for *Australopithecus anamensis*. *Nature* 393, 62–66.

Louchart, A., Wesselman, H., Blumenschine, R.J. et al. 2009. Taphonomic, avian and small-vertebrate indicators of *Ardipithecus ramidus* habitat. *Science* 326, 66–70.

Lovejoy, C.O., Latimer, B., Suwa, G., Asfaw, B. & White, T.D. 2009. Combining prehension and propulsion: the foot of *Ardipithecus ramidus*. *Science* 326, 72–80.

Lovejoy, C.O., Simpson, S.W., White, T.D., Asfaw, B. & Suwa, G. 2009. Careful climbing in the Miocene: the forelimbs of *Ardipithecus ramidus* and humans are primitive. *Science* 326, 70–78.

Lovejoy, C.O., Suwa, G., Simpson, S.W., Matternes, J.H. & White, T.D. 2009. The great divides: *Ardipithecus ramidus* reveals the postcrania of our last common ancestors with African apes. *Science* 326, 100–106.

Lovejoy, C.O., Suwa, G., Spurlock, L., Asfaw, B. & White, T.D. 2009. The pelvis and femur of *Ardipithecus ramidus*: the emergence of upright walking. *Science* 326, 71–77.

Merceron, G., Kostopoulos, D.S., de Bonis, L. et al. 2013. Stable isotope ecology of Miocene bovids from northern Greece and the ape/monkey turnover in the Balkans. *Journal of Human Evolution* 65, 185–198.

Munro, S.J. 2010. Molluscs as ecological indicators in palaeoanthropological contexts. PhD thesis, The Australian National University.

Nelson, S.V. 2013. Chimpanzee fauna isotopes provide new interpretations of fossil ape and hominin ecologies. *Proceedings of the Royal Society* 280, 2013–2324.

Pickford, M. & Senut, B. 2001. The geological and faunal context of late Miocene hominid remains from Lukeino, Kenya. *Comptes Rendus de l'Academie des Sciences de Paris* 332, 145–152.

Pickford, M. & Senut, B. 2005. Hominoid teeth with chimpanzee- and gorilla-like features from the Miocene of Kenya: implications for the chronology of ape-human divergence and biogeography of Miocene hominoids. *Anthropological Science* 113, 95–102.

Pilbeam, D.R. 2004. The anthropoid postcranial axial skeleton: comments on development, variation and evolution. *Journal of Experimental Zoology* 302, 241–267.

Quade, J., Cerling, T.E., Barry, J. et al. 1992. 16 million years of paleodietary change using carbon isotopes in fossil teeth from Pakistan. *Chemical Geology. Isotope Geoscience Section* 94, 183–192.

Rafferty, K.L. 1998. Structural design of the femoral neck in primates. *Journal of Human Evolution* 34, 361–383.

Ruff, C.B. & Higgins, R. 2013. Femoral neck structure and function in early hominins. *American Journal of Physical Anthropology* 150, 512–525.

Senut, B., Pickford, M., Gommery, D. et al. 2001. First hominid from the Miocene (Lukeino Formation, Kenya). *Comptes Rendus de l'Académie des Sciences de Paris* 332, 137–144.

Sikes, N.E. 1999. PlioPleistocene floral context and habitat preferences of sympatric hominid species in East Africa. In T. Bromage & F. Schrenk, Editors, *African Biogeography, Climate Change, and Early Hominid Evolution*, 301–315. Oxford, Oxford University Press.

Susman, R.L. 1994. Fossil evidence for early hominid tool use. *Science* 265, 1570–1573.

Suwa, G., Asfaw, B., Kono, R.T., Kubo, D., Lovejoy, C.O. & White, T.D. 2009. The *Ardipithecus* skull and its implications for hominid origins. *Science* 326, 100–106.

Vignaud, P., Duringer, P., Mackaye, H.T. et al. 2002. Geology and palaeontology of the Upper Miocene Toros-Menalla hominid locality, Chad. *Nature* 418, 152–155.

White, T.D., Lovejoy, C.O., Asfaw, B., Carlson, J.P. & Suwa, G. 2015. Neither chimpanzee nor human, *Ardipithecus* reveals the surprising ancesstry of both. *Proceedings of the National Academy of Sciences* 112, 4877–4884.

White, T.D., Suwa G. & Asfaw, B. 1994. *Australopithecus ramidus*: a new species of early hominid from Aramis, Ethiopia. *Nature* 371, 306–312.

WoldeGabriel, G., Ambrose, S.H., Barboni, D. et al. 2009. The geological, isotopic, botanical, invertebrate, and lower vertebrate surroundings of *Ardipithecus ramidus*. *Science* 326, 65e1–5.

WoldeGabriel, G., Hailie-Selassie, Y., Renne, P.R. et al. 2001. Geology and palaeontology of the late Miocene middle Awash valley, Afar rift, Ethiopia. *Nature* 412, 175–178.

Woldegabriel, G., White, T.D., Suwa, G. et al. 1994. Ecological and temporal placement of early Pliocene hominids at Aramis, Ethiopia. *Nature* 371, 330–333.

Wolpoff, M.H., Senut, B., Pickford, M. & Hawks, J. 2002. *Sahelanthropus* or 'Sahelpithecus'? *Nature* 419, 581–582.

Chapter 16 Putting together the evidence

This chapter attempts to bring together the evidence from the fifteen preceding chapters and does not draw on any one source. It was foreshadowed by my paper with Terry Harrison in the book honouring David Pilbeam, in which we first developed this 'bottom-up' approach to human evolution, and it draws on many seminal papers such as the ones by David Begun, Robin Crompton, Terry Harrison and John Napier.

Alba, D.M., Fortuny, J. & Moyà-Solà, S. 2010. Enamel thickness in the middle Miocene great apes *Anoiapithecus, Pierolapithecus* and Dryopithecus. *Proceedings of the Royal Society* 277, 2237–2245.

Almécija, S., Tallman, M., Alba, D.M. et al. 2007. *Nature Communications*. DOI: 10.1038/ncomms 3888.

Andrews, P. & Cronin, J. 1982. The relationships of *Sivapithecus* and *Ramapithecus* and the evolution of the orang utan. *Nature* 297, 541–546.

Andrews, P. & Harrison, T. 2005. The last common ancestor of apes and humans. In D.E. Lieberman, R.J. Smith & J. Kelley, Editors, *Interpreting the Past: Essays on Human, Primate, and Mammal Evolution in Honor of David Pilbeam*, 103–121. Boston, Brill Academic Publishers, Inc.

Ashton, E.H. & Oxnard, C. 1964. Locomotor patterns in primates. *Proceedings of the Zoological Society of London* 142, 1–28.

Barrett, L., Dunbar, R.I.M. & Lycett, J. 2002. *Human Evolutionary Psychology*. Basingstoke, Palgrave.

Begun, D.R. 2013. The Miocene hominoid radiations. In D.R. Begun, Editor, *A Companion to Paleoanthropology*, 398–416. Oxford, Wiley-Blackwell.

Begun, D.R. & Kivell, T.L. 2011. Knuckle-walking in *Sivapithecus*? The combined effects of homology and homoplasy with possible implications for pongine dispersals. *Journal of Human Evolution* 60, 158–170.

Begun, D.R., Nargolwalla, M.C. & Kordos, L. 2012. European Miocene hominids and the origin of the African ape and human clade. *Evolutionary Anthropology* 21, 10–23.

Chaimanee, Y., Suteethorn, V., Jintsakul, P. et al. 2004. A new orang-utan relative from the late Miocene of Thailand. *Nature* 427, 439–441.

Crast, J., Fragaszy, D., Hayashi, M. & Matsuzawa, T. 2009. Dynamic in-hand movements in adult and young juvenile chimpanzees (*Pan troglodytes*). *American Journal of Physical Anthropology* 138, 274–285.

Harrison, T. 2012. Apes among the tangled branches of human origins. *Science* 327, 532–534.

Harrison, T. & Andrews, P. 2009. The anatomy and systematic position of the early Miocene proconsulid from Meswa Bridge, Kenya. *Journal of Human Evolution* 56, 479–496.

Humphrey, L. & Andrews, P. 2008. Metric variation in the postcanine teeth from Paşalar, Turkey. *Journal of Human Evolution* 54, 503–507.

Hürzeler, J. 1958. *Oreopithecus bambolii* Gervais: a preliminary report. *Verhandlungen der naturforschenden Gesellschaft, Basel* 69, 1–47.

Kelley, J. 1993. Taxonomic implications of sexual dimorphism in *Lufengpithecus*. In W.H. Kimbel & L.B. Martin, Editors, *Species, Species Concepts and Primate Evolution*, 429–458. New York, Plenum Press.

Lukaks, D. & Clutton-Brock, T.H. 2013. The evolution of social monogamy in mammals. *Science* 341, 526–530.

Martin, L.B. & Andrews, P. 1993. Species recognition in middle Miocene hominoids. In W.H. Kimbel & L.B. Martin, Editors, *Species, Species Concepts and Primate Evolution*, 393–428. New York, Plenum Press.

Marzke, M.W. 1997. Precision grips, hand morphology and tools. *American Journal of Physical Anthropology* 102, 91–110.

Marzke, M.W. & Marzke, R.F. 2000. Evolution of the human hand: approaches to acquiring, analyzing and interpreting the anatomical evidence. *Journal of Anatomy* 197, 121–140.

McNulty, K.P. & Vinyard, C.J. 2015. Morphometry, geometry, function and the future. *Anatomical Record* 298, 328–333.

Moyà-Solà, S., Alba, D.M., Almecija, S. et al. 2009. A unique middle Miocene European hominoid and the origins of the great ape and human clade. *Proceedings of the National Academy of Sciences* 106, 1–6.

Moyà-Solà, S. & Köhler, M. 1996. The first *Dryopithecus* skeleton: origins of great ape locomotion. *Nature* 379, 156–159.

Moyà-Solà, S. & Köhler, M. 1997. The phylogenetic relationships of *Oreopithecus bambolii* Gervais, 1872. *Comptes Rendus de l'Académie des Sciences de Paris* 324, 141–148.

Nelson, E., Rolian, C., Cashmore, L. & Shultz, S. 2014. Digit ratios predict polygyny in early apes, Ardipithecus, Neandertals and early modern humans, but not in Australopithecus. *Proceedings of the Royal Society B* 278, 1556–1563.

Nevell, L. & Wood, B. 2008. Cranial base evolution within the hominin clade. *Journal of Anatomy* 212, 455–468.

Pilbeam, D.R. 1982. New hominoid skull material from the Miocene of Pakistan. *Nature* 295, 232–234.

Patel, B.A., Ruff, C.B., Simons, E.L.R. & Organ, J.M. 2013. Humeral cross-sectional shape in suspensory primates and sloths. *The Anatomical Record* 296, 545–556.

Reno, P.L., Melindi, R.S., McCollum, M.A. & Lovejoy, C.O. 2003. Sexual dimorphism in Australopithecus afarensis was similar to that of modern humans. *Proceedings of the National Academy of Sciences* 100, 9404–9409.

Rolian, C. & Gordon, A.D. 2013. Reassessing manual proportions in *Australopithecus afarensis*. *American Journal of Physical Anthropology* 152, 393–406.

Rosenberger, A.L., Halenar, L., Cooke, S.B. & Hartwig, W.C. 2008. Morphology and evolution of the spider monkey, genus *Ateles*. In C.J. Campbell, Editor, *Spider Monkeys: Ecology and Evolution of the Genus Ateles*, 19–50. Cambridge, Cambridge University Press.

Ruff, C.B. & Higgins, R. 2013. Femoral neck structure and function in early hominins. *American Journal of Physical Anthropology* 150, 512–525.

Stevens, N.J., Seiffert, E.R., O'Connor, P.M et al. 2013. Palaeontological evidence for an Oligocene divergence between Old World monkeys and apes. *Nature* (Published online 15 April 2013).

Susman, R.L. 1994. Fossil evidence for early hominid tool use. *Science* 265, 1570–1573.

Szalay, F. & Delson, E. 1979. *Evolutionary History of the Primates*. New York, Academic Press.

Tocheri, M.W., Orr, C.M., Jacofsky, M.C. & Marzke, M.W. 2008. The evolutionary history of the hominin hand since the last common ancestor of *Pan* and *Homo*. *Journal of Anatomy* 212, 544–562.

Tuttle, R.H. 1967. Knuckle-walking and the evolution of hominoid hands. *American Journal of Physical Anthropology* 26, 171–206.

Ward, C.V., Plavcan, J.M. & Manthi, F.K. 2010. Anterior dental evolution in the *Australopithecus anamensis-afarensis* lineage. *Proceedings of the Royal Society B* 365, 3333–3344.

Chapter 17 An ape's view of human evolution

The final chapter is essentially a summary of the rest of the book and does not draw on any single source.

Aiello, L. & Dean, C. 1990. *An Introduction to Human Evolutionary Anatomy*. New York, Academic Press.

Andrews, P. & Harrison, T. 2005. The last common ancestor of apes and humans. In D.E. Lieberman, R.J. Smith & J. Kelley, Editors, *Interpreting the Past: Essays on Human, Primate, and Mammal Evolution in Honor of David Pilbeam*, 103–121. Boston, Brill Academic Publishers, Inc.

Boesch, C. & Boesch-Achermann, H. 2000. *The Chimpanzees of the Tai Forest: Behavioural Ecology and Evolution*. Oxford, Oxford University Press.

Dupanloup, I., Pereira, L., Bertorelle, G. et al. 2003. A recent shift from polygyny to monogamy in humans is suggested by the analysis of worldwide Y-chromosome diversity. *Journal of Molecular Evolution* 57, 85–97.

Gordon, A.D., Green, D.J. & Richmond, B.G. 2008. Strong postcranial size dimorphism in *Australopithecus afarensis*: results from two new resampling methods for multivariate data sets with missing data. *American Journal of Physical Anthropology* 135, 311–328.

Harrison, T. 2012. Apes among the tangled branches of human origins. *Science* 327, 532–534.

Kelley, J. 1993. Taxonomic implications of sexual dimorphism in *Lufengpithecus*. In W.H. Kimbel & L.B. Martin, Editors, *Species, Species Concepts and Primate Evolution*, 429–458. New York, Plenum Press.

Lukaks, D. & Clutton-Brock, T.H. 2013. The evolution of social monogamy in mammals. *Science* 341, 526–530.

McGrew, W.C. 2010. In search of the last common ancestor: new findings on wild chimpanzees. *Philosophical Transactions of the Royal Society of London* 365, 3267–3276.

Nelson, S.V. 2013. Chimpanzee fauna isotopes provide new interpretations of fossil ape and hominin ecologies. *Proceedings of the Royal Society* 280, 2013–2324.

Newton-Fisher, N. 1999. Infant killers of Budongo. *Folia Primatologica* 70, 167–169.

Nishida, T. & Kawanaka, K. 1985. Within-group cannibalism by adult male chimpanzees. *Primates* 26, 274–284.

Patel, B.A., Ruff, C.B., Simons, E.L.R. & Organ, J.M. 2013. Humeral cross-sectional shape in suspensory primates and sloths. *The Anatomical Record* 296, 545–556.

Plummer, T.W. & Stanford, C.B. 2000. Analysis of a bone assemblage made by chimpanzees at Gombe National Park, Tanzania. *Journal of Human Evolution* 39, 345–365.

Pobiner, B.L., DeSilva, J., Sanders, W.J. & Mitani, J.C. 2007. Taphonomic analysis of skeletal remains from chimpanzee hunts at Ngogo, Kibale National Park, Uganda. *Journal of Human Evolution* 52, 614–636.

Pruetz, J.D. 2006. Feeding ecology of savanna chimpanzees (*Pan troglodytes verus*) at Fongoli, Senegal. In G. Hofman & M.M. Robbins, Editors, *Feeding Ecology in Apes and Other Primates*, 161–182. Cambridge, Cambridge University Press.

Raaum, R., Sterner, K.N., Noviello, C.M., Stewart, C.-B. & Disotell, T.R. 2005. Catarrhine primate divergence dates estimated from complete mitochondrial genomes: concordance with fossil and nuclear DNA evidence. *Journal of Human Evolution* 48, 237–257.

Rose, M.D. 1994. Quadrupedalism in some Miocene catarrhines. *Journal of Human Evolution* 26, 387–411.

Sarringhaus, L.A., MacLatchy, L.M. & Mitani, J.A. 2014. Locomotor and postural development of wild chimpanzees. *Journal of Human Evolution* 66, 29–38.

Smith, C.C., Morgan, M.E. & Pilbeam, D. 2010. Isotopic ecology and dietary profiles of Liberian chimpanzees. *Journal of Human Evolution* 58, 43–55.

Stanford, C.B. & Bunn, H.T. (Editors) 2001. *Meat-Eating & Human Evolution*, 305–331. Oxford, Oxford University Press.

Watts, D.P. 2008. Scavenging by chimpanzees at Ngogo and the relevance of chimpanzee scavenging to early hominin behavioural ecology. *Journal of Human Evolution* 54, 125–133.

Wood, B. & Harrison, T. 2011. The evolutionary context of the first hominins. *Nature* 470, 347–352.

Yamagiwa, J. & Basabose, A.K. 2006. Effects of fruit scarcity on foraging strategies of sympatric gorillas and chimpanzees. In G. Hofman & M.M. Robbins, Editors, *Feeding Ecology in Apes and Other Primates*, 73–96. Cambridge, Cambridge University Press.

Index